CRIMSON EMPIRE
クリムゾン・エンパイア
~ Circumstances to serve a noble ~

We devote our life proudly.
my life for you. For all you.

Quin Rose 2008

- STORY -

The setting is a country of aristocrats: a tributary nation for Luxonne. *Crimson Empire* is a love adventure game about a maid, Sheila, who works in the luxurious royal castle. But behind the lavish façade, the castle is home to a savage—and bloody—political war.

Strong and skilled, Sheila uses her position as a maid to hide her true profession: bodyguard to Prince Edvard. Sheila carries a dark past of enslavement and murder. Now she survives day to day, with only a small wish in her heart.

While navigating the power struggle between Prince Edvard and his brother, the deceptive Prince Justin, Sheila must understand and use the dangerous people who surround her. But although a brilliant fighter and tactician, Sheila is unskilled when it comes to love and friendships. Such a gap between her power and her heart could lead to a dire ending indeed!

Crimson Empire Character Information

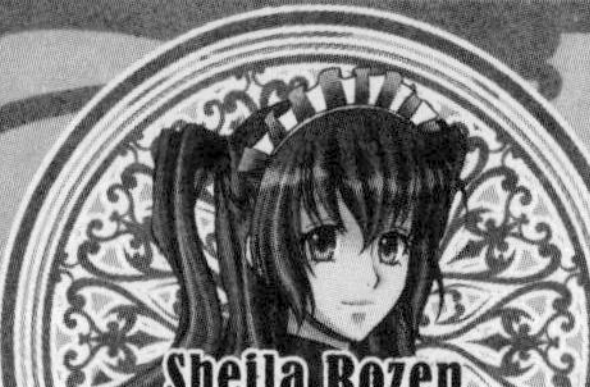

Sheila Rozen

The intensely loyal head maid to Prince Edvard—and his secret bodyguard. She's a skilled leader and shrewdly political, in addition to being fierce in combat. She doesn't hide her roots as a slave.

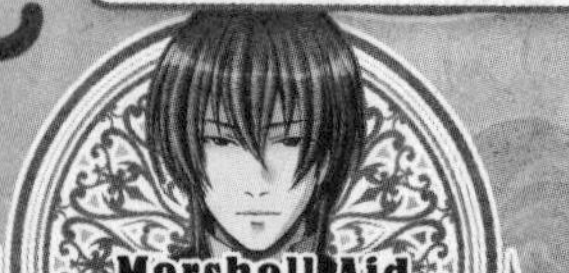

Marshall Aid

VA: Ken Narita

Prince Justin's head servant. He argues with Sheila in public but doesn't dislike her. In private, they're intimate enough to spar peacefully.

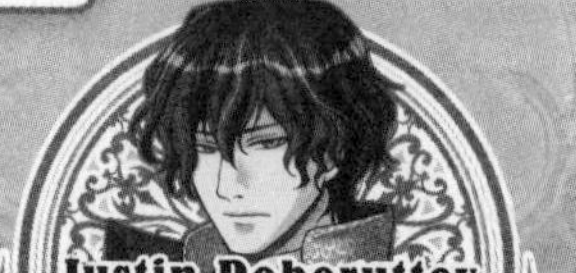

Justin Roberuttey

VA: Daisuke Hirakawa

The eldest prince, and Edvard's older half-brother. Since his mother is of lower status, Justin falls below his younger brother in line for the throne.

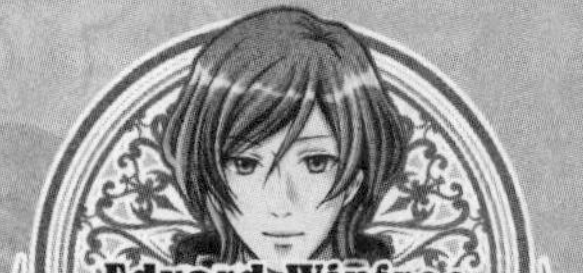

Edvard Winfree

VA: Kenichi Suzumura

Sheila's master. While friendly and regal on the surface, he's very condescending. He thinks of Sheila as more than a subordinate and loves her more than his own family... or so he *claims*.

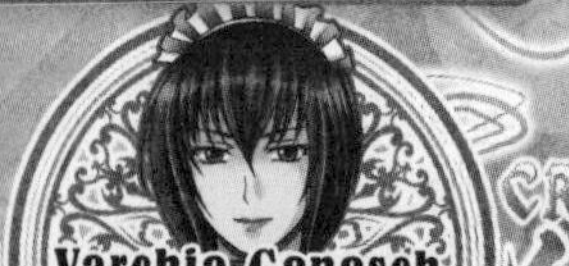

Varchia Ganasch

VA: Mitsuki Saiga

Varchia, the vice-maid, is a close friend of Sheila's, and is a former slave. Her actions and words are always painfully neutral. She's trustworthy and helps Sheila in both public and private.

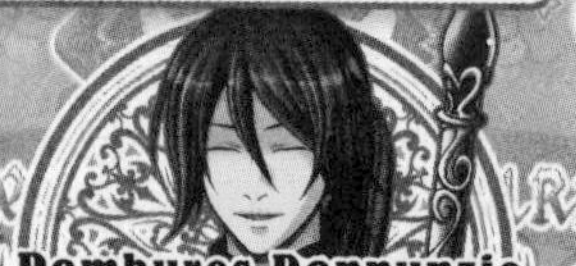

Rambures Dannunzio

VA: Taniyama Kisho

A commoner who was knighted after saving the king. He loves to lurk in his room and brew concoctions—which often stink and explode—instead of interacting with the nobility.

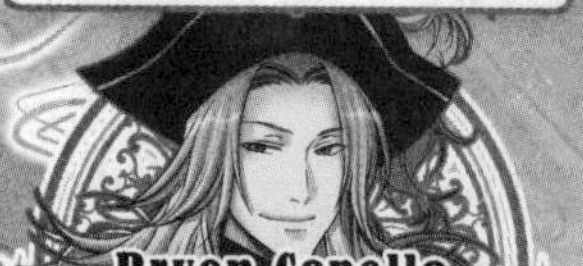

Bryon Capella

VA: Tatsuhisa Suzuki

Son of the marquis who one day will inherit the position and become an important pillar of the country. He seems cheerful and carefree, but rather guarded. Like his sister, he adores Sheila.

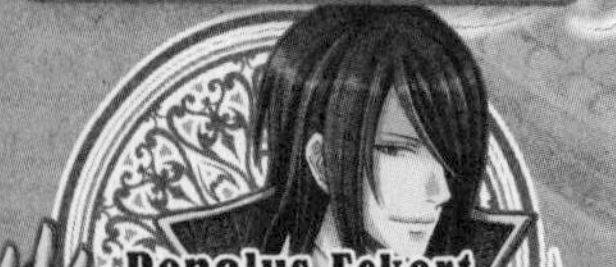

Ronalus Eckert

VA: Daisuke Kisho

Another guest in the royal castle, Ronalus is the servant to the Queen of Luxonne. Although he enjoys a higher status by serving the queen, he has a good relationship with other servants. His role is to monitor Meissen.

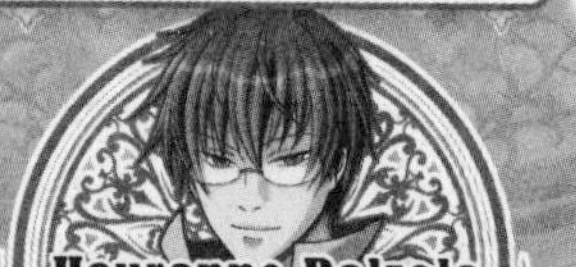

Hauranne Balzola

VA: Daisuke Namikawa

A wizard staying in the royal castle who is treated as a guest, but he's been in the castle longer than anyone. He's lived a *long* life...and his real age doesn't match his looks.

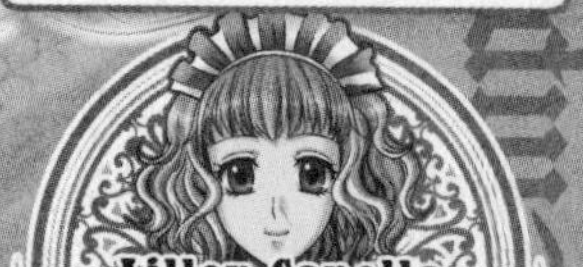

Lilley Capella

VA: Miyazaki Ui

Another battle maid, but of noble birth, Lilley is fiercely loyal to Sheila. She has innate skill, and her strength is second only to Sheila's. She and her brother Bryon are very close.

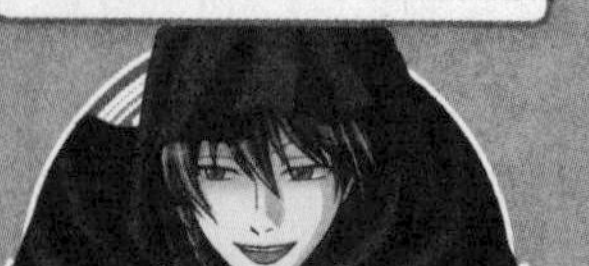

Curtis Nile

VA: Akira Ishida

A deadly assassin who specializes in poisons. He raised Sheila, and nearly killed her with his vicious training. Ever since, their relationship has been strained, to say the least.

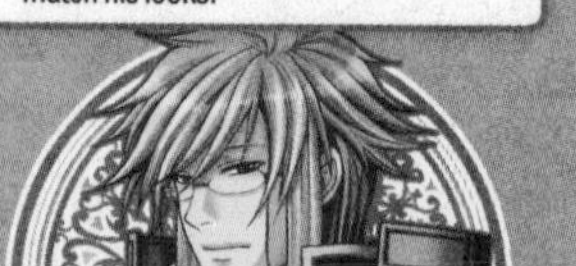

Michael Faust

VA: Hikaru Midorikawa

A demon who made a contract with Meissen. He's dangerously strong, monologues frequently, and is oddly nervous. His mental instability feeds his pessimism.

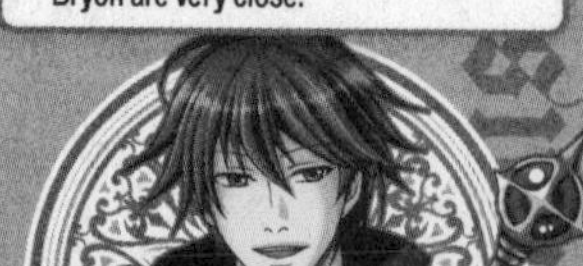

Meissen Hildegarde

VA: Hiro Shimono

Meissen has a tendency to wander, and he's traveled all over the world. His ladykiller persona hides a powerful wizard. He's searching for the truth and is trying to become a sage...supposedly.

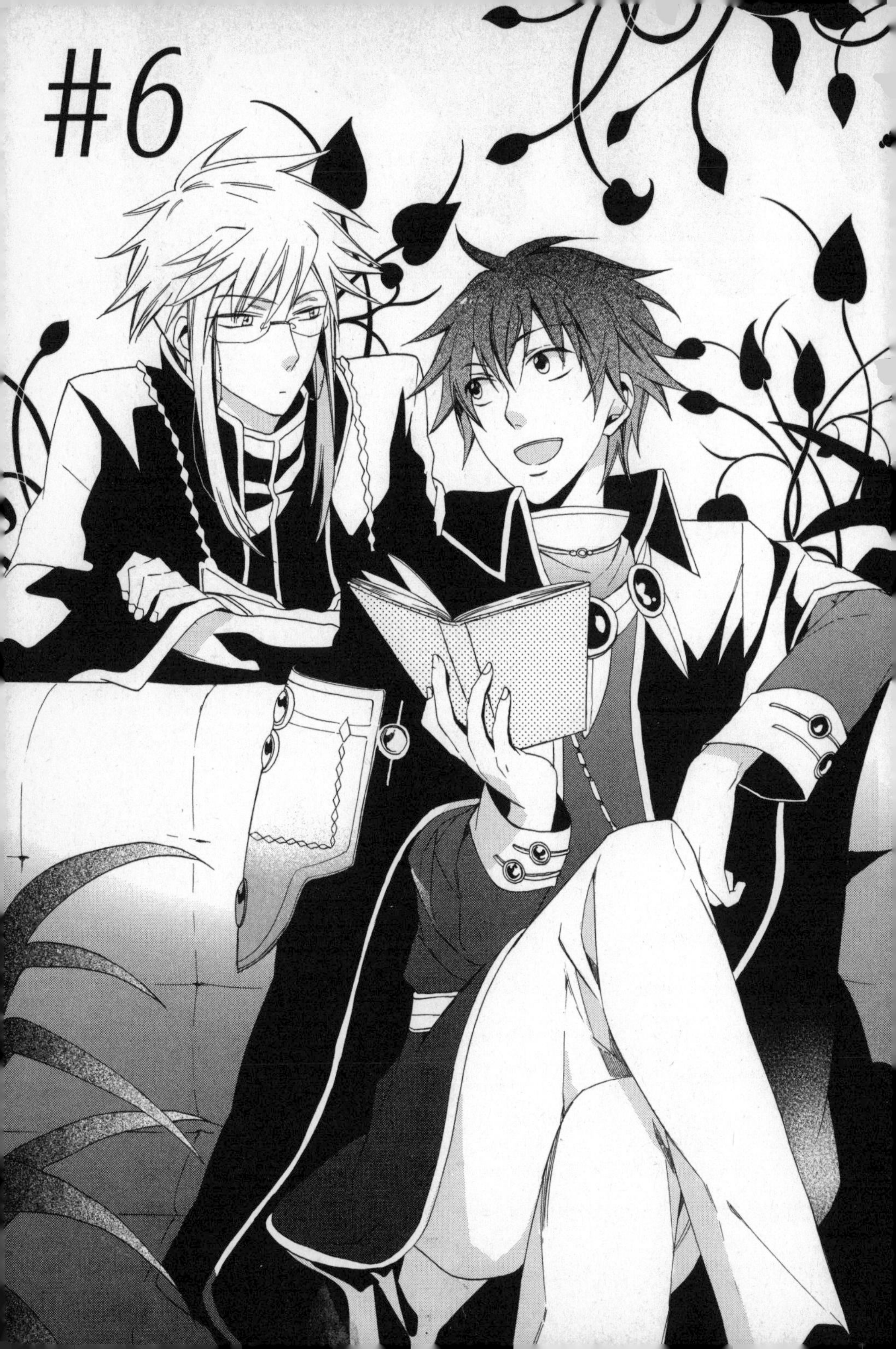
#6

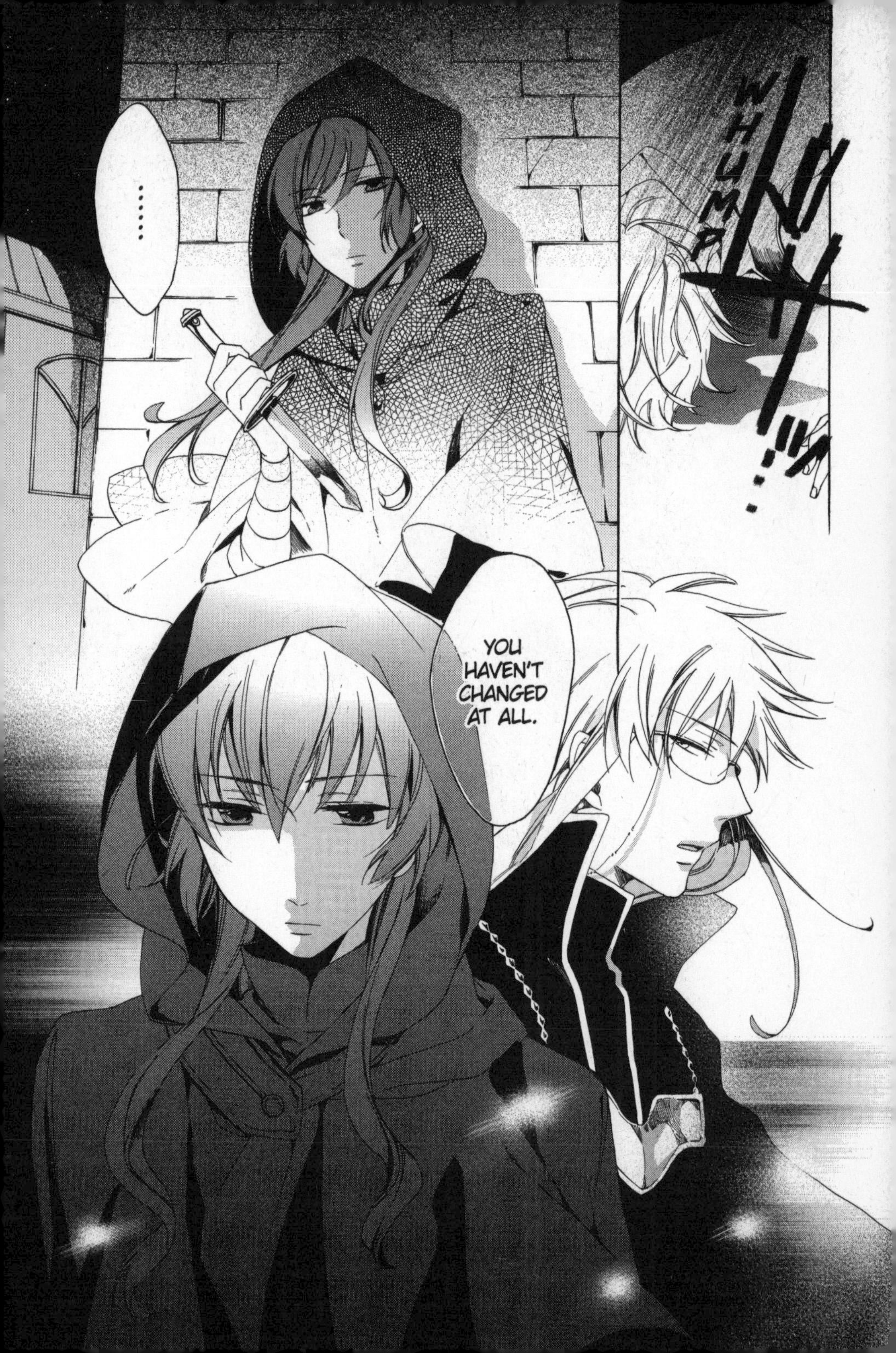
WHUMP
......
YOU HAVEN'T CHANGED AT ALL.

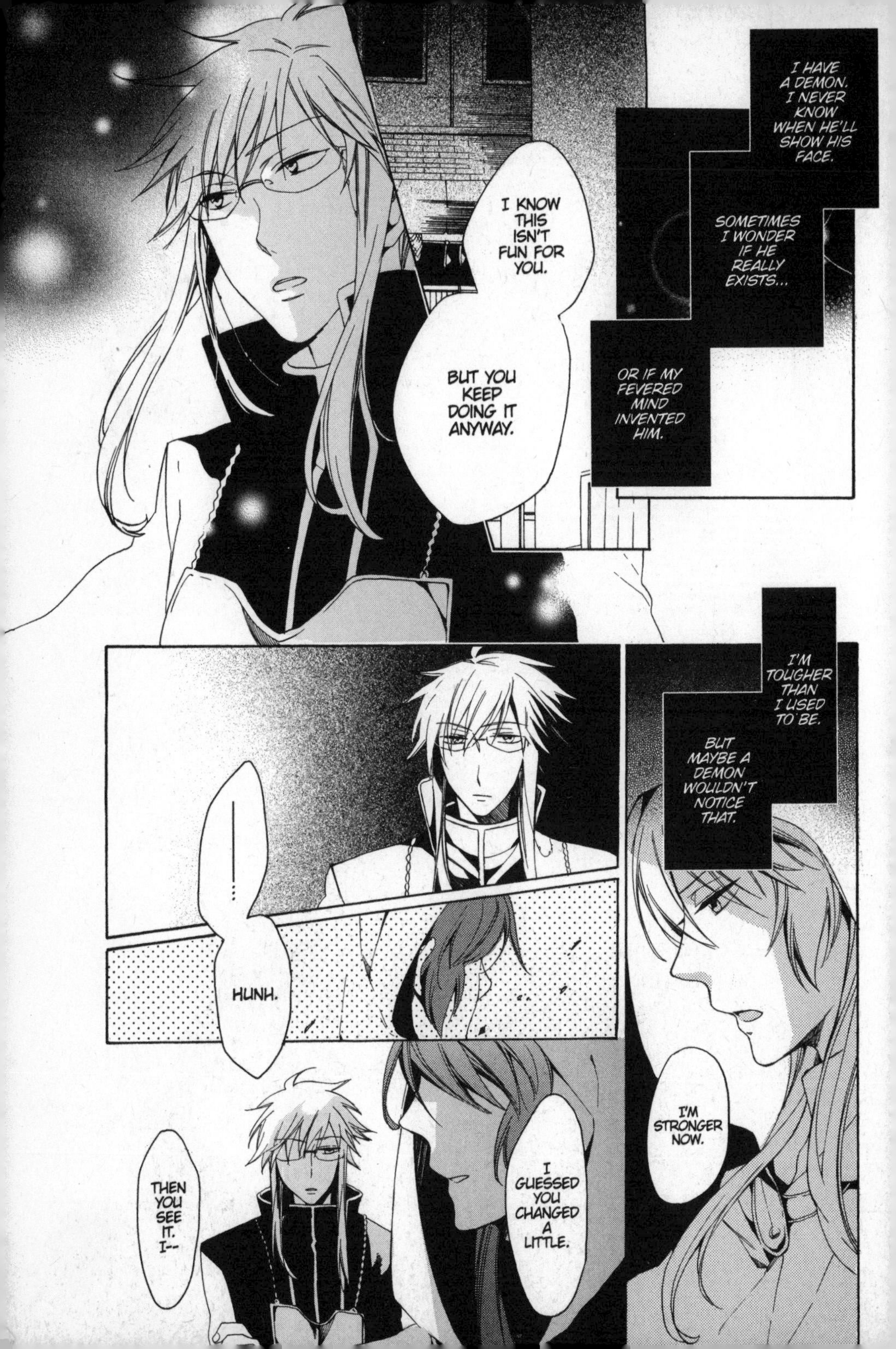

I HAVE A DEMON. I NEVER KNOW WHEN HE'LL SHOW HIS FACE.
SOMETIMES I WONDER IF HE REALLY EXISTS...
OR IF MY FEVERED MIND INVENTED HIM.
I KNOW THIS ISN'T FUN FOR YOU.
BUT YOU KEEP DOING IT ANYWAY.
I'M TOUGHER THAN I USED TO BE.
BUT MAYBE A DEMON WOULDN'T NOTICE THAT.
I'M STRONGER NOW.
......
HUNH.
I GUESSED YOU CHANGED A LITTLE.
THEN YOU SEE IT. I--

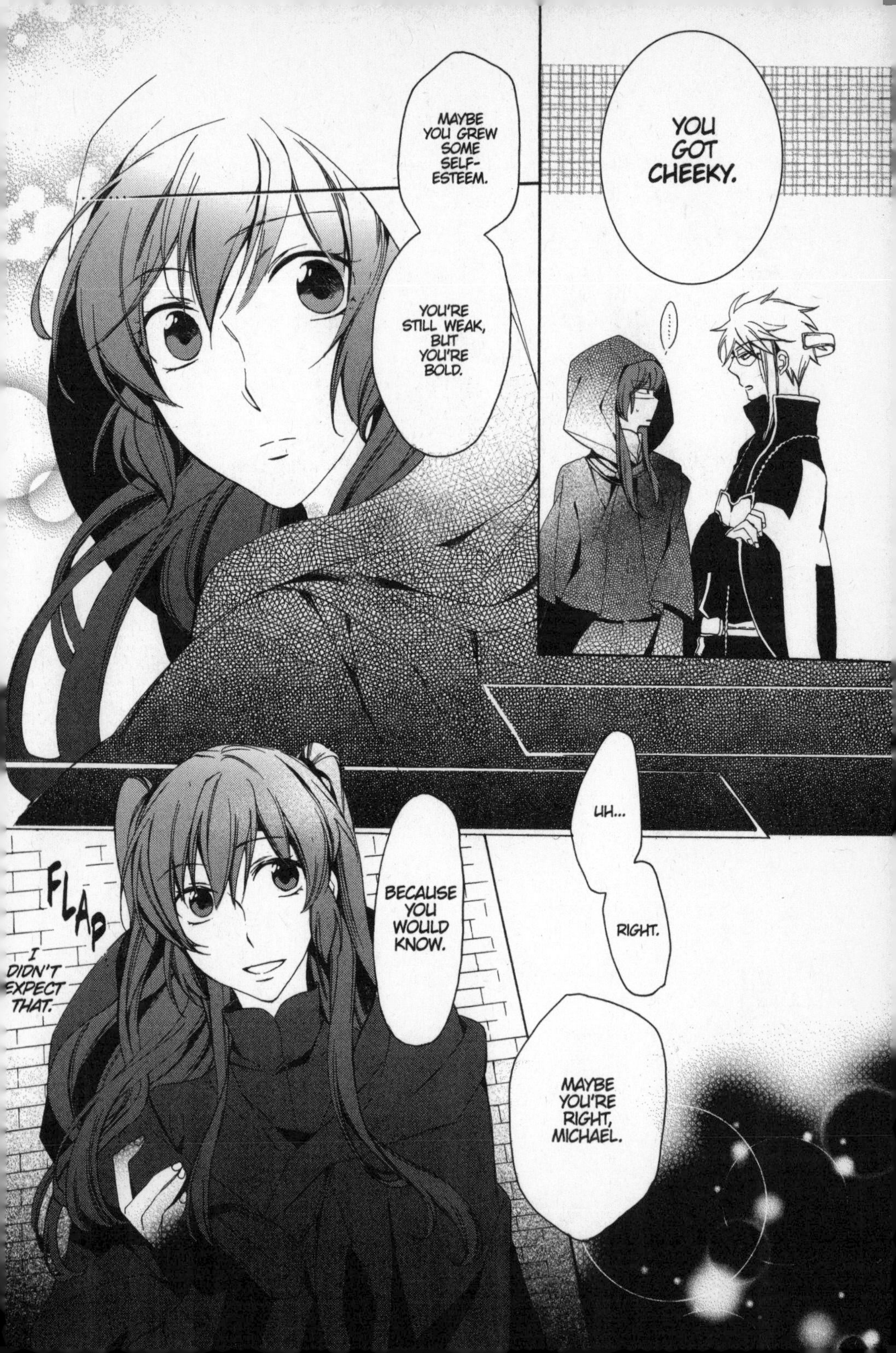
YOU GOT CHEEKY.
...!
MAYBE YOU GREW SOME SELF-ESTEEM.
YOU'RE STILL WEAK, BUT YOU'RE BOLD.
UH... RIGHT.
BECAUSE YOU WOULD KNOW.
FLAP
I DIDN'T EXPECT THAT.
MAYBE YOU'RE RIGHT, MICHAEL.

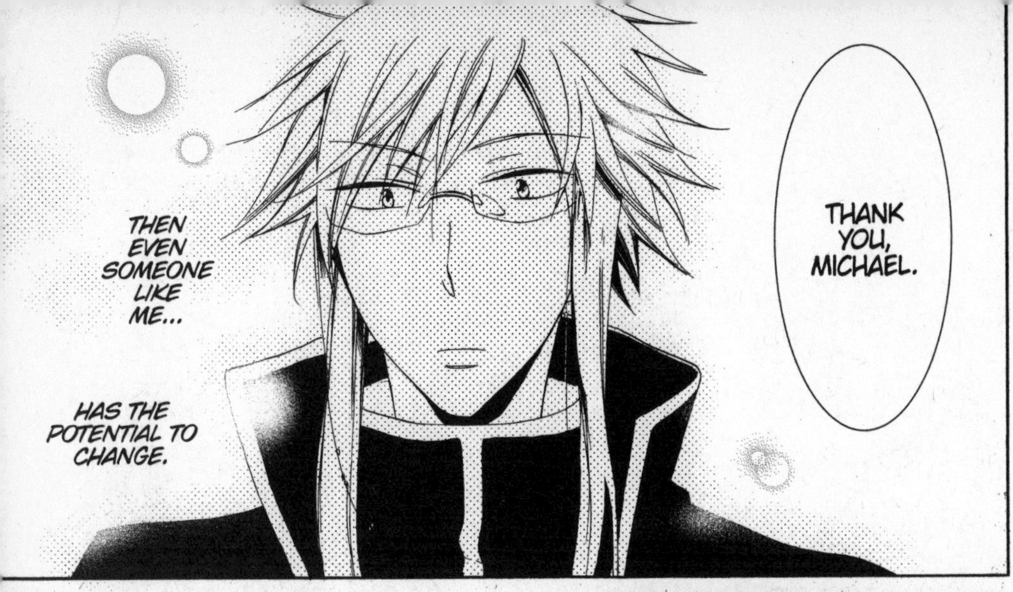
THANK YOU, MICHAEL.
THEN EVEN SOMEONE LIKE ME...
HAS THE POTENTIAL TO CHANGE.

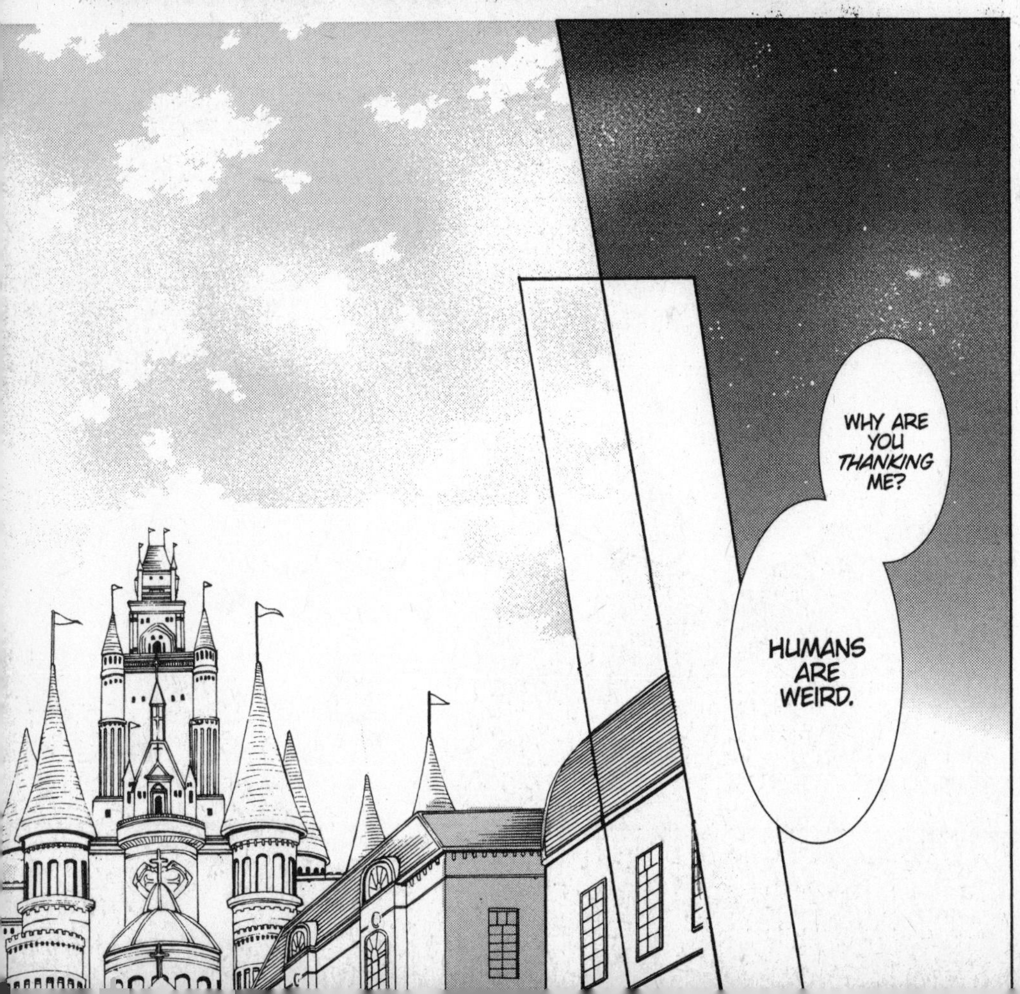
WHY ARE YOU *THANKING* ME?
HUMANS ARE WEIRD.

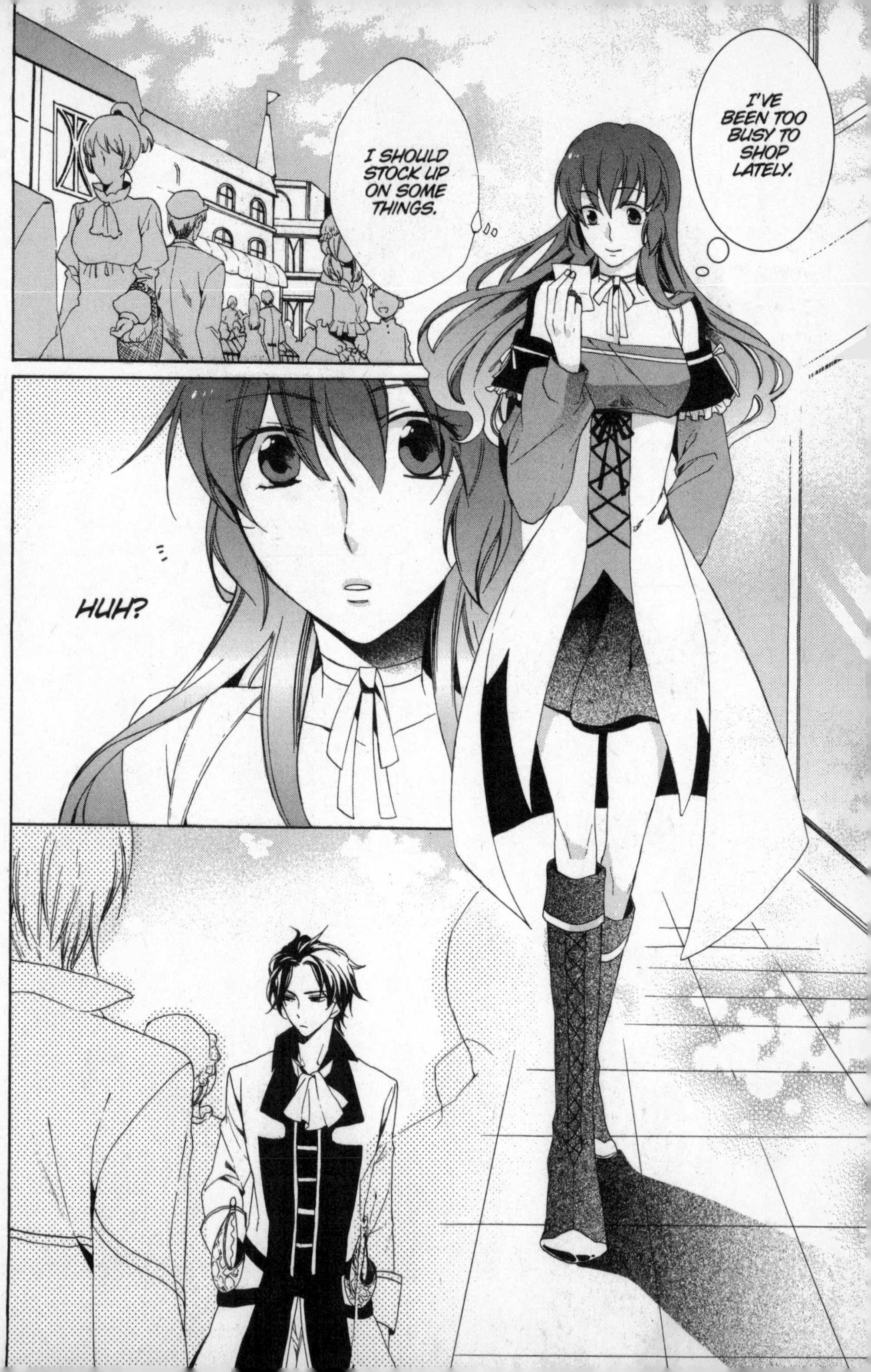
I'VE BEEN TOO BUSY TO SHOP LATELY.
I SHOULD STOCK UP ON SOME THINGS.
HUH?

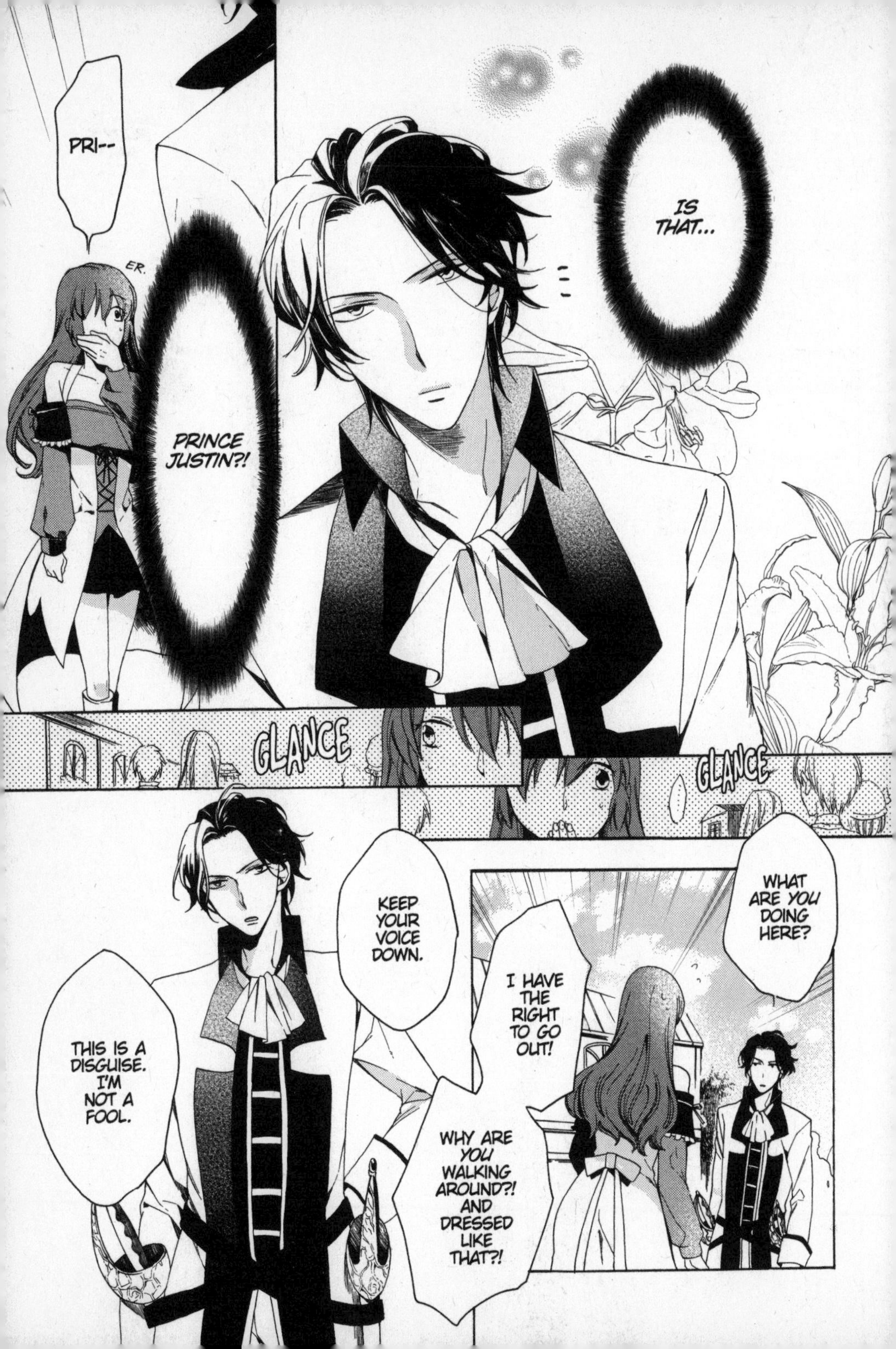
IS THAT...
PRINCE JUSTIN?!
PRI--
ER.
GLANCE
GLANCE
WHAT ARE YOU DOING HERE?
KEEP YOUR VOICE DOWN.
I HAVE THE RIGHT TO GO OUT!
WHY ARE YOU WALKING AROUND?! AND DRESSED LIKE THAT?!
THIS IS A DISGUISE. I'M NOT A FOOL.

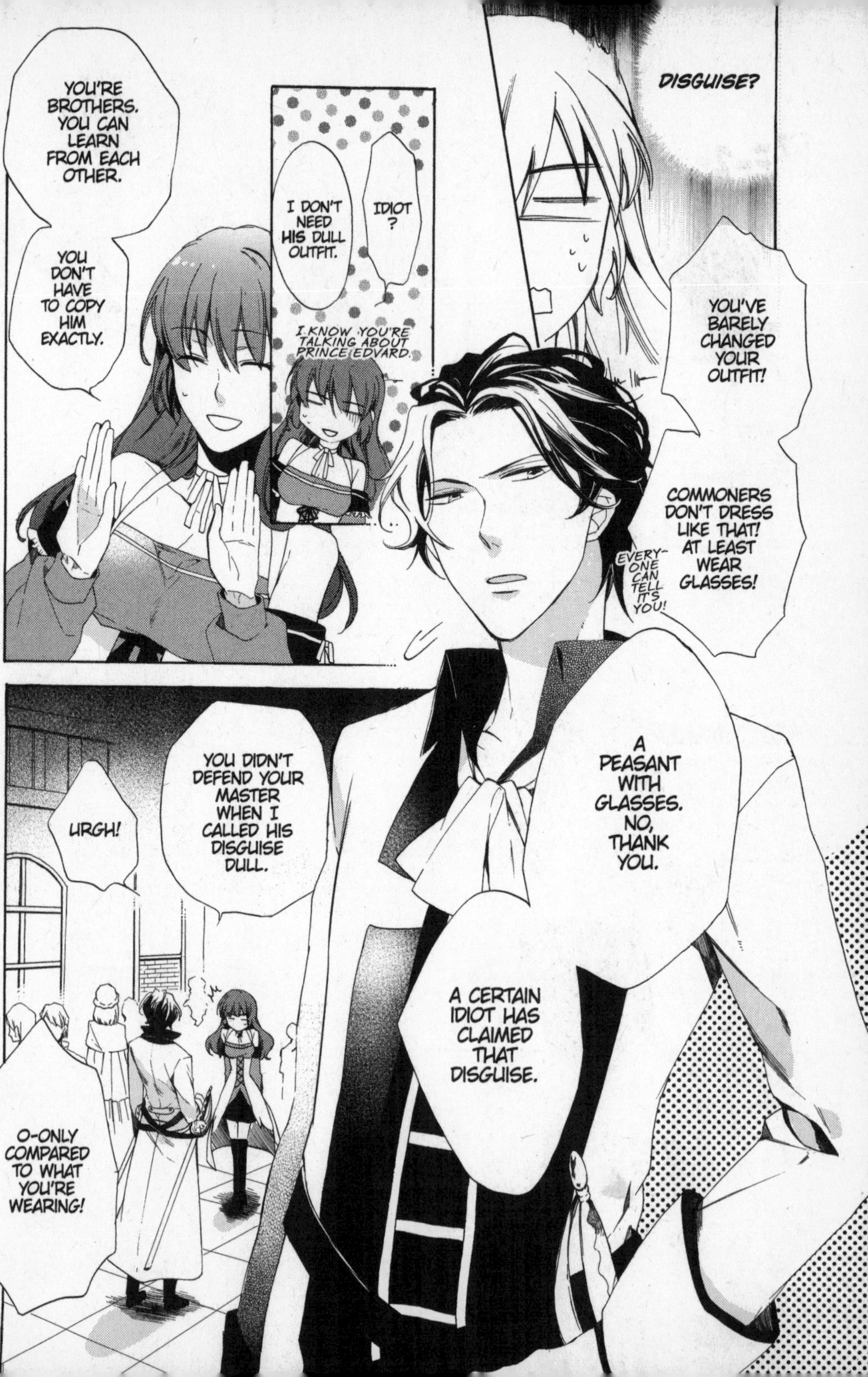
DISGUISE?
YOU'VE BARELY CHANGED YOUR OUTFIT!
COMMONERS DON'T DRESS LIKE THAT! AT LEAST WEAR GLASSES!
EVERYONE CAN TELL IT'S YOU!
A PEASANT WITH GLASSES. NO, THANK YOU.
A CERTAIN IDIOT HAS CLAIMED THAT DISGUISE.
IDIOT?
I DON'T NEED HIS DULL OUTFIT.
I KNOW YOU'RE TALKING ABOUT PRINCE EDVARD.
YOU'RE BROTHERS. YOU CAN LEARN FROM EACH OTHER.
YOU DON'T HAVE TO COPY HIM EXACTLY.
YOU DIDN'T DEFEND YOUR MASTER WHEN I CALLED HIS DISGUISE DULL.
URGH!
O-ONLY COMPARED TO WHAT YOU'RE WEARING!

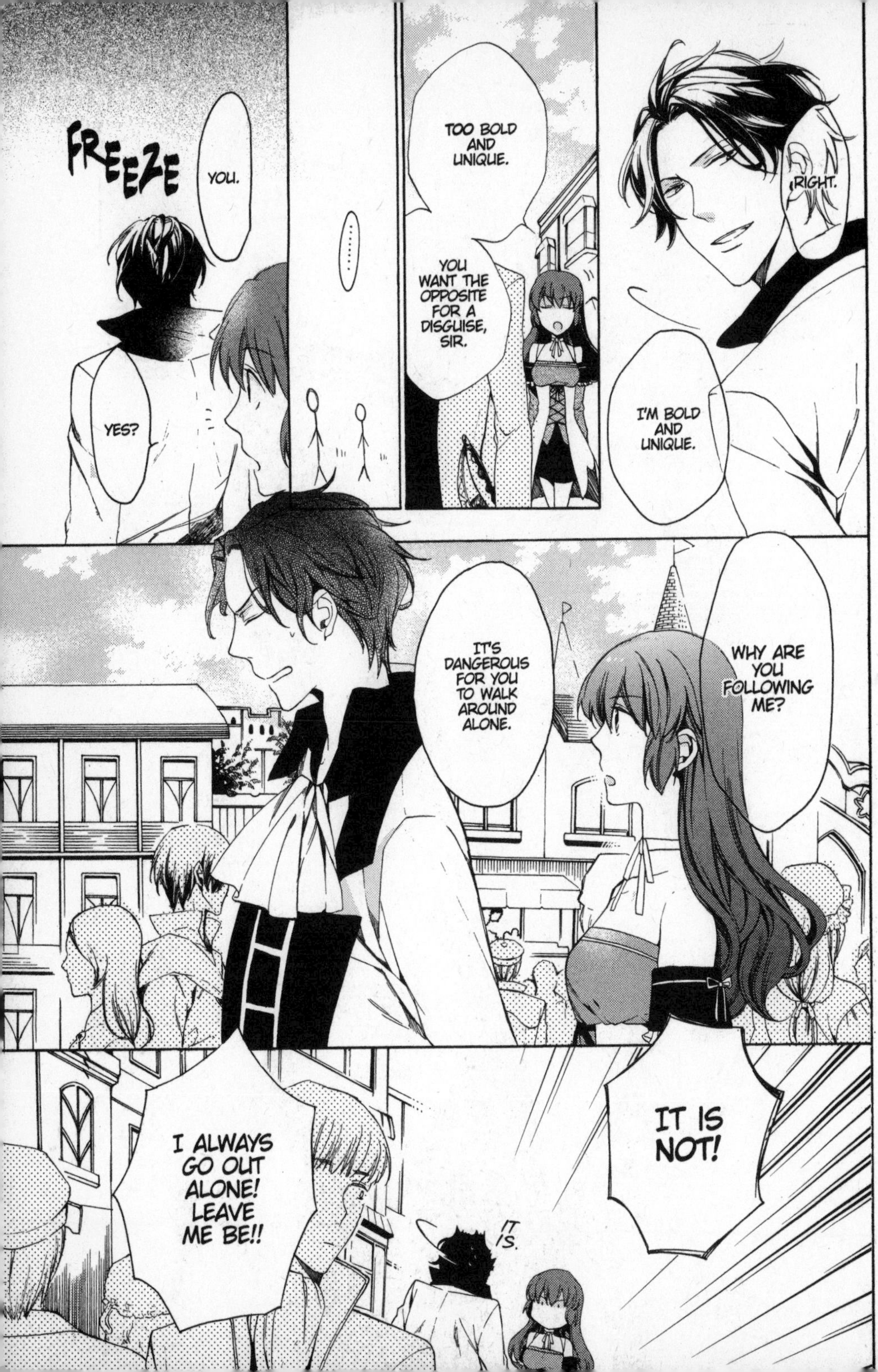
RIGHT.
I'M BOLD AND UNIQUE.
TOO BOLD AND UNIQUE.
YOU WANT THE OPPOSITE FOR A DISGUISE, SIR.
......
YOU.
FREEZE
YES?
WHY ARE YOU FOLLOWING ME?
IT'S DANGEROUS FOR YOU TO WALK AROUND ALONE.
IT IS NOT!
IT IS.
I ALWAYS GO OUT ALONE! LEAVE ME BE!!

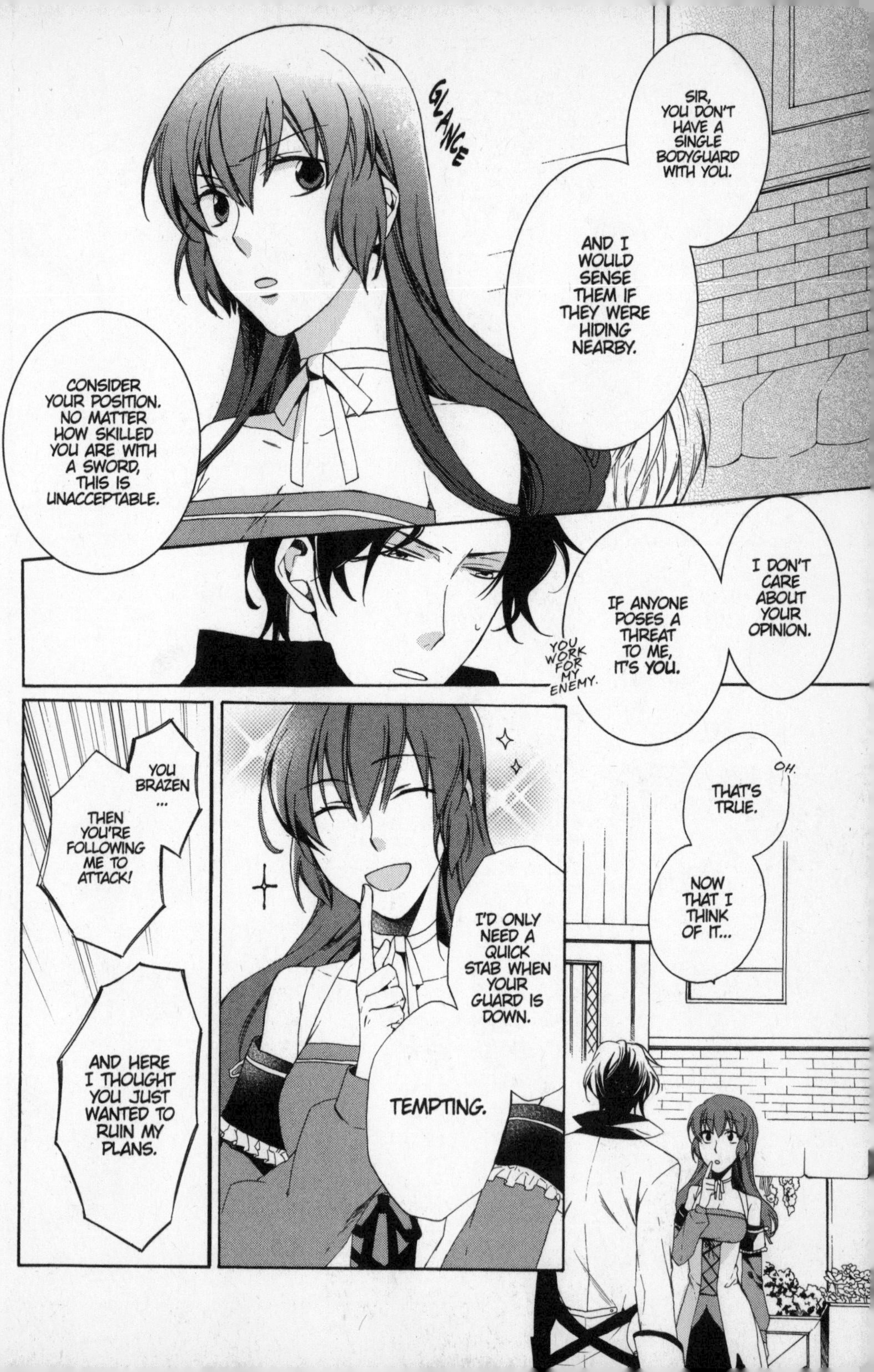
SIR, YOU DON'T HAVE A SINGLE BODYGUARD WITH YOU.
AND I WOULD SENSE THEM IF THEY WERE HIDING NEARBY.
GLANCE
CONSIDER YOUR POSITION. NO MATTER HOW SKILLED YOU ARE WITH A SWORD, THIS IS UNACCEPTABLE.
I DON'T CARE ABOUT YOUR OPINION.
IF ANYONE POSES A THREAT TO ME, IT'S YOU.
YOU WORK FOR MY ENEMY.
OH.
THAT'S TRUE.
NOW THAT I THINK OF IT...
I'D ONLY NEED A QUICK STAB WHEN YOUR GUARD IS DOWN.
TEMPTING.
YOU BRAZEN ...
THEN YOU'RE FOLLOWING ME TO ATTACK!
AND HERE I THOUGHT YOU JUST WANTED TO RUIN MY PLANS.

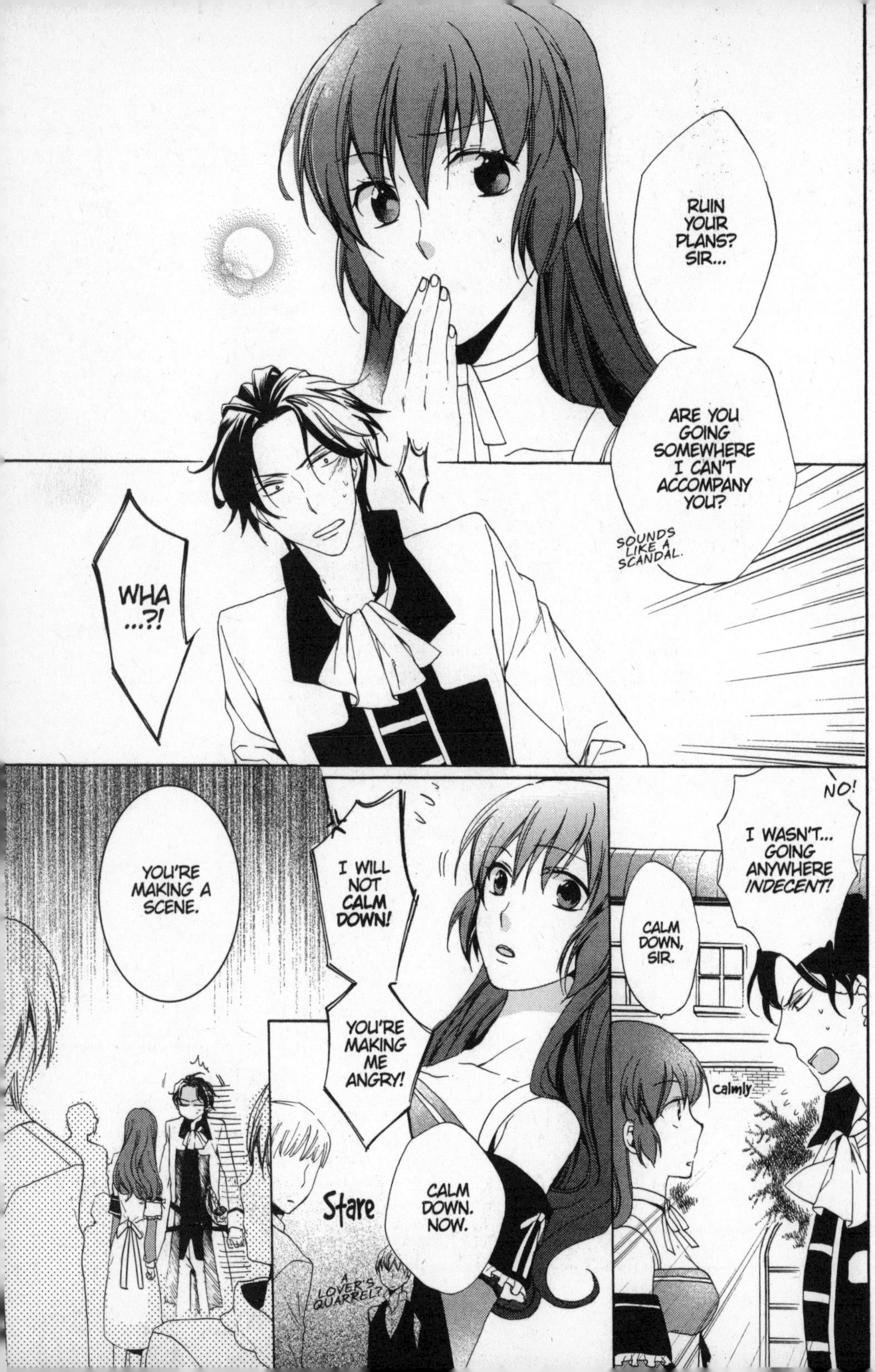
RUIN YOUR PLANS? SIR...
ARE YOU GOING SOMEWHERE I CAN'T ACCOMPANY YOU?
SOUNDS LIKE A SCANDAL.
WHA ...?!
NO!
I WASN'T... GOING ANYWHERE *INDECENT!*
CALM DOWN, SIR.
calmly
I WILL NOT CALM DOWN!
YOU'RE MAKING ME ANGRY!
CALM DOWN. NOW.
YOU'RE MAKING A SCENE.
Stare
A LOVER'S QUARREL?

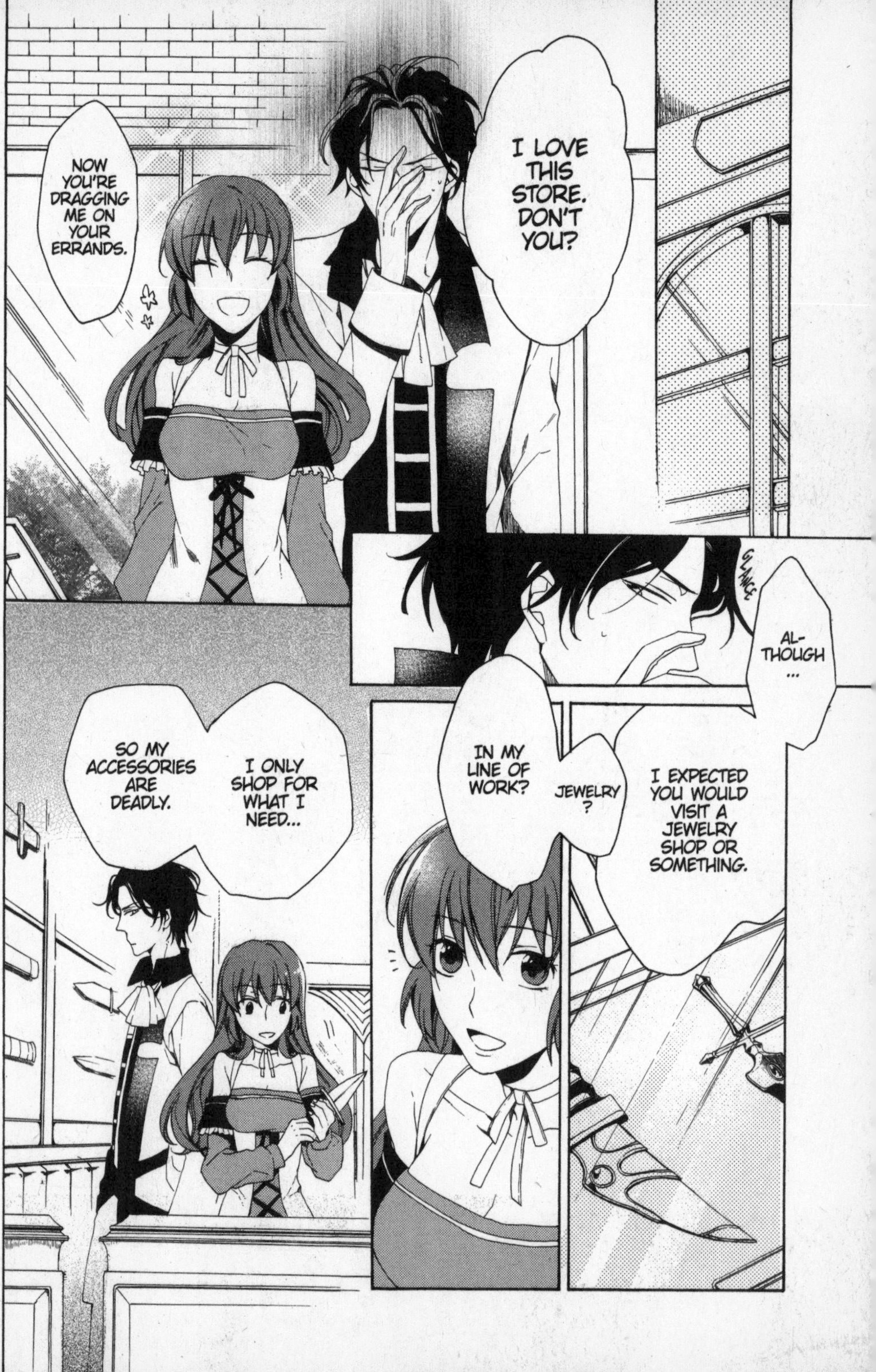
I LOVE THIS STORE. DON'T YOU?
NOW YOU'RE DRAGGING ME ON YOUR ERRANDS.
GLANCE
AL-THOUGH...
I EXPECTED YOU WOULD VISIT A JEWELRY SHOP OR SOMETHING.
JEWELRY?
IN MY LINE OF WORK?
I ONLY SHOP FOR WHAT I NEED...
SO MY ACCESSORIES ARE DEADLY.

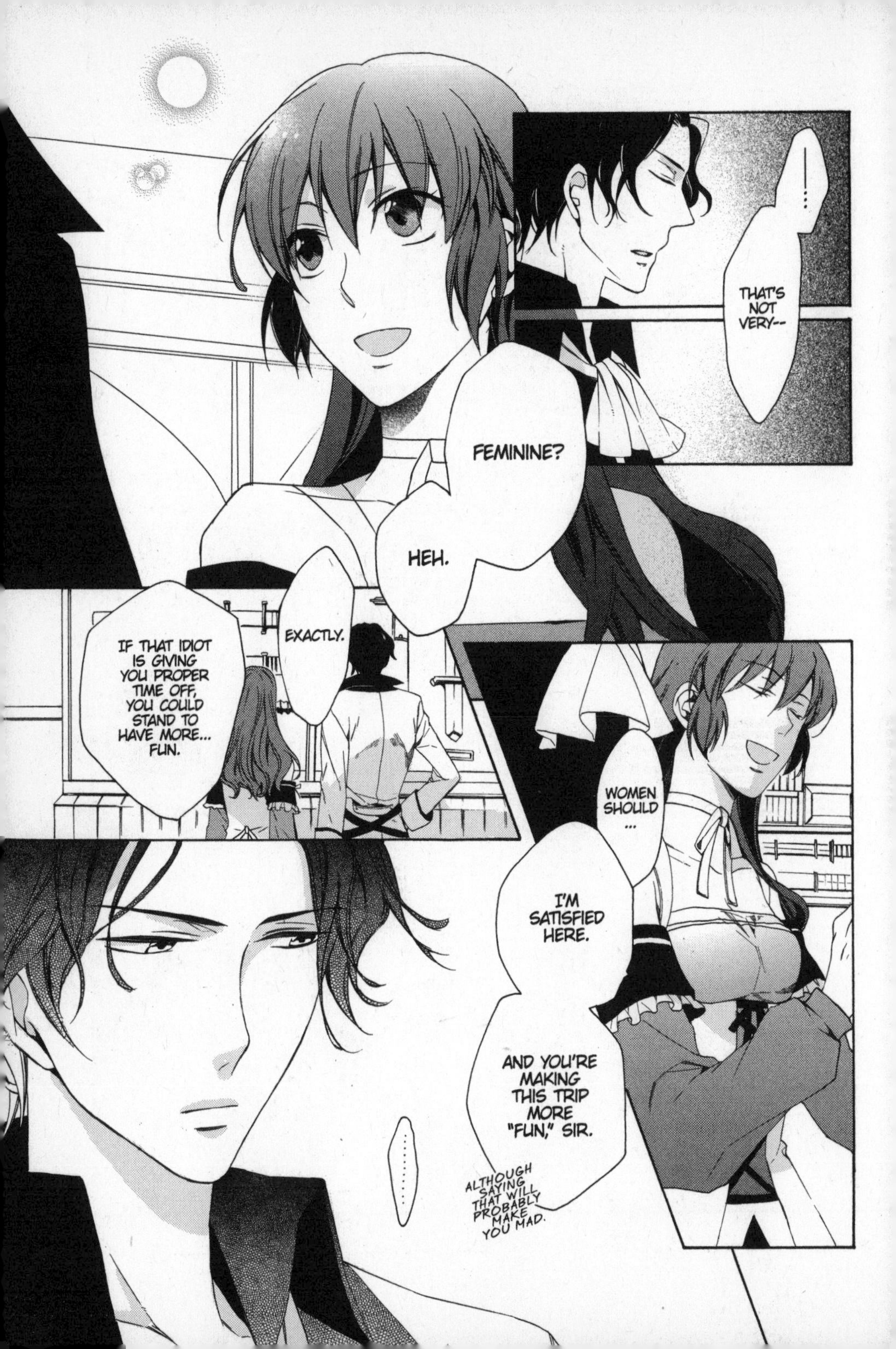

.....
THAT'S NOT VERY--
FEMININE?
HEH.
EXACTLY.
WOMEN SHOULD ...
IF THAT IDIOT IS GIVING YOU PROPER TIME OFF, YOU COULD STAND TO HAVE MORE... FUN.
I'M SATISFIED HERE.
AND YOU'RE MAKING THIS TRIP MORE "FUN," SIR.
ALTHOUGH SAYING THAT WILL PROBABLY MAKE YOU MAD.
......

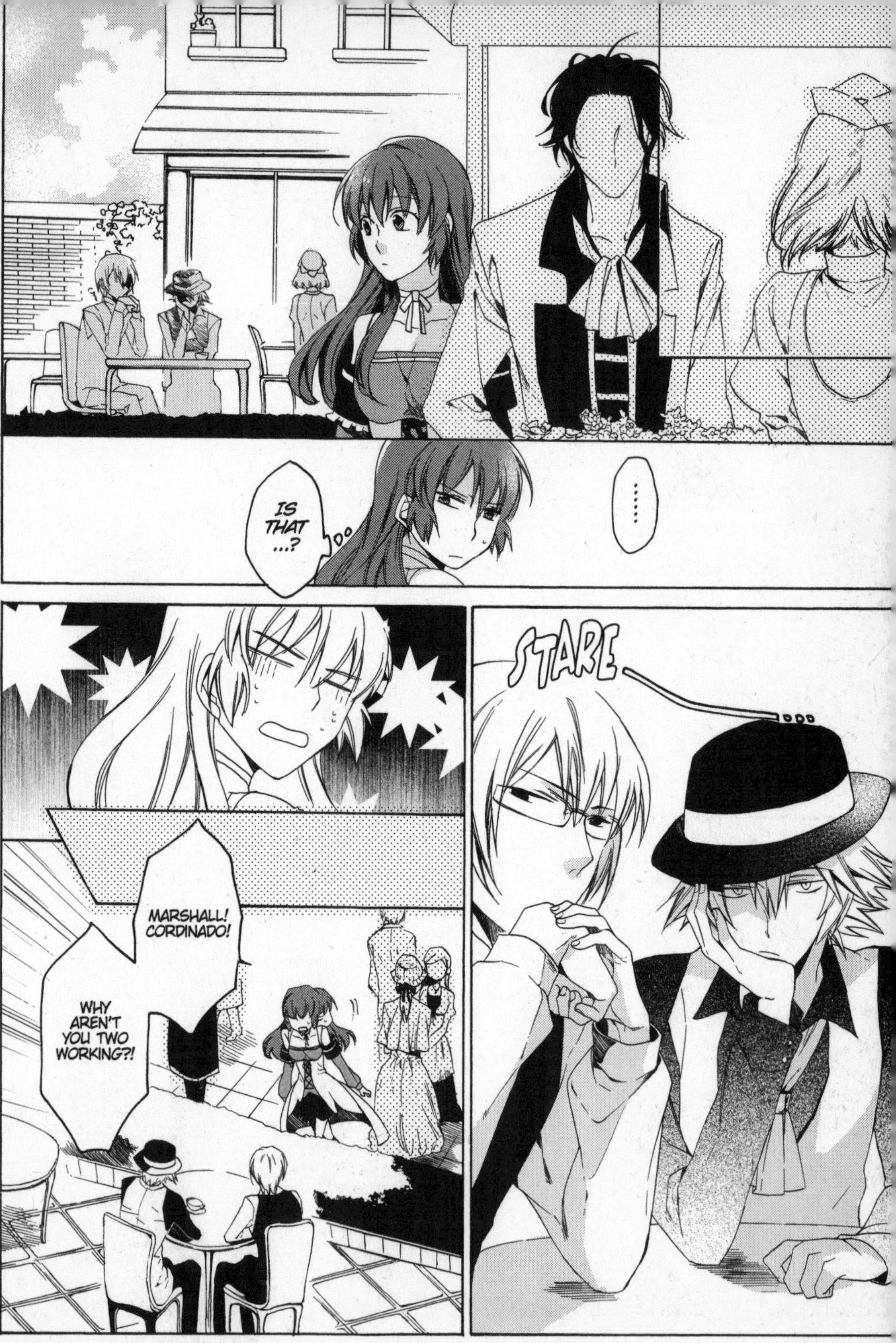
......
IS THAT ...?
STARE
MARSHALL! CORDINADO!
WHY AREN'T YOU TWO WORKING?!

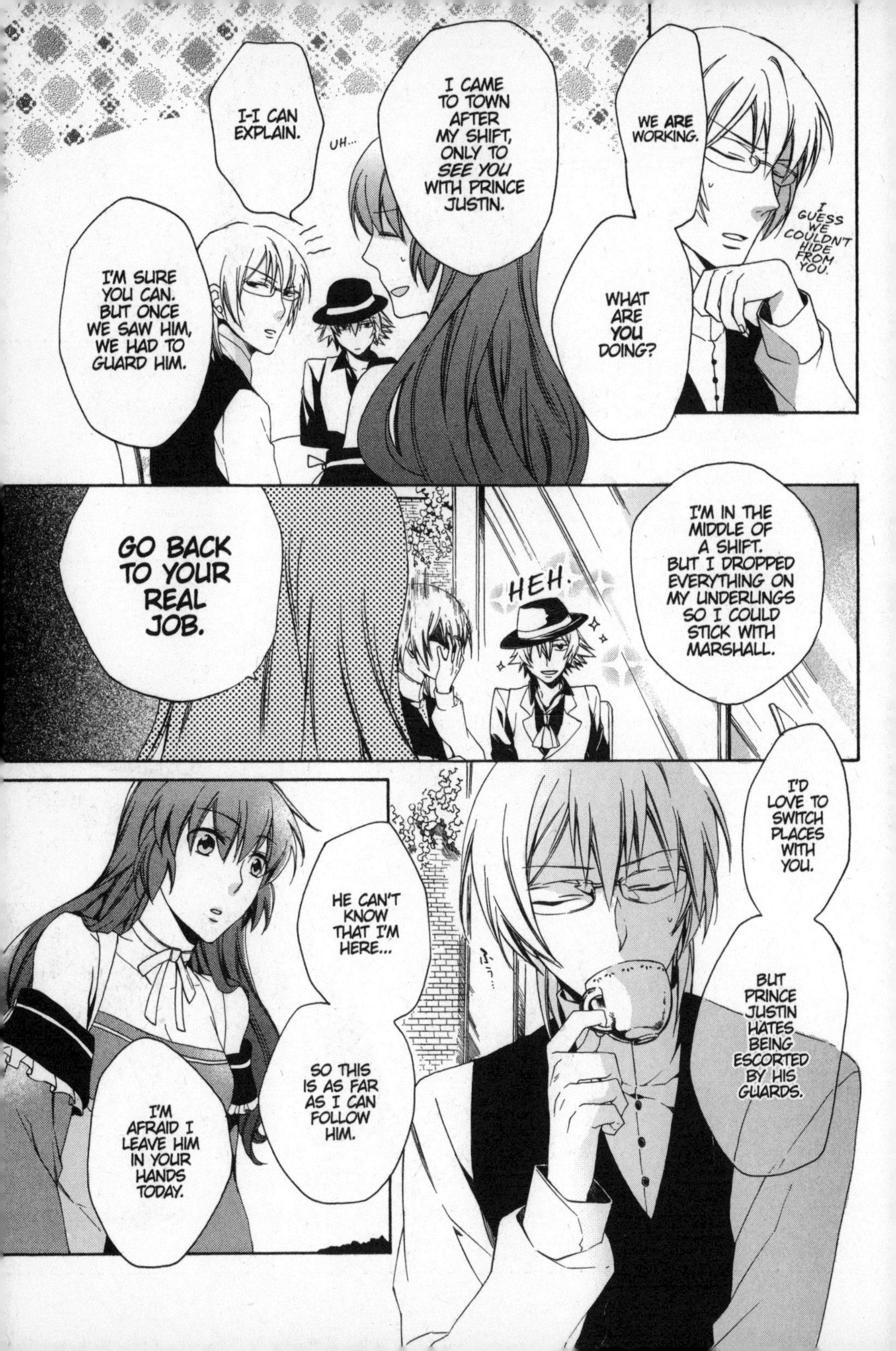
WE ARE WORKING.
I GUESS WE COULDN'T HIDE FROM YOU.
WHAT ARE YOU DOING?
I CAME TO TOWN AFTER MY SHIFT, ONLY TO SEE YOU WITH PRINCE JUSTIN.
UH...
I-I CAN EXPLAIN.
I'M SURE YOU CAN. BUT ONCE WE SAW HIM, WE HAD TO GUARD HIM.
I'M IN THE MIDDLE OF A SHIFT. BUT I DROPPED EVERYTHING ON MY UNDERLINGS SO I COULD STICK WITH MARSHALL.
HEH.
GO BACK TO YOUR REAL JOB.
I'D LOVE TO SWITCH PLACES WITH YOU.
BUT PRINCE JUSTIN HATES BEING ESCORTED BY HIS GUARDS.
HE CAN'T KNOW THAT I'M HERE...
SO THIS IS AS FAR AS I CAN FOLLOW HIM.
I'M AFRAID I LEAVE HIM IN YOUR HANDS TODAY.

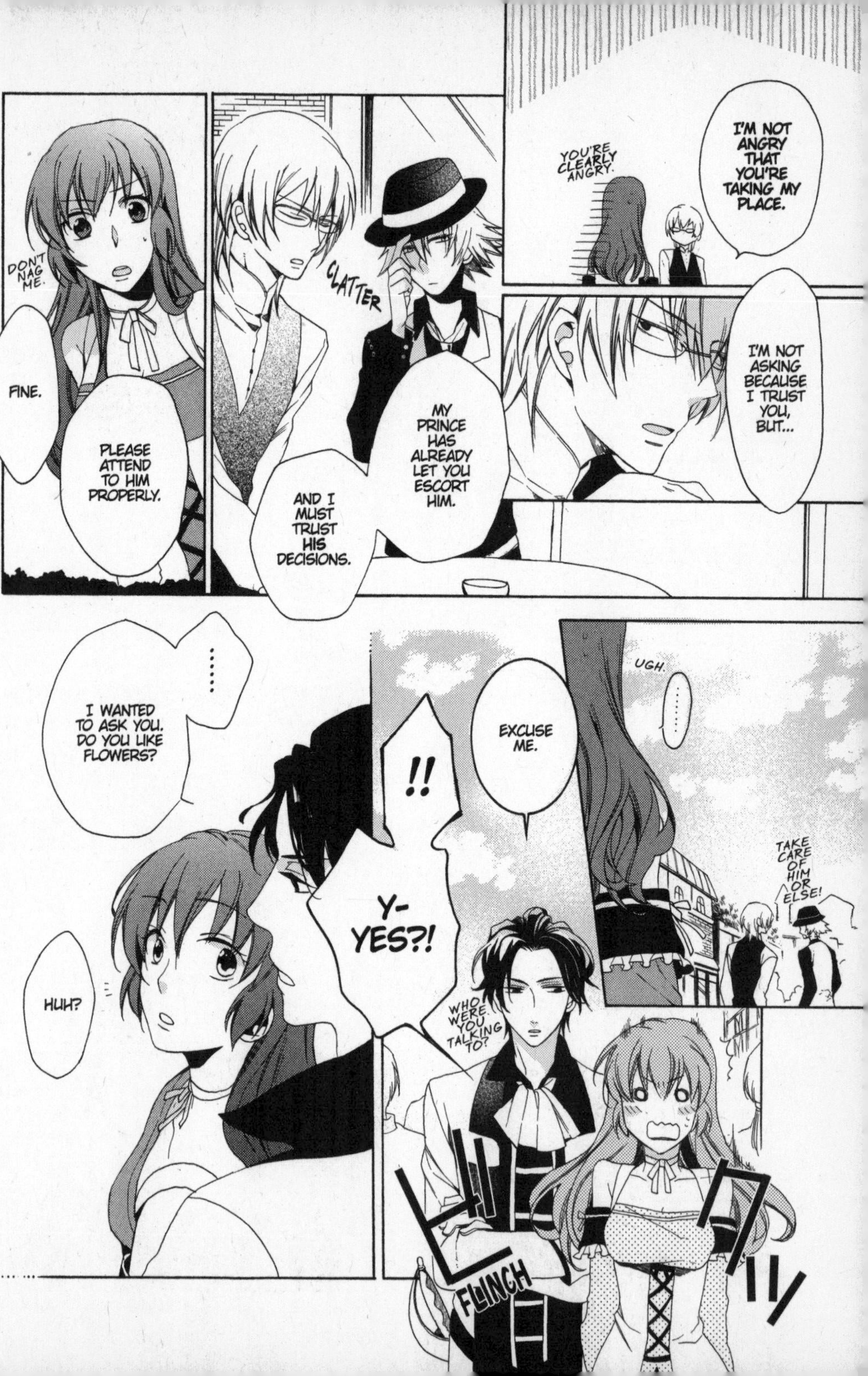
I'M NOT ANGRY THAT YOU'RE TAKING MY PLACE.
YOU'RE CLEARLY ANGRY.
I'M NOT ASKING BECAUSE I TRUST YOU, BUT...
CLATTER
MY PRINCE HAS ALREADY LET YOU ESCORT HIM.
AND I MUST TRUST HIS DECISIONS.
DON'T NAG ME.
FINE.
PLEASE ATTEND TO HIM PROPERLY.
UGH.
......
EXCUSE ME.
TAKE CARE OF HIM OR ELSE!
WHO WERE YOU TALKING TO?
!!
Y-YES?!
FLINCH
......
I WANTED TO ASK YOU. DO YOU LIKE FLOWERS?
HUH?

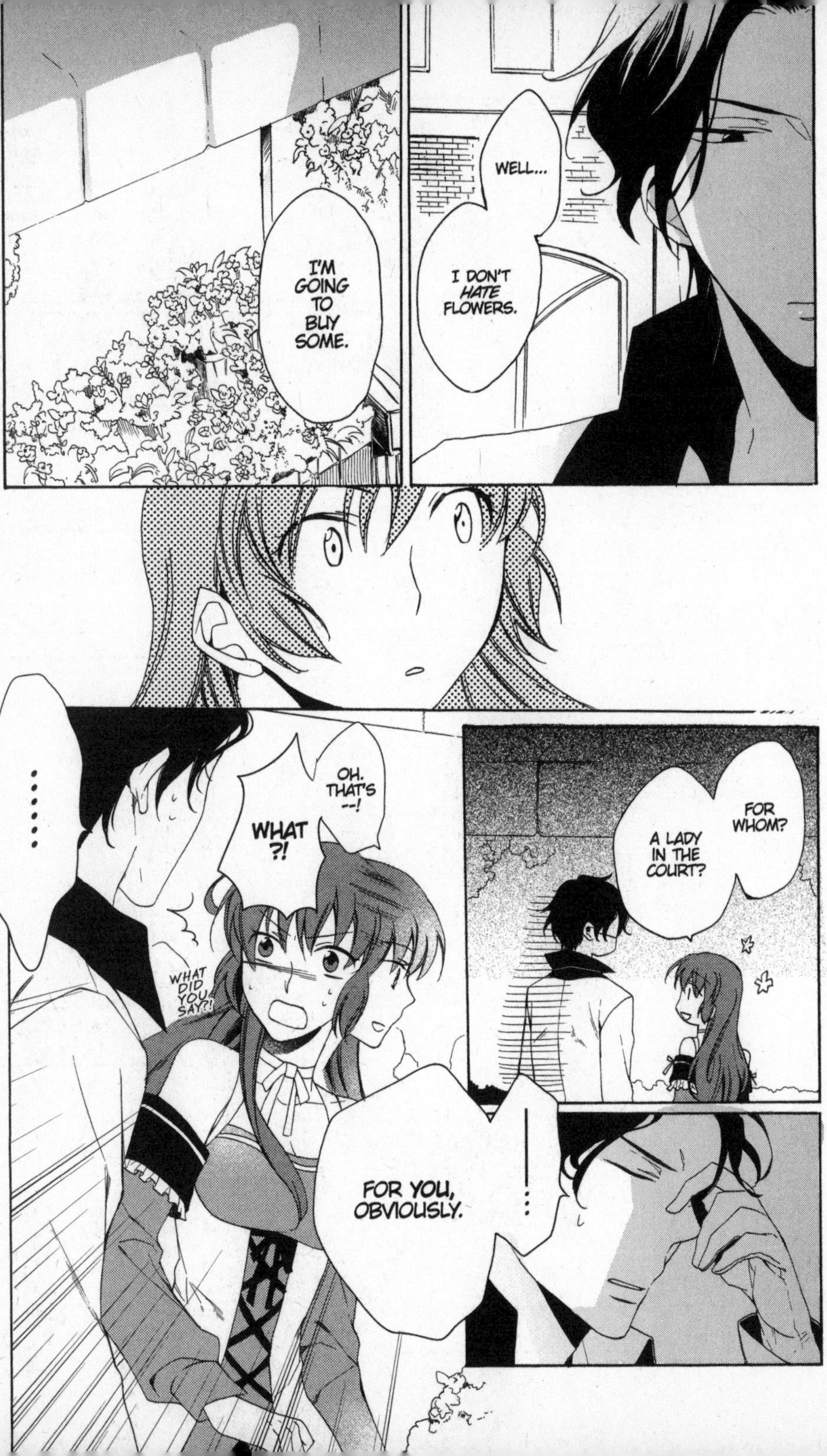
WELL...
I DON'T *HATE* FLOWERS.
I'M GOING TO BUY SOME.
FOR WHOM?
A LADY IN THE COURT?
......
FOR YOU, OBVIOUSLY.
OH. THAT'S --!
WHAT ?!
WHAT DID YOU SAY?!
......

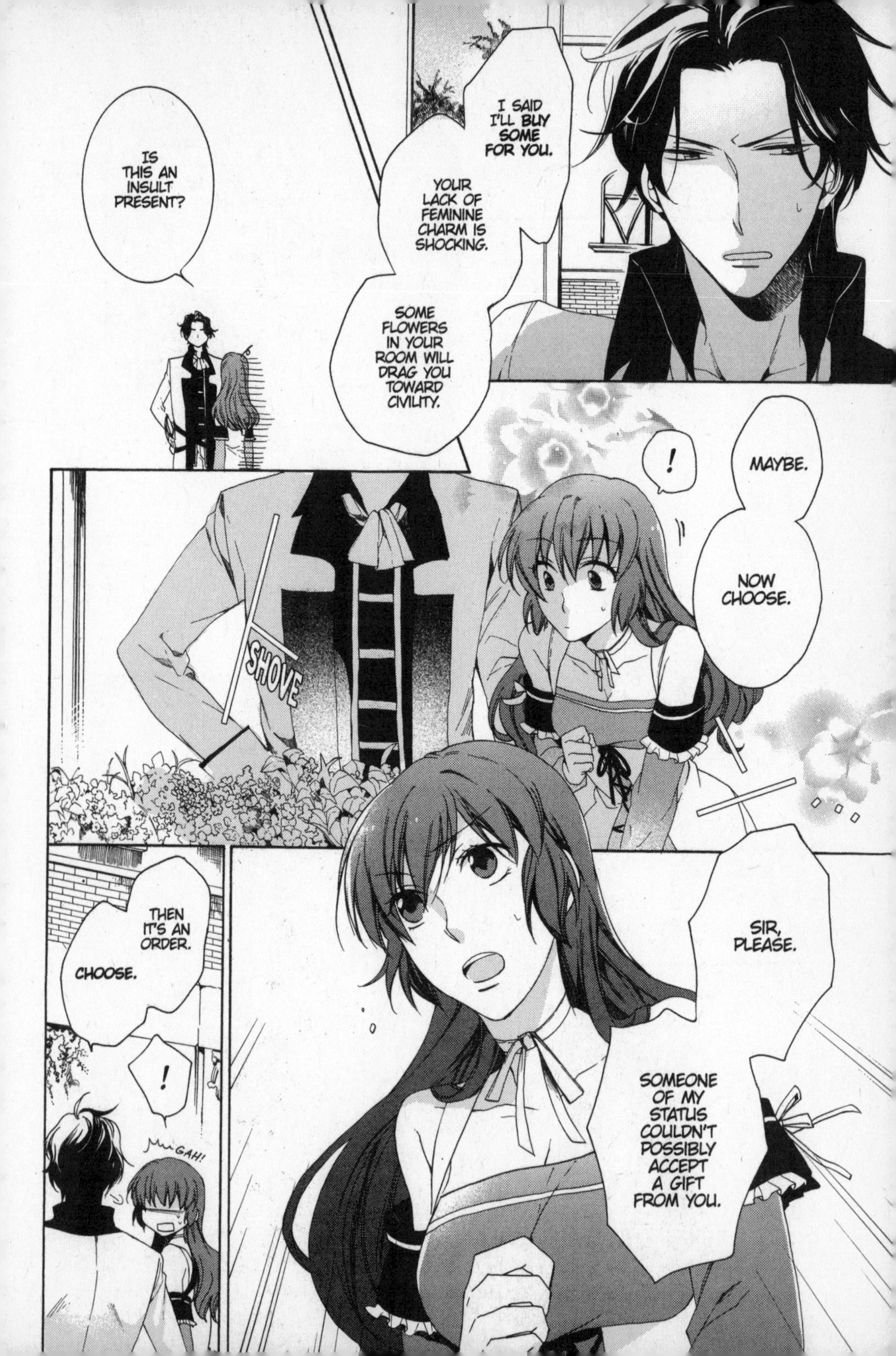
I SAID I'LL BUY SOME FOR YOU.
YOUR LACK OF FEMININE CHARM IS SHOCKING.
SOME FLOWERS IN YOUR ROOM WILL DRAG YOU TOWARD CIVILITY.
IS THIS AN INSULT PRESENT?
MAYBE.
NOW CHOOSE.
!
SHOVE
...
SIR, PLEASE.
SOMEONE OF MY STATUS COULDN'T POSSIBLY ACCEPT A GIFT FROM YOU.
THEN IT'S AN ORDER.
CHOOSE.
!
MUGAH!

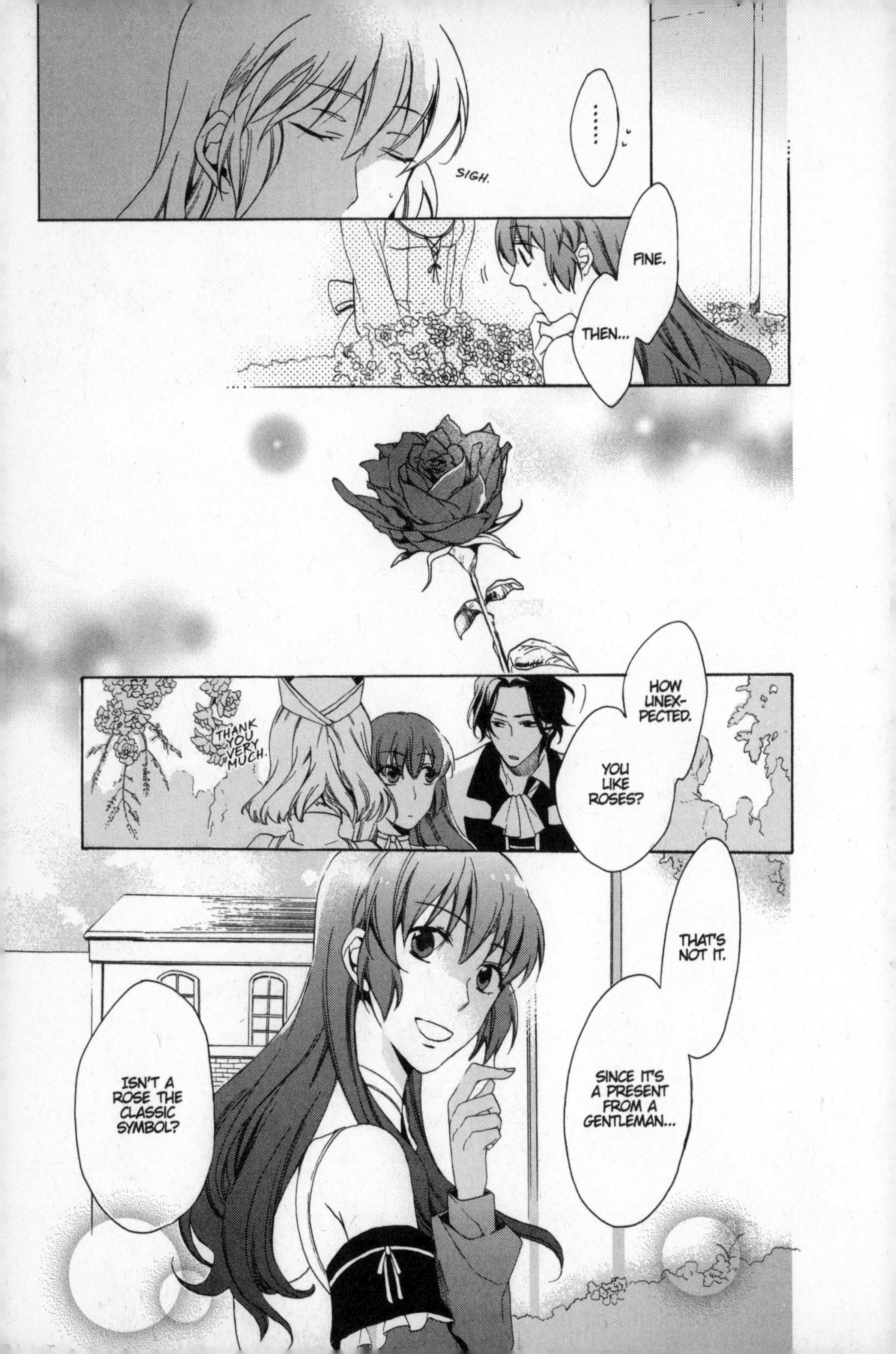
......
SIGH.
FINE. THEN...
......
HOW UNEX-PECTED.
YOU LIKE ROSES?
THANK YOU VERY MUCH.
THAT'S NOT IT.
SINCE IT'S A PRESENT FROM A GENTLEMAN...
ISN'T A ROSE THE CLASSIC SYMBOL?

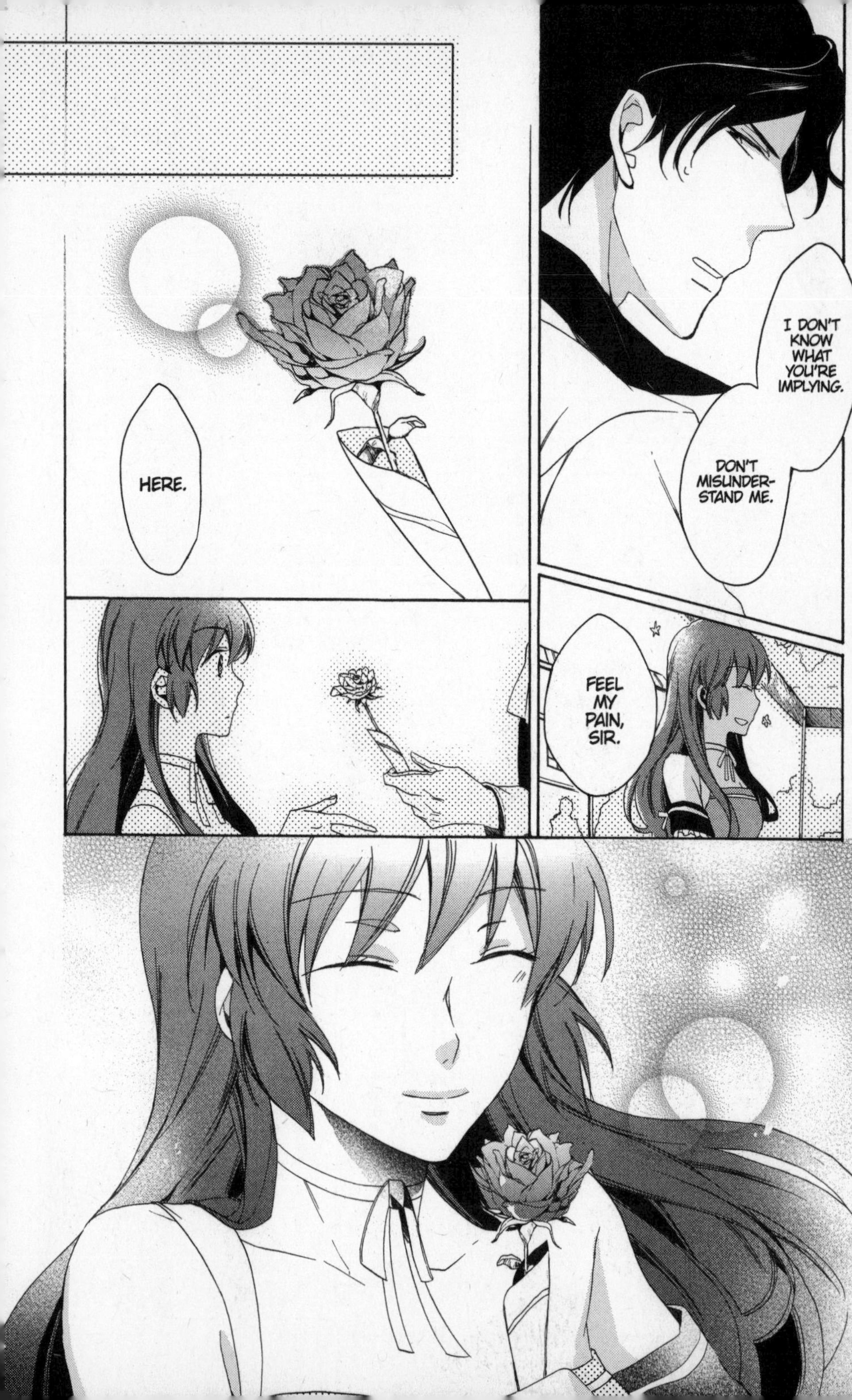
I DON'T KNOW WHAT YOU'RE IMPLYING.
DON'T MISUNDERSTAND ME.
HERE.
FEEL MY PAIN, SIR.

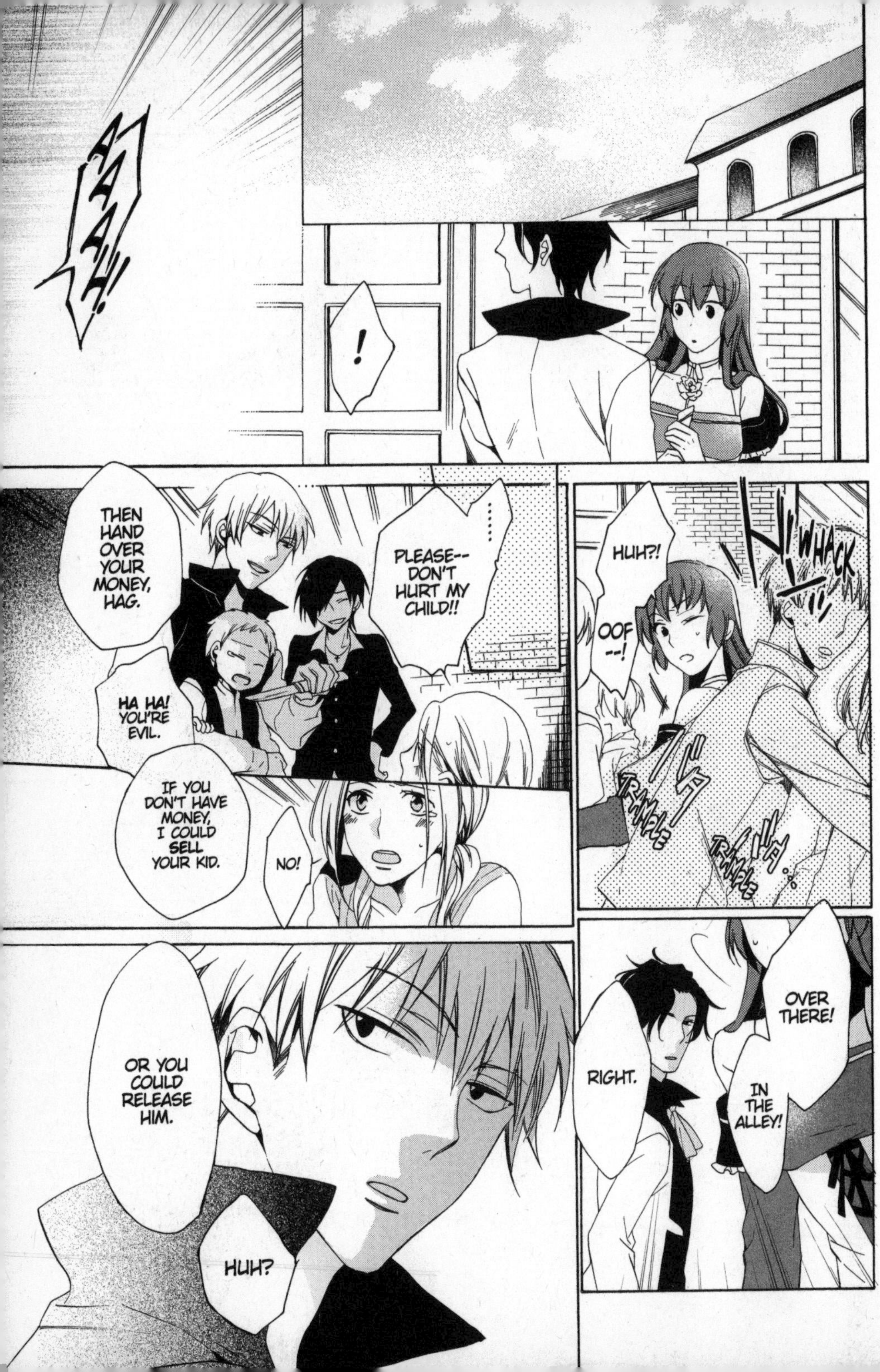
!
AAAAH!!
HUH?!
WHACK
OOF--!
TRAMPLE
TRAMPLE
.....
PLEASE-- DON'T HURT MY CHILD!!
THEN HAND OVER YOUR MONEY, HAG.
HA HA! YOU'RE EVIL.
NO!
IF YOU DON'T HAVE MONEY, I COULD SELL YOUR KID.
OVER THERE!
IN THE ALLEY!
RIGHT.
OR YOU COULD RELEASE HIM.
HUH?

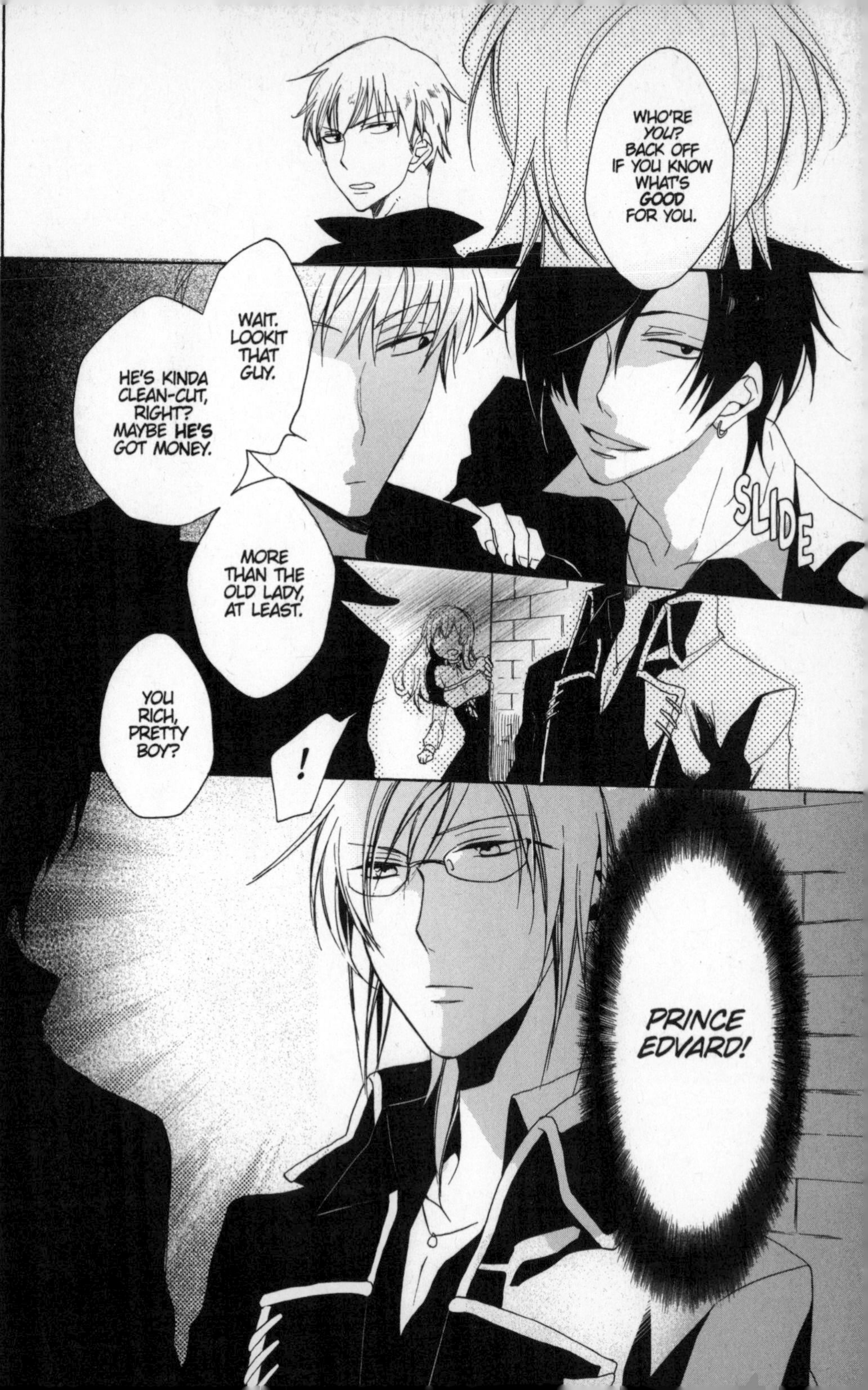
WHO'RE YOU? BACK OFF IF YOU KNOW WHAT'S GOOD FOR YOU.
WAIT. LOOKIT THAT GUY.
HE'S KINDA CLEAN-CUT, RIGHT? MAYBE HE'S GOT MONEY.
SLIDE
MORE THAN THE OLD LADY, AT LEAST.
YOU RICH, PRETTY BOY?
!
PRINCE EDVARD!

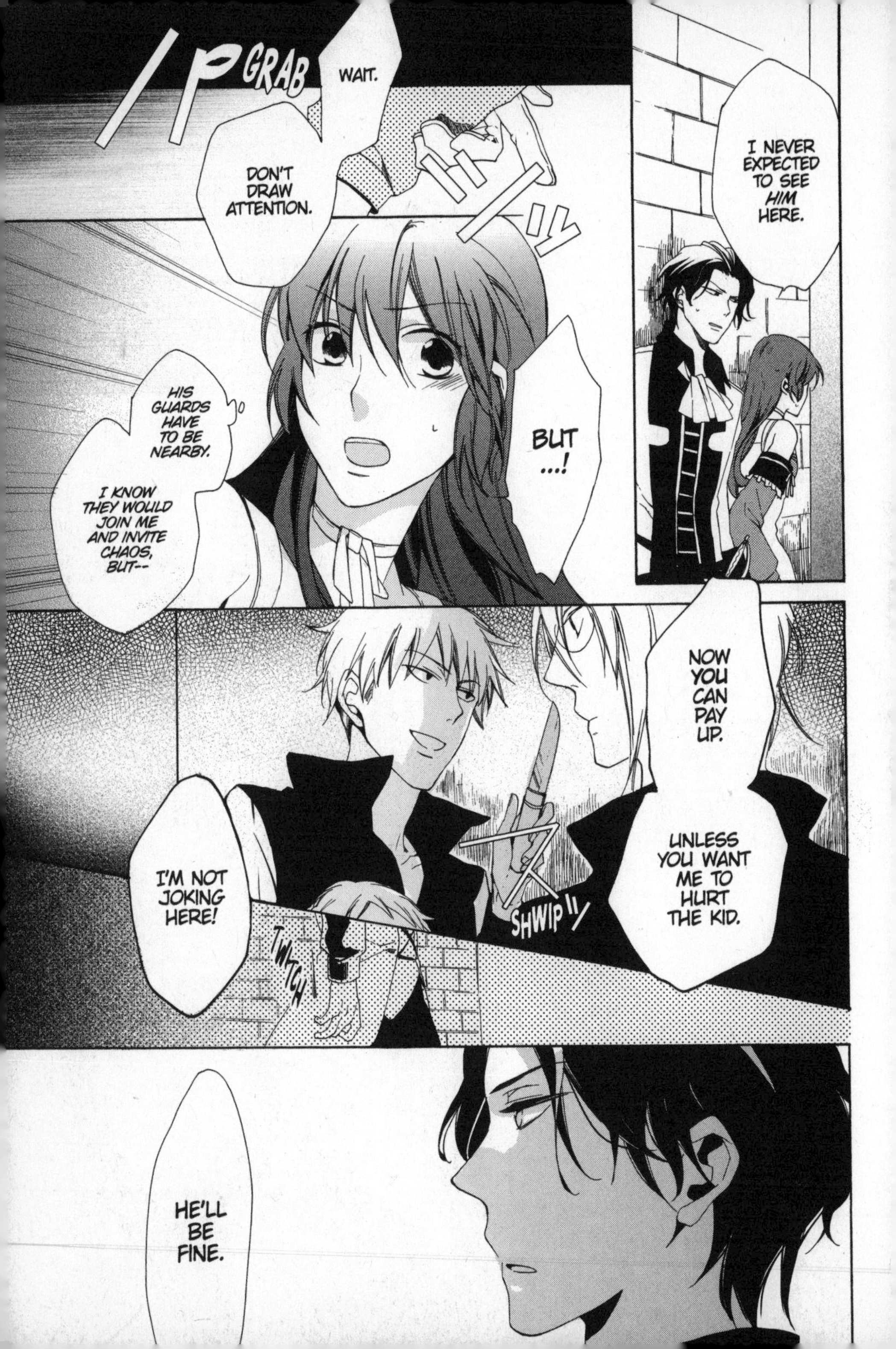
I NEVER EXPECTED TO SEE HIM HERE.
GRAB
WAIT.
DON'T DRAW ATTENTION.
BUT ...!
HIS GUARDS HAVE TO BE NEARBY.
I KNOW THEY WOULD JOIN ME AND INVITE CHAOS, BUT--
NOW YOU CAN PAY UP.
UNLESS YOU WANT ME TO HURT THE KID.
SHWIP
I'M NOT JOKING HERE!
TWITCH
HE'LL BE FINE.

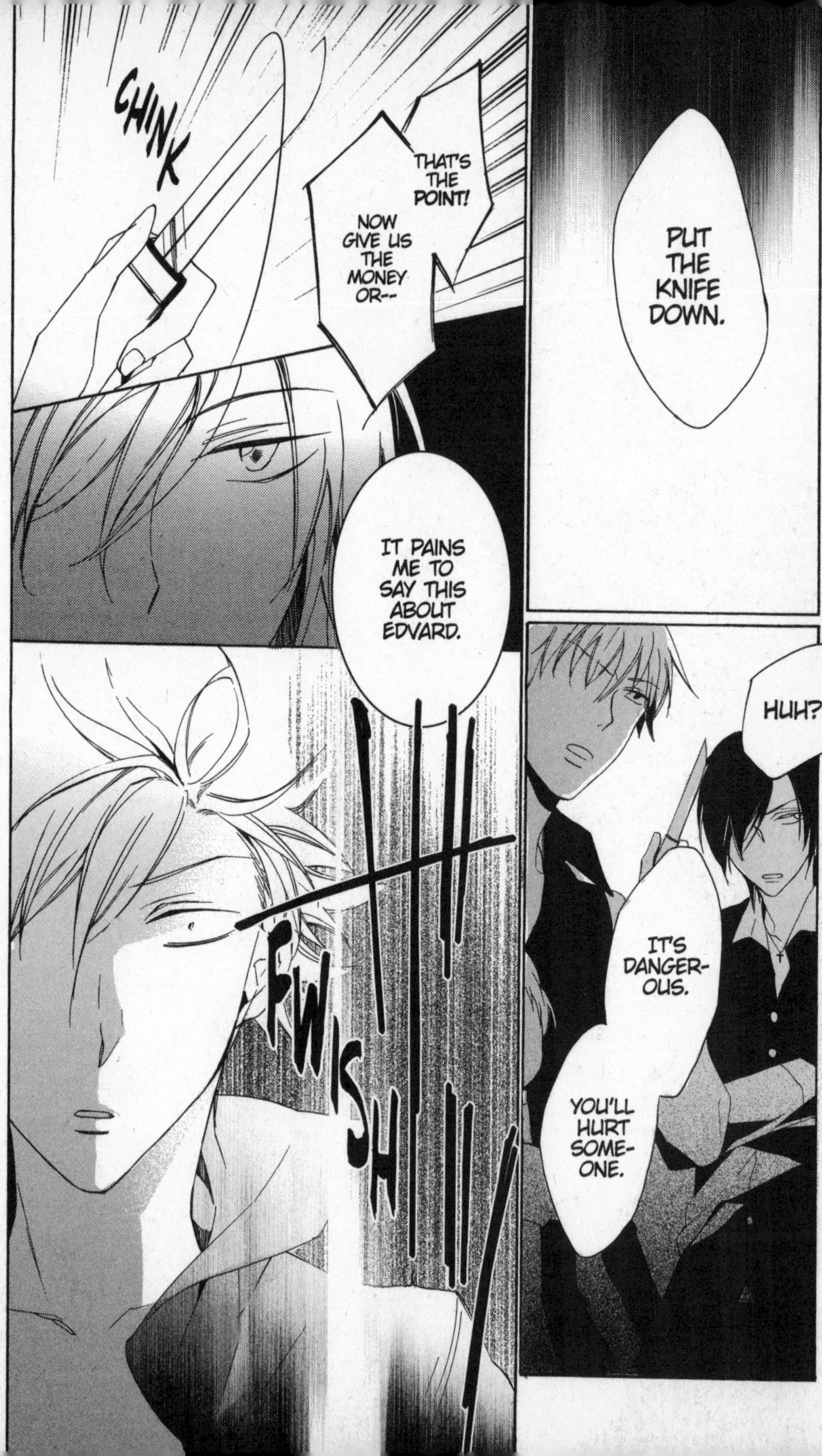
PUT THE KNIFE DOWN.
CHINK
THAT'S THE POINT!
NOW GIVE US THE MONEY OR--
IT PAINS ME TO SAY THIS ABOUT EDVARD.
HUH?
IT'S DANGER-OUS.
YOU'LL HURT SOME-ONE.
FWISH

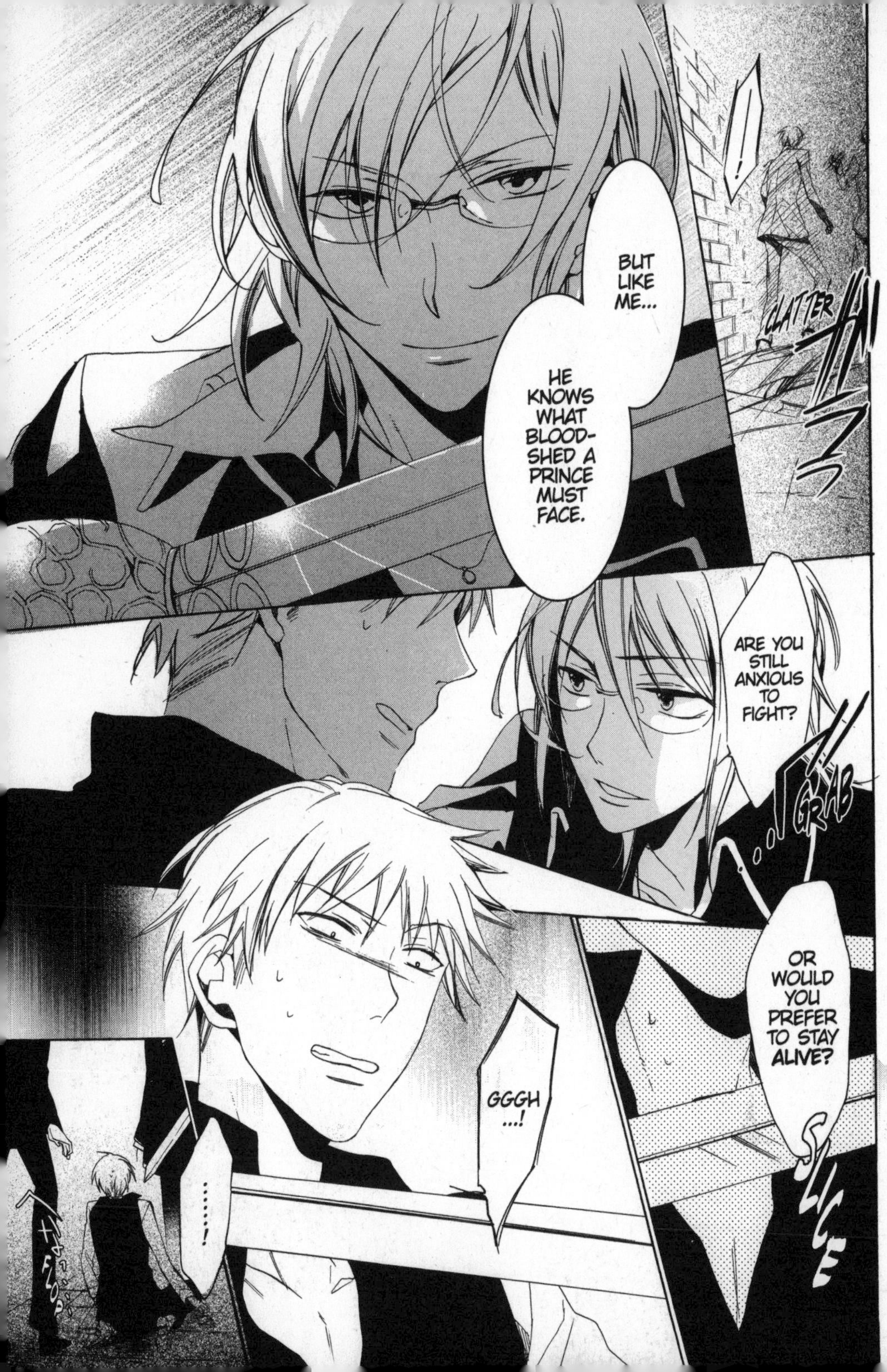
!
CLATTER
BUT LIKE ME...
HE KNOWS WHAT BLOOD-SHED A PRINCE MUST FACE.
ARE YOU STILL ANXIOUS TO FIGHT?
GRAB
...
OR WOULD YOU PREFER TO STAY ALIVE?
SLICE
GGGH ...!
......!

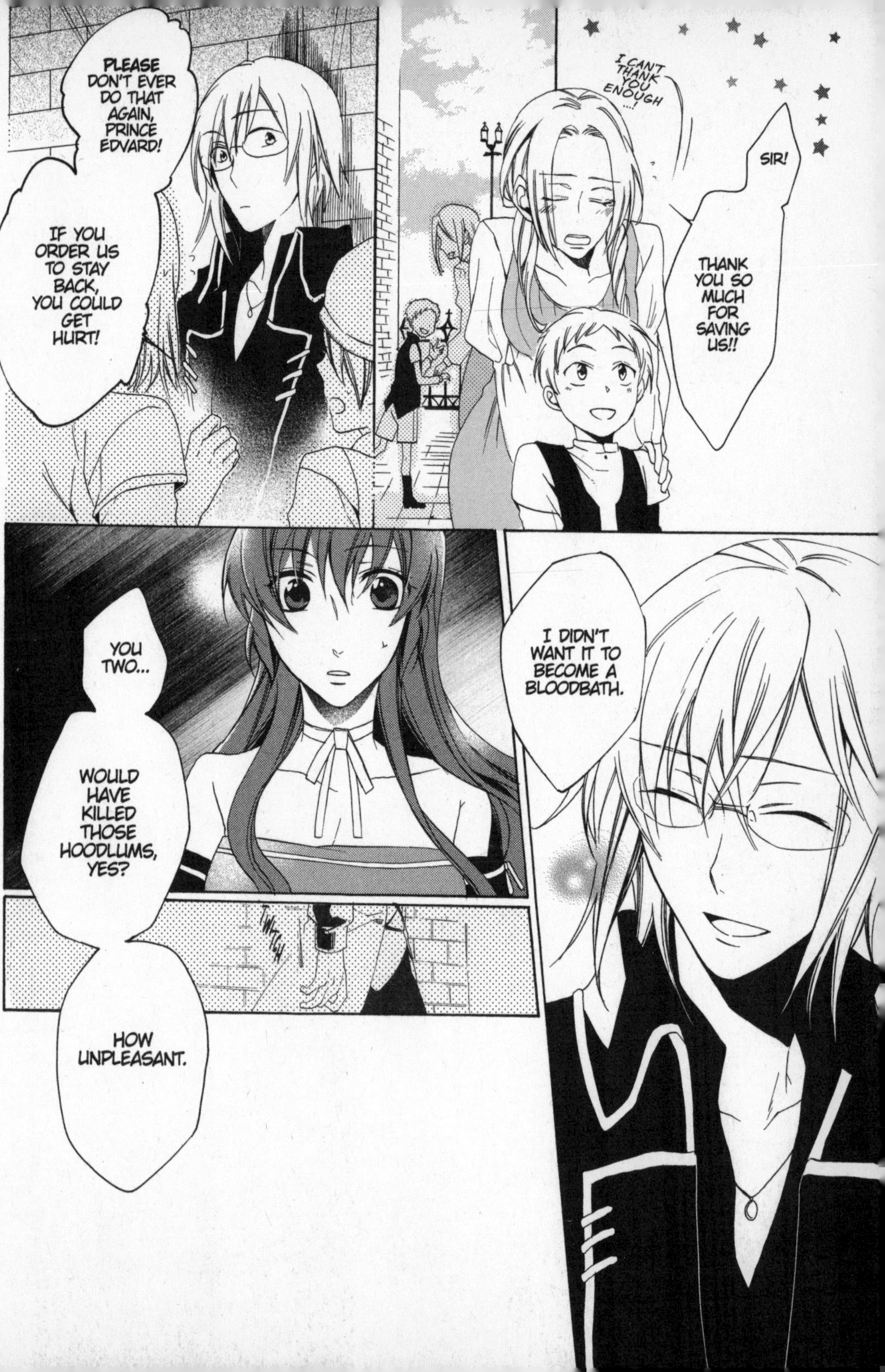
SIR!
THANK YOU SO MUCH FOR SAVING US!!
I CAN'T THANK YOU ENOUGH...!
PLEASE DON'T EVER DO THAT AGAIN, PRINCE EDVARD!
IF YOU ORDER US TO STAY BACK, YOU COULD GET HURT!
I DIDN'T WANT IT TO BECOME A BLOODBATH.
YOU TWO...
WOULD HAVE KILLED THOSE HOODLUMS, YES?
TWITCH
HOW UNPLEASANT.

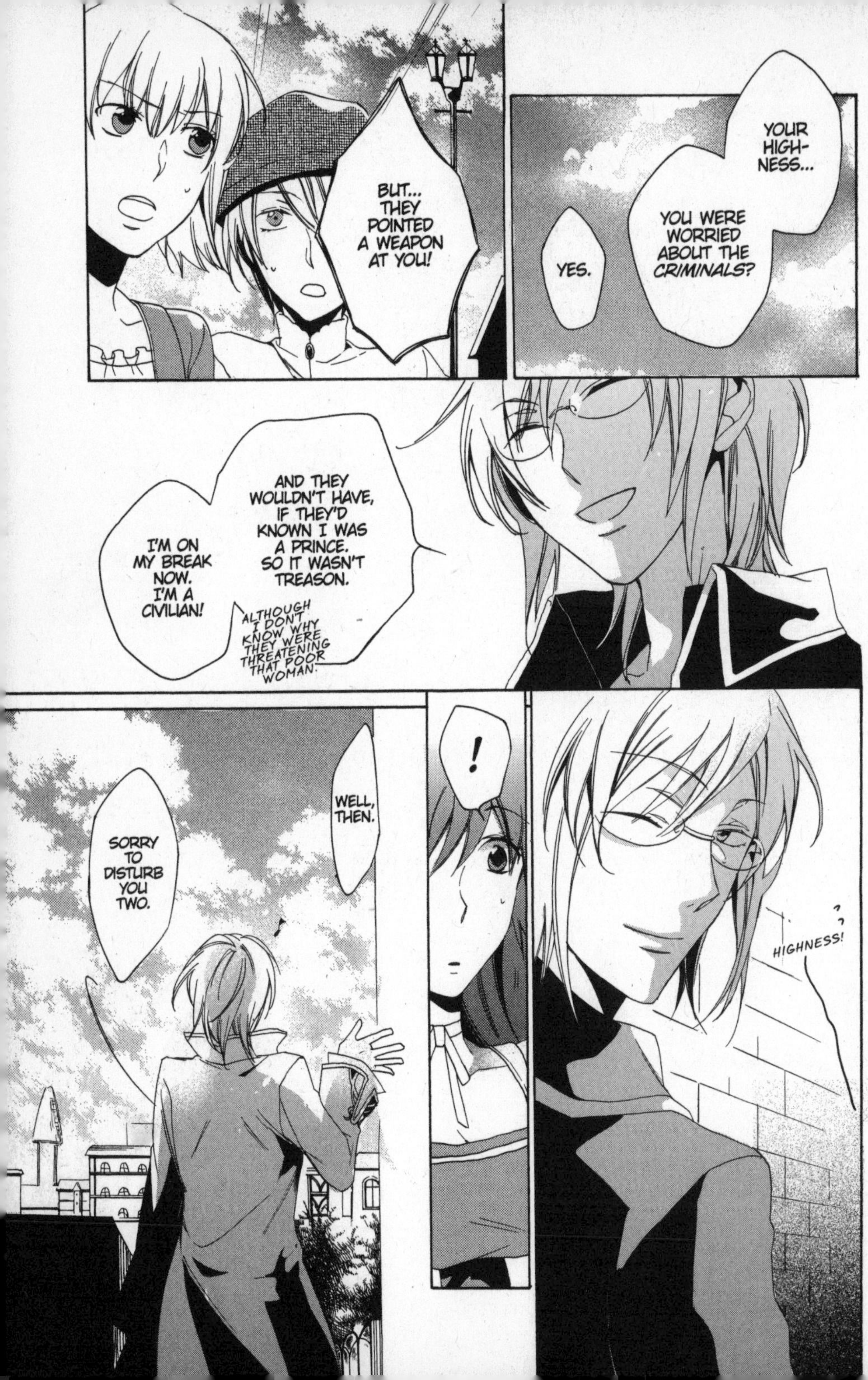
YOUR HIGH-NESS...
YOU WERE WORRIED ABOUT THE *CRIMINALS*?
YES.
BUT... THEY POINTED A WEAPON AT YOU!
AND THEY WOULDN'T HAVE, IF THEY'D KNOWN I WAS A PRINCE. SO IT WASN'T TREASON.
I'M ON MY BREAK NOW. I'M A CIVILIAN!
ALTHOUGH I DON'T KNOW WHY THEY WERE THREATENING THAT POOR WOMAN.
HIGHNESS!
!
WELL, THEN.
SORRY TO DISTURB YOU TWO.

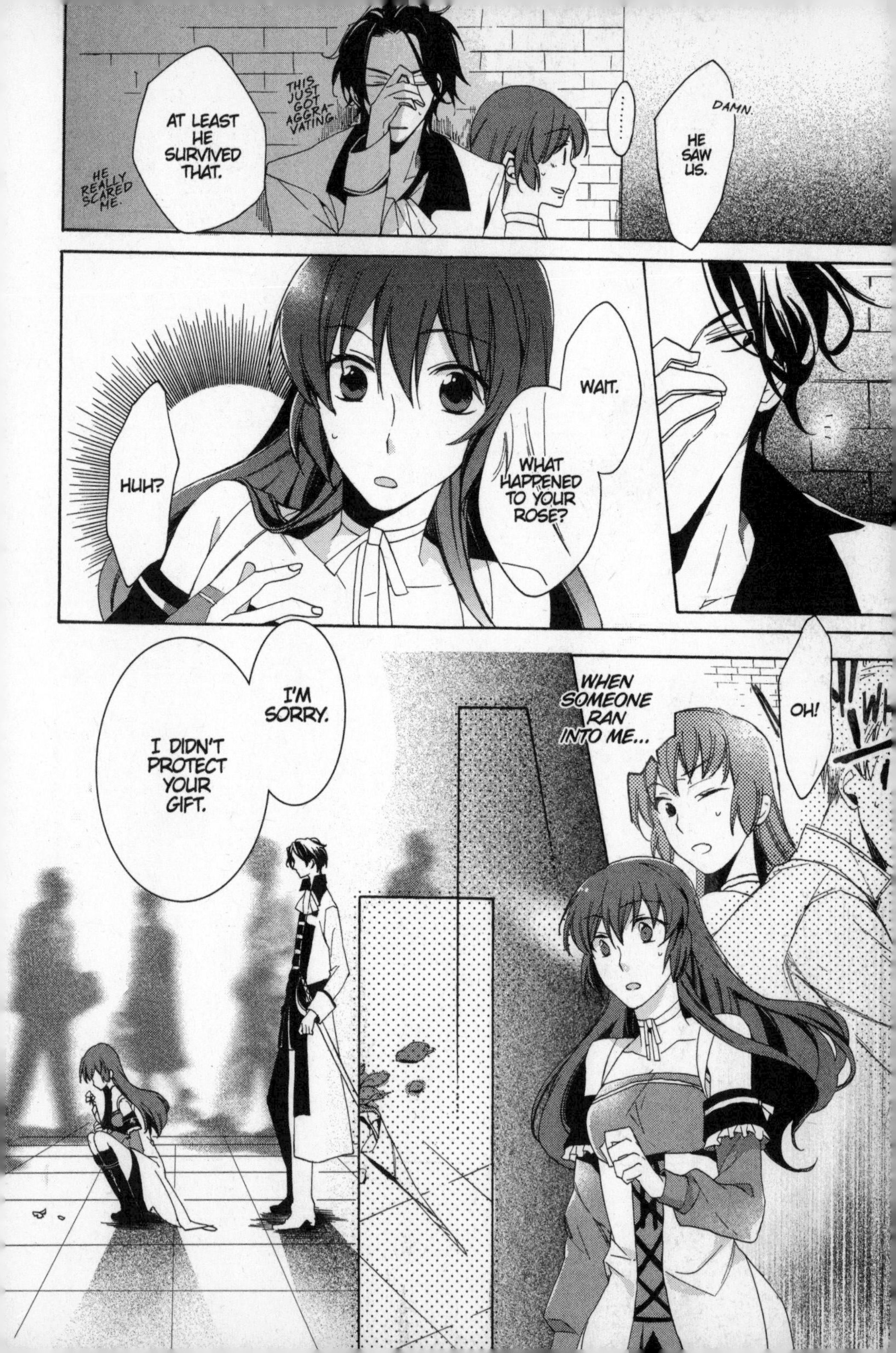
DAMN.
HE SAW US.
......
THIS JUST GOT AGGRAVATING.
AT LEAST HE SURVIVED THAT.
HE REALLY SCARED ME.
WAIT.
WHAT HAPPENED TO YOUR ROSE?
HUH?
OH!
WHEN SOMEONE RAN INTO ME...
I'M SORRY.
I DIDN'T PROTECT YOUR GIFT.

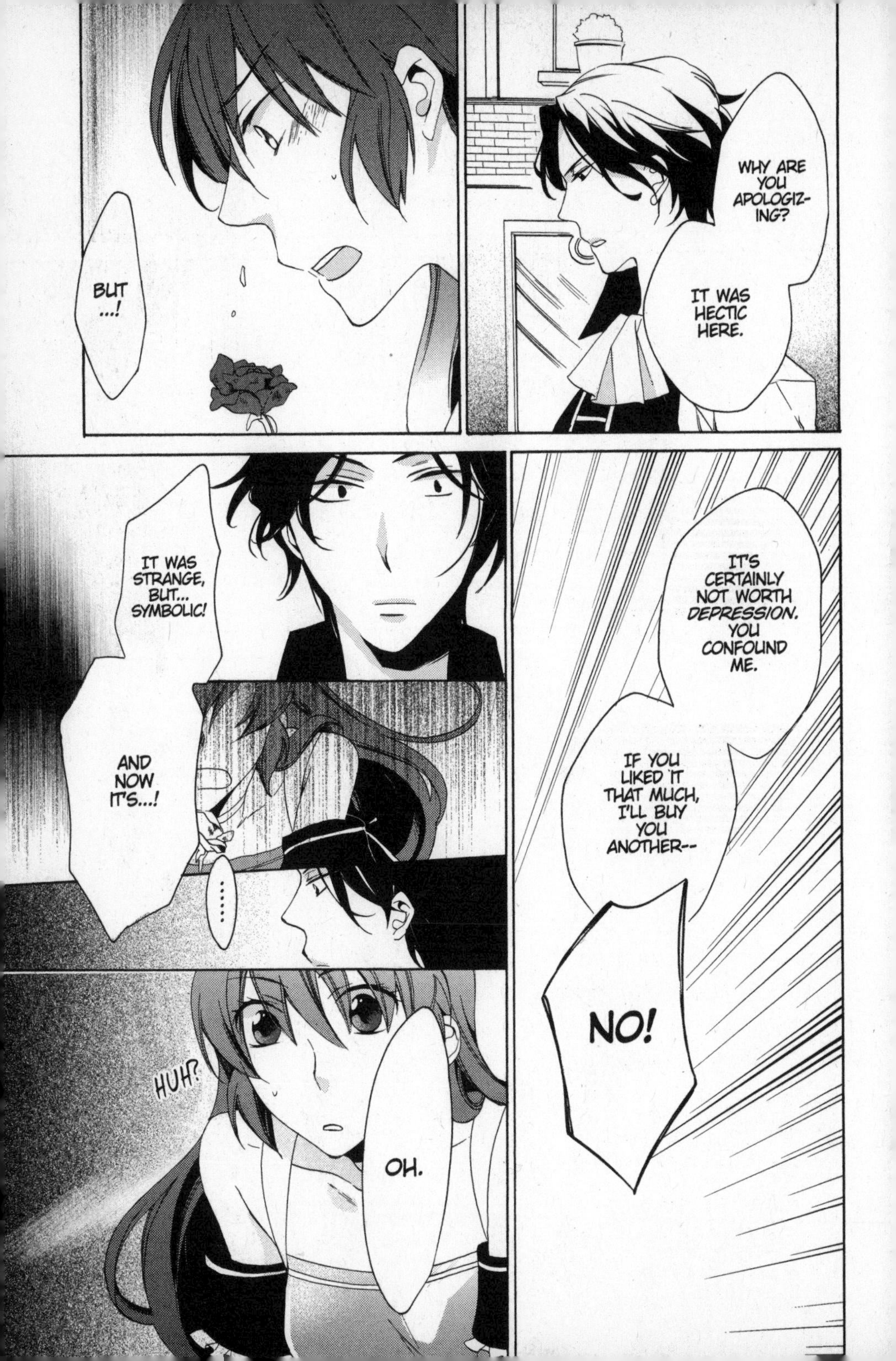

WHY ARE YOU APOLOGIZING?
IT WAS HECTIC HERE.
BUT ...!
IT'S CERTAINLY NOT WORTH *DEPRESSION*. YOU CONFOUND ME.
IF YOU LIKED IT THAT MUCH, I'LL BUY YOU ANOTHER--
NO!
IT WAS STRANGE, BUT... SYMBOLIC!
AND NOW IT'S...!
......
HUH?
OH.

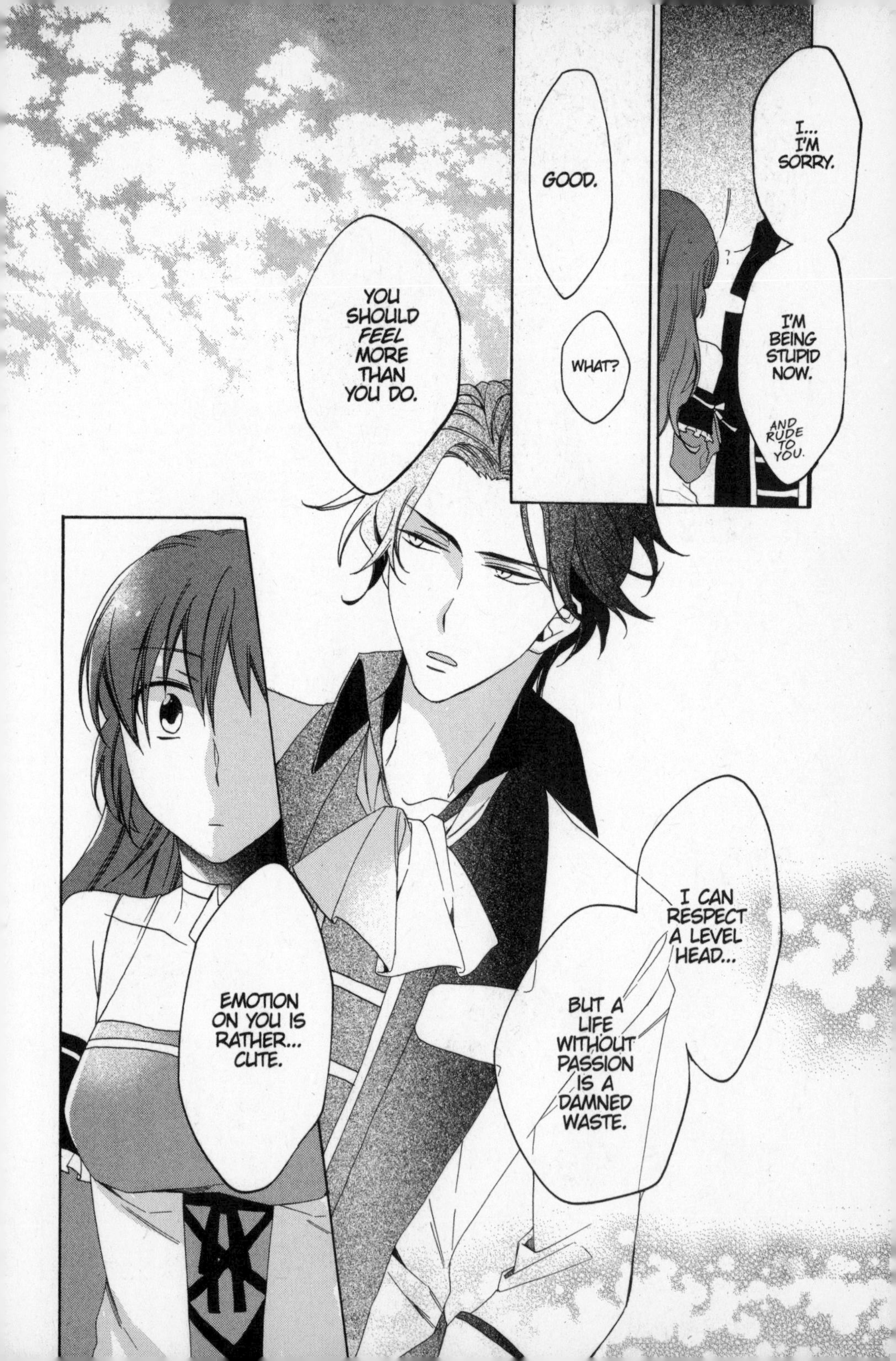

I... I'M SORRY.
I'M BEING STUPID NOW.
AND RUDE TO YOU.
GOOD.
WHAT?
YOU SHOULD FEEL MORE THAN YOU DO.
I CAN RESPECT A LEVEL HEAD...
BUT A LIFE WITHOUT PASSION IS A DAMNED WASTE.
EMOTION ON YOU IS RATHER... CUTE.

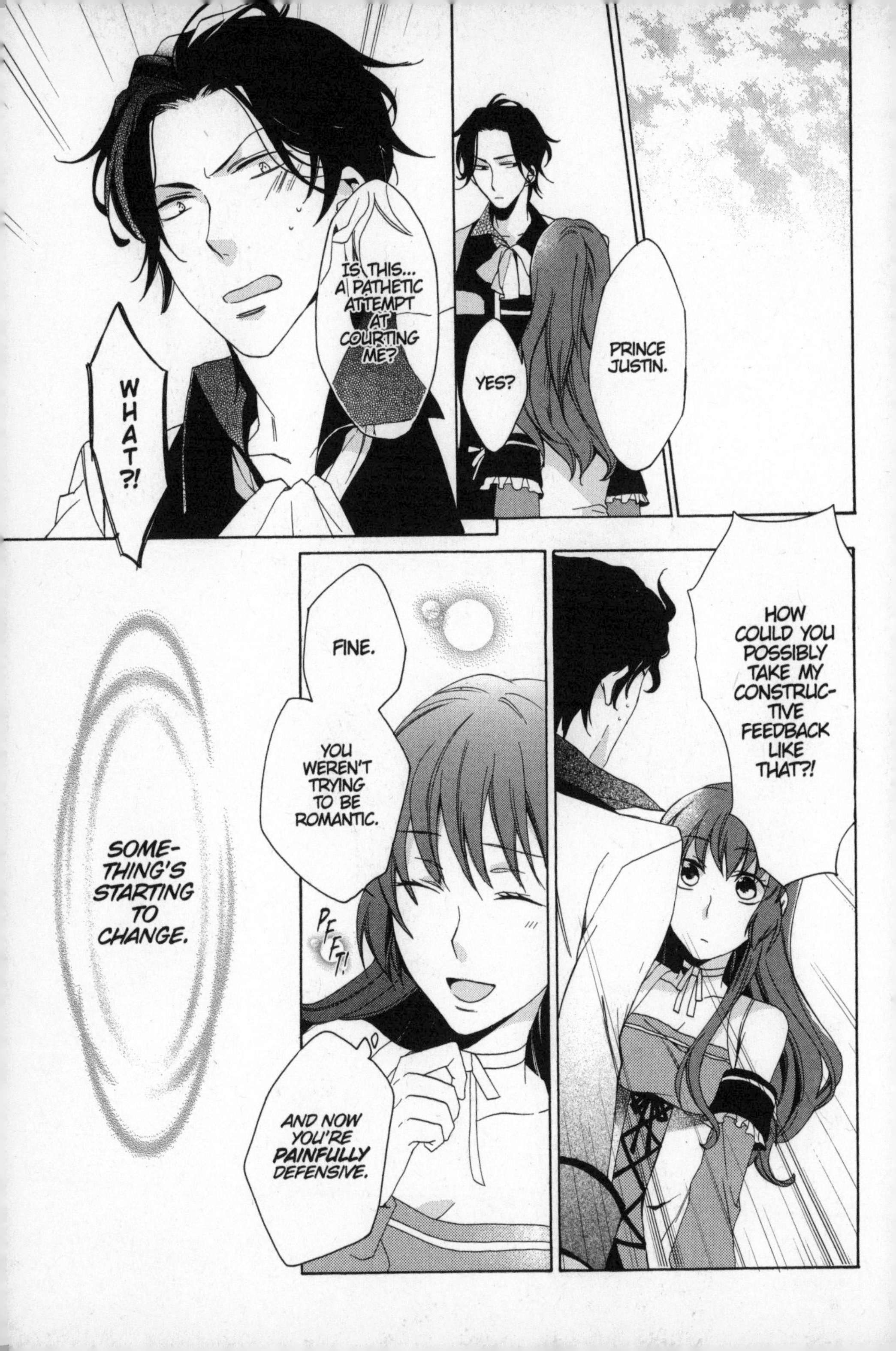
PRINCE JUSTIN.
YES?
IS THIS... A PATHETIC ATTEMPT AT COURTING ME?
WHAT?!
HOW COULD YOU POSSIBLY TAKE MY CONSTRUC-TIVE FEEDBACK LIKE THAT?!
FINE.
YOU WEREN'T TRYING TO BE ROMANTIC.
PFFT!
AND NOW YOU'RE PAINFULLY DEFENSIVE.
SOME-THING'S STARTING TO CHANGE.

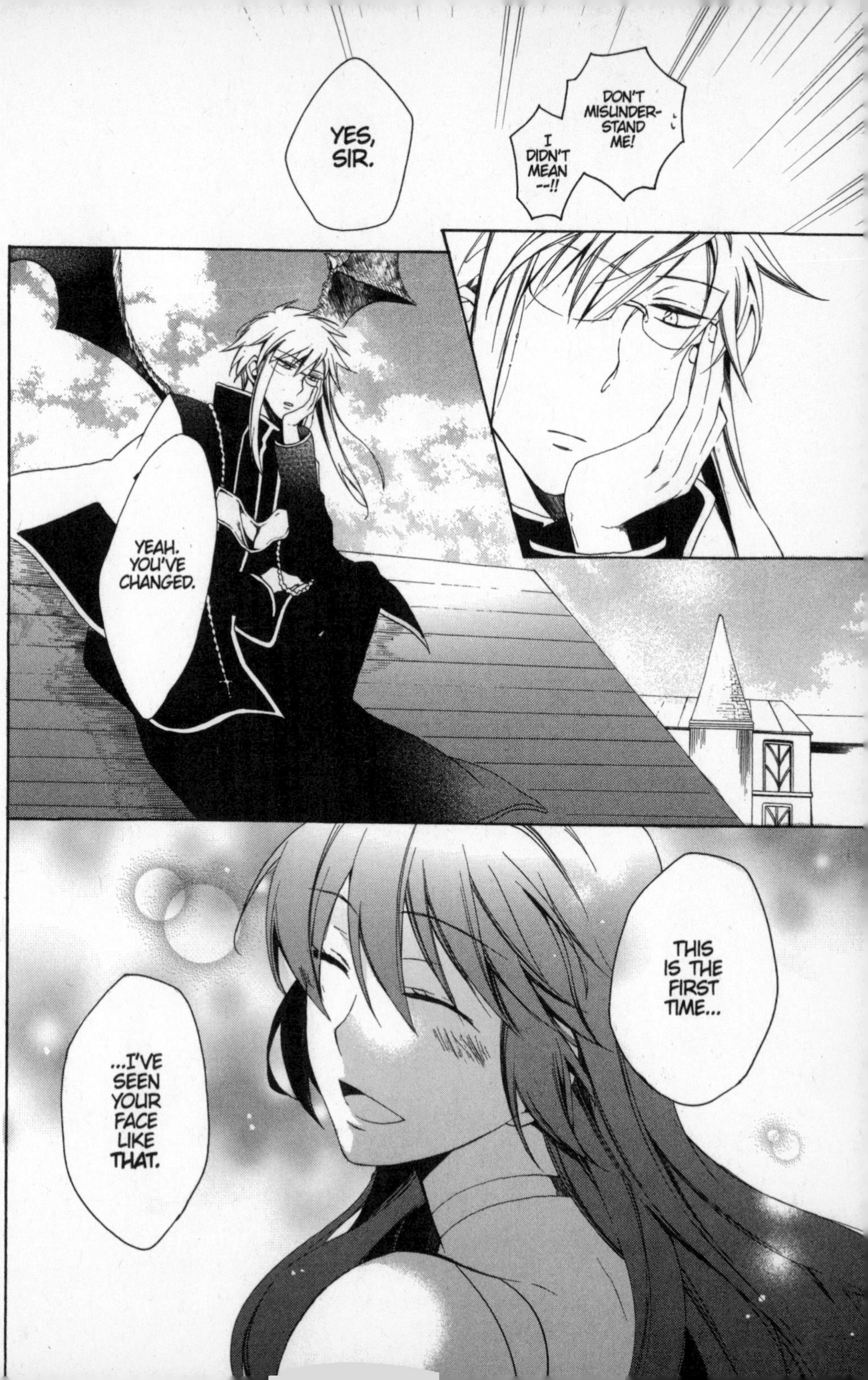
DON'T MISUNDER-STAND ME!
I DIDN'T MEAN --!!
YES, SIR.
YEAH. YOU'VE CHANGED.
THIS IS THE FIRST TIME...
...I'VE SEEN YOUR FACE LIKE THAT.

CRIMSON EMPIRE

Circumstances to Serve a Noble

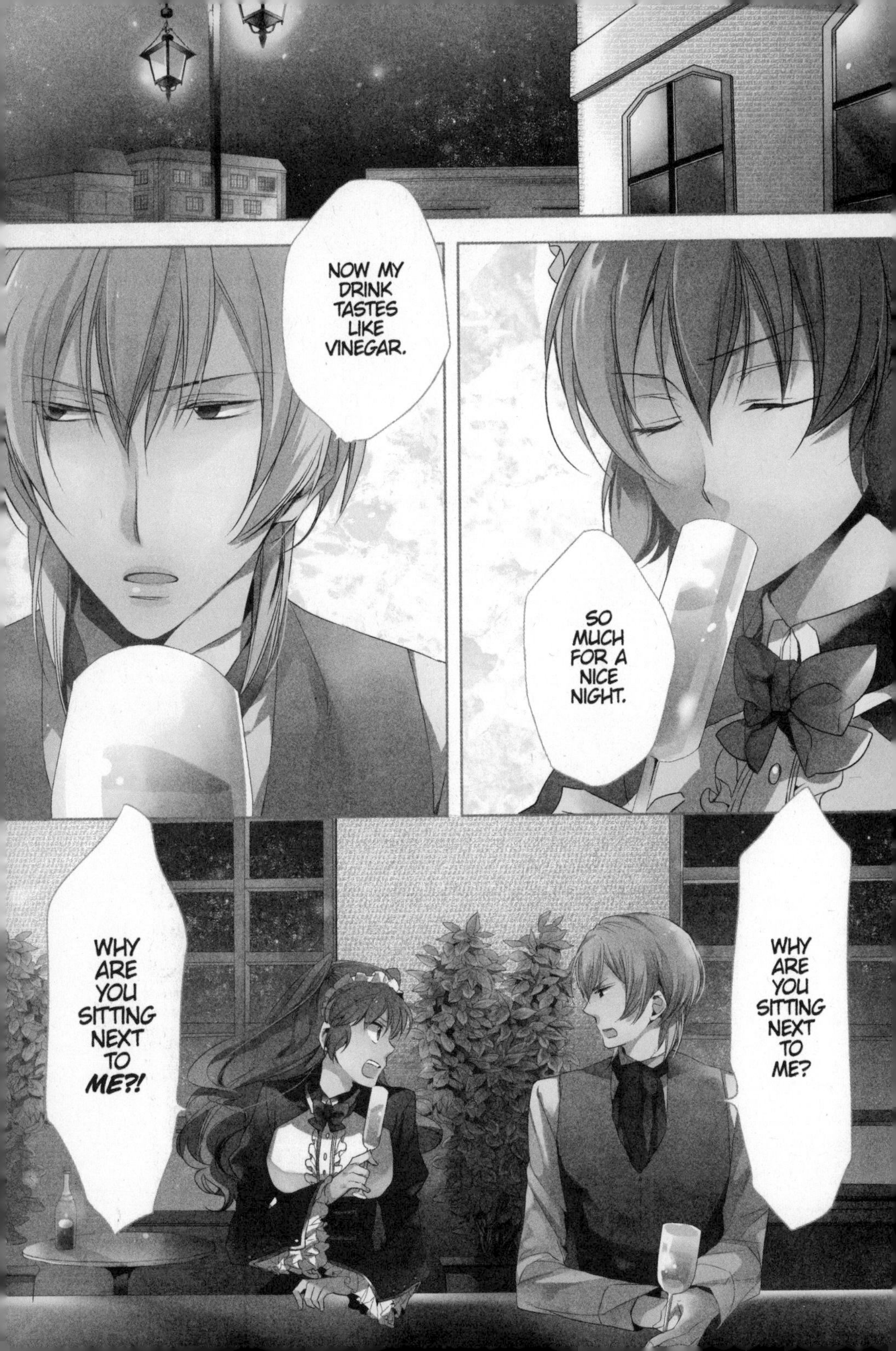
SO MUCH FOR A NICE NIGHT.
NOW MY DRINK TASTES LIKE VINEGAR.
WHY ARE YOU SITTING NEXT TO ME?
WHY ARE YOU SITTING NEXT TO *ME*?!

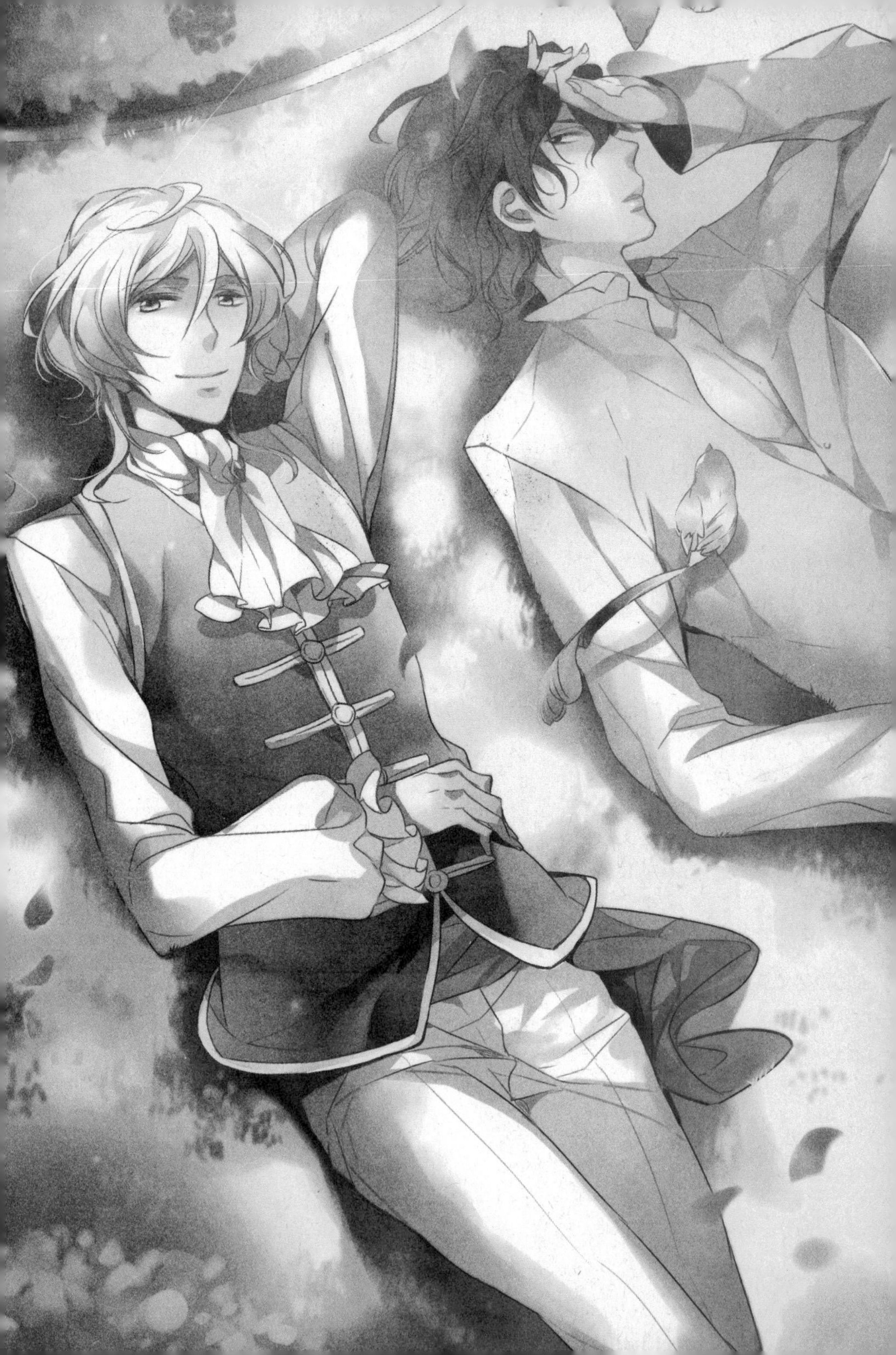

#7

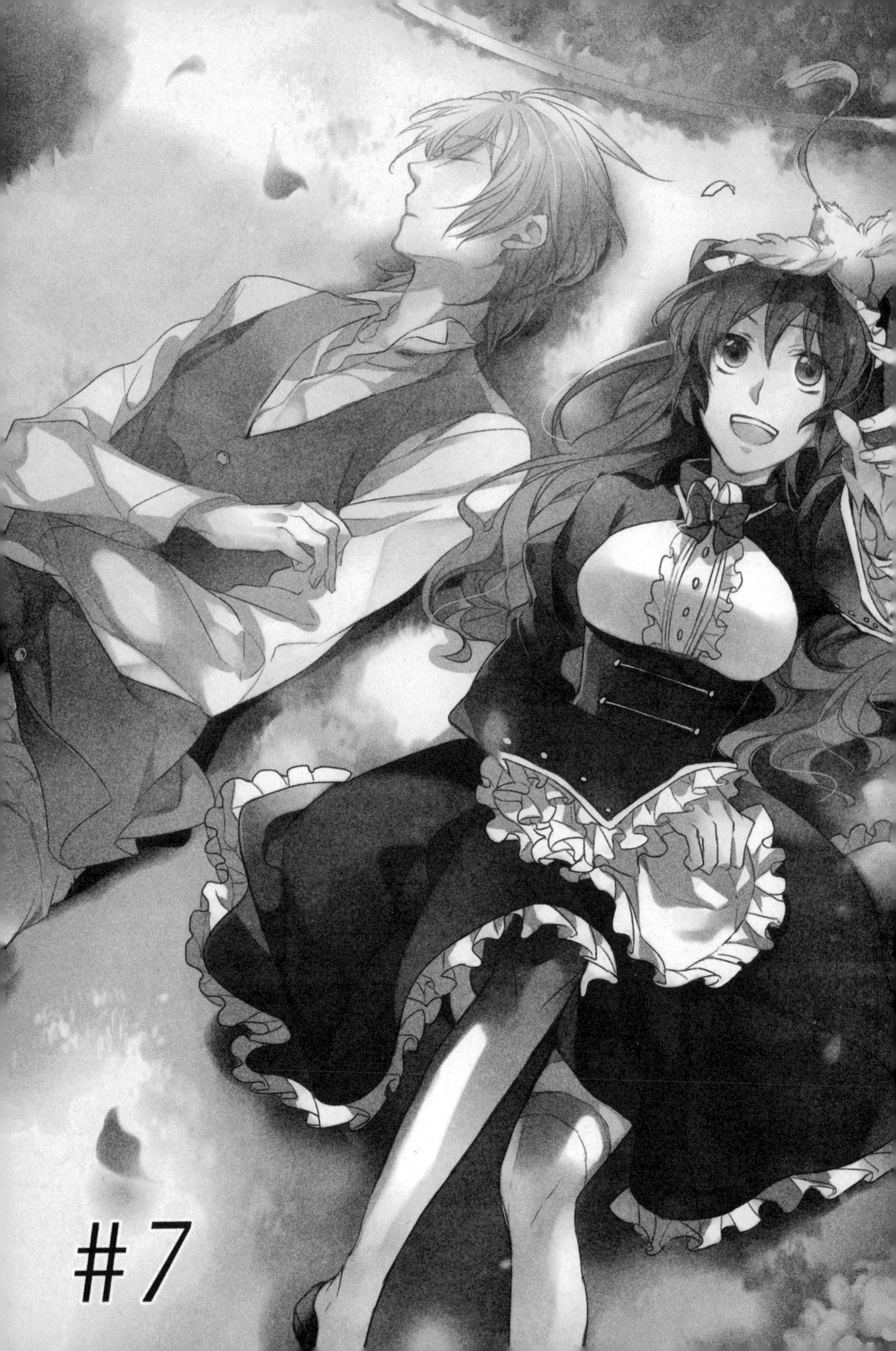

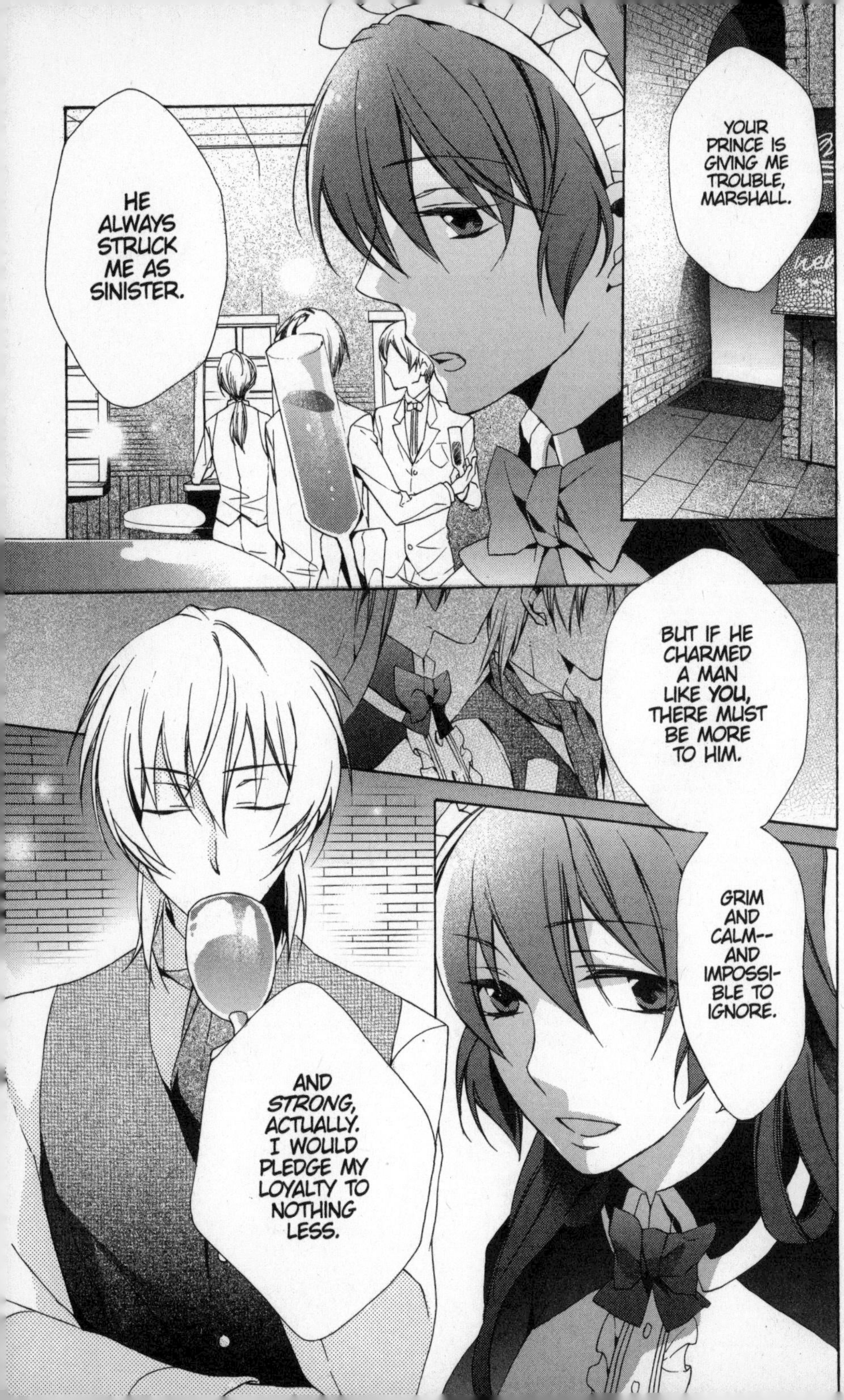
YOUR PRINCE IS GIVING ME TROUBLE, MARSHALL.
HE ALWAYS STRUCK ME AS SINISTER.
BUT IF HE CHARMED A MAN LIKE YOU, THERE MUST BE MORE TO HIM.
GRIM AND CALM--AND IMPOSSIBLE TO IGNORE.
AND *STRONG*, ACTUALLY. I WOULD PLEDGE MY LOYALTY TO NOTHING LESS.

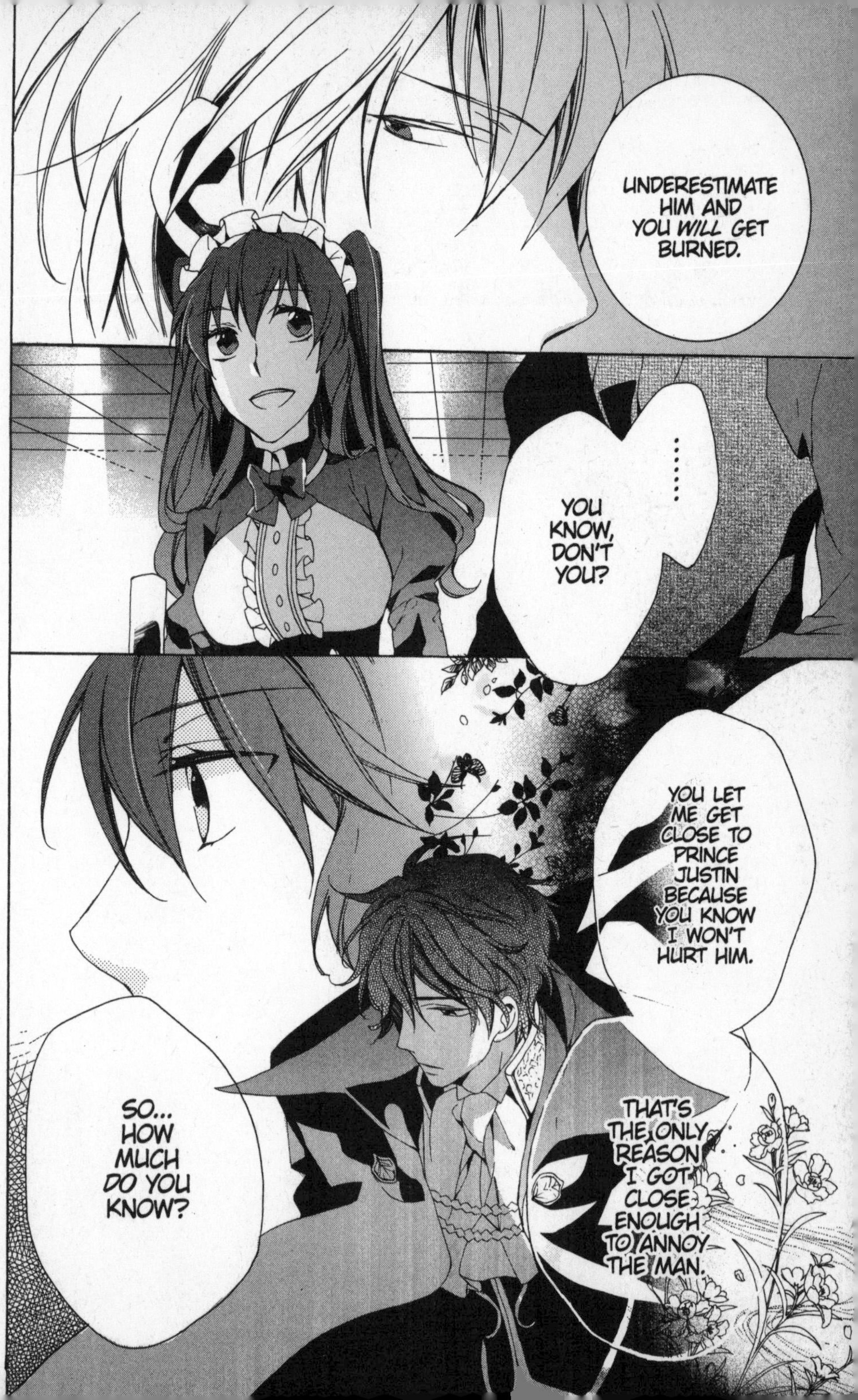
UNDERESTIMATE HIM AND YOU *WILL* GET BURNED.
......
YOU KNOW, DON'T YOU?
YOU LET ME GET CLOSE TO PRINCE JUSTIN BECAUSE YOU KNOW I WON'T HURT HIM.
THAT'S THE ONLY REASON I GOT CLOSE ENOUGH TO ANNOY THE MAN.
SO... HOW MUCH *DO* YOU KNOW?

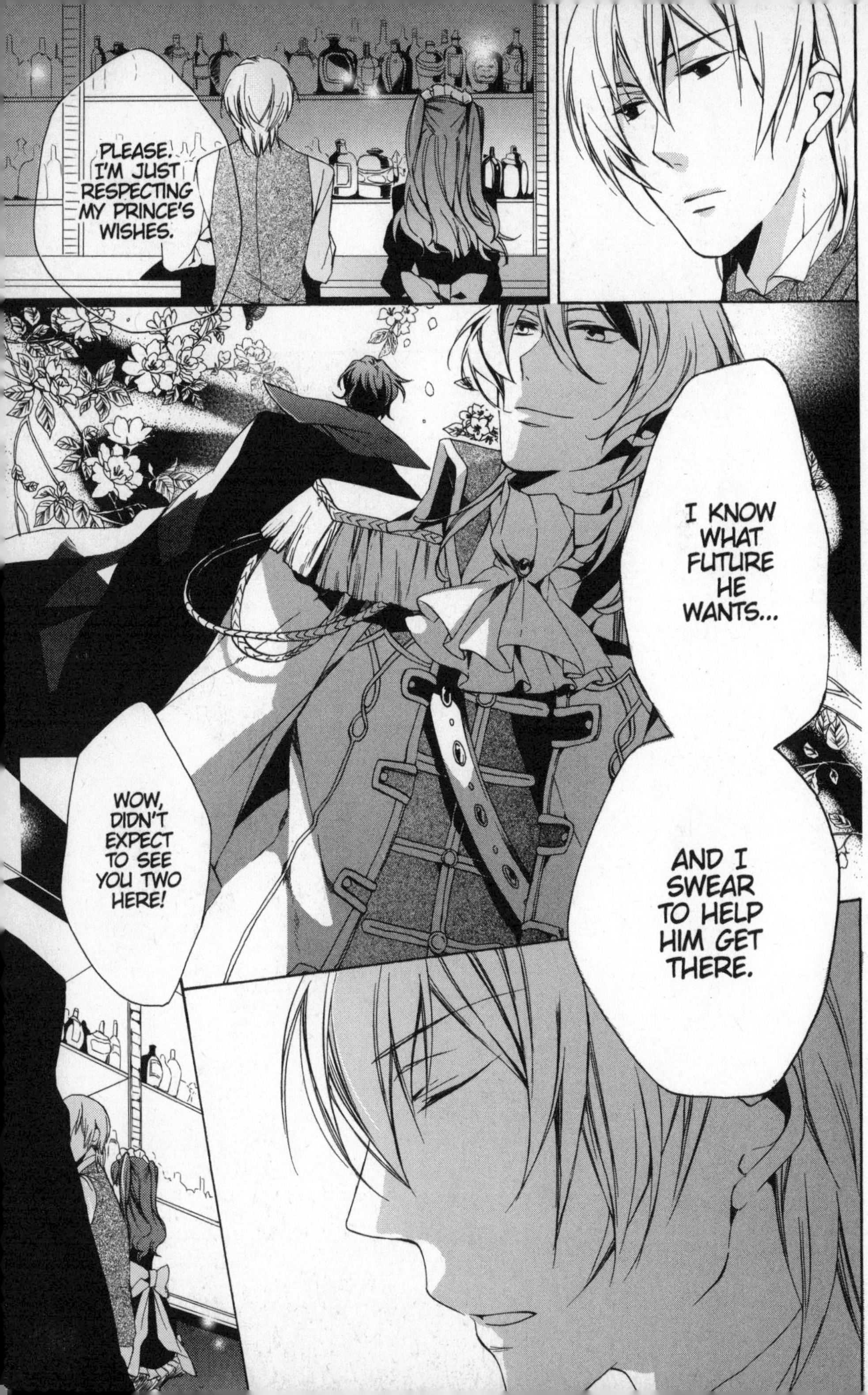
PLEASE. I'M JUST RESPECTING MY PRINCE'S WISHES.
I KNOW WHAT FUTURE HE WANTS...
AND I SWEAR TO HELP HIM GET THERE.
WOW, DIDN'T EXPECT TO SEE YOU TWO HERE!

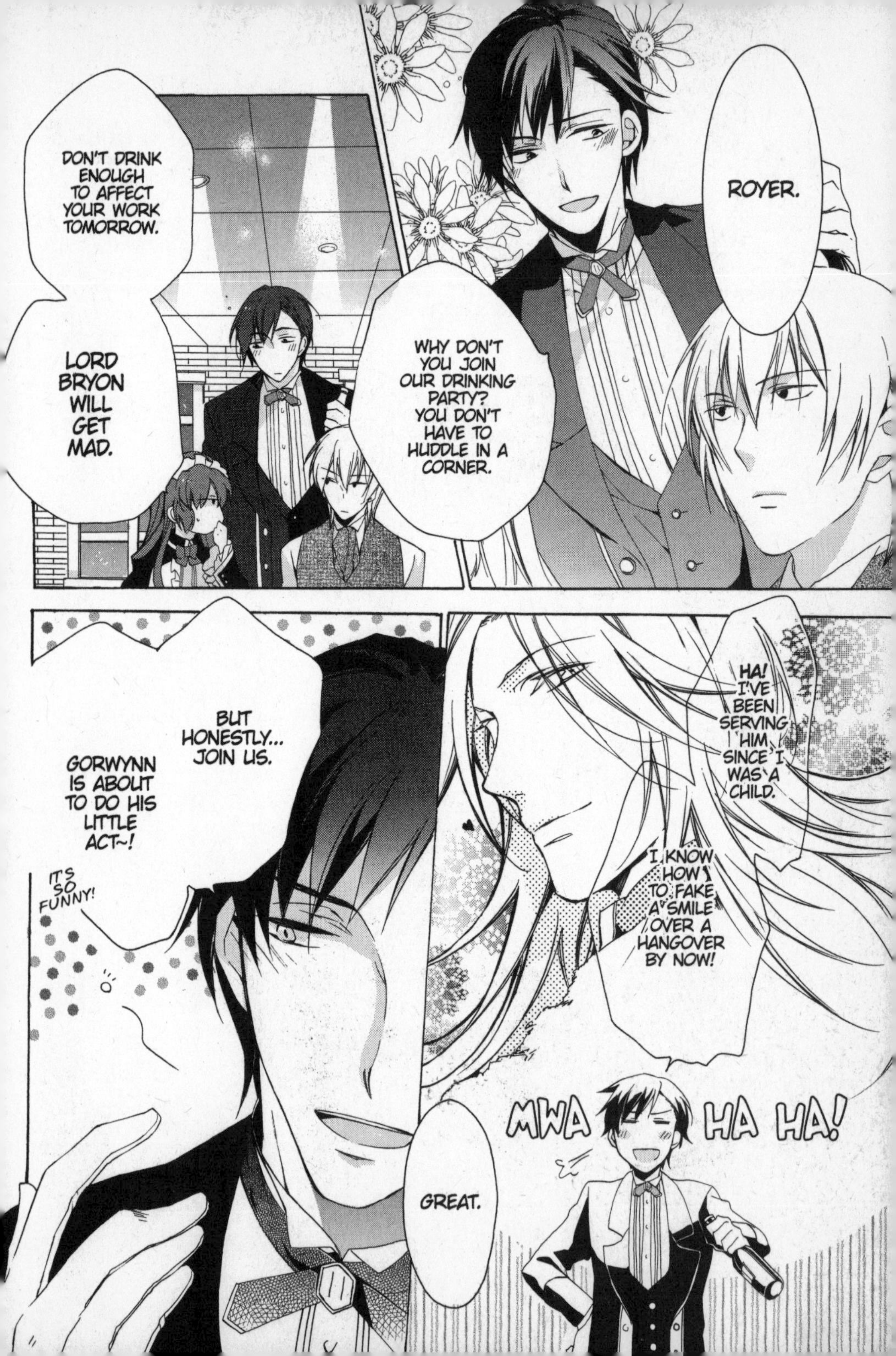
ROYER.
WHY DON'T YOU JOIN OUR DRINKING PARTY? YOU DON'T HAVE TO HUDDLE IN A CORNER.
DON'T DRINK ENOUGH TO AFFECT YOUR WORK TOMORROW.
LORD BRYON WILL GET MAD.
HA! I'VE BEEN SERVING HIM SINCE I WAS A CHILD.
I KNOW HOW TO FAKE A SMILE OVER A HANGOVER BY NOW!
MWA HA HA!
BUT HONESTLY... JOIN US.
GORWYNN IS ABOUT TO DO HIS LITTLE ACT~!
IT'S SO FUNNY!
GREAT.

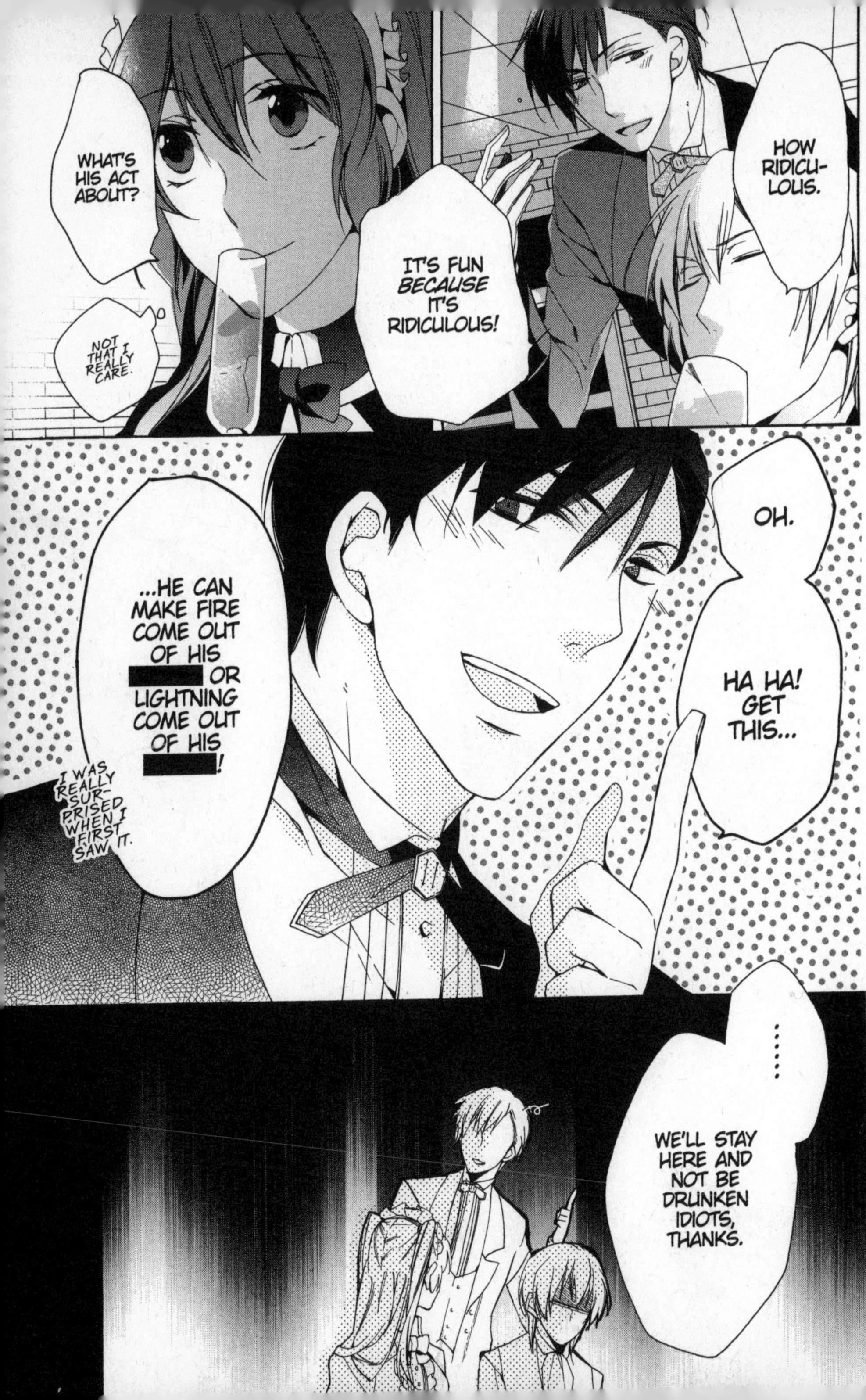
HOW RIDICULOUS.
IT'S FUN *BECAUSE* IT'S RIDICULOUS!
WHAT'S HIS ACT ABOUT?
NOT THAT I REALLY CARE.
OH.
HA HA! GET THIS...
...HE CAN MAKE FIRE COME OUT OF HIS [redacted] OR LIGHTNING COME OUT OF HIS [redacted]!
I WAS REALLY SURPRISED WHEN I FIRST SAW IT.
......
WE'LL STAY HERE AND NOT BE DRUNKEN IDIOTS, THANKS.

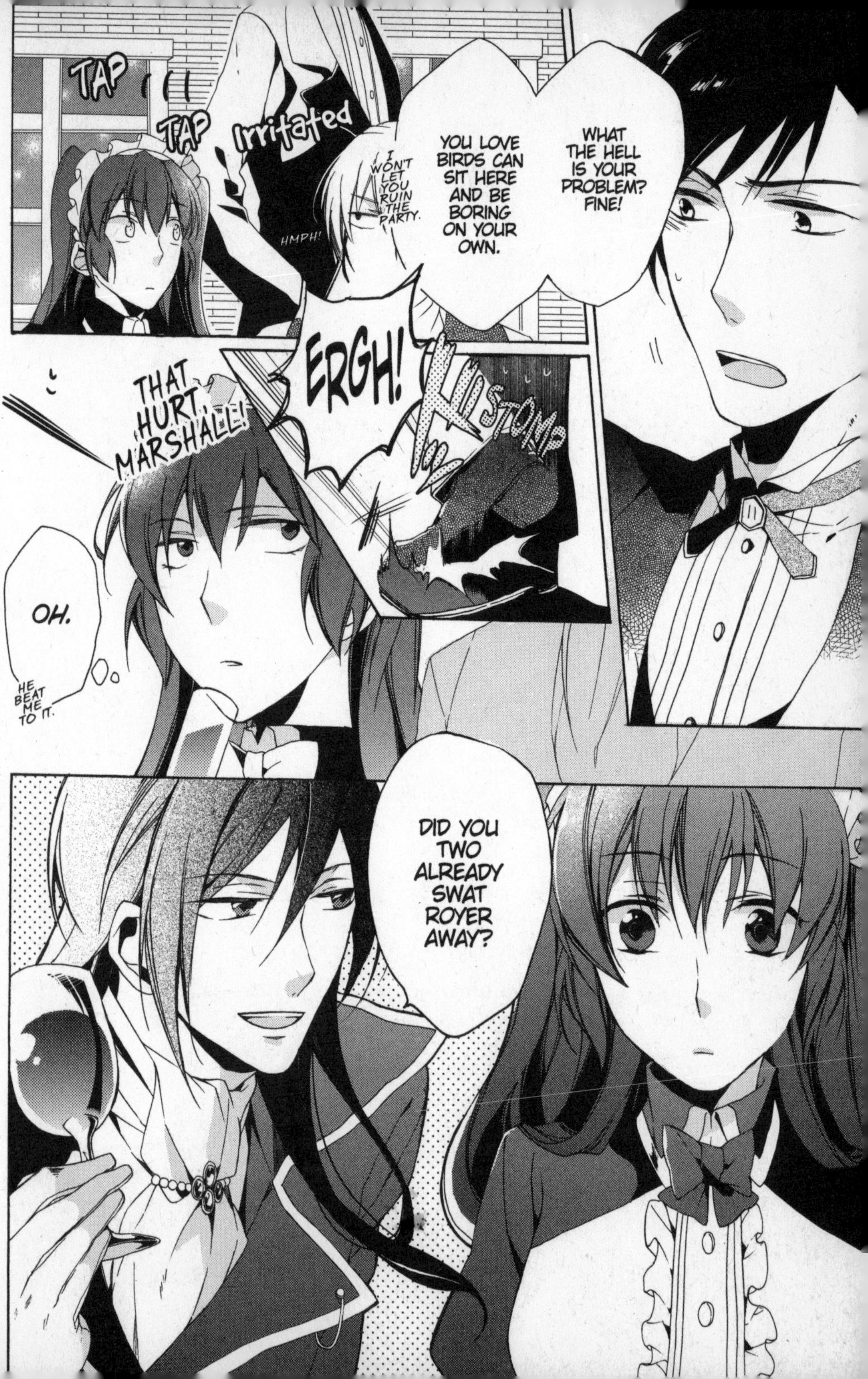
WHAT THE HELL IS YOUR PROBLEM? FINE!
YOU LOVE BIRDS CAN SIT HERE AND BE BORING ON YOUR OWN.
I WON'T LET YOU RUIN THE PARTY.
HMPH!
Irritated
TAP
TAP
ERGH!
STOMP
THAT HURT, MARSHALL!
OH.
HE BEAT ME TO IT.
DID YOU TWO ALREADY SWAT ROYER AWAY?

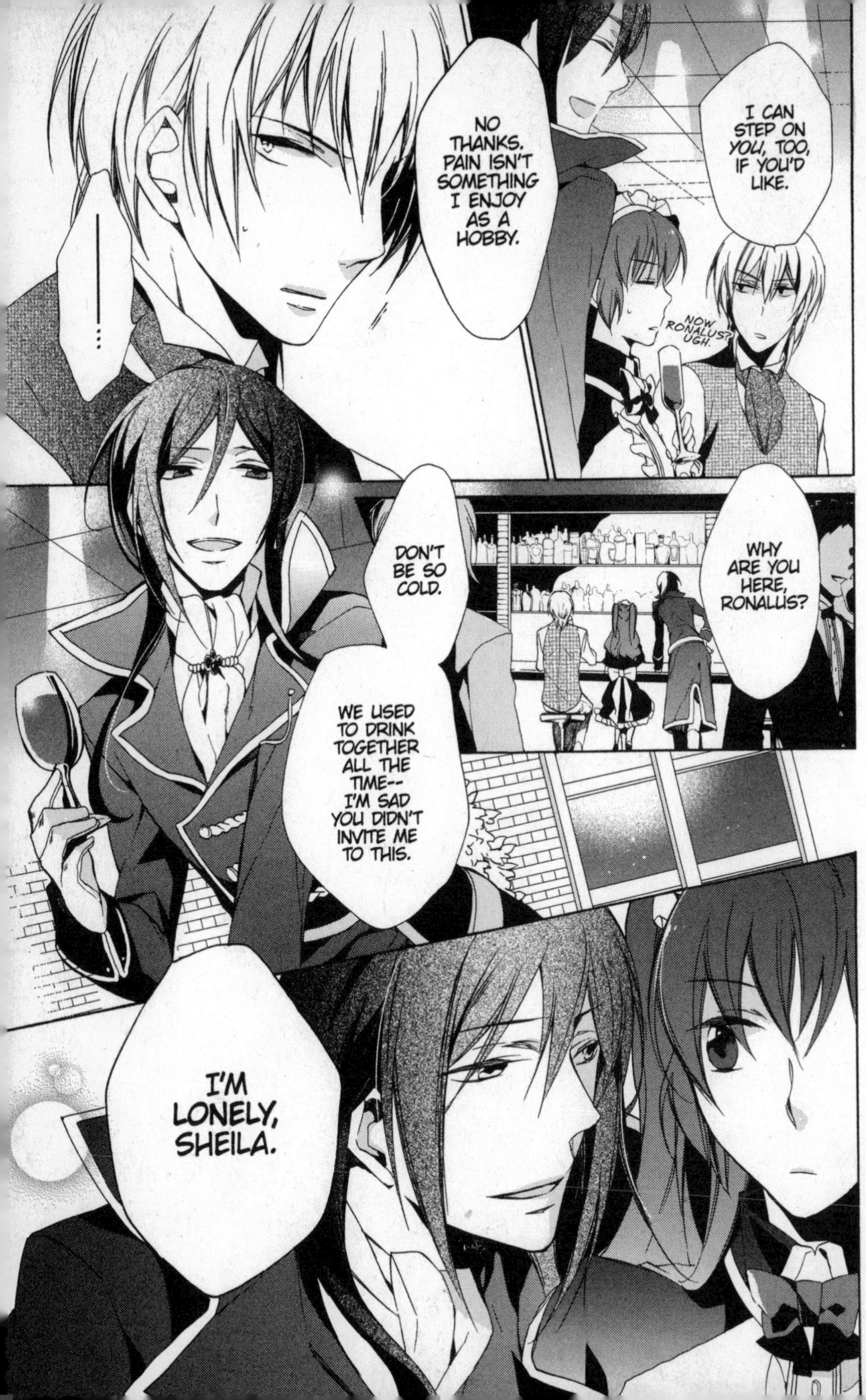
I CAN STEP ON YOU, TOO, IF YOU'D LIKE.
NO THANKS. PAIN ISN'T SOMETHING I ENJOY AS A HOBBY.
NOW RONALUS? UGH.
......
WHY ARE YOU HERE, RONALUS?
DON'T BE SO COLD.
WE USED TO DRINK TOGETHER ALL THE TIME-- I'M SAD YOU DIDN'T INVITE ME TO THIS.
I'M LONELY, SHEILA.

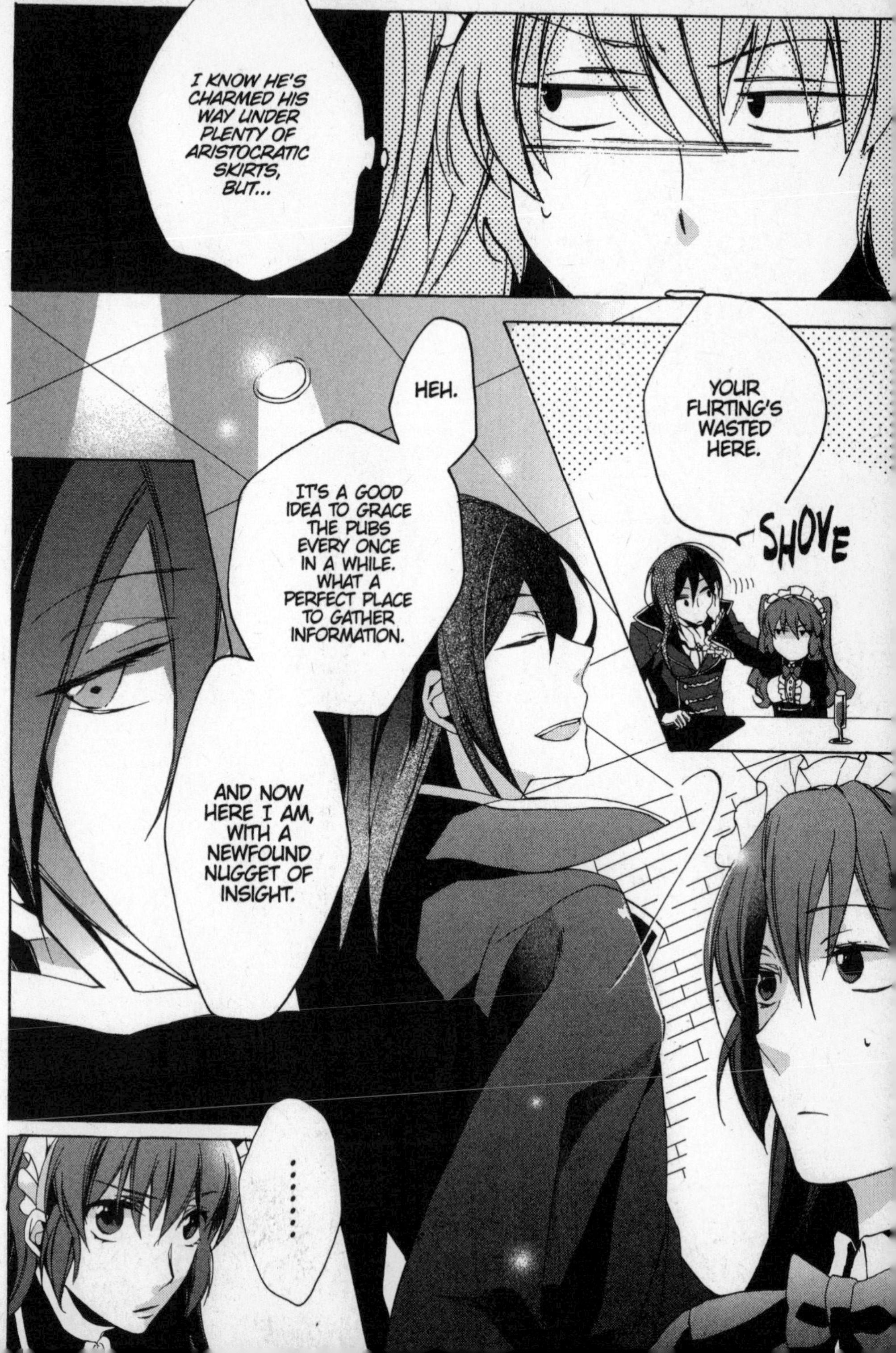
I KNOW HE'S CHARMED HIS WAY UNDER PLENTY OF ARISTOCRATIC SKIRTS, BUT...
YOUR FLIRTING'S WASTED HERE.
SHOVE
HEH.
IT'S A GOOD IDEA TO GRACE THE PUBS EVERY ONCE IN A WHILE. WHAT A PERFECT PLACE TO GATHER INFORMATION.
AND NOW HERE I AM, WITH A NEWFOUND NUGGET OF INSIGHT.
......

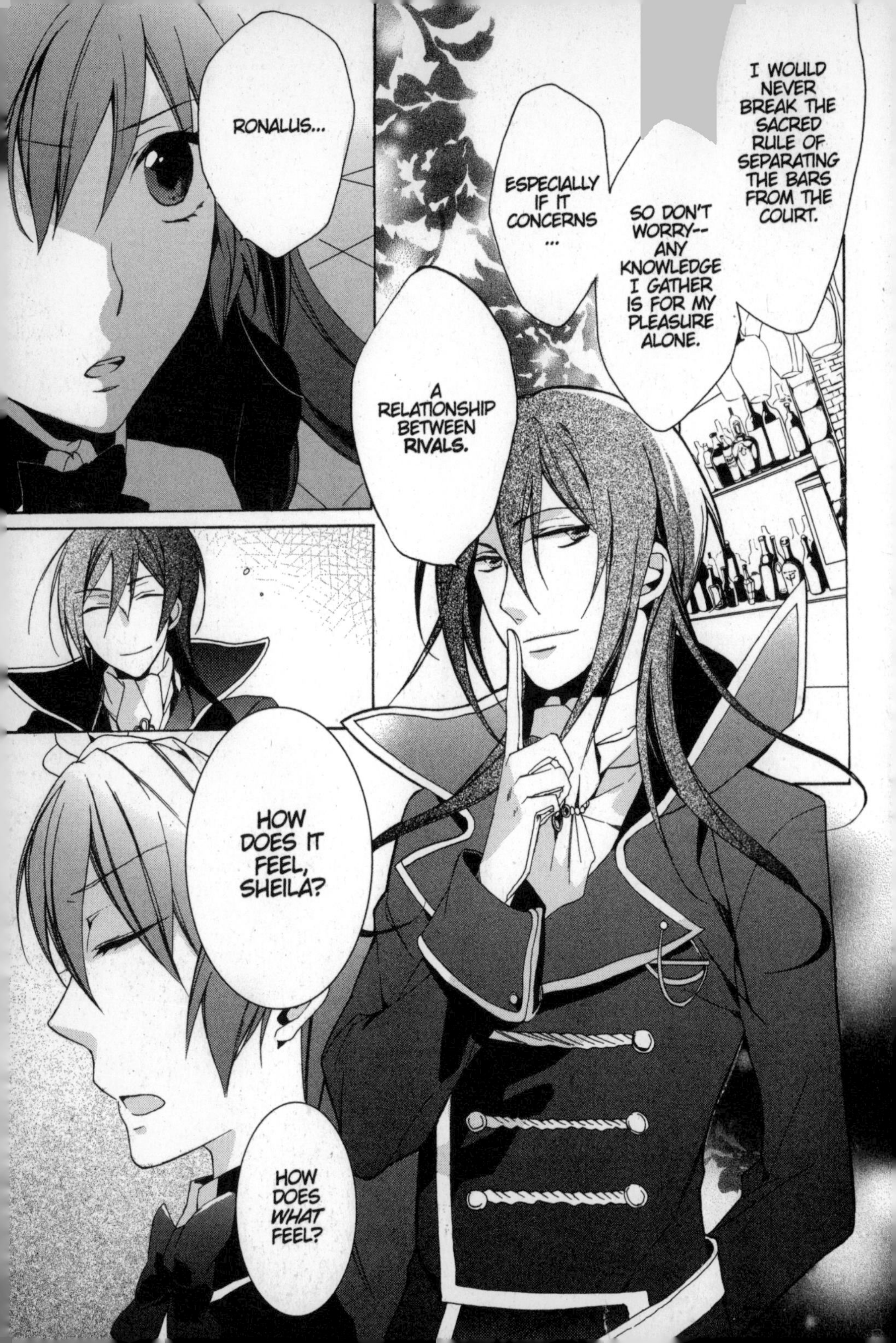
I WOULD NEVER BREAK THE SACRED RULE OF SEPARATING THE BARS FROM THE COURT.
SO DON'T WORRY-- ANY KNOWLEDGE I GATHER IS FOR MY PLEASURE ALONE.
ESPECIALLY IF IT CONCERNS ...
A RELATIONSHIP BETWEEN RIVALS.
RONALUS...
HOW DOES IT FEEL, SHEILA?
HOW DOES *WHAT* FEEL?

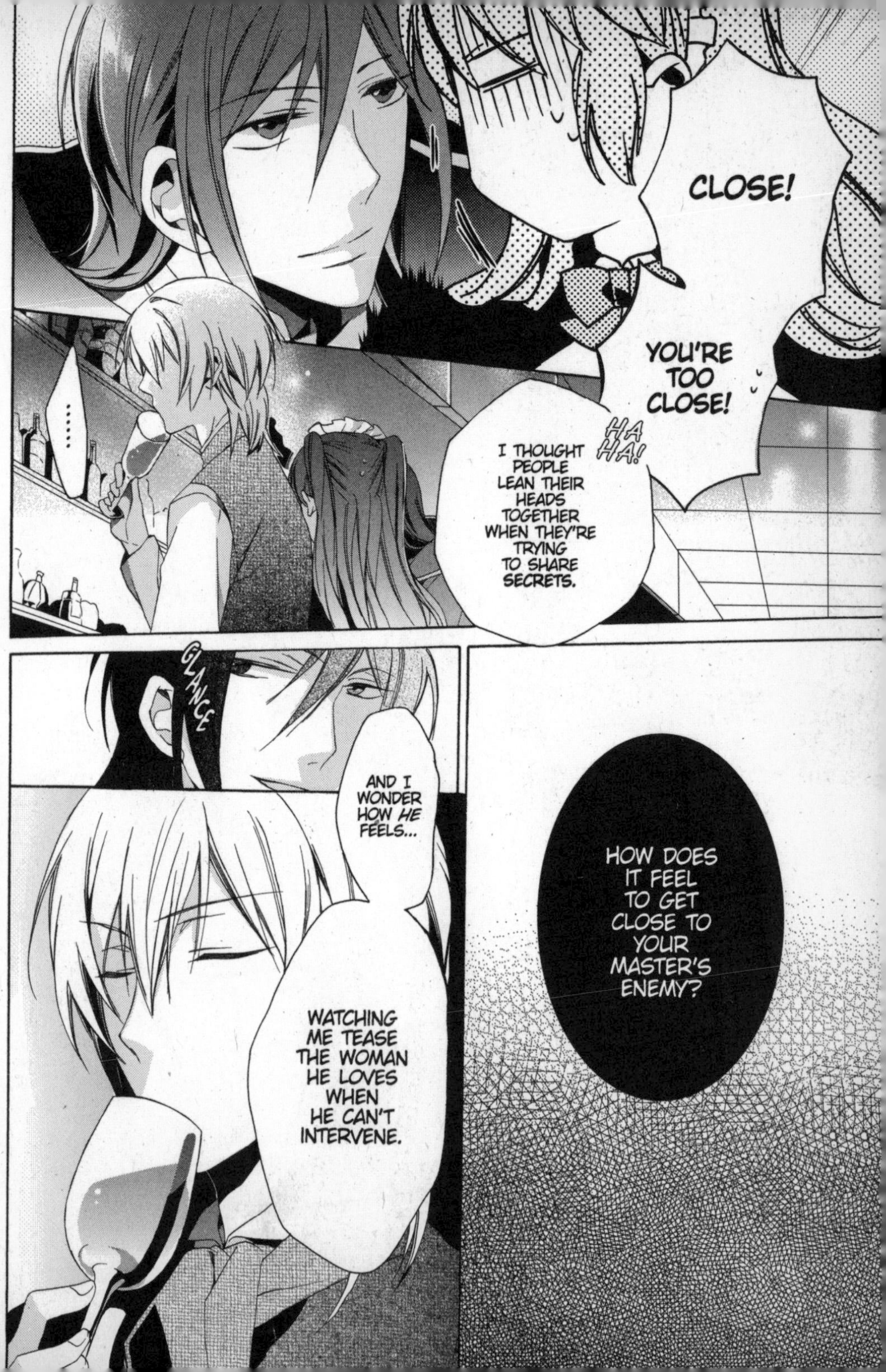
CLOSE!
YOU'RE TOO CLOSE!
HA HA!
I THOUGHT PEOPLE LEAN THEIR HEADS TOGETHER WHEN THEY'RE TRYING TO SHARE SECRETS.
......
HOW DOES IT FEEL TO GET CLOSE TO YOUR MASTER'S ENEMY?
GLANCE
AND I WONDER HOW *HE* FEELS...
WATCHING ME TEASE THE WOMAN HE LOVES WHEN HE CAN'T INTERVENE.

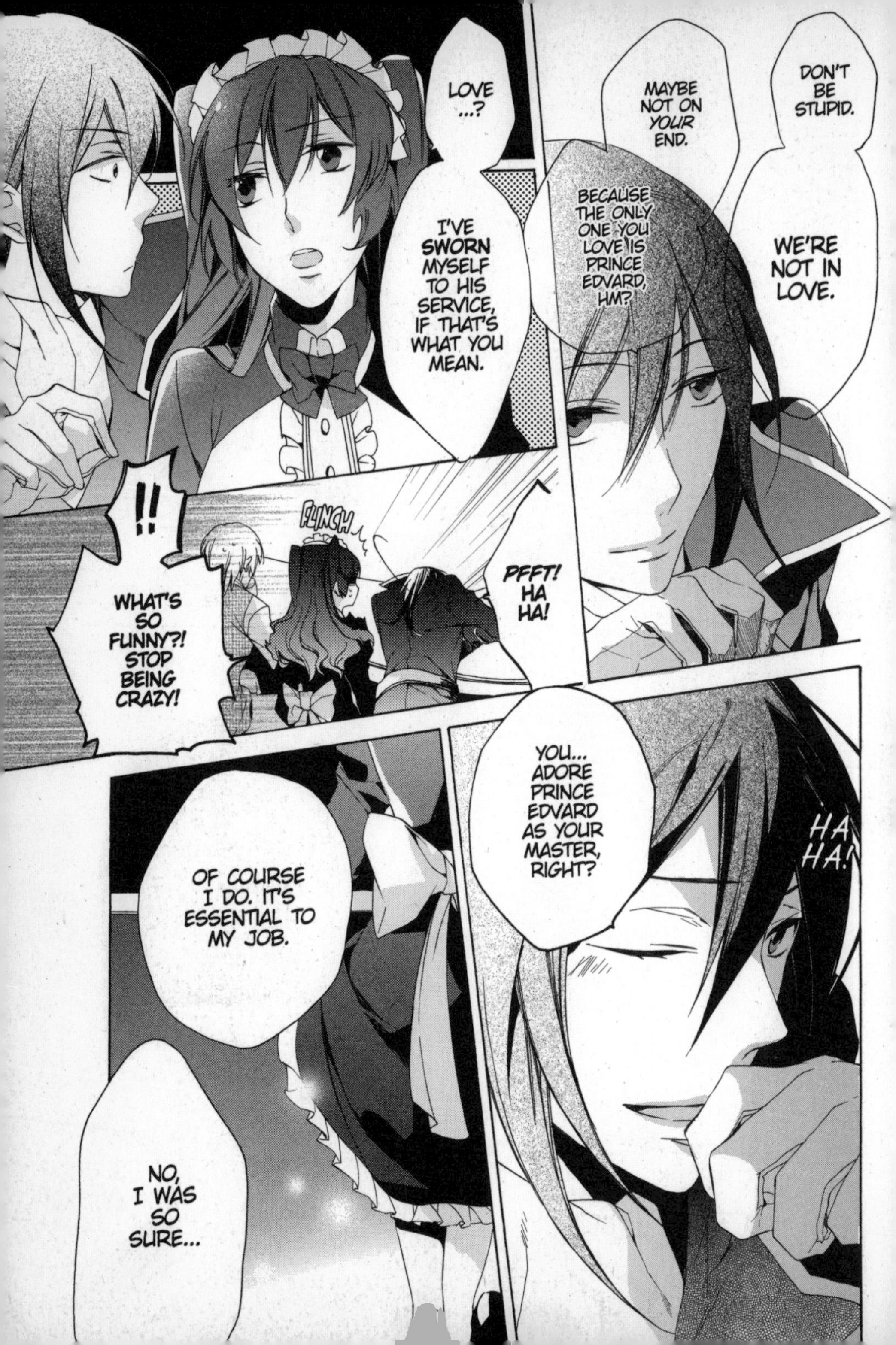
DON'T BE STUPID.
MAYBE NOT ON YOUR END.
WE'RE NOT IN LOVE.
BECAUSE THE ONLY ONE YOU LOVE IS PRINCE EDVARD, HM?
PFFT! HA HA!
LOVE ...?
I'VE SWORN MYSELF TO HIS SERVICE, IF THAT'S WHAT YOU MEAN.
FLINCH
!!
WHAT'S SO FUNNY?! STOP BEING CRAZY!
HA HA!
YOU... ADORE PRINCE EDVARD AS YOUR MASTER, RIGHT?
OF COURSE I DO. IT'S ESSENTIAL TO MY JOB.
NO, I WAS SO SURE...

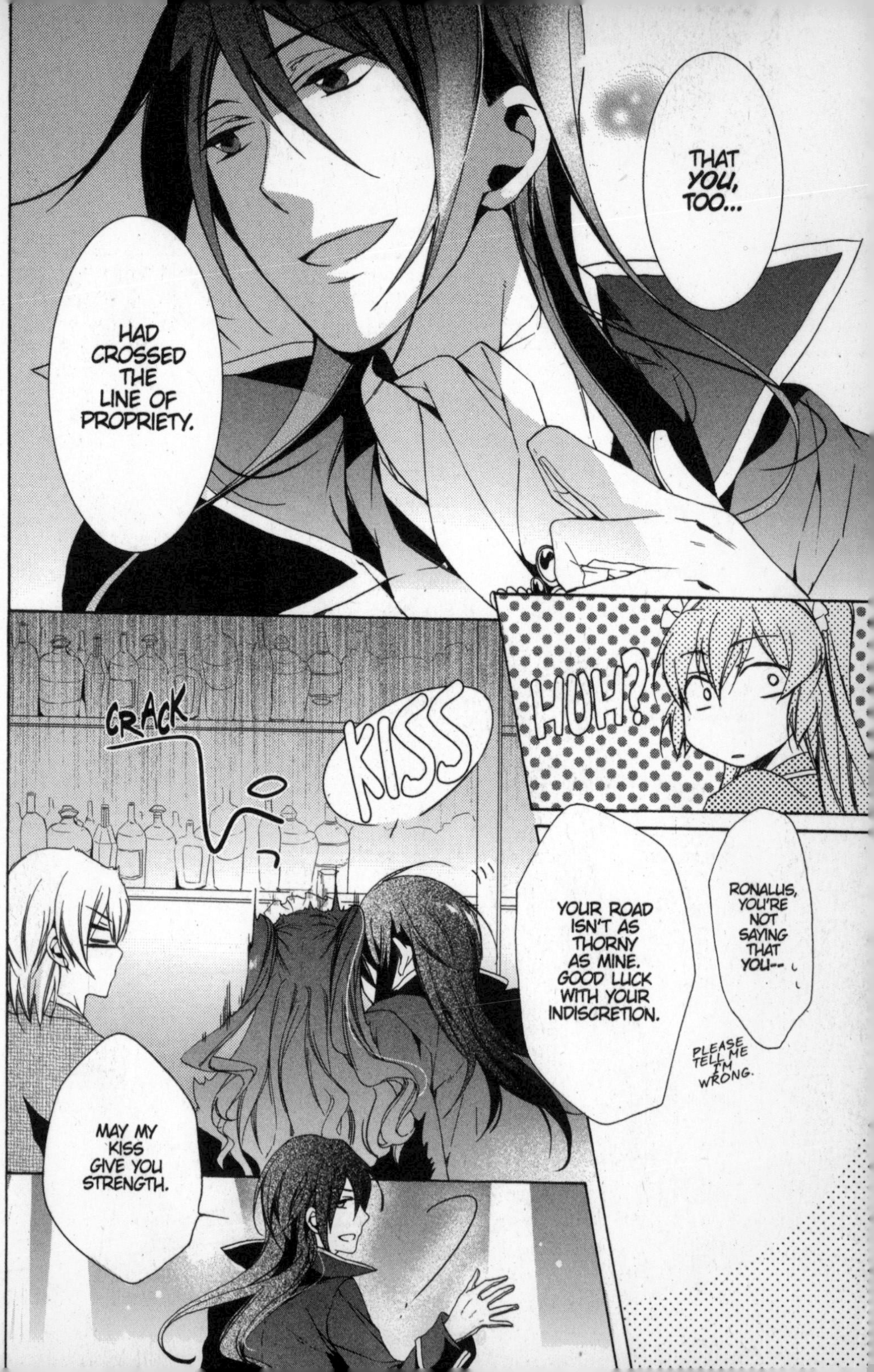
THAT YOU, TOO...
HAD CROSSED THE LINE OF PROPRIETY.
HUH?
KISS
CRACK
RONALUS, YOU'RE NOT SAYING THAT YOU--
PLEASE TELL ME I'M WRONG.
YOUR ROAD ISN'T AS THORNY AS MINE. GOOD LUCK WITH YOUR INDISCRETION.
MAY MY KISS GIVE YOU STRENGTH.

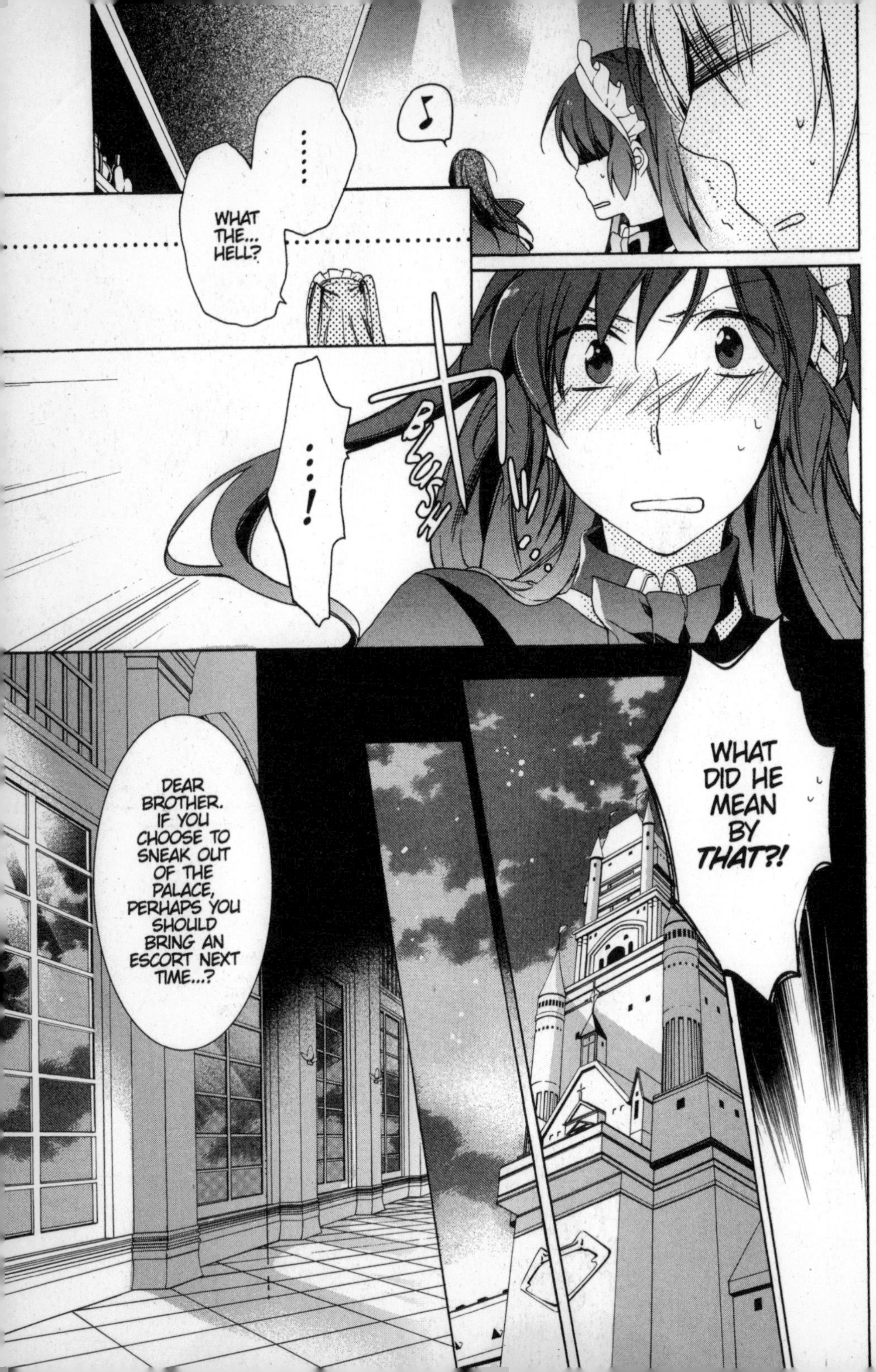
♪
...... WHAT THE... HELL?
BLUSH
...!
WHAT DID HE MEAN BY THAT?!
DEAR BROTHER. IF YOU CHOOSE TO SNEAK OUT OF THE PALACE, PERHAPS YOU SHOULD BRING AN ESCORT NEXT TIME...?

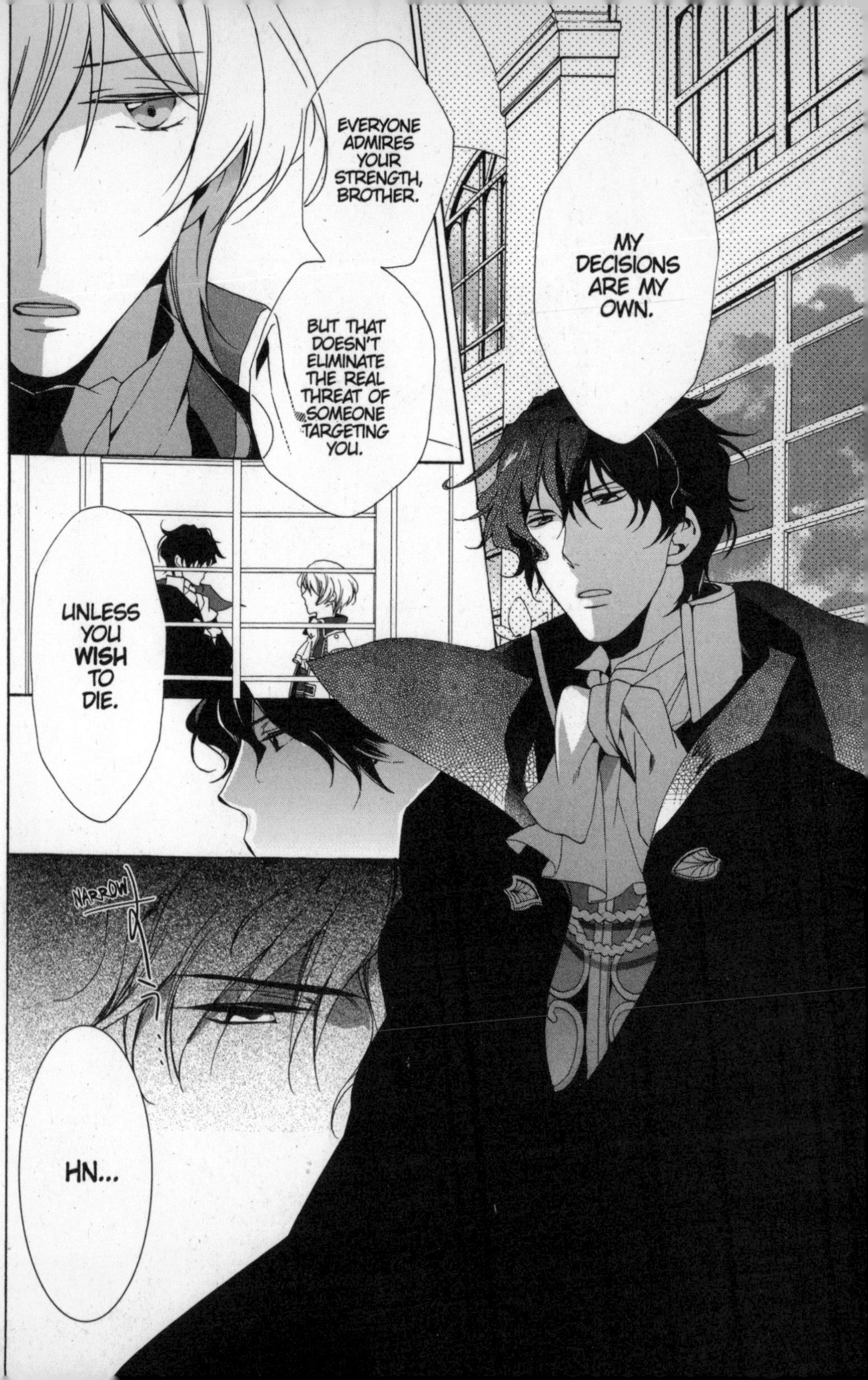
MY DECISIONS ARE MY OWN.
EVERYONE ADMIRES YOUR STRENGTH, BROTHER.
BUT THAT DOESN'T ELIMINATE THE REAL THREAT OF SOMEONE TARGETING YOU.
UNLESS YOU WISH TO DIE.
NARROW
HN...

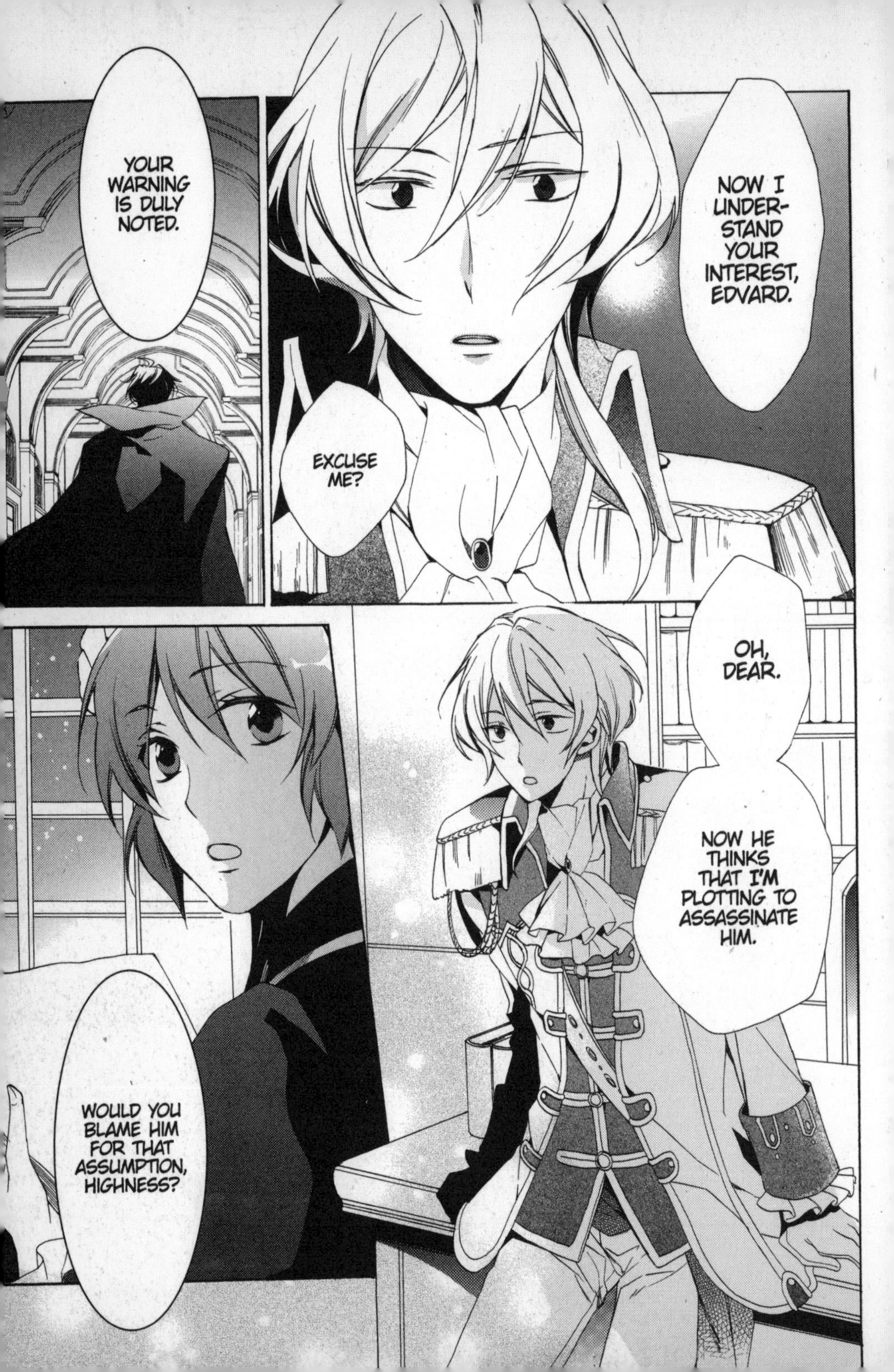
NOW I UNDER-STAND YOUR INTEREST, EDVARD.
EXCUSE ME?
YOUR WARNING IS DULY NOTED.
OH, DEAR.
NOW HE THINKS THAT I'M PLOTTING TO ASSASSINATE HIM.
WOULD YOU BLAME HIM FOR THAT ASSUMPTION, HIGHNESS?

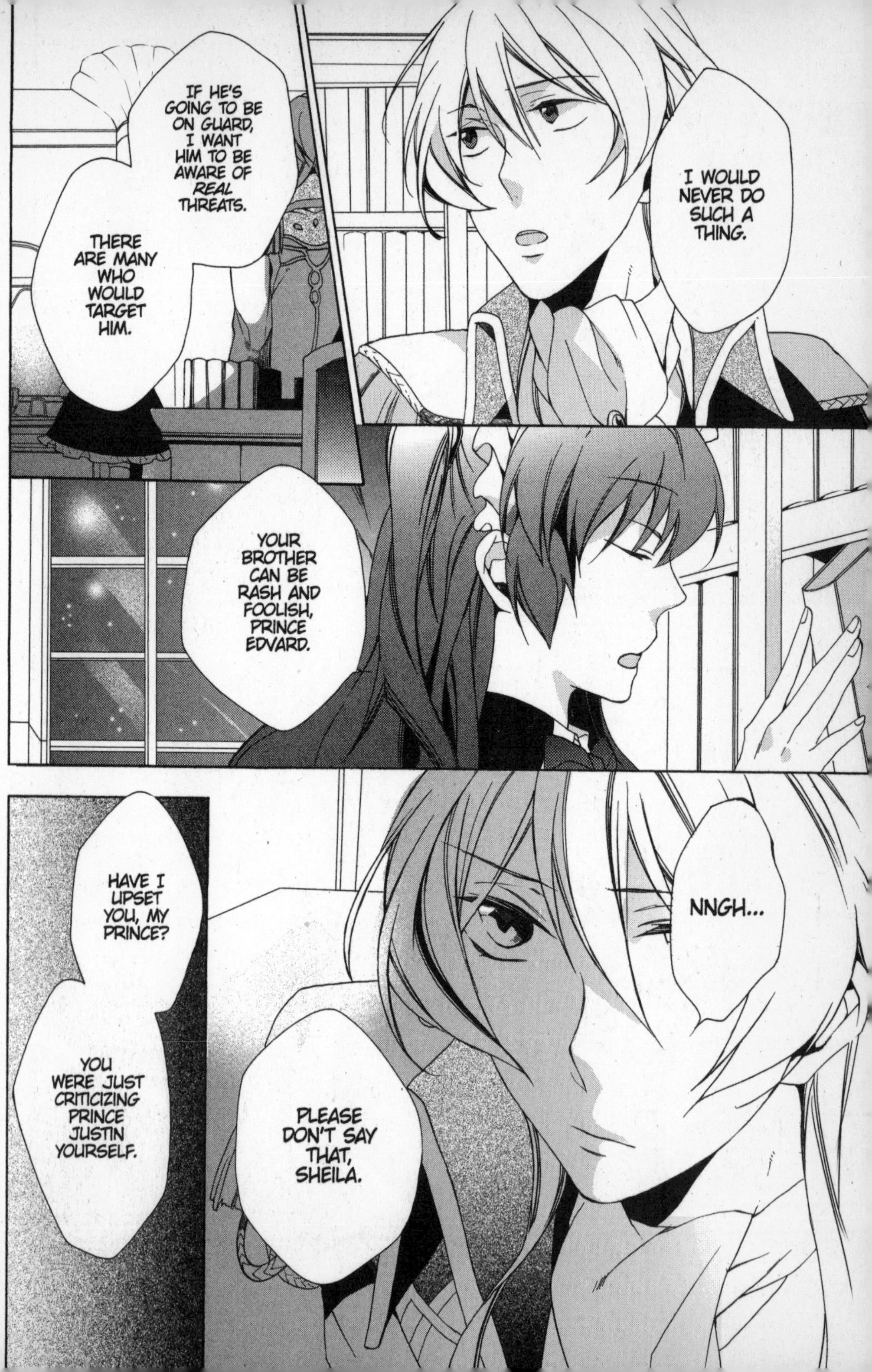
I WOULD NEVER DO SUCH A THING.
IF HE'S GOING TO BE ON GUARD, I WANT HIM TO BE AWARE OF *REAL* THREATS.
THERE ARE MANY WHO WOULD TARGET HIM.
YOUR BROTHER CAN BE RASH AND FOOLISH, PRINCE EDVARD.
NNGH...
PLEASE DON'T SAY THAT, SHEILA.
HAVE I UPSET YOU, MY PRINCE?
YOU WERE JUST CRITICIZING PRINCE JUSTIN YOURSELF.

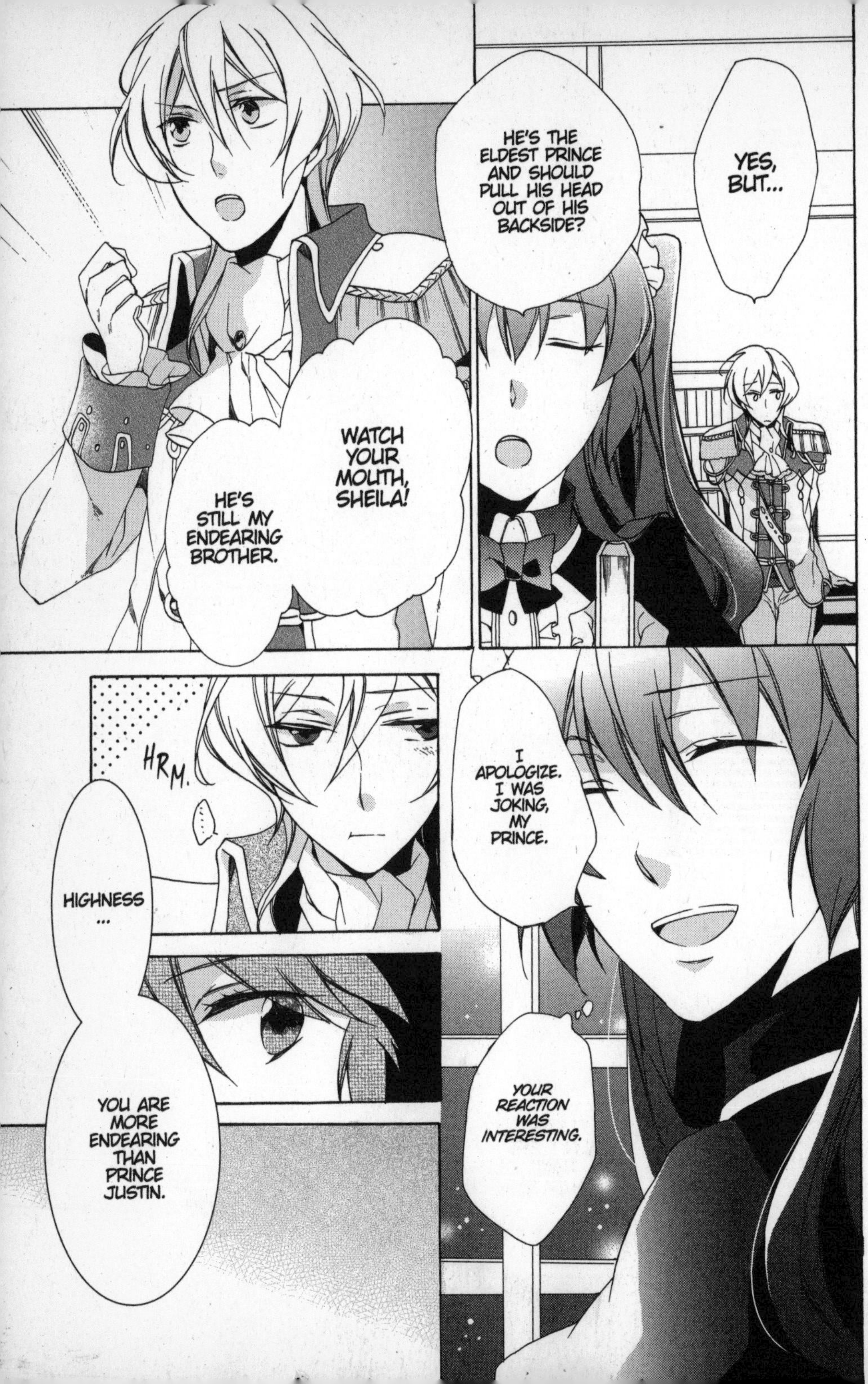
YES, BUT...
HE'S THE ELDEST PRINCE AND SHOULD PULL HIS HEAD OUT OF HIS BACKSIDE?
WATCH YOUR MOUTH, SHEILA!
HE'S STILL MY ENDEARING BROTHER.
I APOLOGIZE. I WAS JOKING, MY PRINCE.
YOUR REACTION WAS INTERESTING.
HRM.
...
HIGHNESS ...
YOU ARE MORE ENDEARING THAN PRINCE JUSTIN.

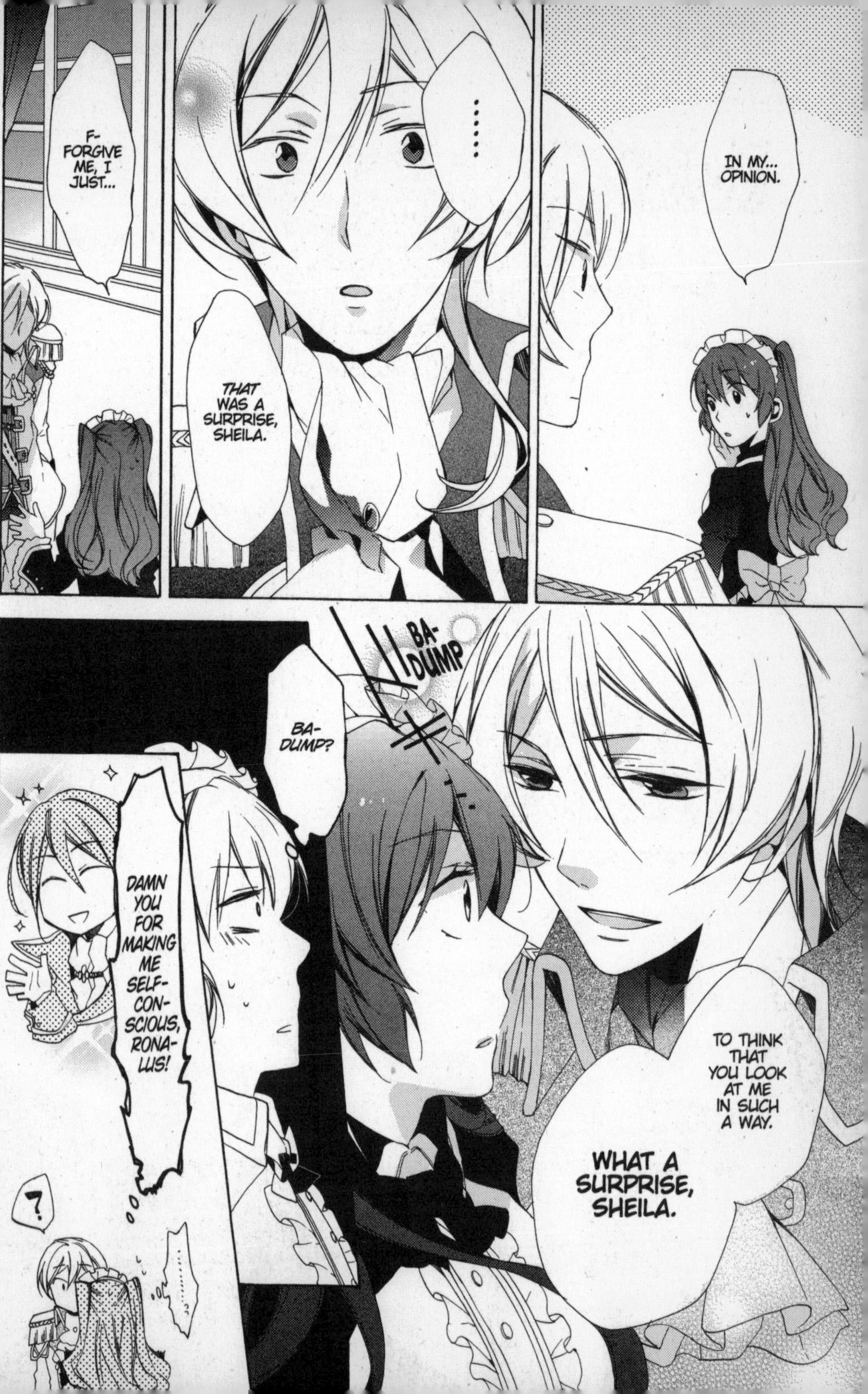
IN MY... OPINION.
......
THAT WAS A SURPRISE, SHEILA.
F-FORGIVE ME, I JUST...
BA-DUMP
TO THINK THAT YOU LOOK AT ME IN SUCH A WAY.
WHAT A SURPRISE, SHEILA.
BA-DUMP?
DAMN YOU FOR MAKING ME SELF-CONSCIOUS, RONALUS!
?
......

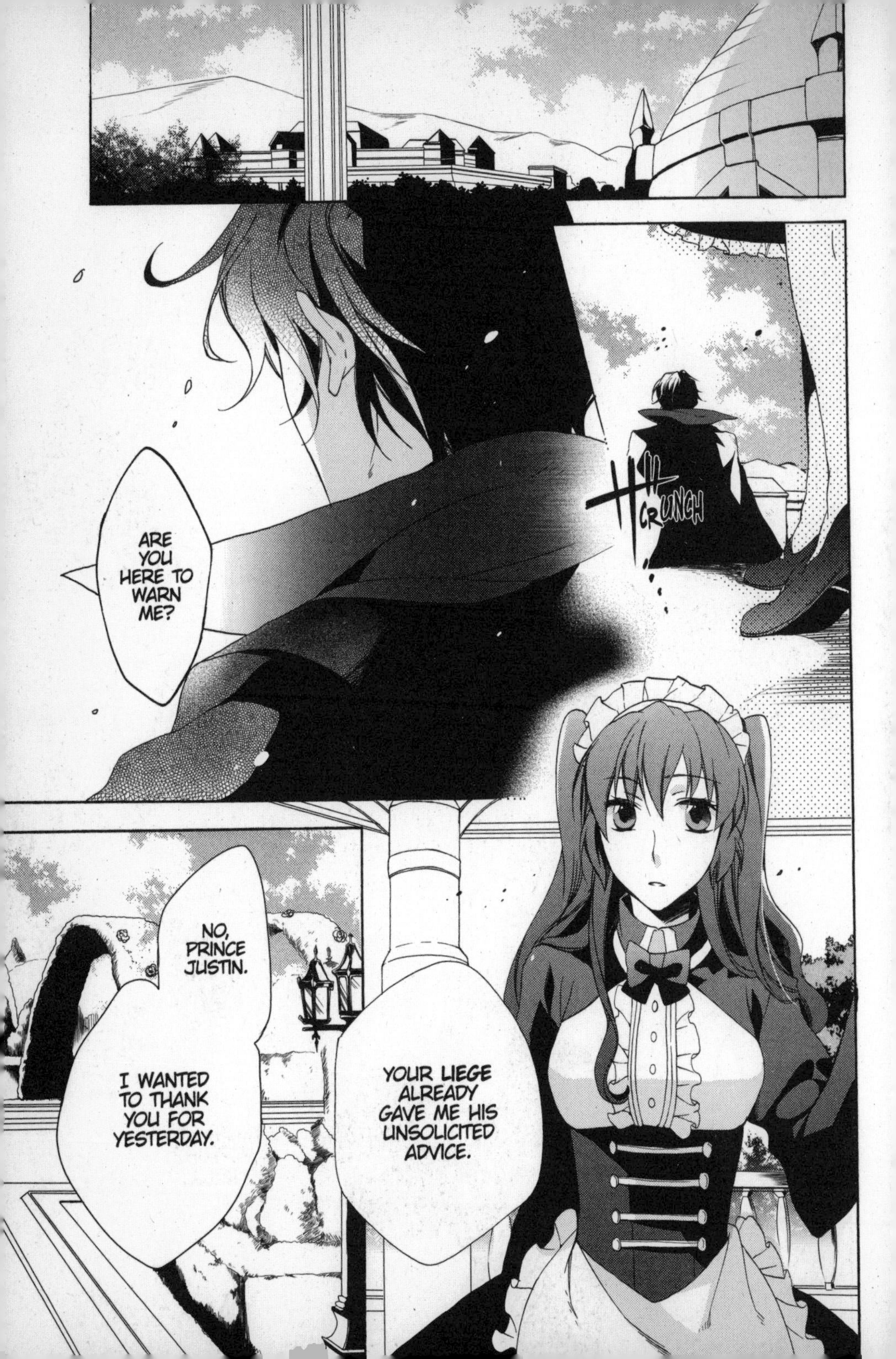
CRUNCH
ARE YOU HERE TO WARN ME?
YOUR LIEGE ALREADY GAVE ME HIS UNSOLICITED ADVICE.
NO, PRINCE JUSTIN.
I WANTED TO THANK YOU FOR YESTERDAY.

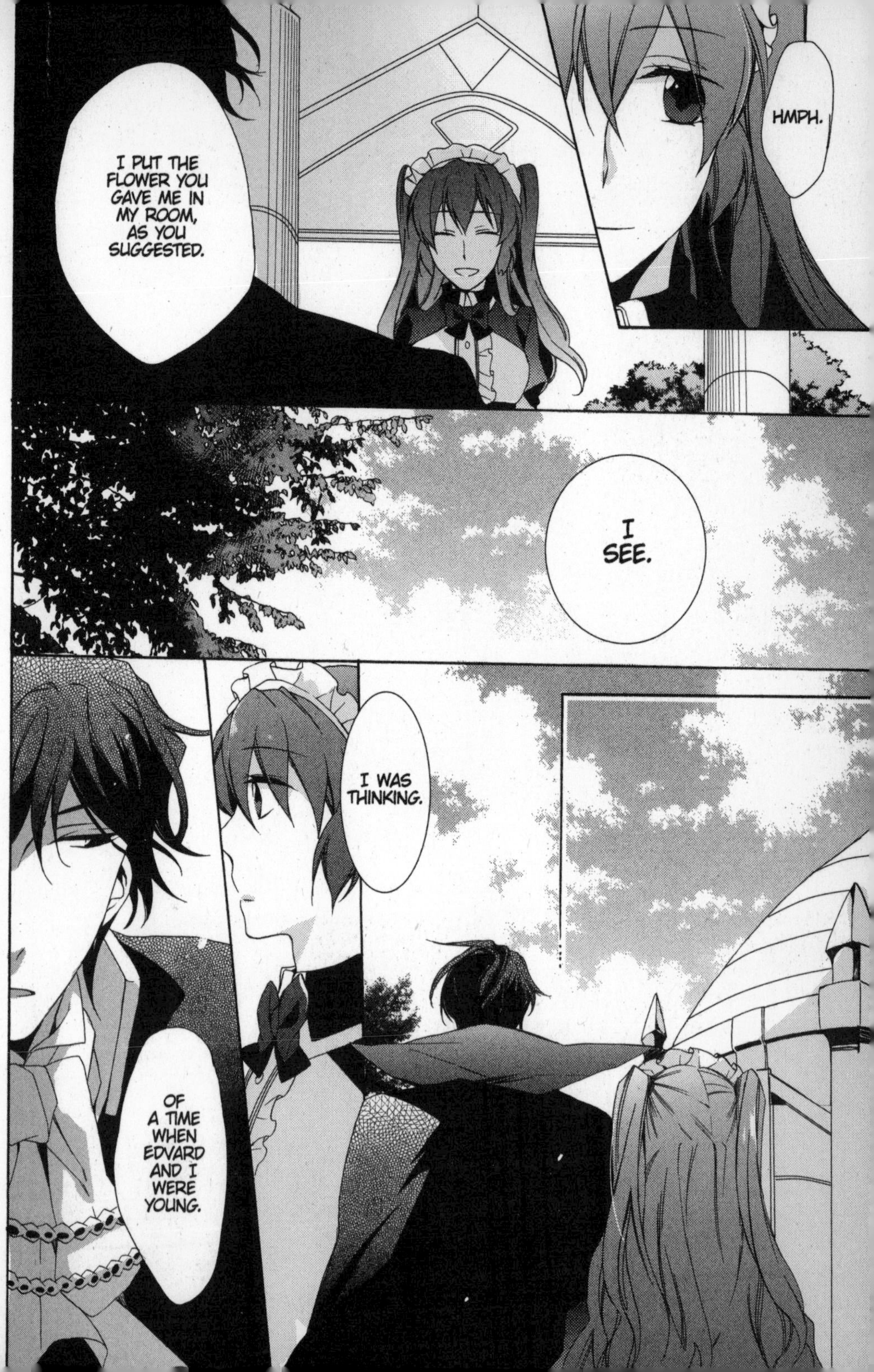
HMPH.
I PUT THE FLOWER YOU GAVE ME IN MY ROOM, AS YOU SUGGESTED.
I SEE.
...
I WAS THINKING.
OF A TIME WHEN EDVARD AND I WERE YOUNG.

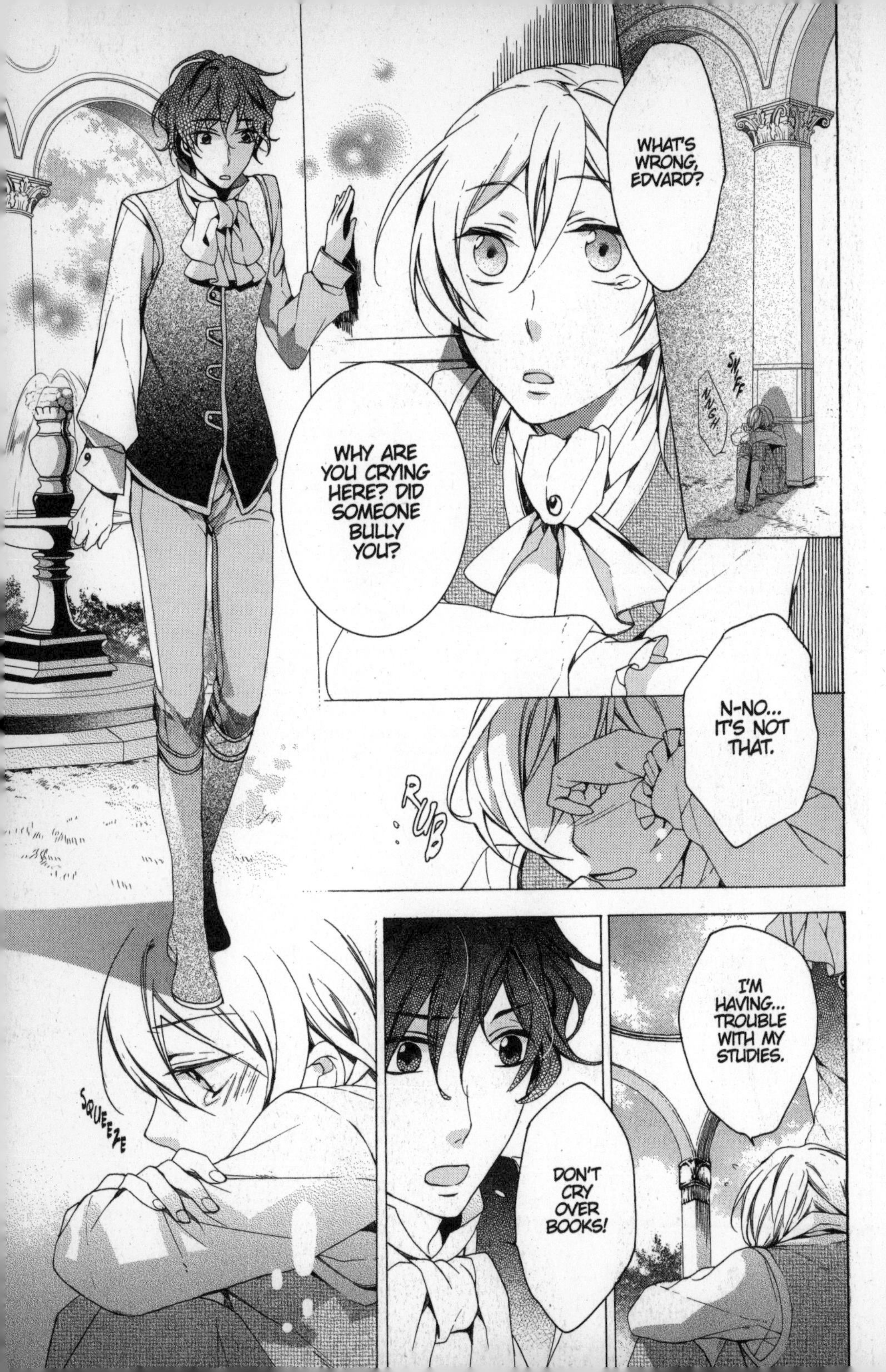
SNIFF
NNGH
WHAT'S WRONG, EDVARD?
WHY ARE YOU CRYING HERE? DID SOMEONE BULLY YOU?
N-NO... IT'S NOT THAT.
RUB
I'M HAVING... TROUBLE WITH MY STUDIES.
DON'T CRY OVER BOOKS!
SQUEEZE

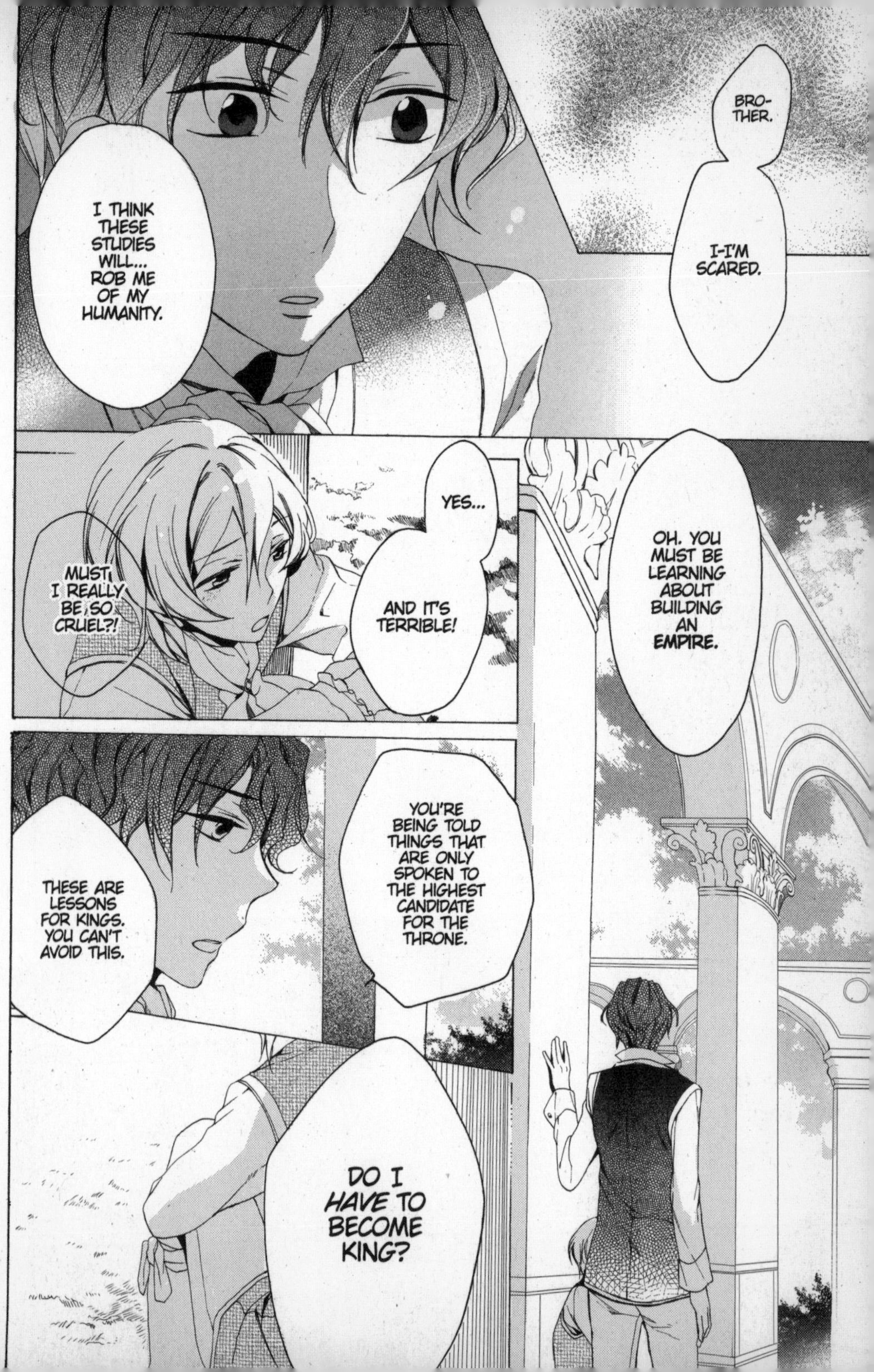
BRO-THER.
I-I'M SCARED.
I THINK THESE STUDIES WILL... ROB ME OF MY HUMANITY.
OH. YOU MUST BE LEARNING ABOUT BUILDING AN EMPIRE.
YES...
AND IT'S TERRIBLE!
MUST I REALLY BE SO CRUEL?!
YOU'RE BEING TOLD THINGS THAT ARE ONLY SPOKEN TO THE HIGHEST CANDIDATE FOR THE THRONE.
THESE ARE LESSONS FOR KINGS. YOU CAN'T AVOID THIS.
DO I *HAVE* TO BECOME KING?

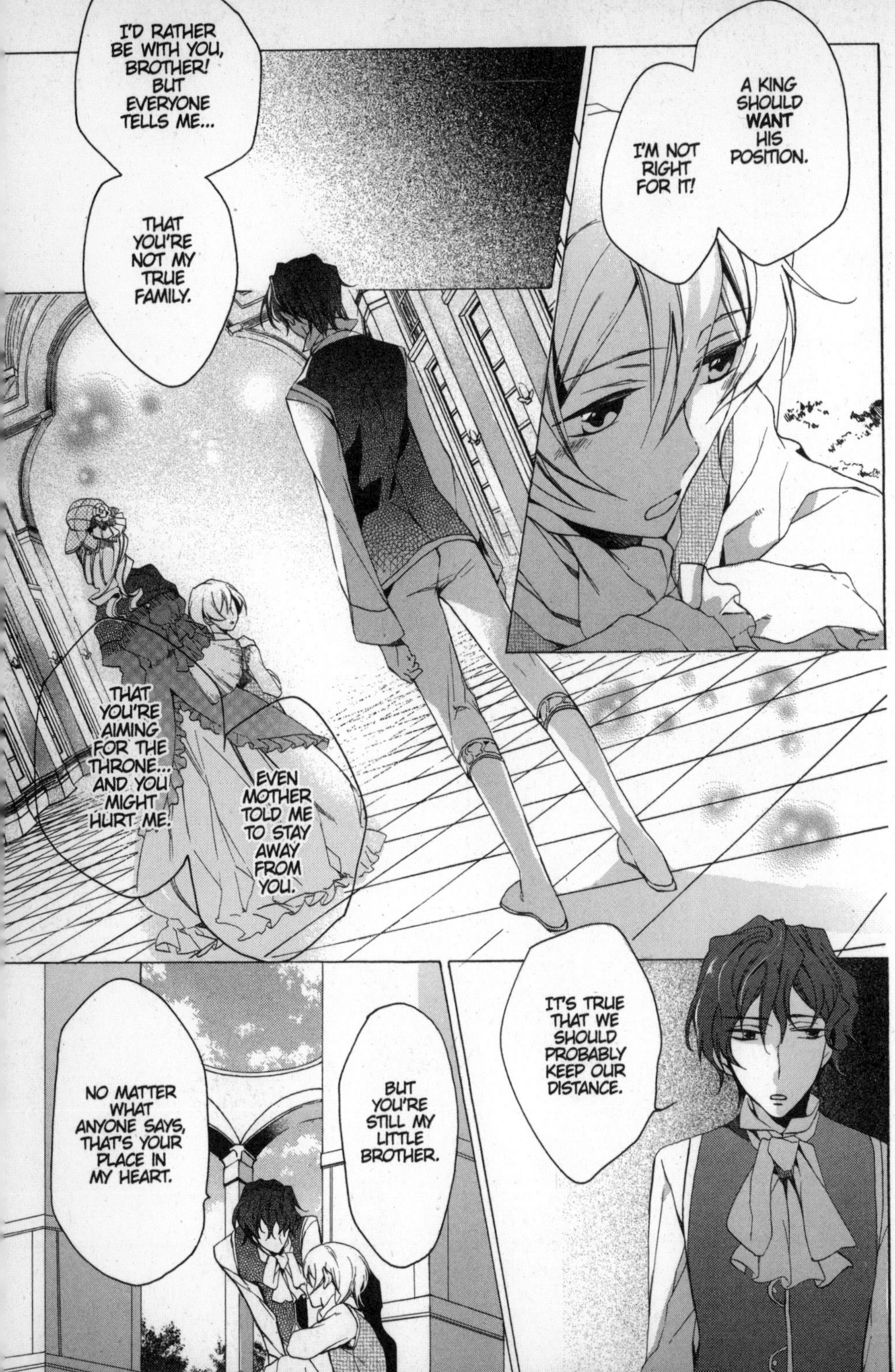
A KING SHOULD WANT HIS POSITION.
I'M NOT RIGHT FOR IT!
I'D RATHER BE WITH YOU, BROTHER! BUT EVERYONE TELLS ME...
THAT YOU'RE NOT MY TRUE FAMILY.
THAT YOU'RE AIMING FOR THE THRONE... AND YOU MIGHT HURT ME.
EVEN MOTHER TOLD ME TO STAY AWAY FROM YOU.
IT'S TRUE THAT WE SHOULD PROBABLY KEEP OUR DISTANCE.
BUT YOU'RE STILL MY LITTLE BROTHER.
NO MATTER WHAT ANYONE SAYS, THAT'S YOUR PLACE IN MY HEART.

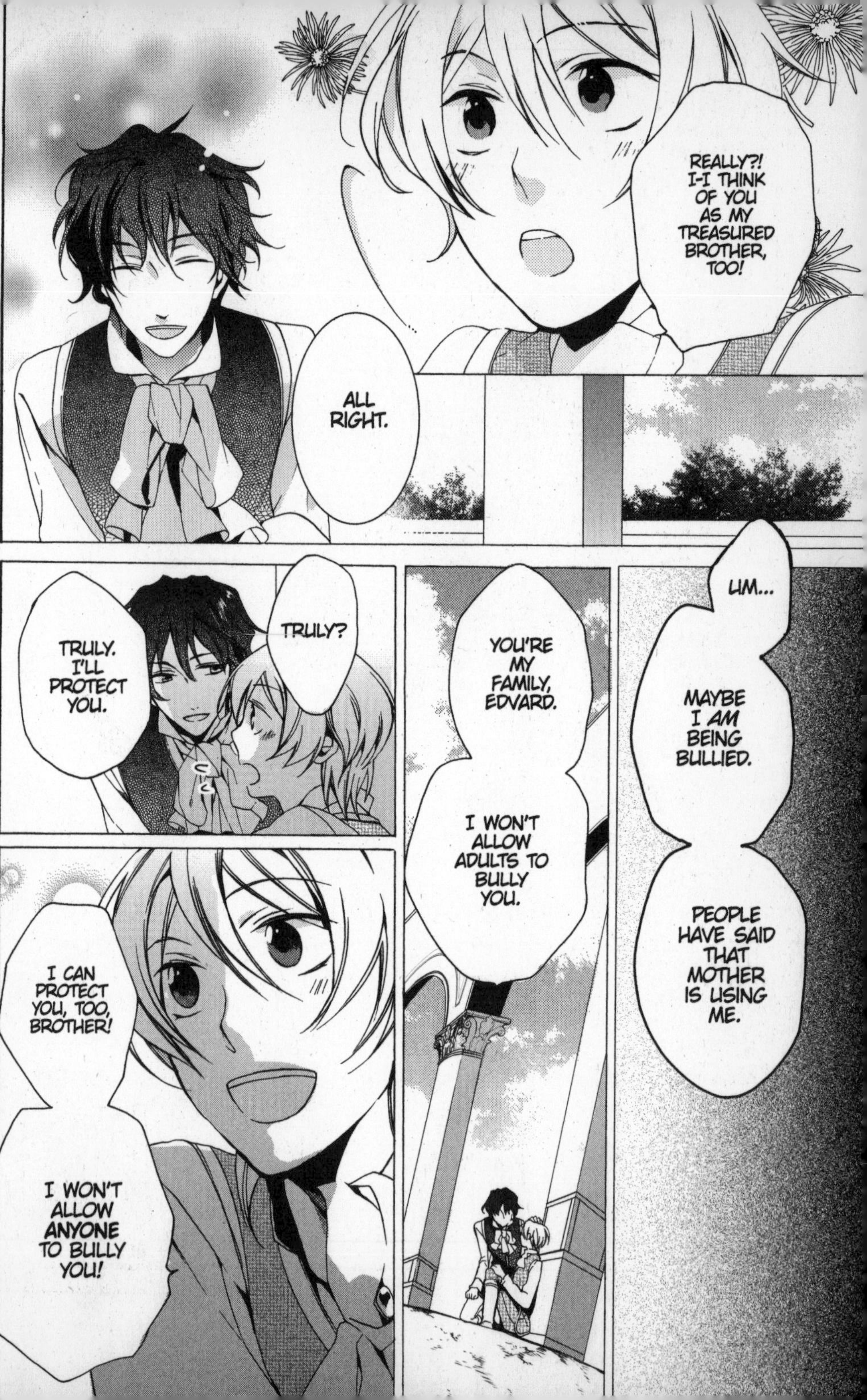

REALLY?! I-I THINK OF YOU AS MY TREASURED BROTHER, TOO!
ALL RIGHT.
UM...
MAYBE I *AM* BEING BULLIED.
PEOPLE HAVE SAID THAT MOTHER IS USING ME.
YOU'RE MY FAMILY, EDVARD.
I WON'T ALLOW ADULTS TO BULLY YOU.
TRULY?
TRULY. I'LL PROTECT YOU.
I CAN PROTECT YOU, TOO, BROTHER!
I WON'T ALLOW ANYONE TO BULLY YOU!

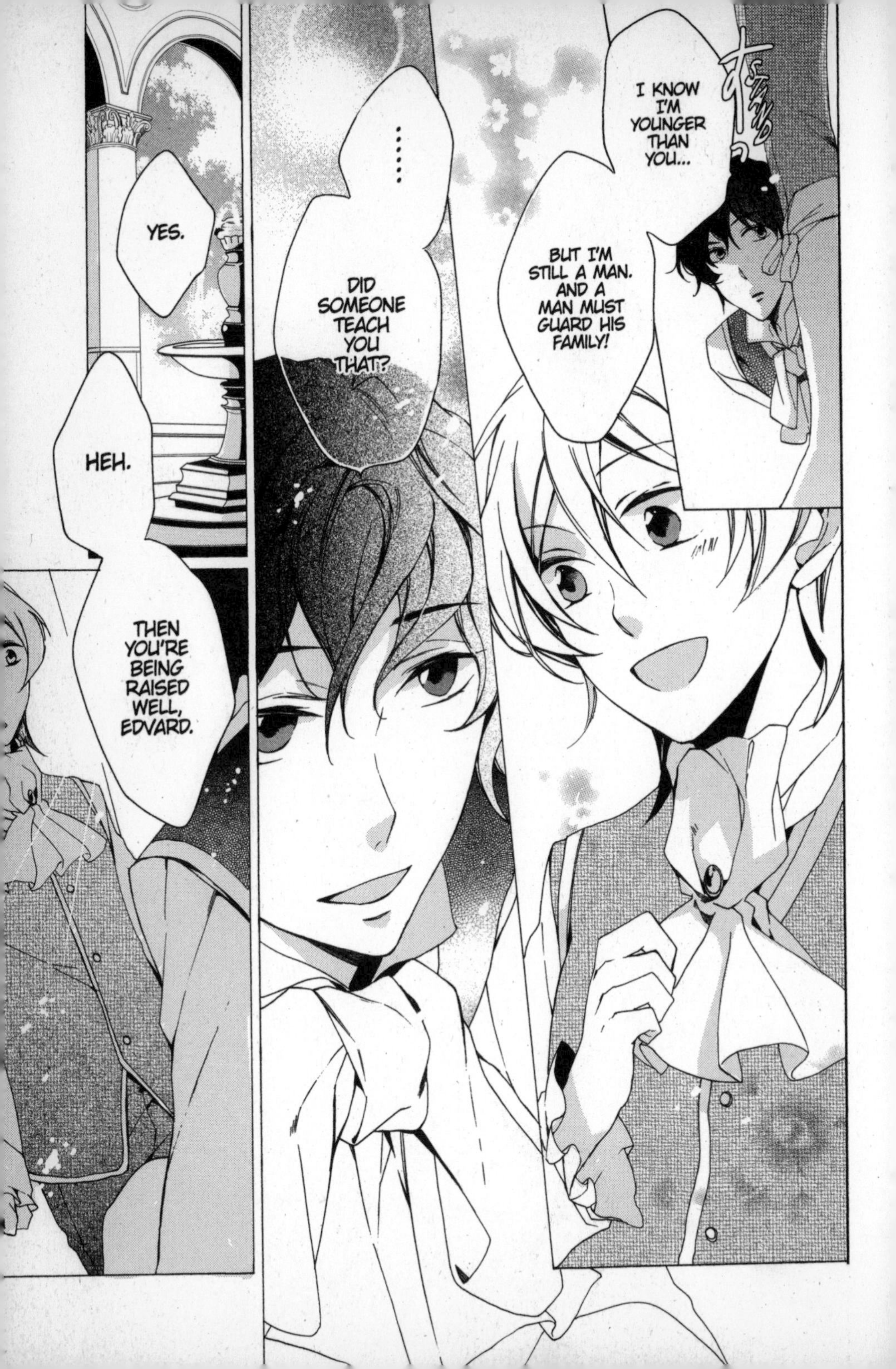
I KNOW I'M YOUNGER THAN YOU...
STAND
BUT I'M STILL A MAN. AND A MAN MUST GUARD HIS FAMILY!
......
DID SOMEONE TEACH YOU THAT?
YES.
HEH.
THEN YOU'RE BEING RAISED WELL, EDVARD.

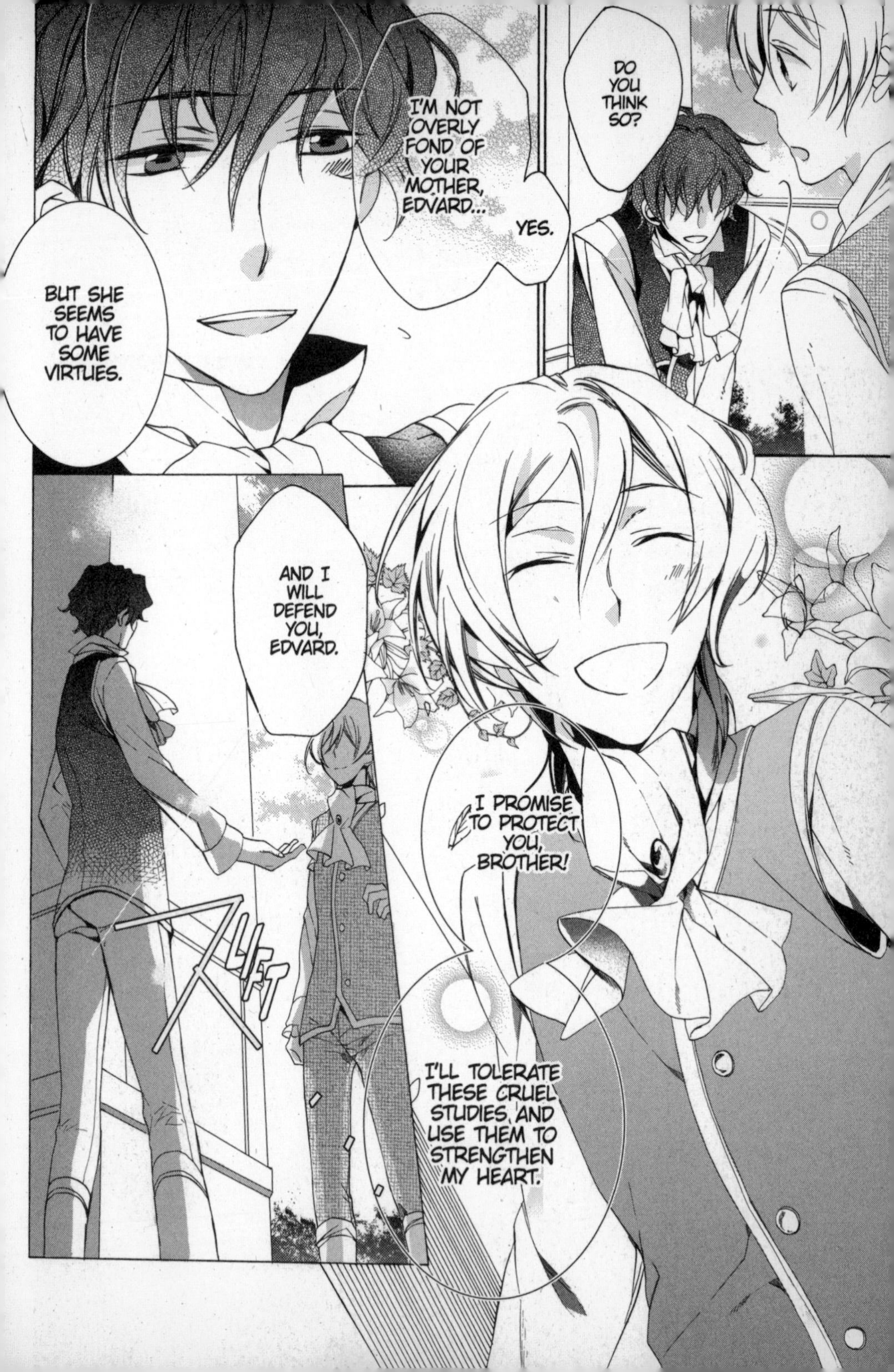
DO YOU THINK SO?
I'M NOT OVERLY FOND OF YOUR MOTHER, EDVARD...
YES.
BUT SHE SEEMS TO HAVE SOME VIRTUES.
I PROMISE TO PROTECT YOU, BROTHER!
I'LL TOLERATE THESE CRUEL STUDIES, AND USE THEM TO STRENGTHEN MY HEART.
AND I WILL DEFEND YOU, EDVARD.
FLIFT

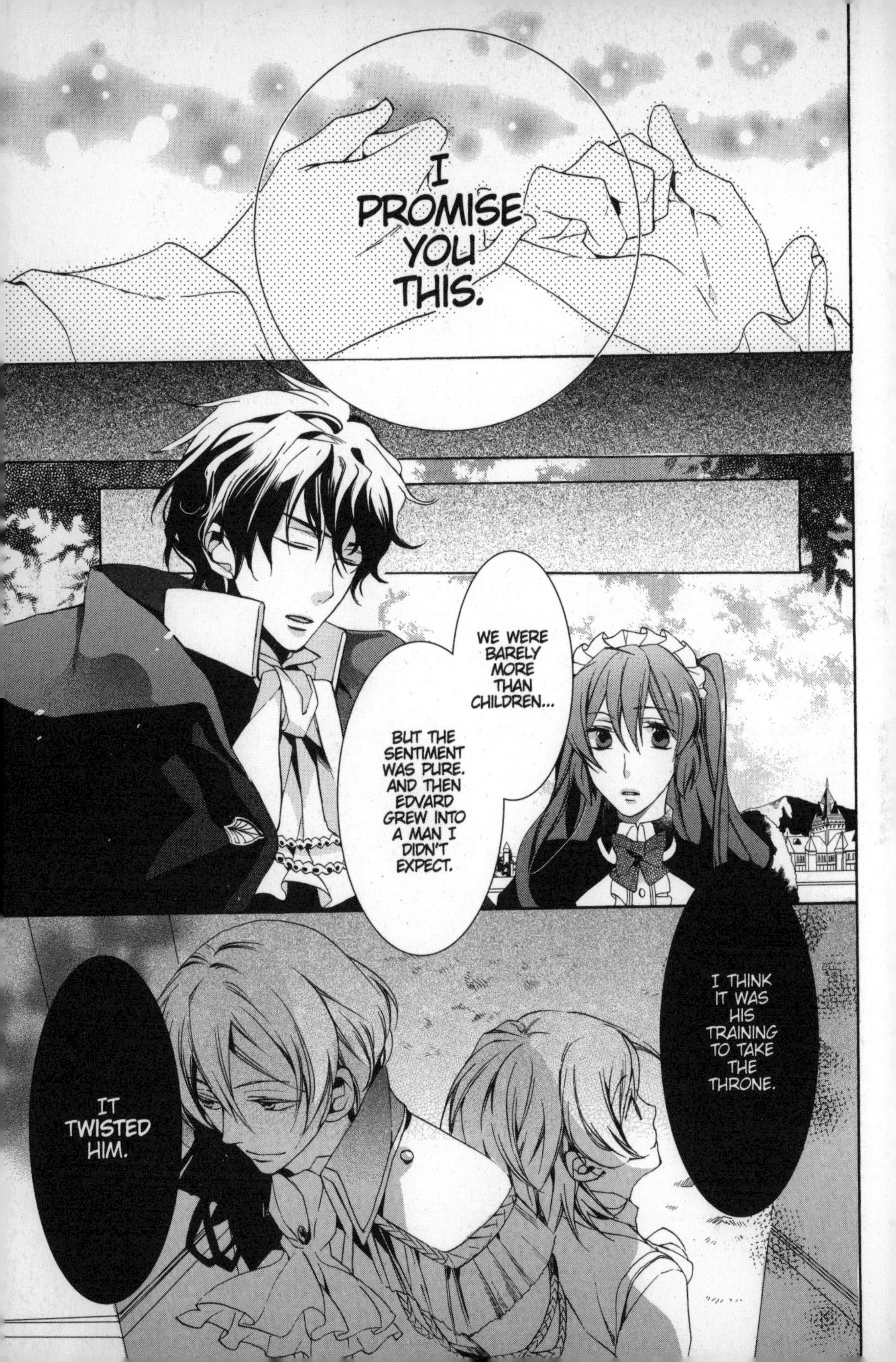
I PROMISE YOU THIS.
WE WERE BARELY MORE THAN CHILDREN...
BUT THE SENTIMENT WAS PURE. AND THEN EDVARD GREW INTO A MAN I DIDN'T EXPECT.
I THINK IT WAS HIS TRAINING TO TAKE THE THRONE.
IT TWISTED HIM.

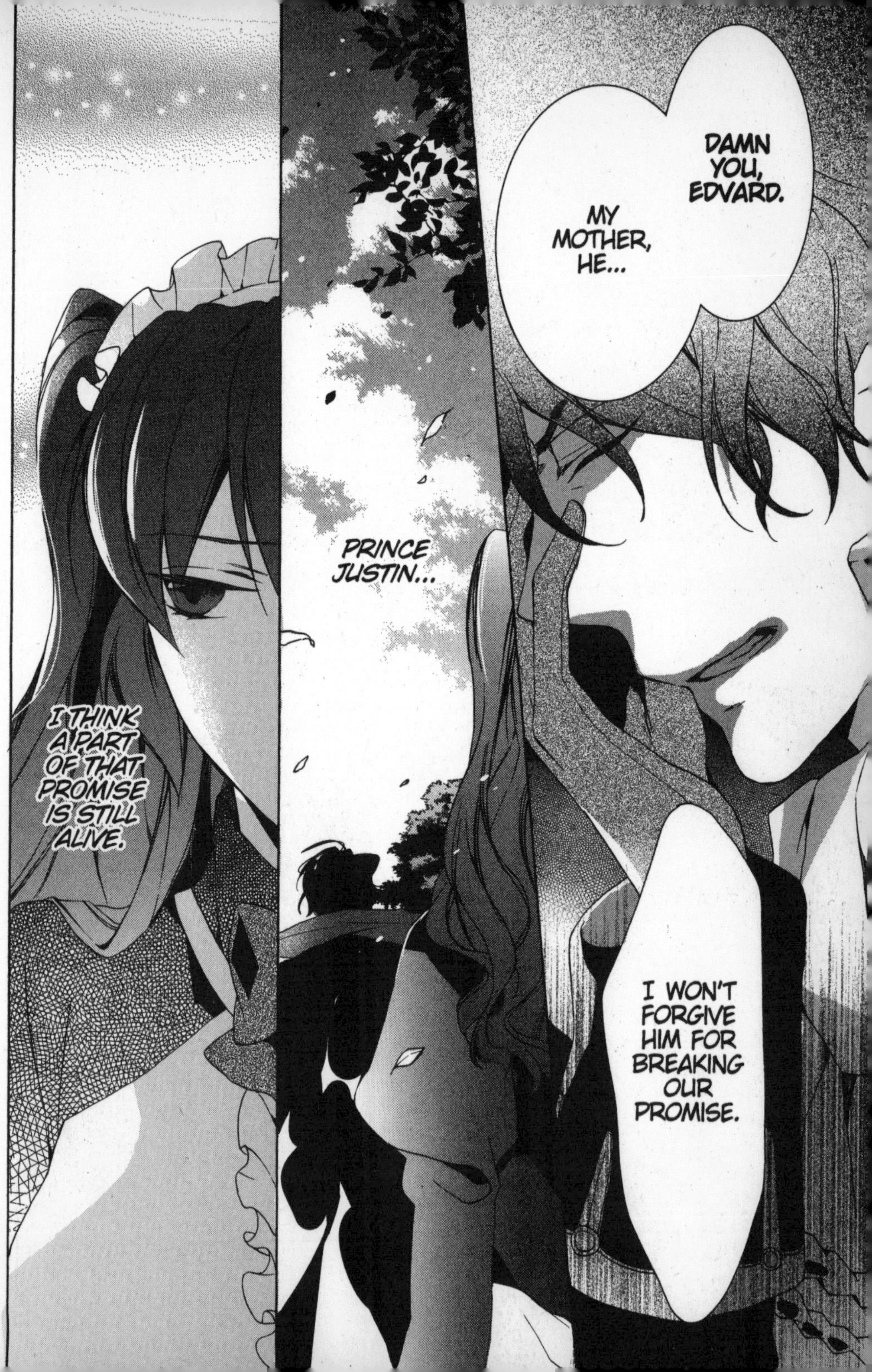
DAMN YOU, EDVARD.
MY MOTHER, HE...
I WON'T FORGIVE HIM FOR BREAKING OUR PROMISE.
PRINCE JUSTIN...
I THINK A PART OF THAT PROMISE IS STILL ALIVE.

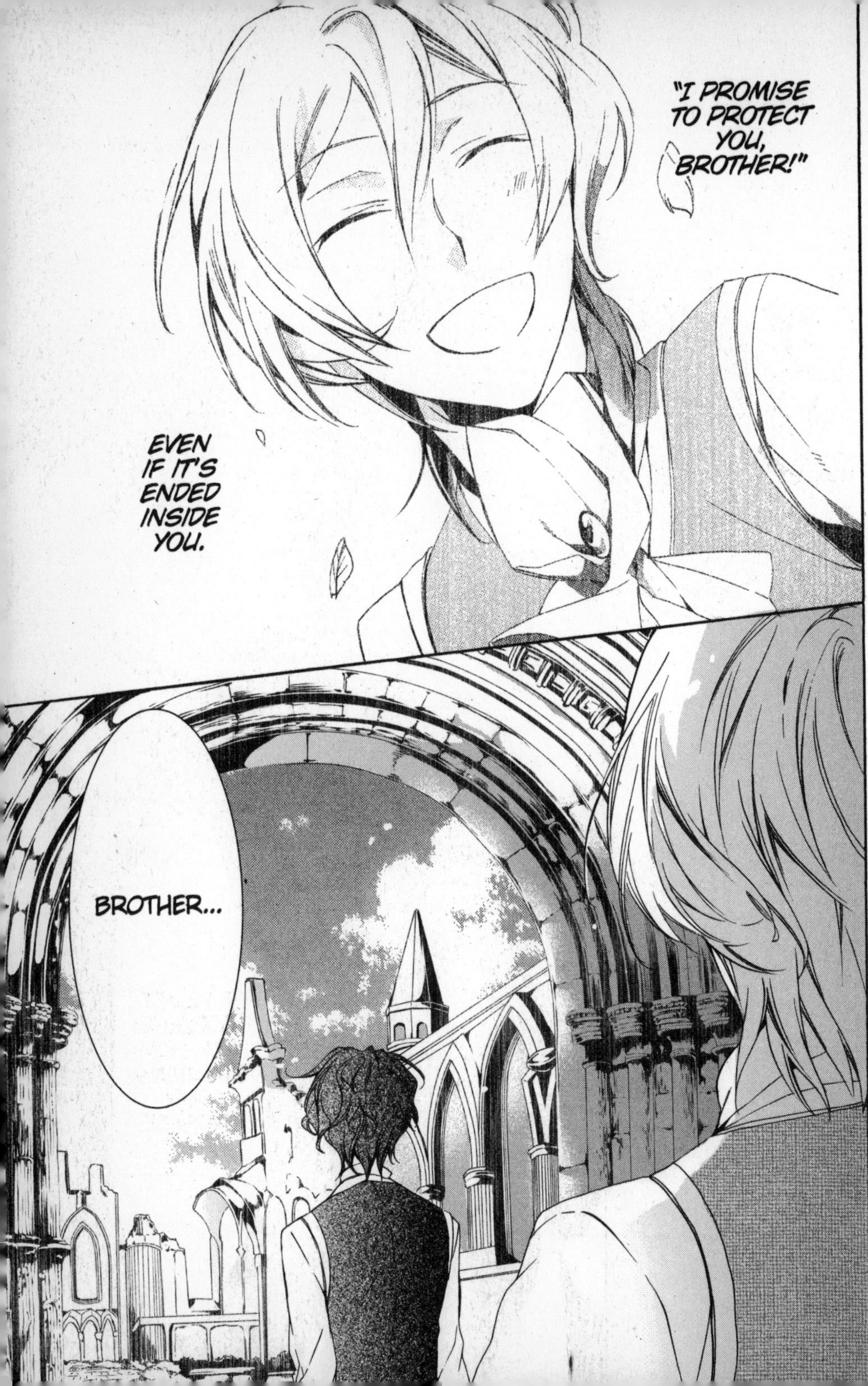
"I PROMISE TO PROTECT YOU, BROTHER!"
EVEN IF IT'S ENDED INSIDE YOU.
BROTHER...

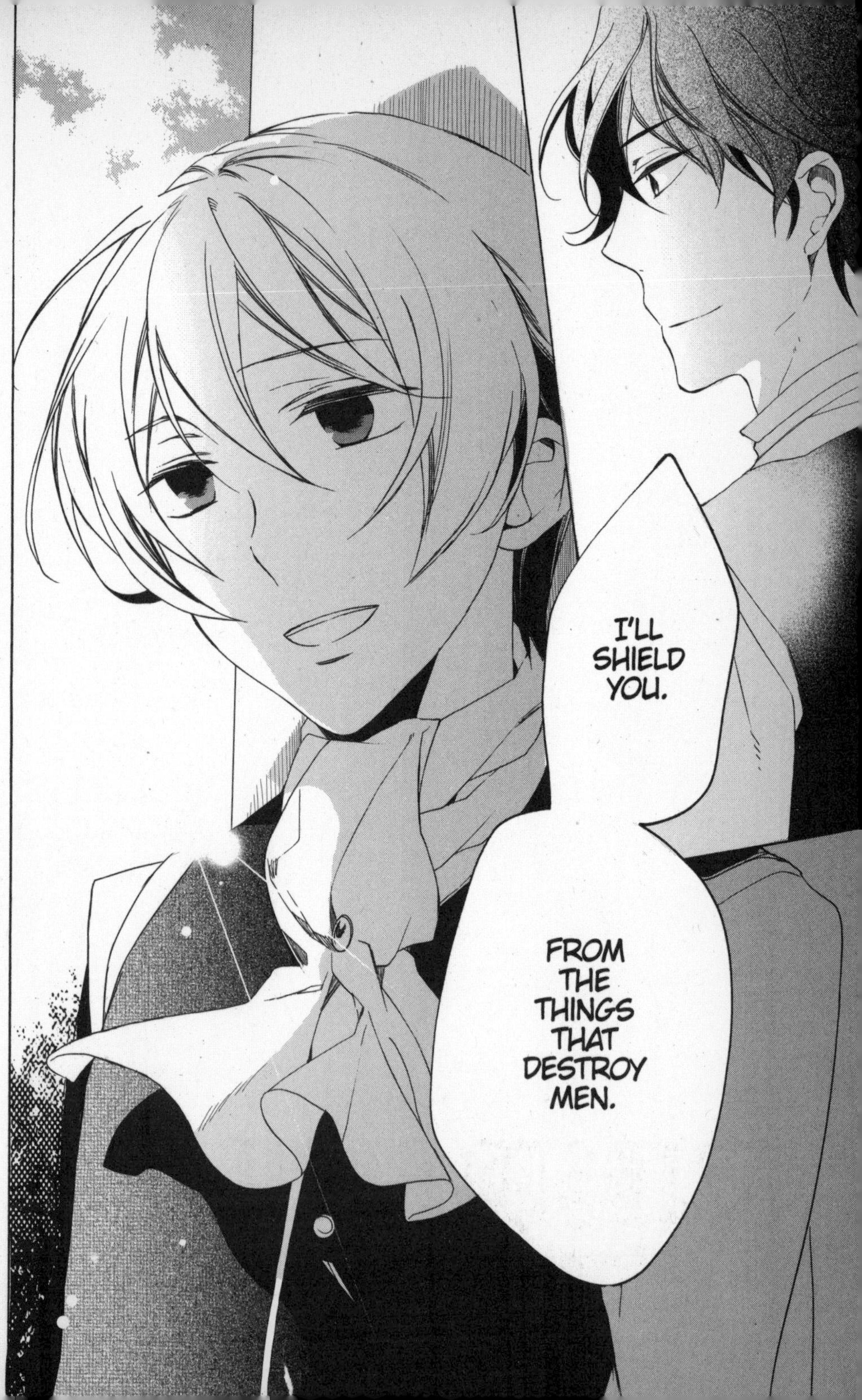
I'LL SHIELD YOU.
FROM THE THINGS THAT DESTROY MEN.

CRIMSON EMPIRE

Circumstances to serve a noble

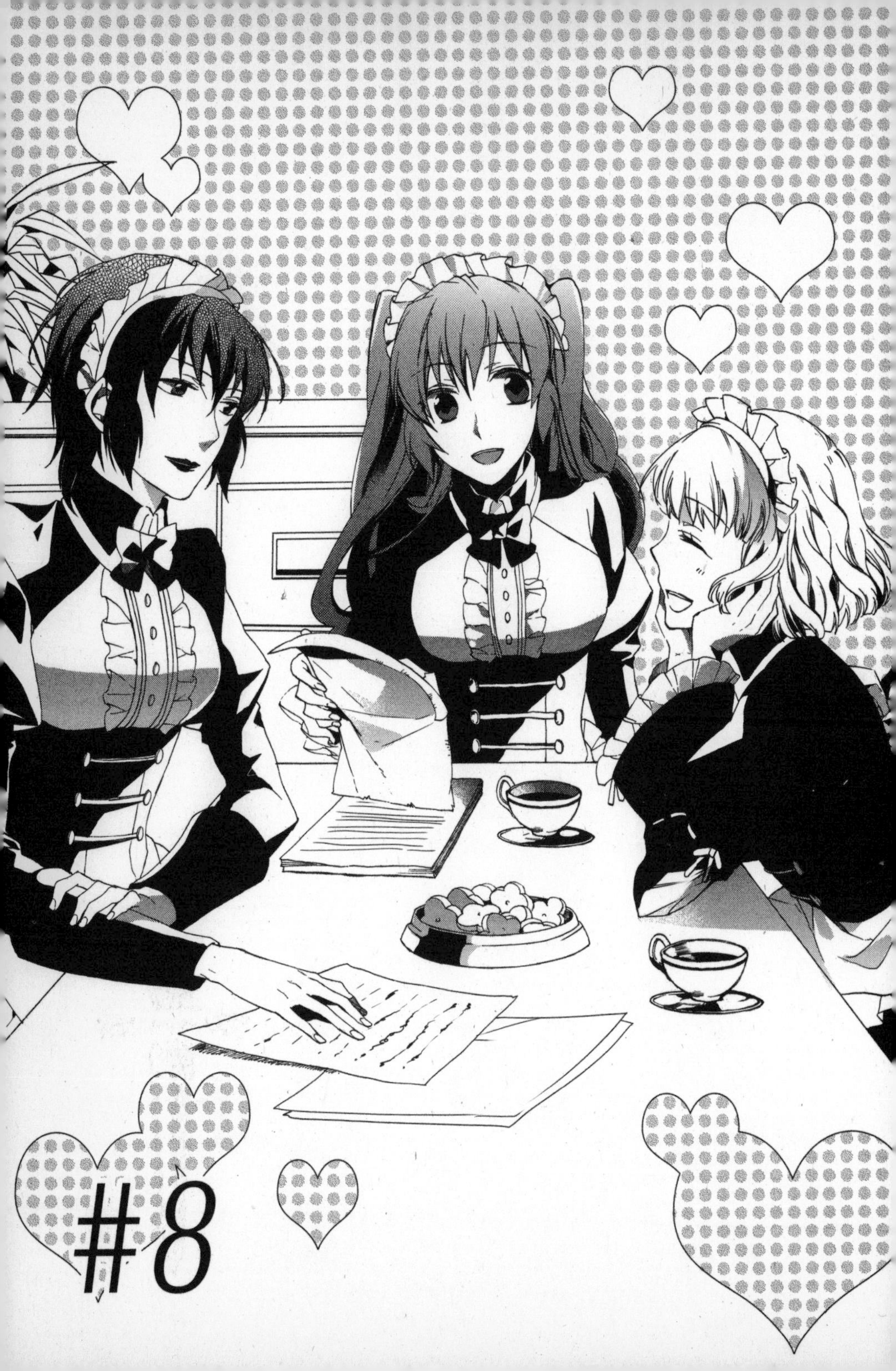
#8

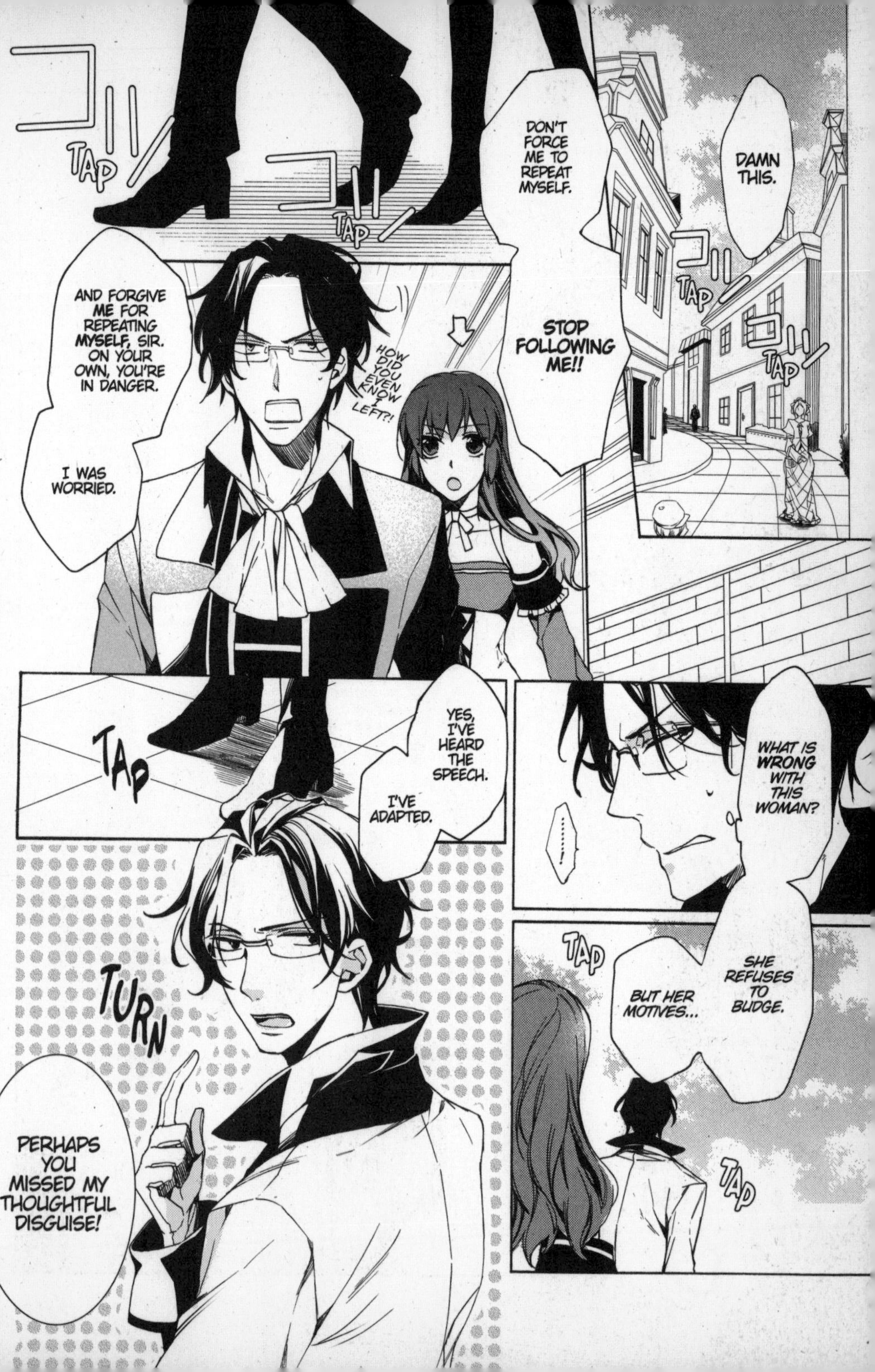
DAMN THIS.
TAP
TAP
DON'T FORCE ME TO REPEAT MYSELF.
STOP FOLLOWING ME!!
TAP
TAP
AND FORGIVE ME FOR REPEATING MYSELF, SIR. ON YOUR OWN, YOU'RE IN DANGER.
HOW DID YOU EVEN KNOW I LEFT?!
I WAS WORRIED.
WHAT IS WRONG WITH THIS WOMAN?
......!
TAP
YES, I'VE HEARD THE SPEECH.
I'VE ADAPTED.
TAP
SHE REFUSES TO BUDGE.
BUT HER MOTIVES...
TAP
TURN
PERHAPS YOU MISSED MY THOUGHTFUL DISGUISE!

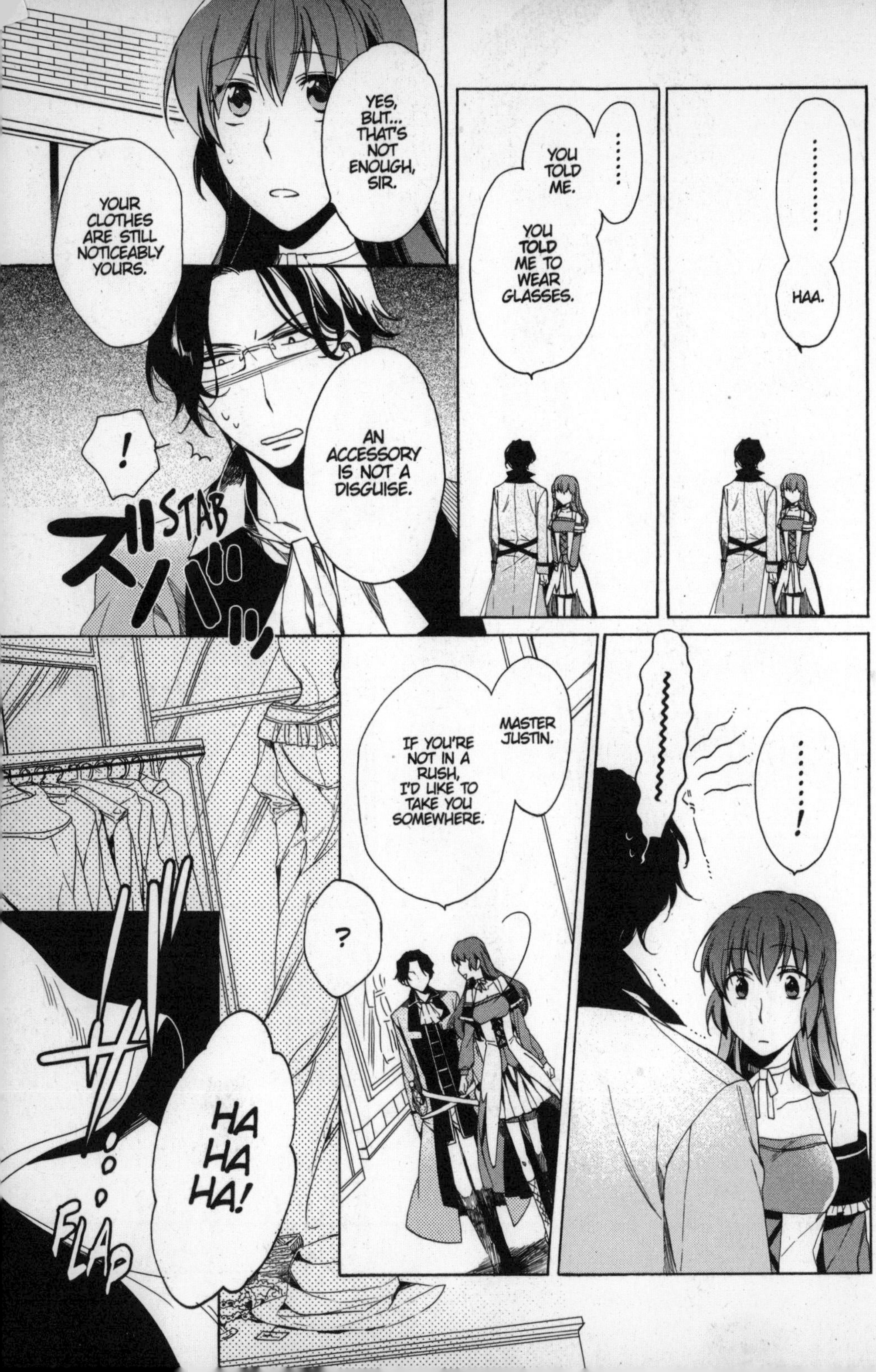
......
HAA.
......
YOU TOLD ME.
YOU TOLD ME TO WEAR GLASSES.
YES, BUT... THAT'S NOT ENOUGH, SIR.
YOUR CLOTHES ARE STILL NOTICEABLY YOURS.
AN ACCESSORY IS NOT A DISGUISE.
!
STAB
......!
MASTER JUSTIN.
IF YOU'RE NOT IN A RUSH, I'D LIKE TO TAKE YOU SOMEWHERE.
?
HA HA HA!
FLAP

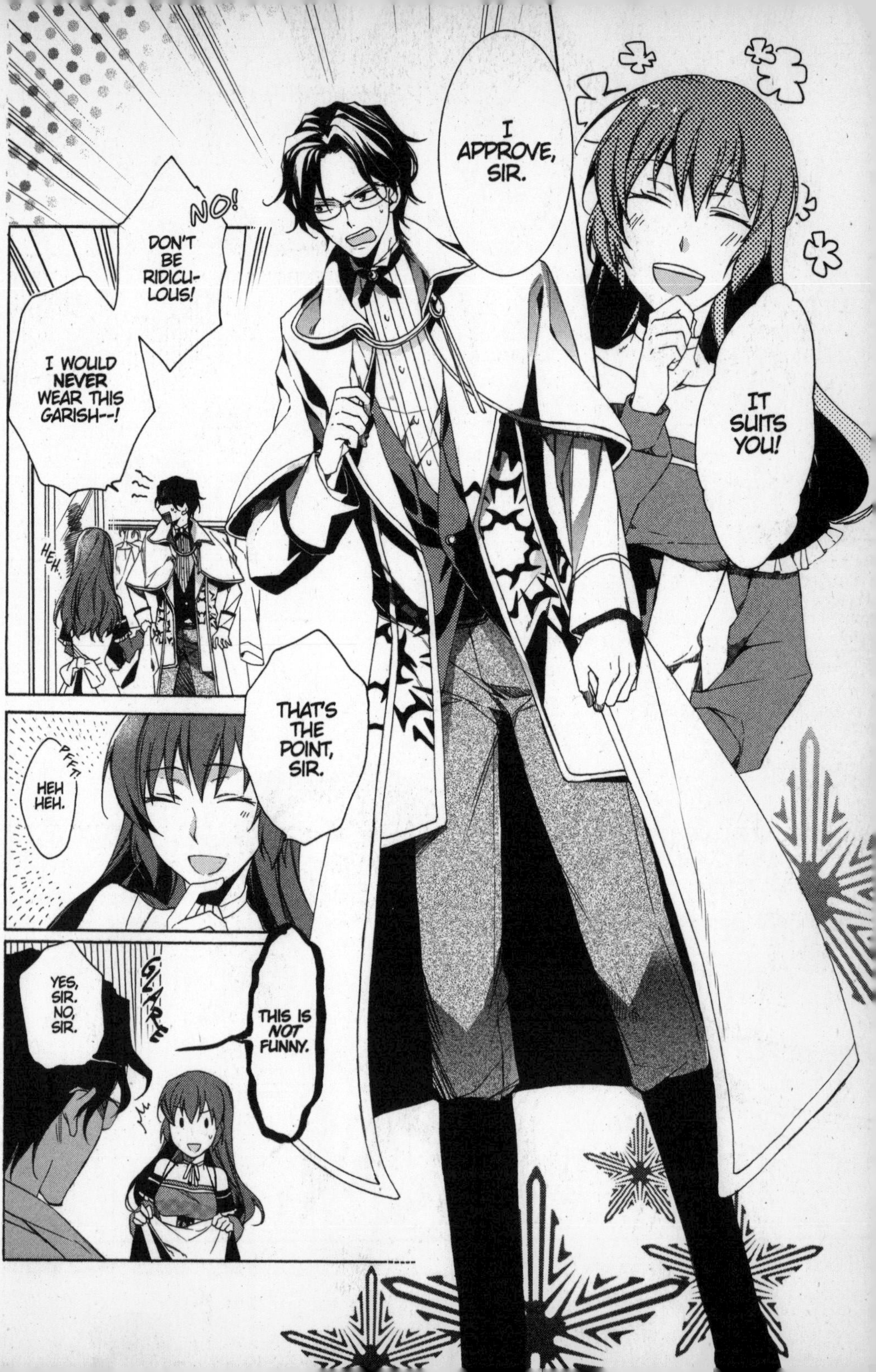
I APPROVE, SIR.
IT SUITS YOU!
NO!
DON'T BE RIDICULOUS!
I WOULD NEVER WEAR THIS GARISH--!
HEH...
THAT'S THE POINT, SIR.
PFFT!
HEH HEH.
THIS IS *NOT* FUNNY.
GLARE
YES, SIR. NO, SIR.

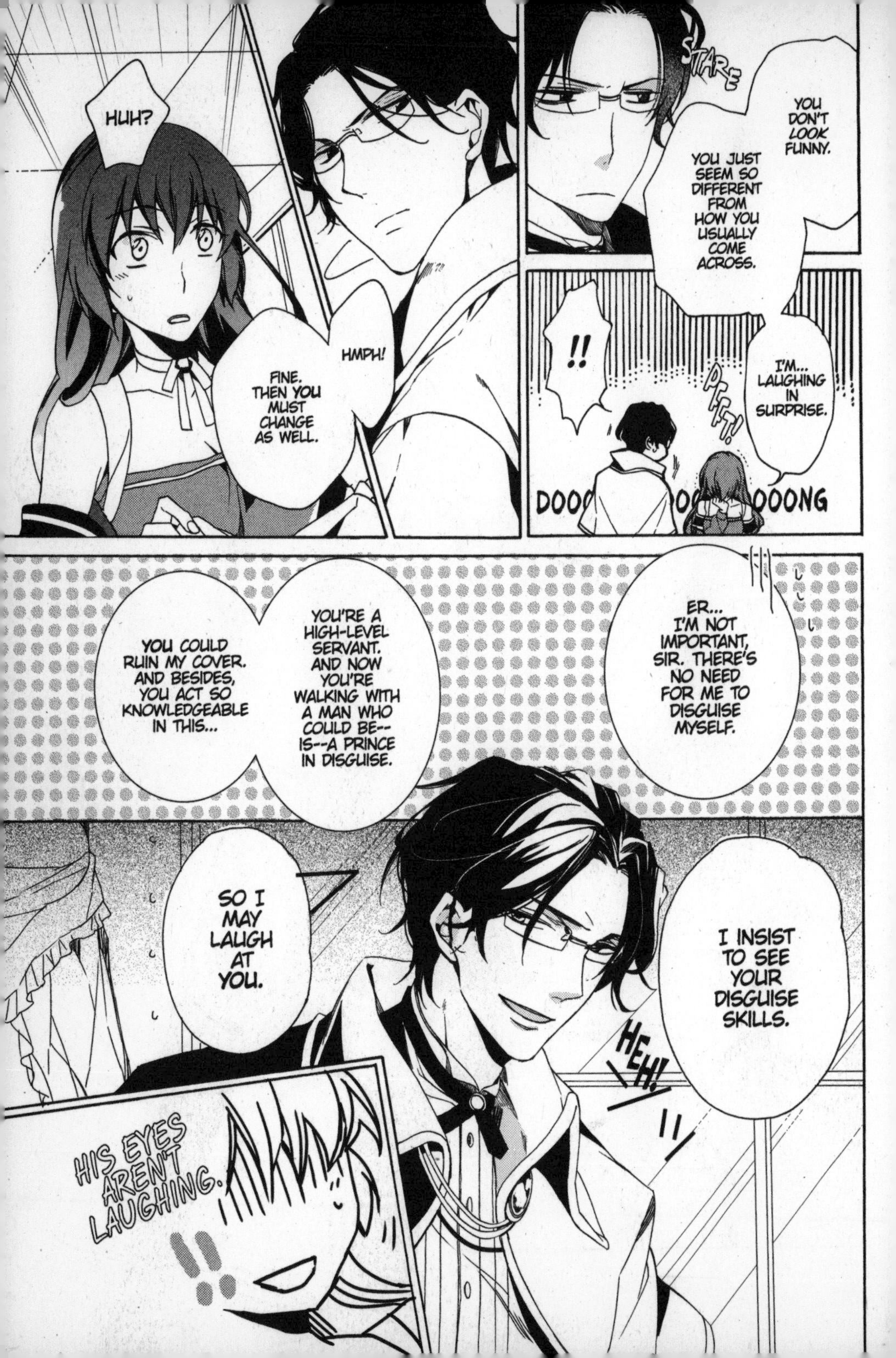
STARE
YOU DON'T LOOK FUNNY.
YOU JUST SEEM SO DIFFERENT FROM HOW YOU USUALLY COME ACROSS.
!!
PFFT!
I'M... LAUGHING IN SURPRISE.
DOOO OO OOONG
HUH?
HMPH!
FINE. THEN YOU MUST CHANGE AS WELL.
ER... I'M NOT IMPORTANT, SIR. THERE'S NO NEED FOR ME TO DISGUISE MYSELF.
YOU'RE A HIGH-LEVEL SERVANT. AND NOW YOU'RE WALKING WITH A MAN WHO COULD BE-- IS--A PRINCE IN DISGUISE.
YOU COULD RUIN MY COVER. AND BESIDES, YOU ACT SO KNOWLEDGEABLE IN THIS...
I INSIST TO SEE YOUR DISGUISE SKILLS.
HEH!
SO I MAY LAUGH AT YOU.
HIS EYES AREN'T LAUGHING.

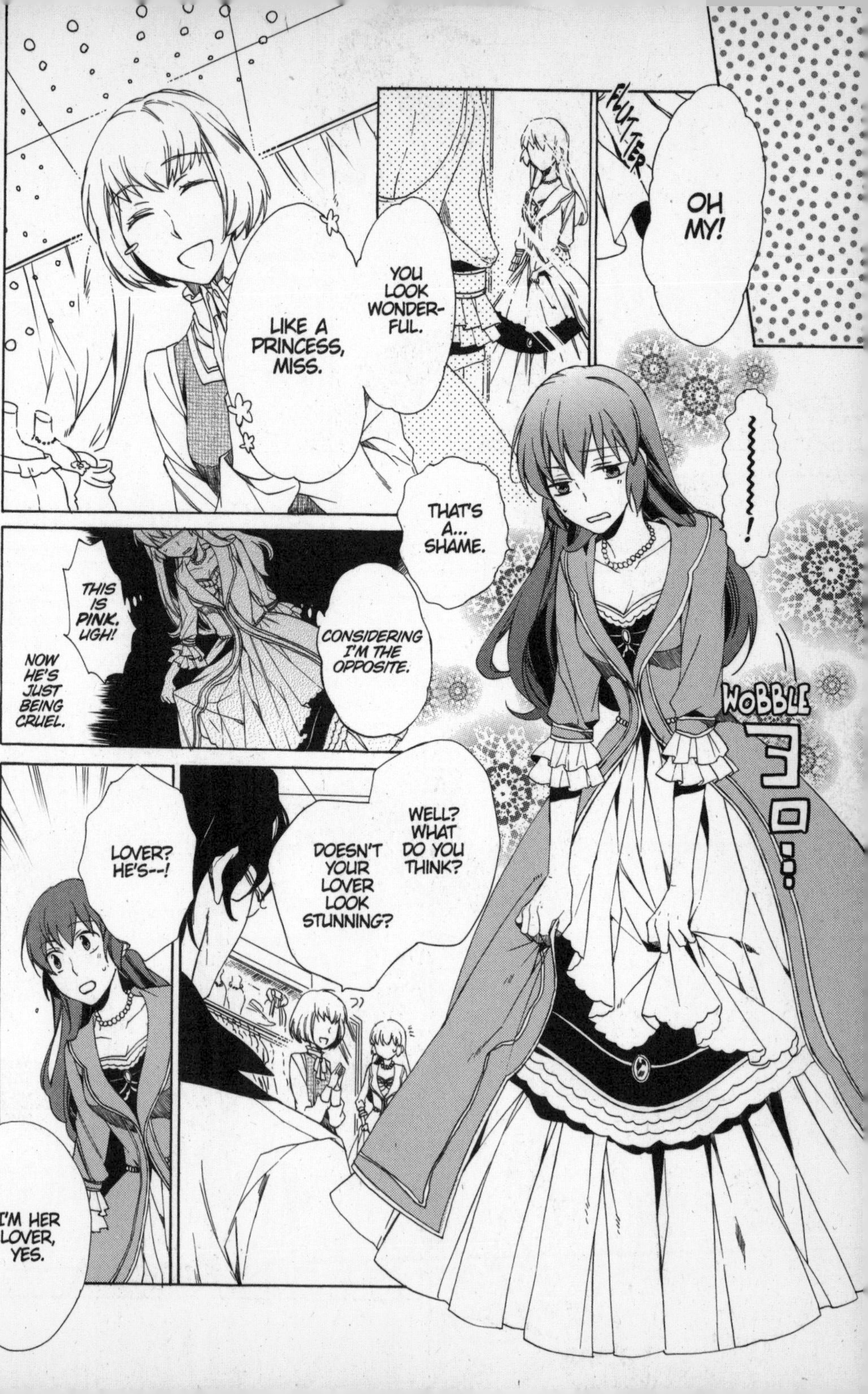
OH MY!
FLUTTER
YOU LOOK WONDERFUL.
LIKE A PRINCESS, MISS.
~~~~~!
WOBBLE
ヨロ‥
THAT'S A... SHAME.
CONSIDERING I'M THE OPPOSITE.
THIS IS PINK. UGH!
NOW HE'S JUST BEING CRUEL.
WELL? WHAT DO YOU THINK?
DOESN'T YOUR LOVER LOOK STUNNING?
LOVER? HE'S--!
I'M HER LOVER, YES.
~~~~~

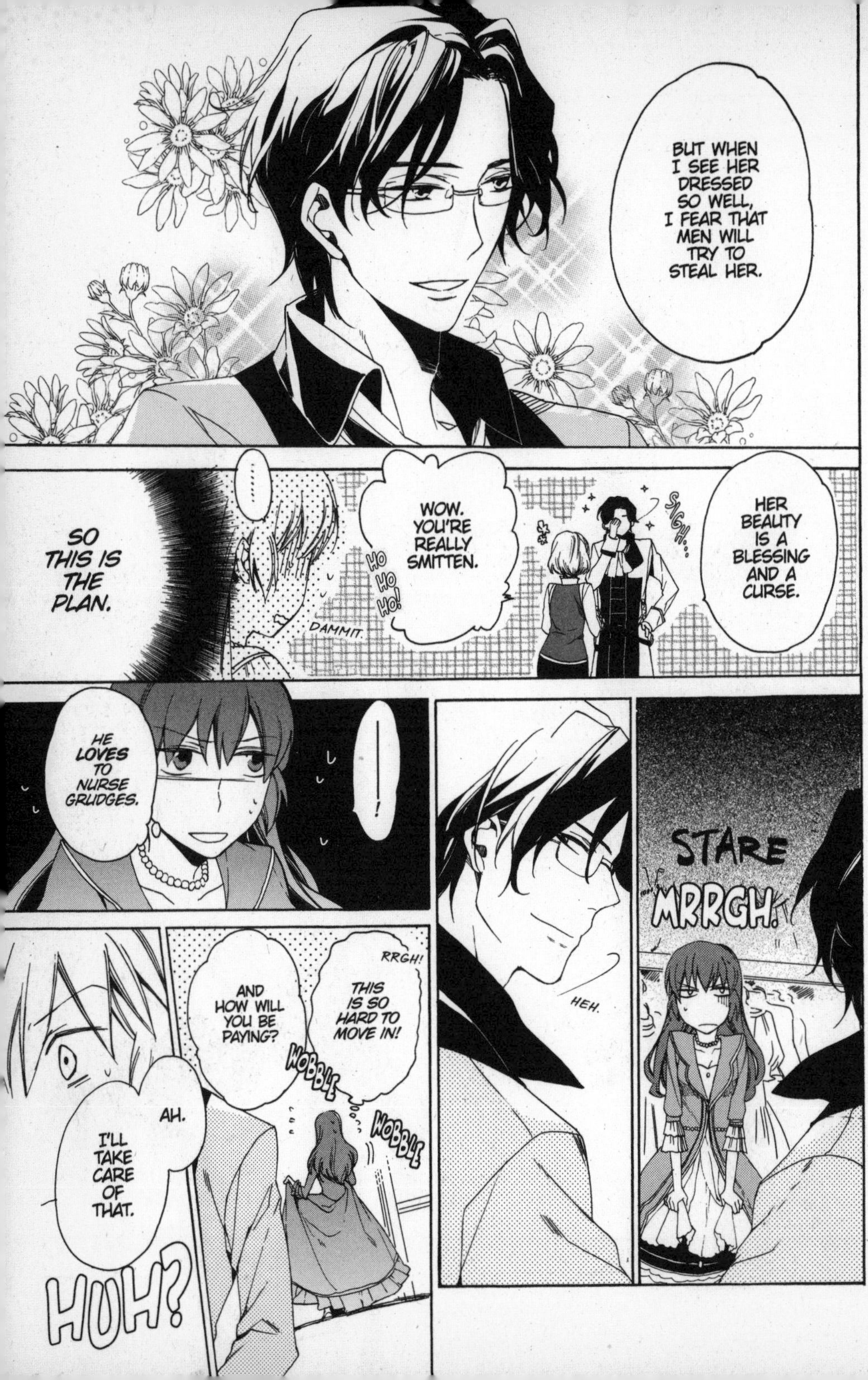
BUT WHEN I SEE HER DRESSED SO WELL, I FEAR THAT MEN WILL TRY TO STEAL HER.
SIGH...
HER BEAUTY IS A BLESSING AND A CURSE.
WOW. YOU'RE REALLY SMITTEN.
HO HO HO!
......
DAMMIT.
SO THIS IS THE PLAN.
STARE
MRRGH.
HEH.
!
HE LOVES TO NURSE GRUDGES.
RRGH!
THIS IS SO HARD TO MOVE IN!
WOBBLE
WOBBLE
AND HOW WILL YOU BE PAYING?
AH.
I'LL TAKE CARE OF THAT.
HUH?

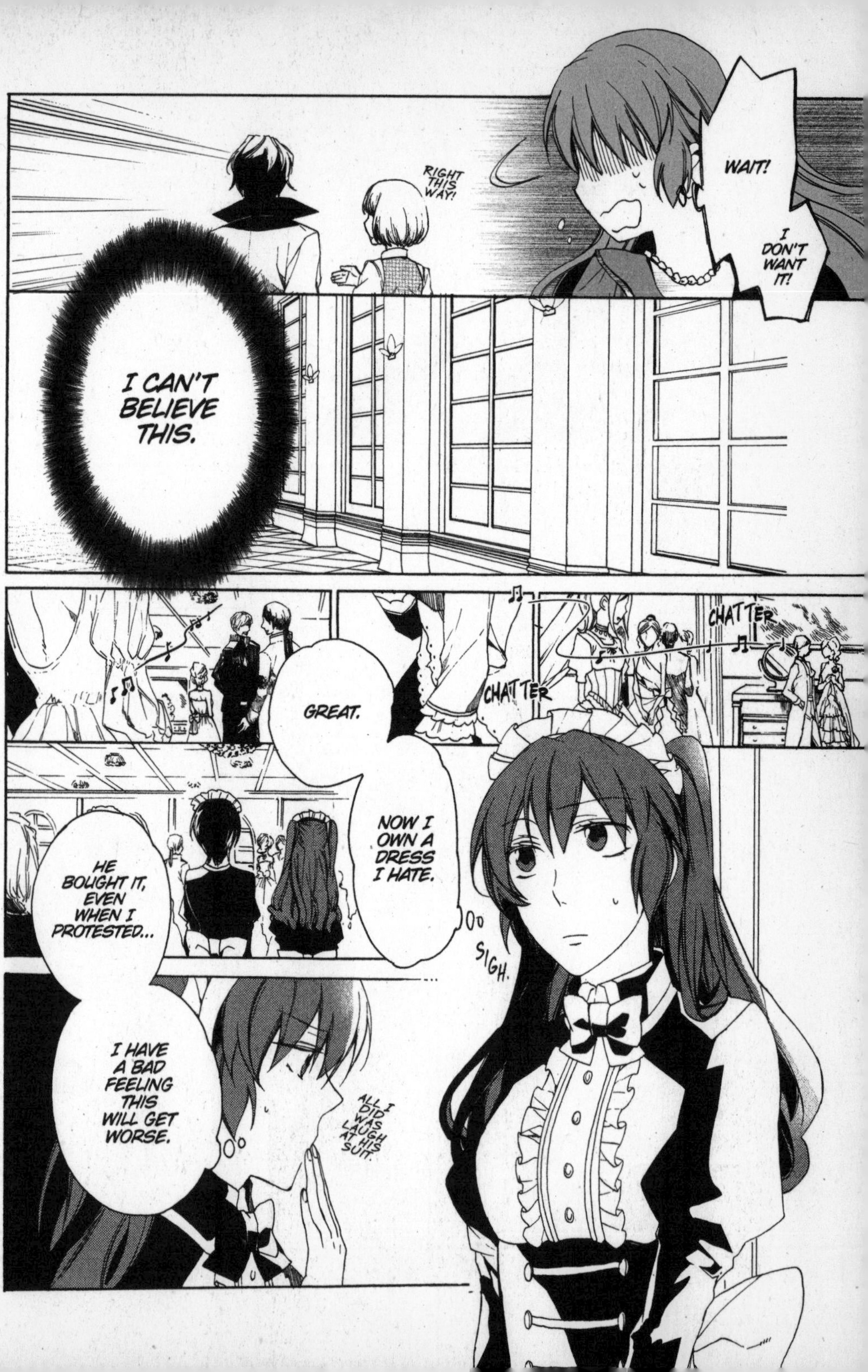
WAIT!
I DON'T WANT IT!
RIGHT THIS WAY!
I CAN'T BELIEVE THIS.
CHATTER
CHATTER
GREAT.
NOW I OWN A DRESS I HATE.
SIGH.
...
HE BOUGHT IT, EVEN WHEN I PROTESTED...
ALL I DID WAS LAUGH AT HIS SUIT.
I HAVE A BAD FEELING THIS WILL GET WORSE.

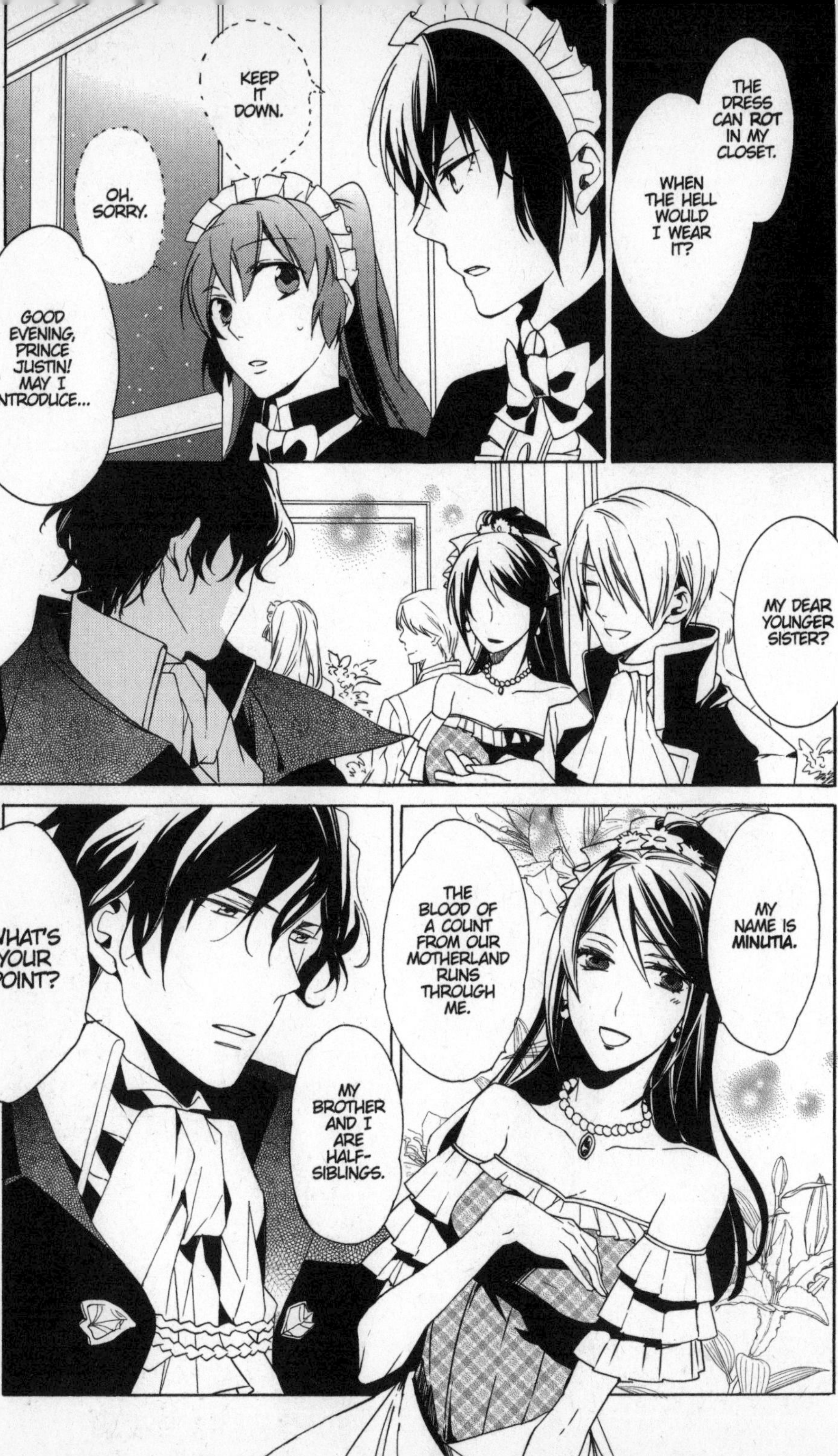
THE DRESS CAN ROT IN MY CLOSET.
WHEN THE HELL WOULD I WEAR IT?
KEEP IT DOWN.
OH. SORRY.
GOOD EVENING, PRINCE JUSTIN! MAY I INTRODUCE...
MY DEAR YOUNGER SISTER?
MY NAME IS MINUTIA.
THE BLOOD OF A COUNT FROM OUR MOTHERLAND RUNS THROUGH ME.
MY BROTHER AND I ARE HALF-SIBLINGS.
WHAT'S YOUR POINT?

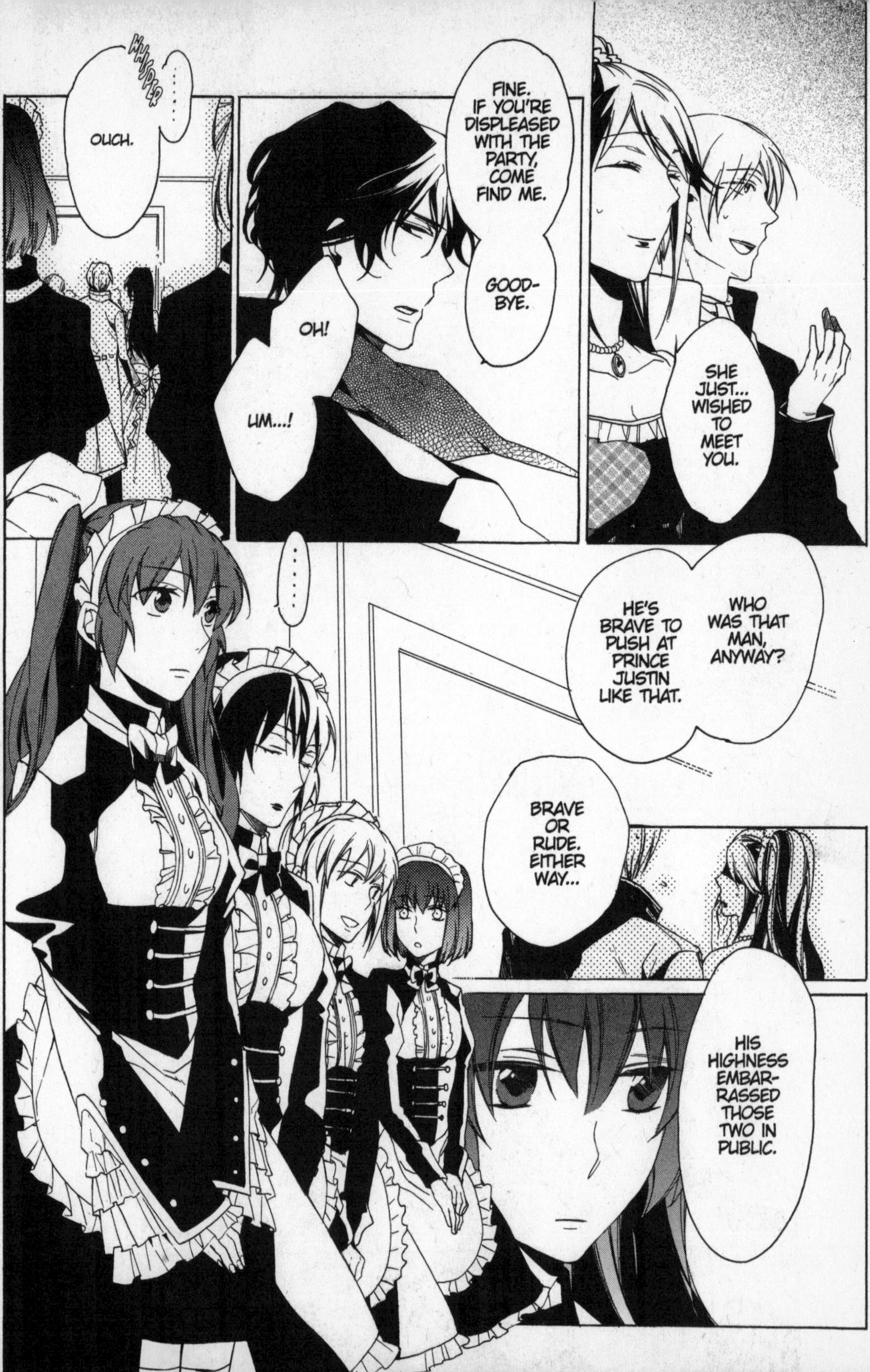
SHE JUST... WISHED TO MEET YOU.
FINE. IF YOU'RE DISPLEASED WITH THE PARTY, COME FIND ME.
GOOD-BYE.
OH!
UM...!
WHISPER
......
OUCH.
WHO WAS THAT MAN, ANYWAY?
HE'S BRAVE TO PUSH AT PRINCE JUSTIN LIKE THAT.
BRAVE OR RUDE. EITHER WAY...
HIS HIGHNESS EMBARRASSED THOSE TWO IN PUBLIC.
......

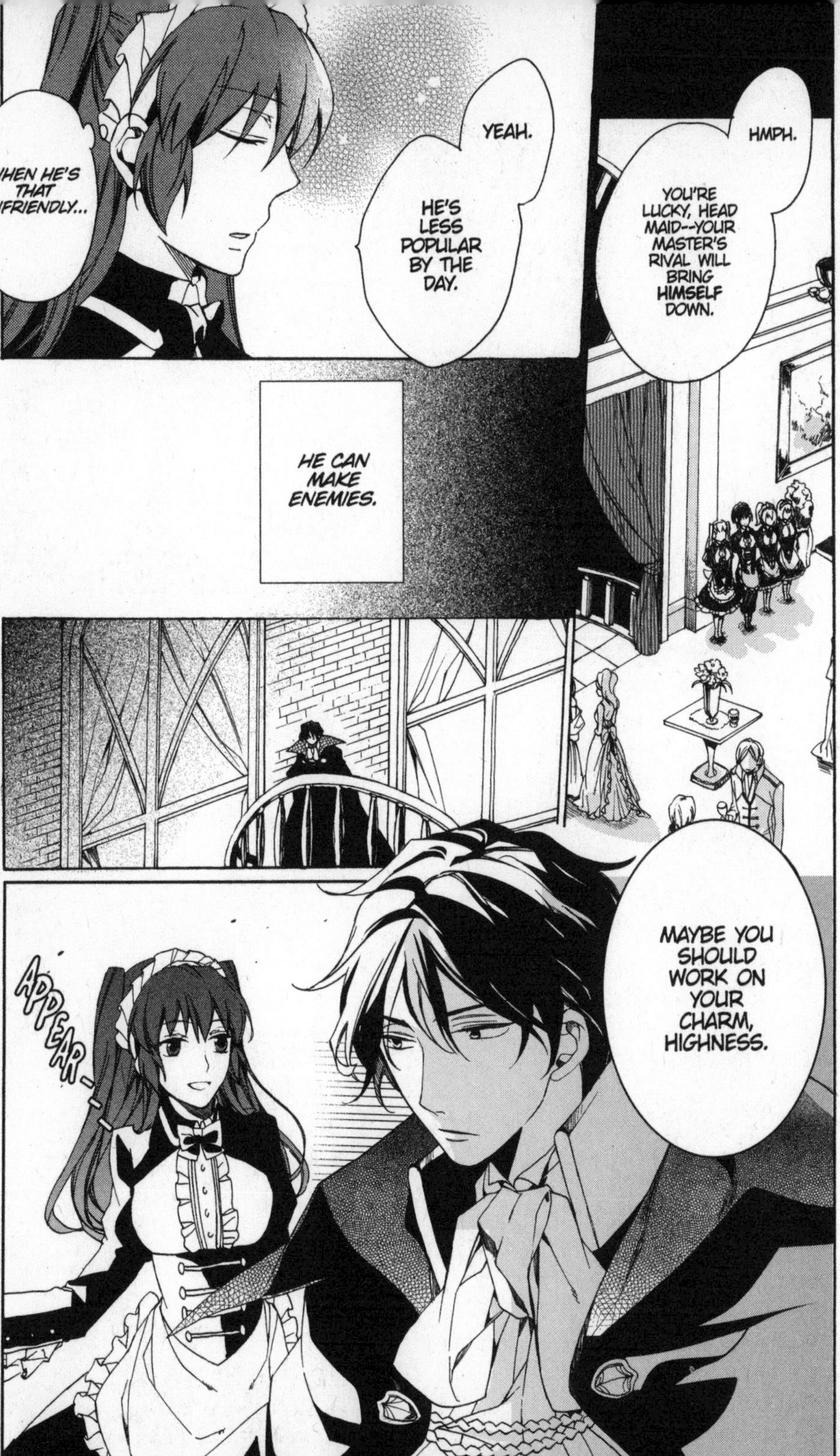
HMPH.
YOU'RE LUCKY, HEAD MAID--YOUR MASTER'S RIVAL WILL BRING HIMSELF DOWN.
YEAH.
HE'S LESS POPULAR BY THE DAY.
WHEN HE'S THAT UNFRIENDLY...
HE CAN MAKE ENEMIES.
MAYBE YOU SHOULD WORK ON YOUR CHARM, HIGHNESS.
APPEAR--

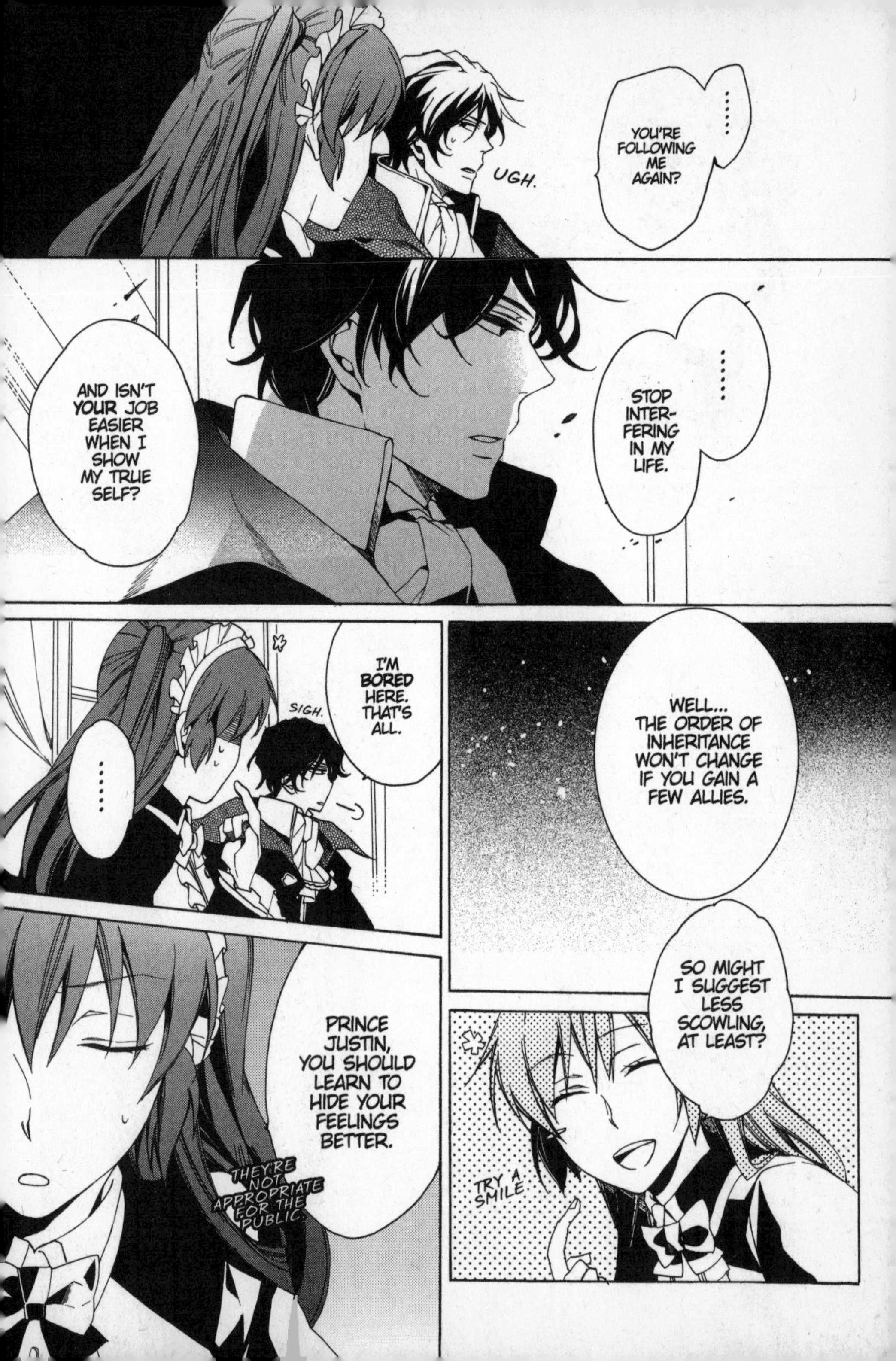
......
YOU'RE FOLLOWING ME AGAIN?
UGH.
......
STOP INTERFERING IN MY LIFE.
AND ISN'T YOUR JOB EASIER WHEN I SHOW MY TRUE SELF?
WELL... THE ORDER OF INHERITANCE WON'T CHANGE IF YOU GAIN A FEW ALLIES.
I'M BORED HERE. THAT'S ALL.
SIGH.
......
SO MIGHT I SUGGEST LESS SCOWLING, AT LEAST?
TRY A SMILE
PRINCE JUSTIN, YOU SHOULD LEARN TO HIDE YOUR FEELINGS BETTER.
THEY'RE NOT APPROPRIATE FOR THE PUBLIC.

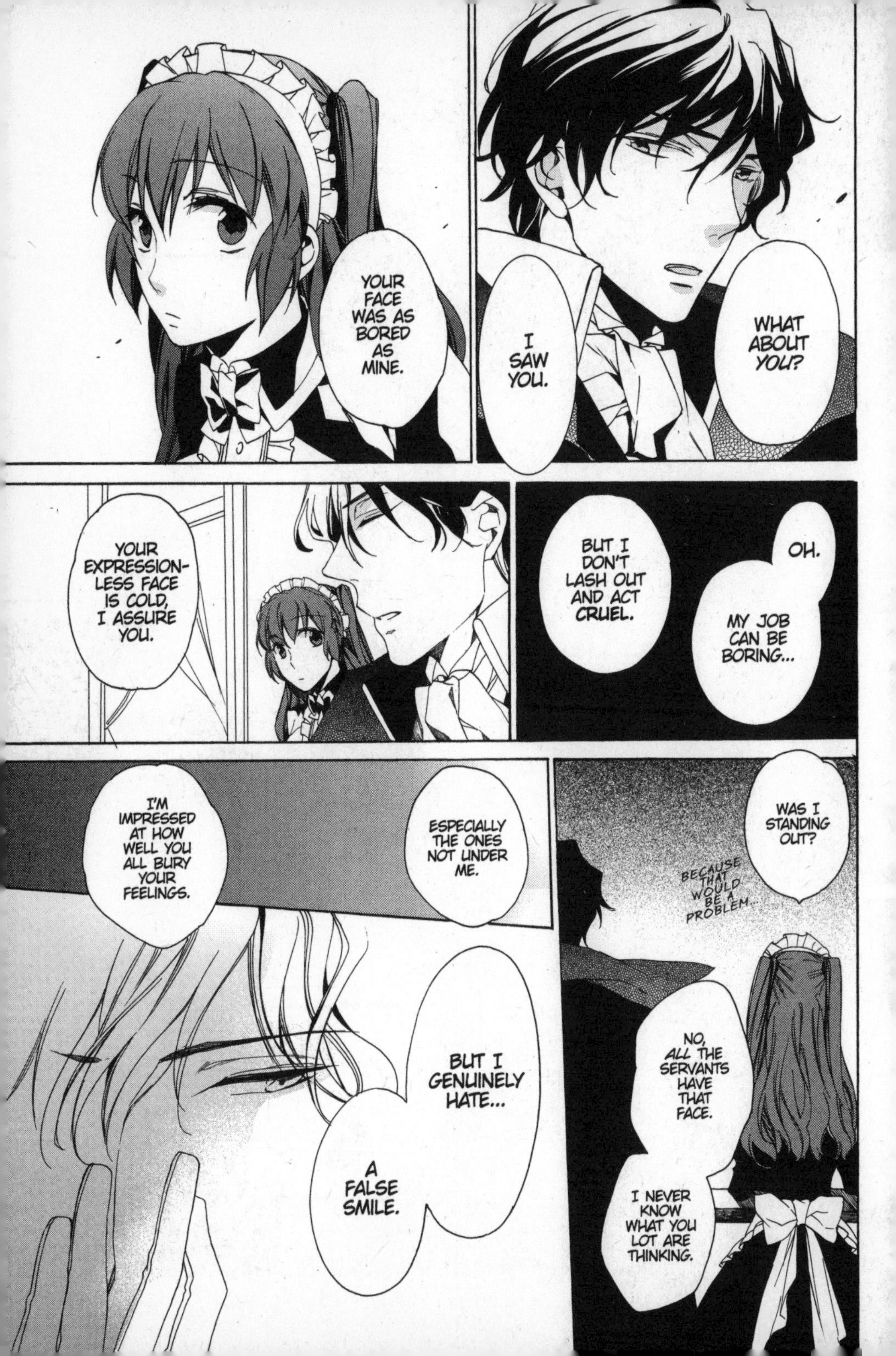
WHAT ABOUT YOU?
I SAW YOU.
YOUR FACE WAS AS BORED AS MINE.
OH.
MY JOB CAN BE BORING...
BUT I DON'T LASH OUT AND ACT CRUEL.
YOUR EXPRESSIONLESS FACE IS COLD, I ASSURE YOU.
WAS I STANDING OUT?
BECAUSE THAT WOULD BE A PROBLEM...
NO, ALL THE SERVANTS HAVE THAT FACE.
I NEVER KNOW WHAT YOU LOT ARE THINKING.
ESPECIALLY THE ONES NOT UNDER ME.
I'M IMPRESSED AT HOW WELL YOU ALL BURY YOUR FEELINGS.
BUT I GENUINELY HATE...
A FALSE SMILE.

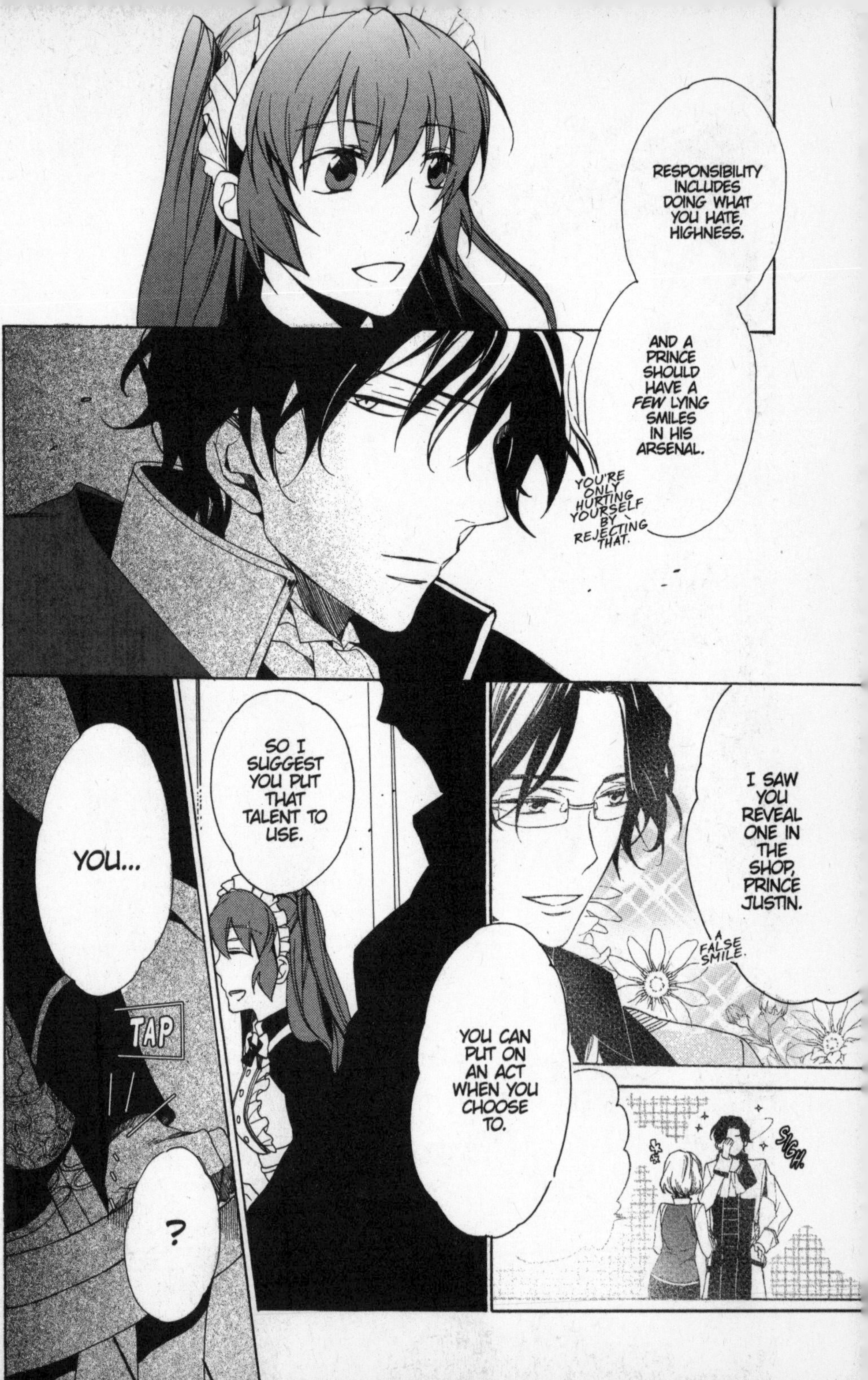
RESPONSIBILITY INCLUDES DOING WHAT YOU HATE, HIGHNESS.
AND A PRINCE SHOULD HAVE A *FEW* LYING SMILES IN HIS ARSENAL.
YOU'RE ONLY HURTING YOURSELF BY REJECTING THAT.
I SAW YOU REVEAL ONE IN THE SHOP, PRINCE JUSTIN.
A FALSE SMILE.
SIGH.
YOU CAN PUT ON AN ACT WHEN YOU CHOOSE TO.
SO I SUGGEST YOU PUT THAT TALENT TO USE.
YOU...
TAP
?

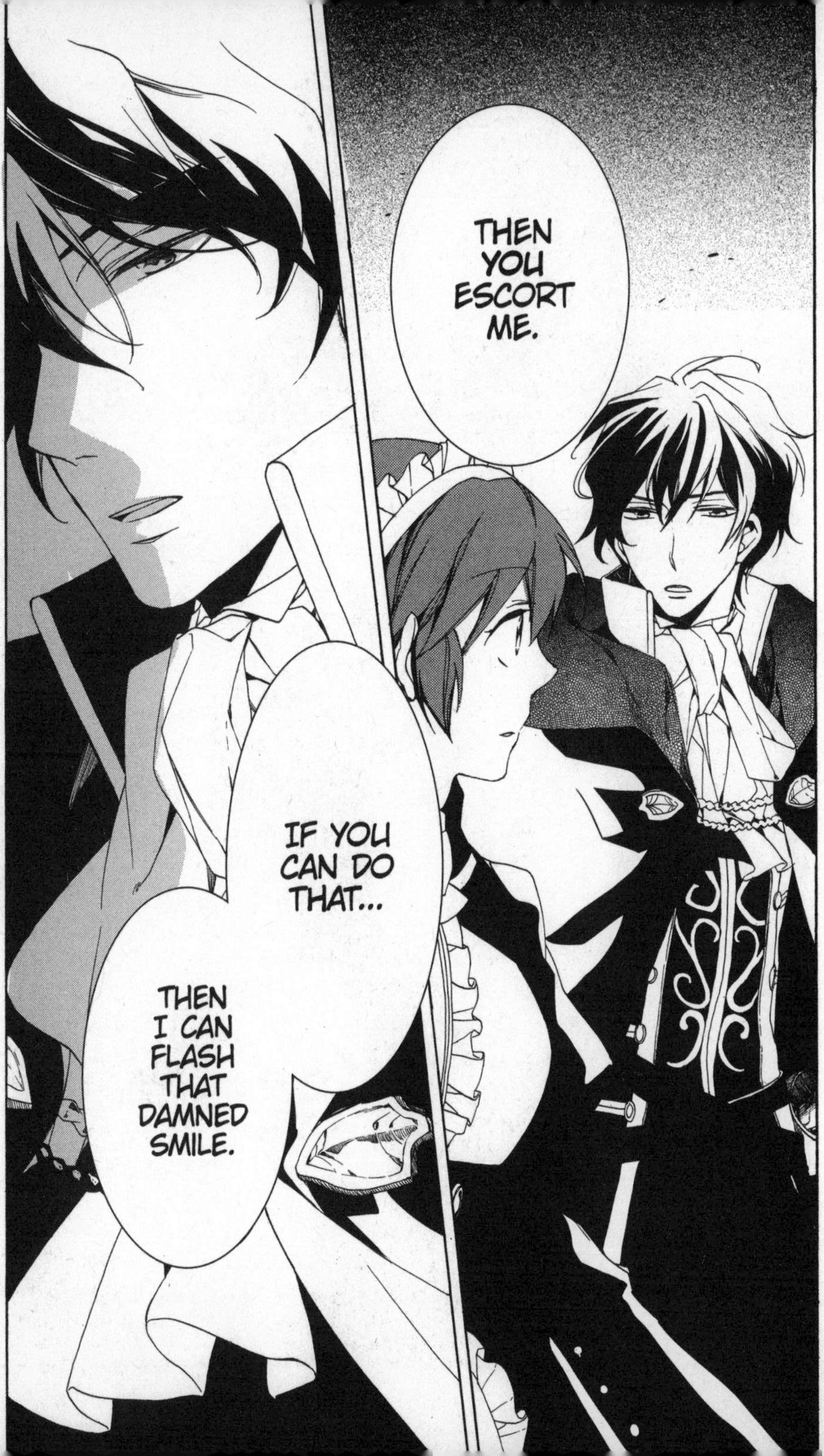
THEN YOU ESCORT ME.
IF YOU CAN DO THAT...
THEN I CAN FLASH THAT DAMNED SMILE.

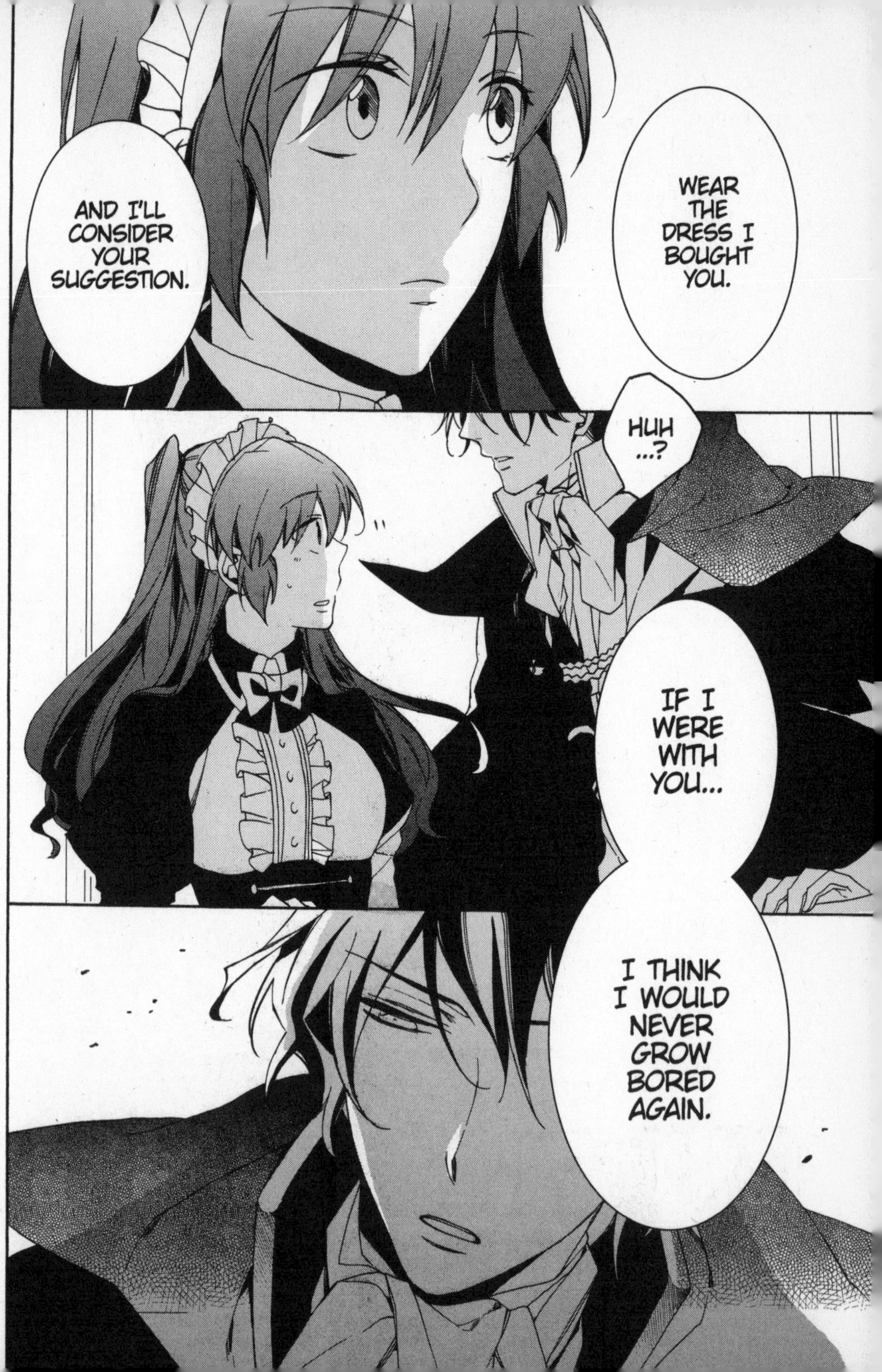
WEAR THE DRESS I BOUGHT YOU.
AND I'LL CONSIDER YOUR SUGGESTION.
HUH ...?
IF I WERE WITH YOU...
I THINK I WOULD NEVER GROW BORED AGAIN.

CRIMSON EMPIRE
CIRCUMSTANCES TO SERVE A NOBLE

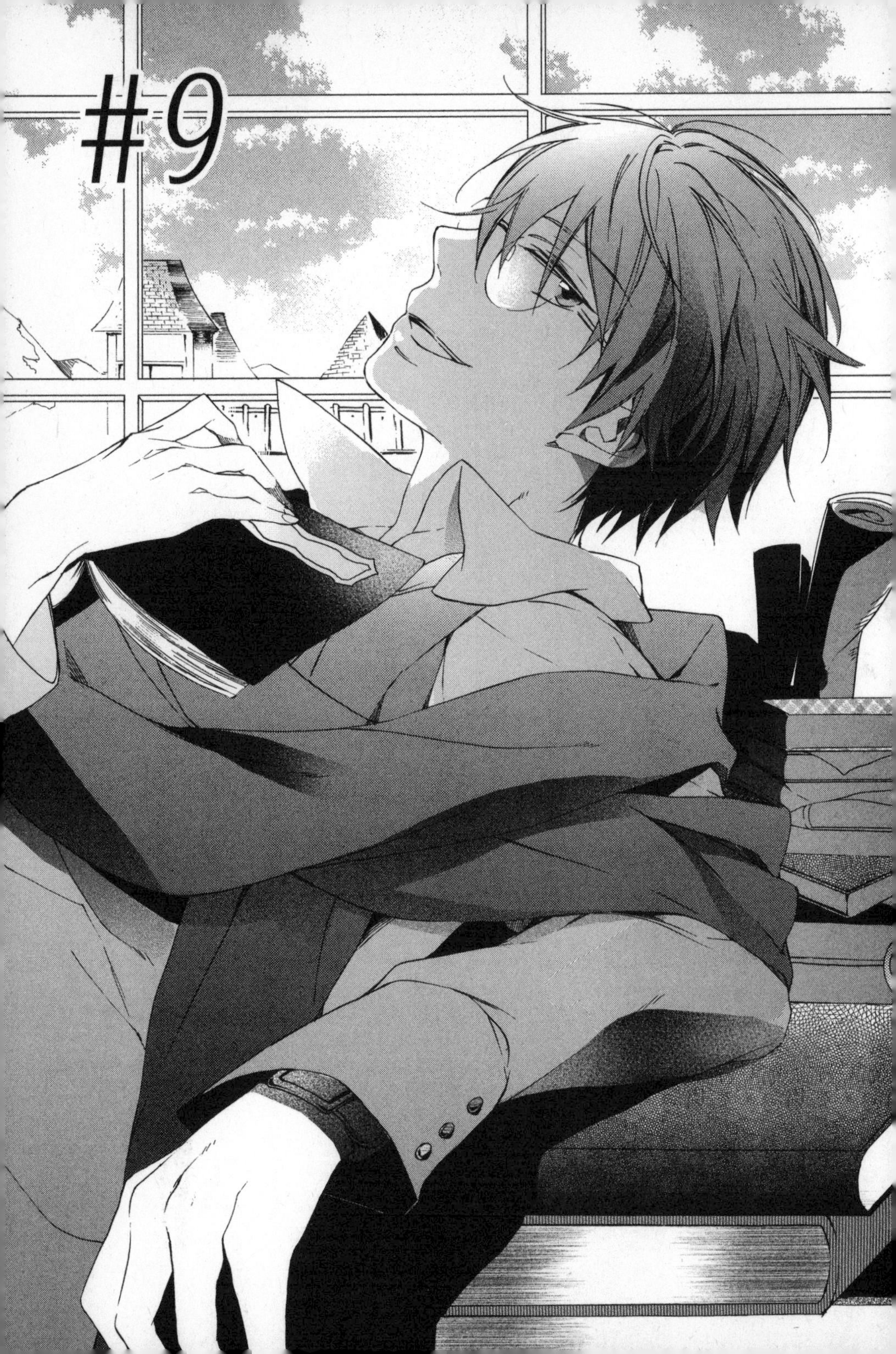
#9

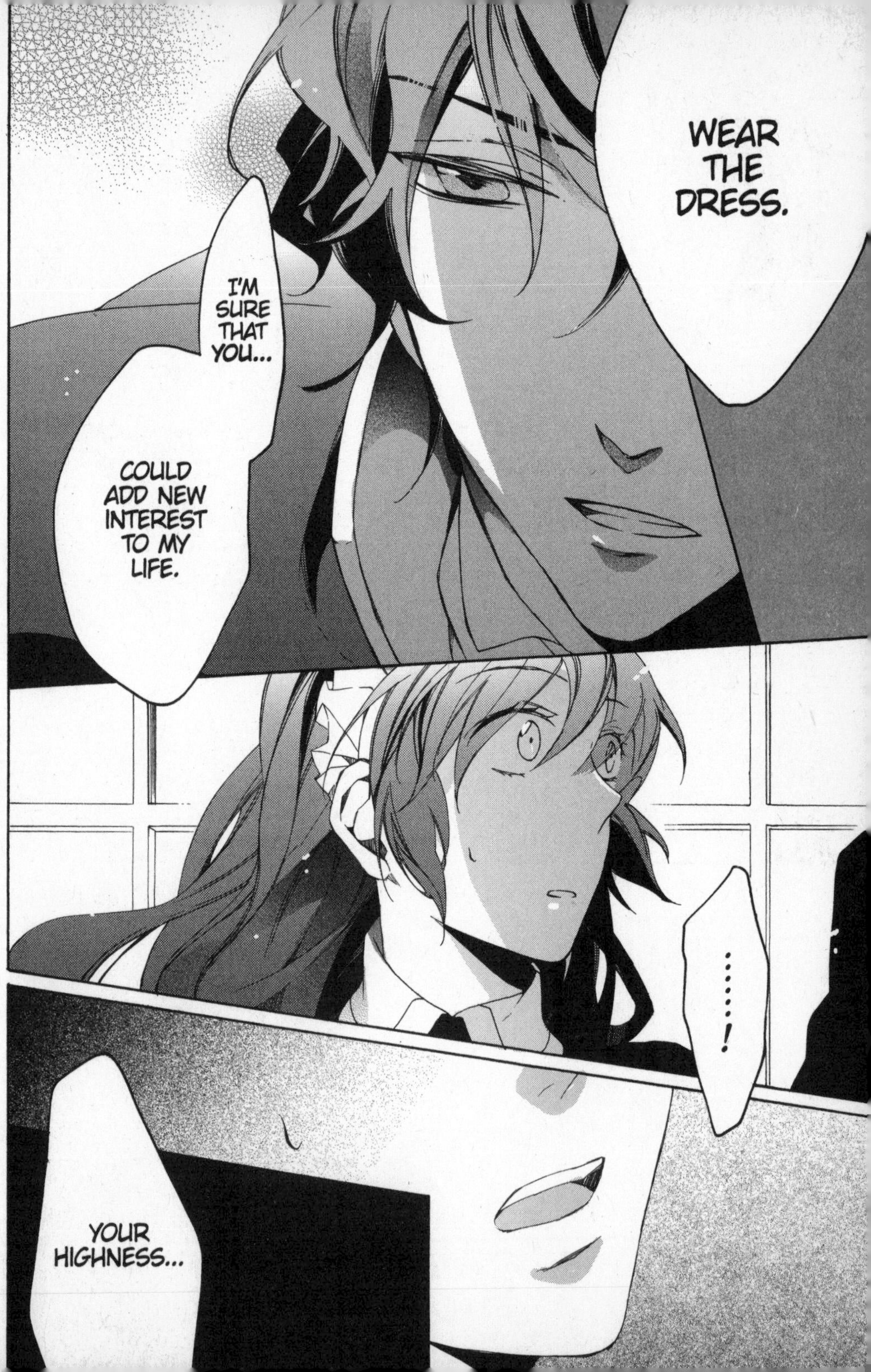
WEAR THE DRESS.
I'M SURE THAT YOU...
COULD ADD NEW INTEREST TO MY LIFE.
......!
YOUR HIGHNESS...

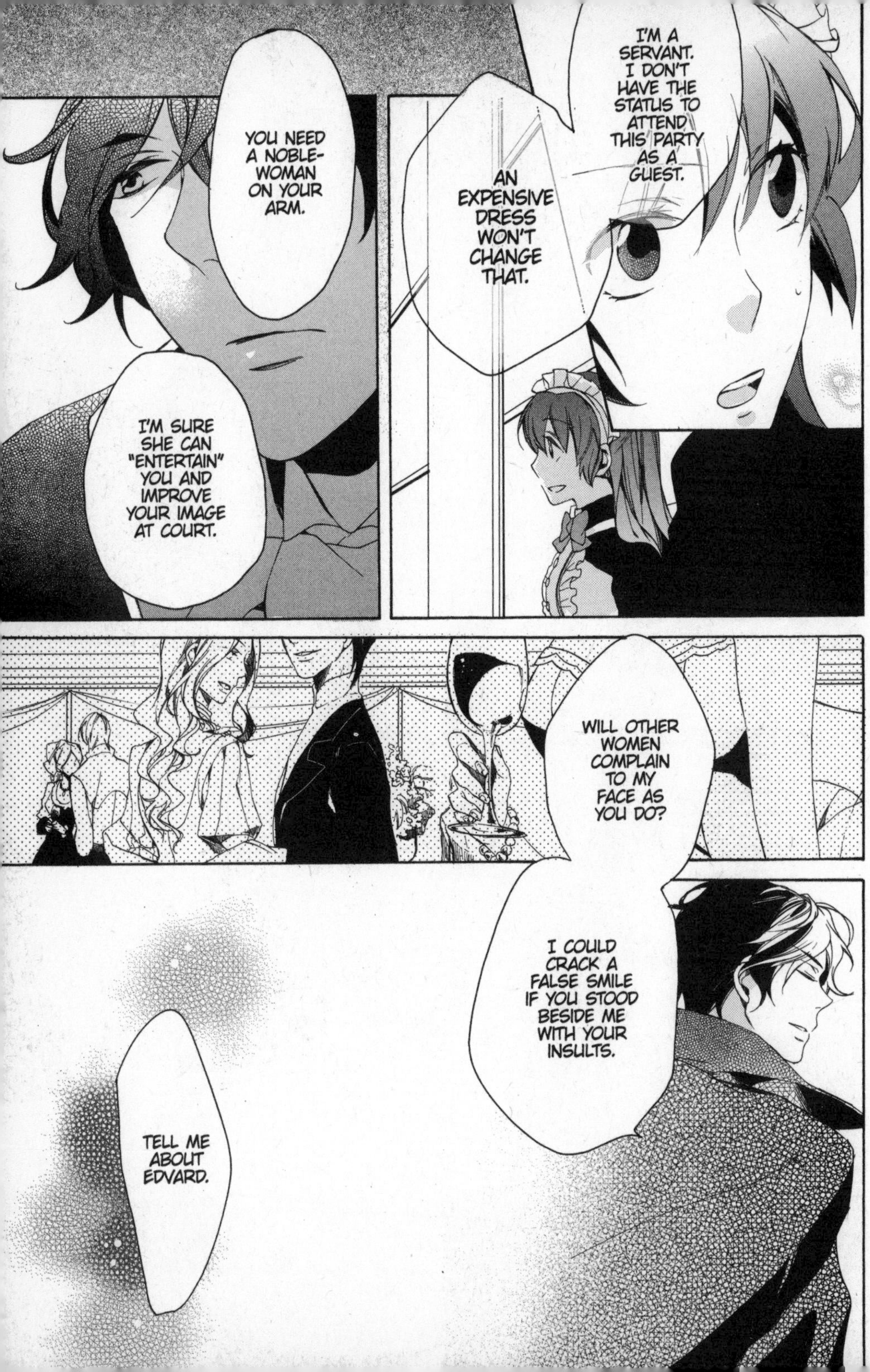
I'M A SERVANT. I DON'T HAVE THE STATUS TO ATTEND THIS PARTY AS A GUEST.
AN EXPENSIVE DRESS WON'T CHANGE THAT.
YOU NEED A NOBLE-WOMAN ON YOUR ARM.
I'M SURE SHE CAN "ENTERTAIN" YOU AND IMPROVE YOUR IMAGE AT COURT.
WILL OTHER WOMEN COMPLAIN TO MY FACE AS YOU DO?
I COULD CRACK A FALSE SMILE IF YOU STOOD BESIDE ME WITH YOUR INSULTS.
TELL ME ABOUT EDVARD.

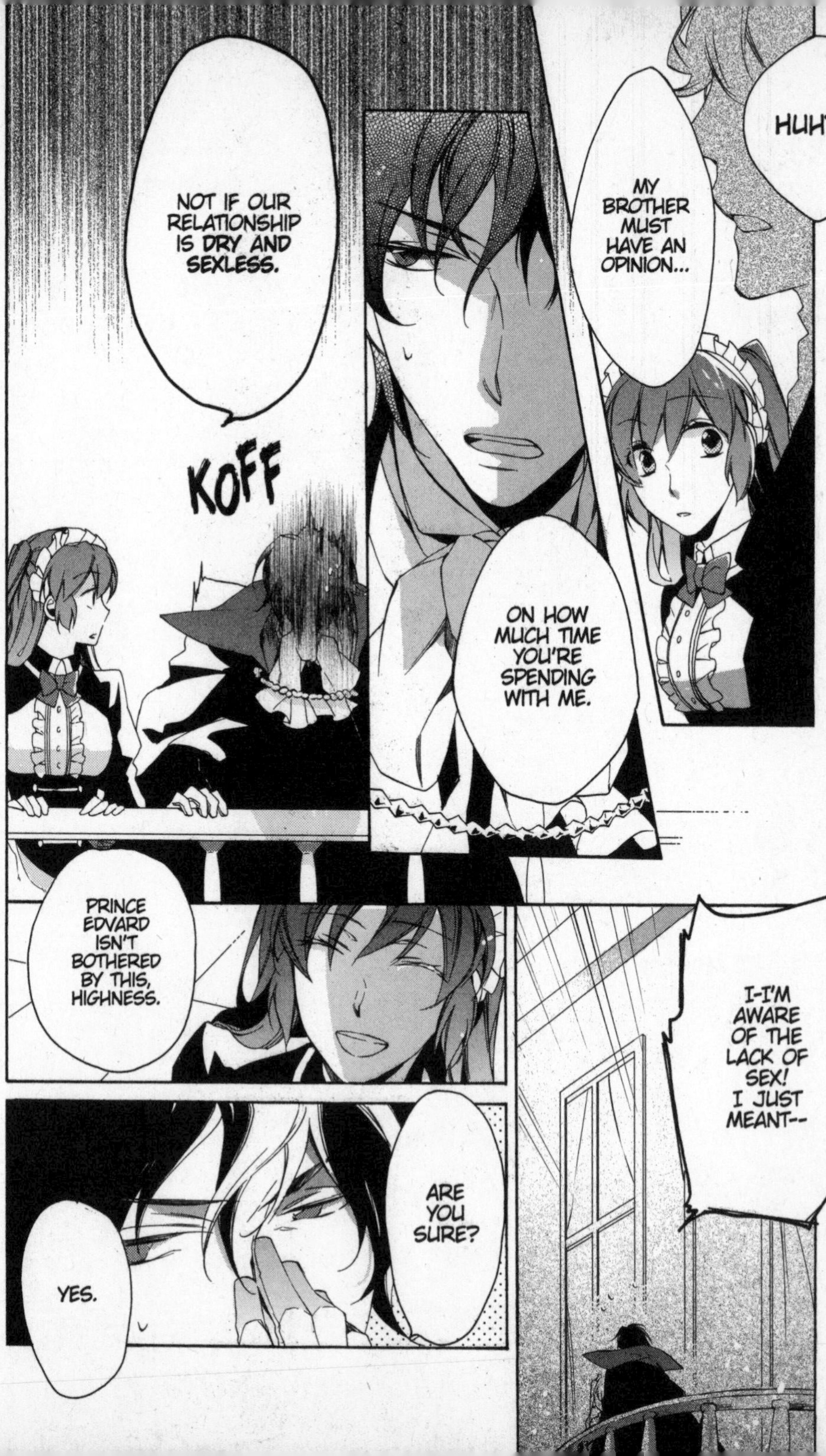
HUH?
MY BROTHER MUST HAVE AN OPINION...
ON HOW MUCH TIME YOU'RE SPENDING WITH ME.
NOT IF OUR RELATIONSHIP IS DRY AND SEXLESS.
KOFF
I-I'M AWARE OF THE LACK OF SEX! I JUST MEANT--
PRINCE EDVARD ISN'T BOTHERED BY THIS, HIGHNESS.
ARE YOU SURE?
YES.

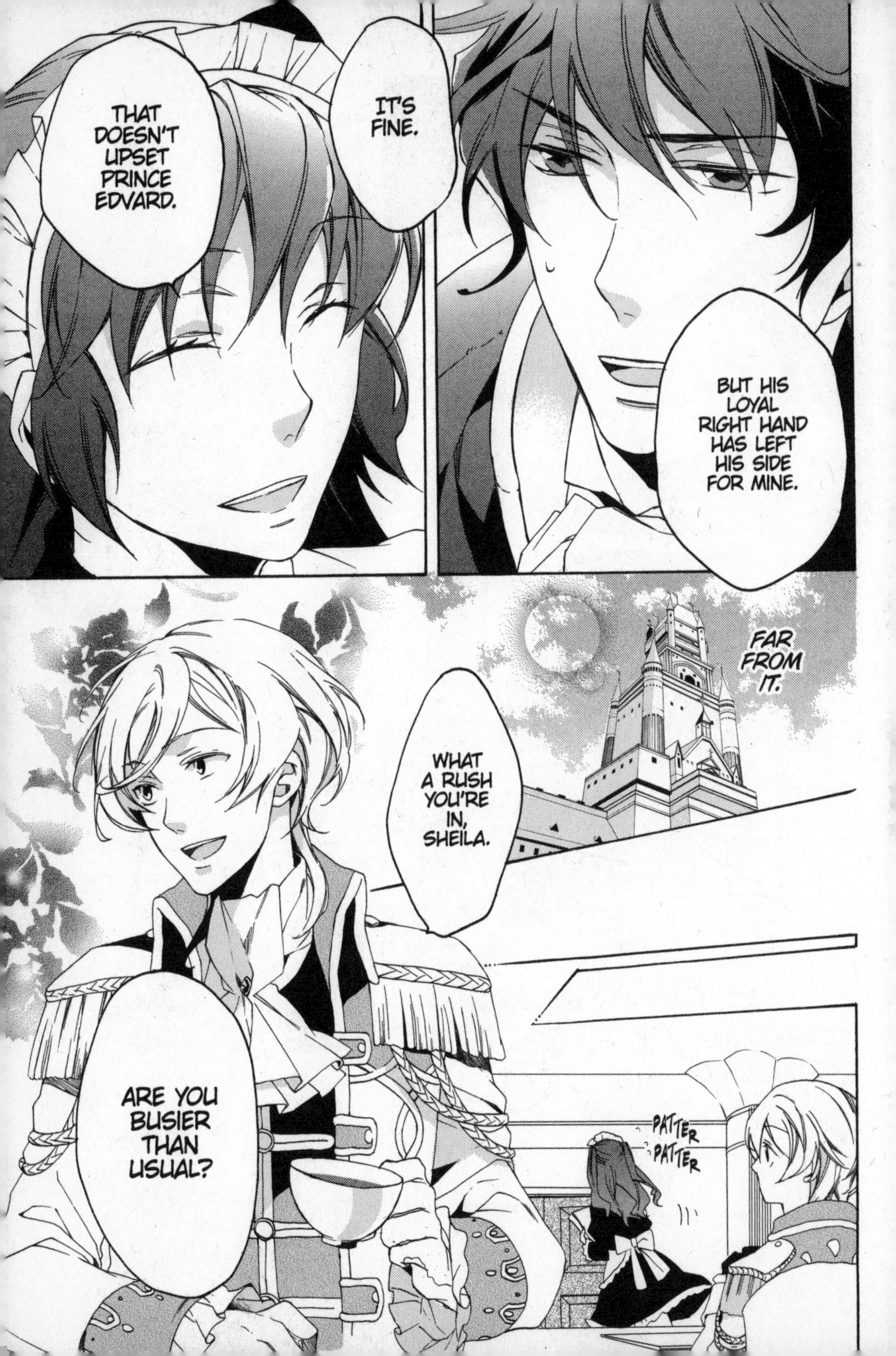
IT'S FINE.
BUT HIS LOYAL RIGHT HAND HAS LEFT HIS SIDE FOR MINE.
THAT DOESN'T UPSET PRINCE EDVARD.
FAR FROM IT.
PATTER PATTER
WHAT A RUSH YOU'RE IN, SHEILA.
ARE YOU BUSIER THAN USUAL?

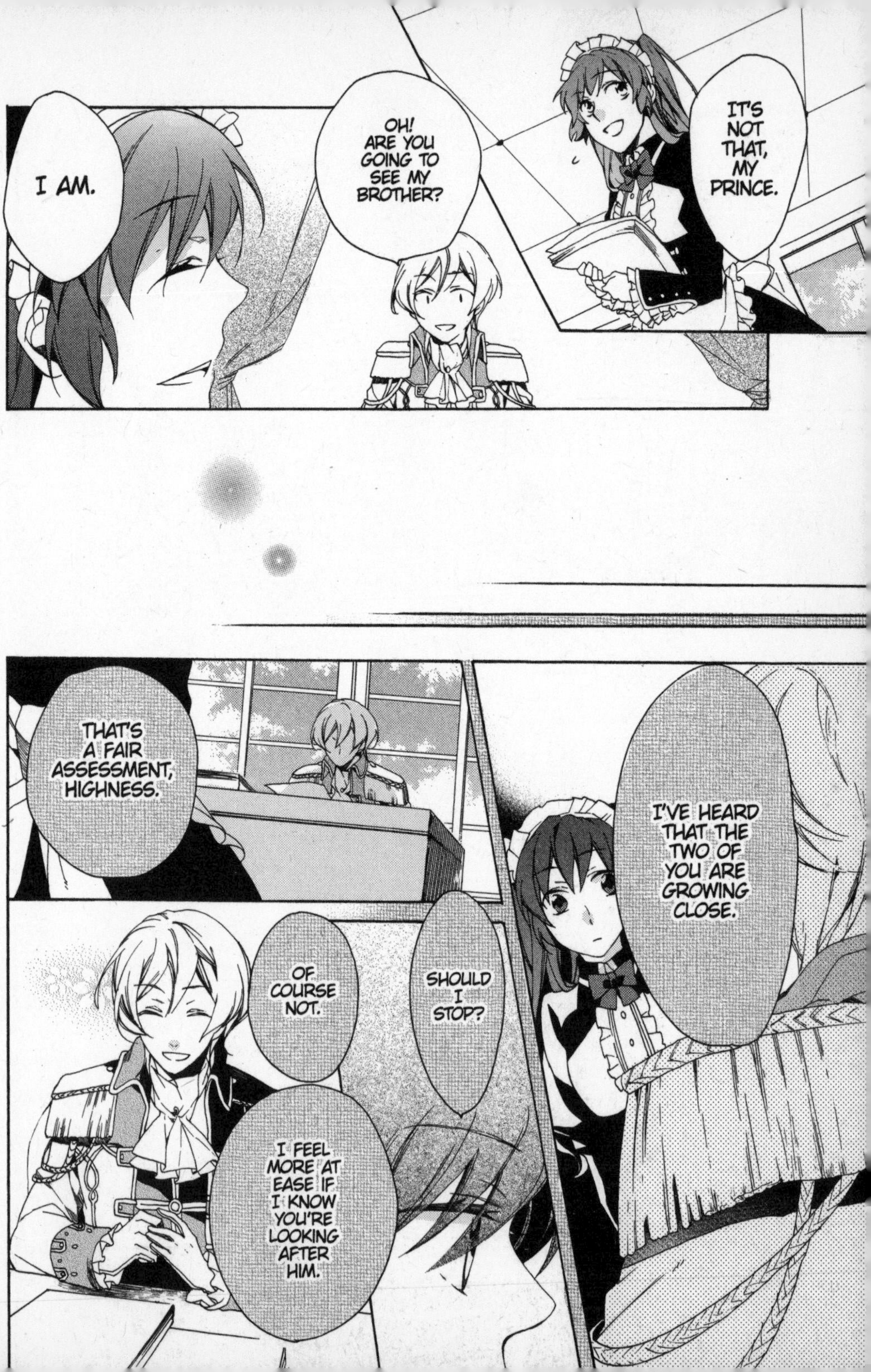
IT'S NOT THAT, MY PRINCE.
OH! ARE YOU GOING TO SEE MY BROTHER?
I AM.
I'VE HEARD THAT THE TWO OF YOU ARE GROWING CLOSE.
THAT'S A FAIR ASSESSMENT, HIGHNESS.
SHOULD I STOP?
OF COURSE NOT.
I FEEL MORE AT EASE IF I KNOW YOU'RE LOOKING AFTER HIM.

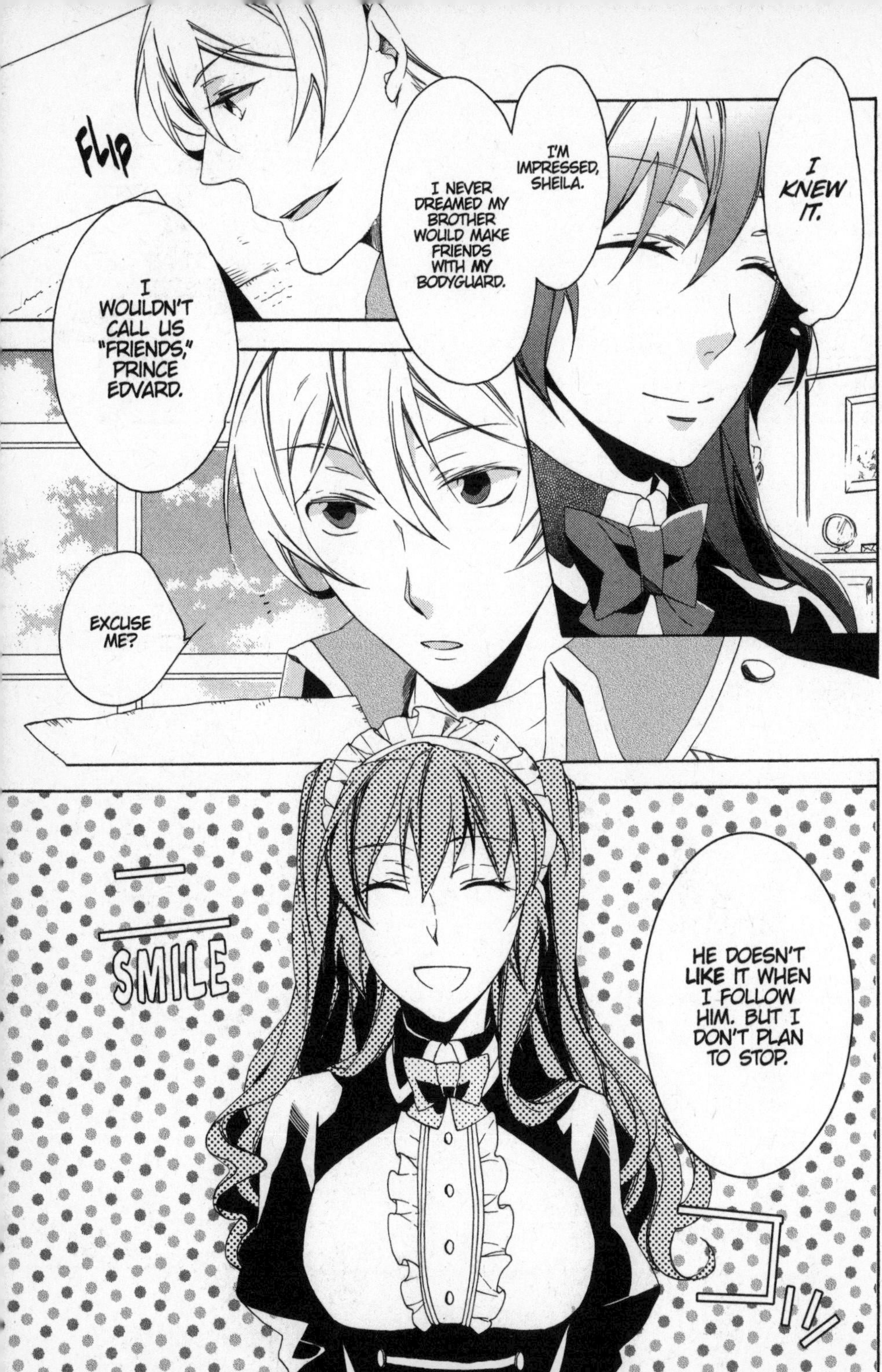
I KNEW IT.
I'M IMPRESSED, SHEILA.
I NEVER DREAMED MY BROTHER WOULD MAKE FRIENDS WITH MY BODYGUARD.
FLIP
I WOULDN'T CALL US "FRIENDS," PRINCE EDVARD.
EXCUSE ME?
HE DOESN'T LIKE IT WHEN I FOLLOW HIM. BUT I DON'T PLAN TO STOP.
SMILE

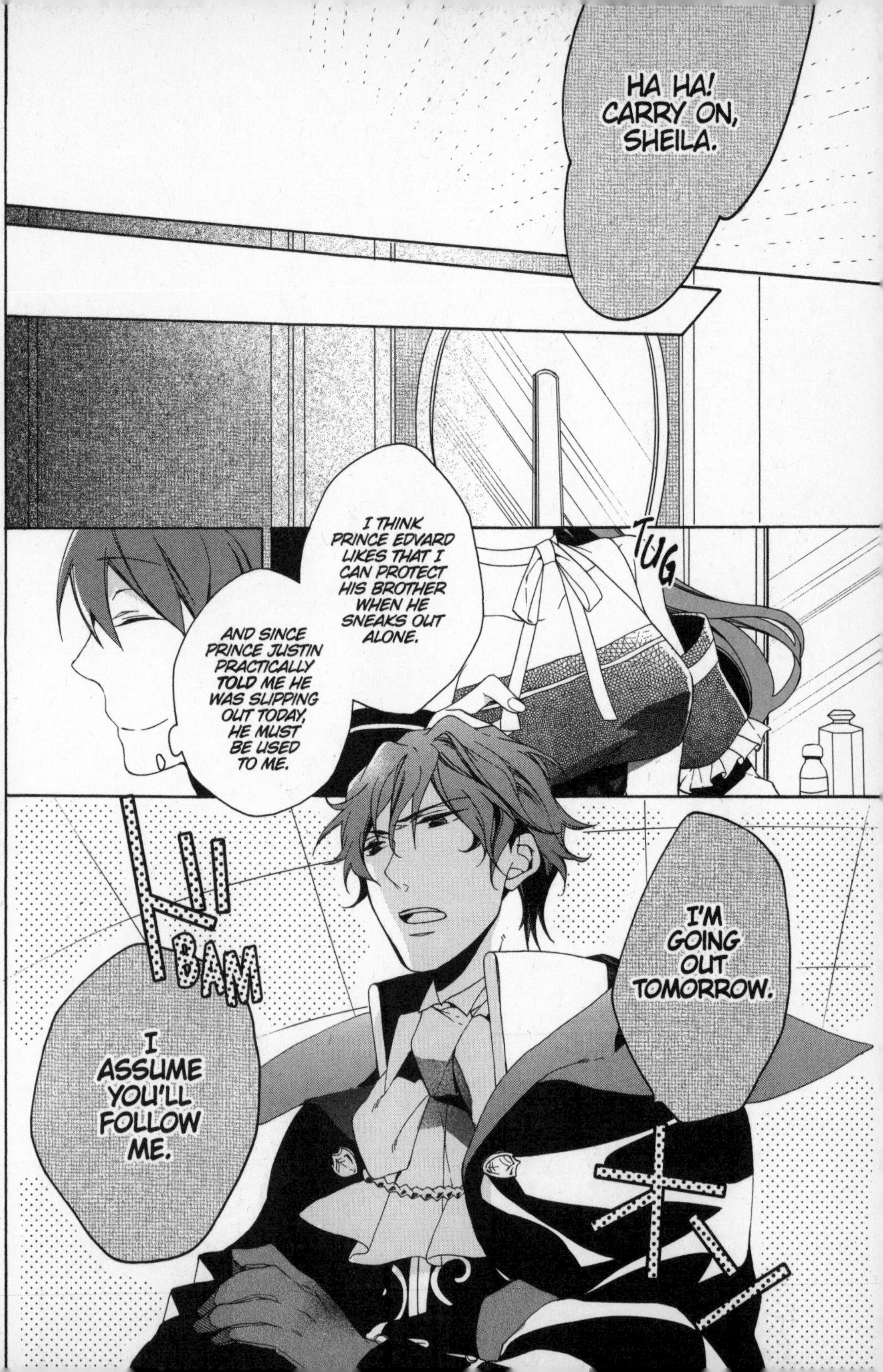
HA HA! CARRY ON, SHEILA.
TUG
I THINK PRINCE EDVARD LIKES THAT I CAN PROTECT HIS BROTHER WHEN HE SNEAKS OUT ALONE.
AND SINCE PRINCE JUSTIN PRACTICALLY TOLD ME HE WAS SLIPPING OUT TODAY, HE MUST BE USED TO ME.
I'M GOING OUT TOMORROW.
BAM
I ASSUME YOU'LL FOLLOW ME.

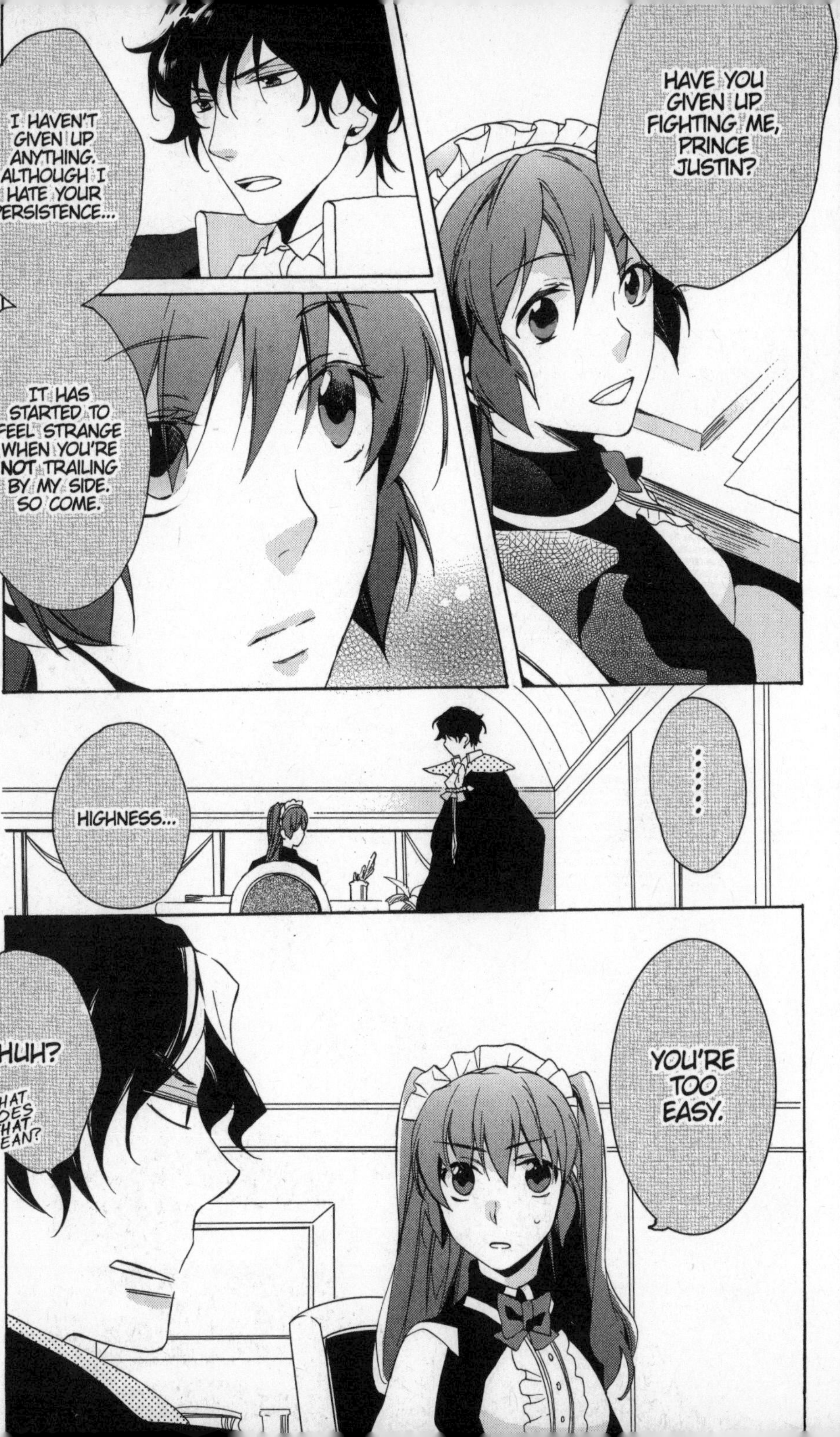
HAVE YOU GIVEN UP FIGHTING ME, PRINCE JUSTIN?
I HAVEN'T GIVEN UP ANYTHING. ALTHOUGH I HATE YOUR PERSISTENCE...
IT HAS STARTED TO FEEL STRANGE WHEN YOU'RE NOT TRAILING BY MY SIDE. SO COME.
......
HIGHNESS...
YOU'RE TOO EASY.
HUH?
WHAT DOES THAT MEAN?

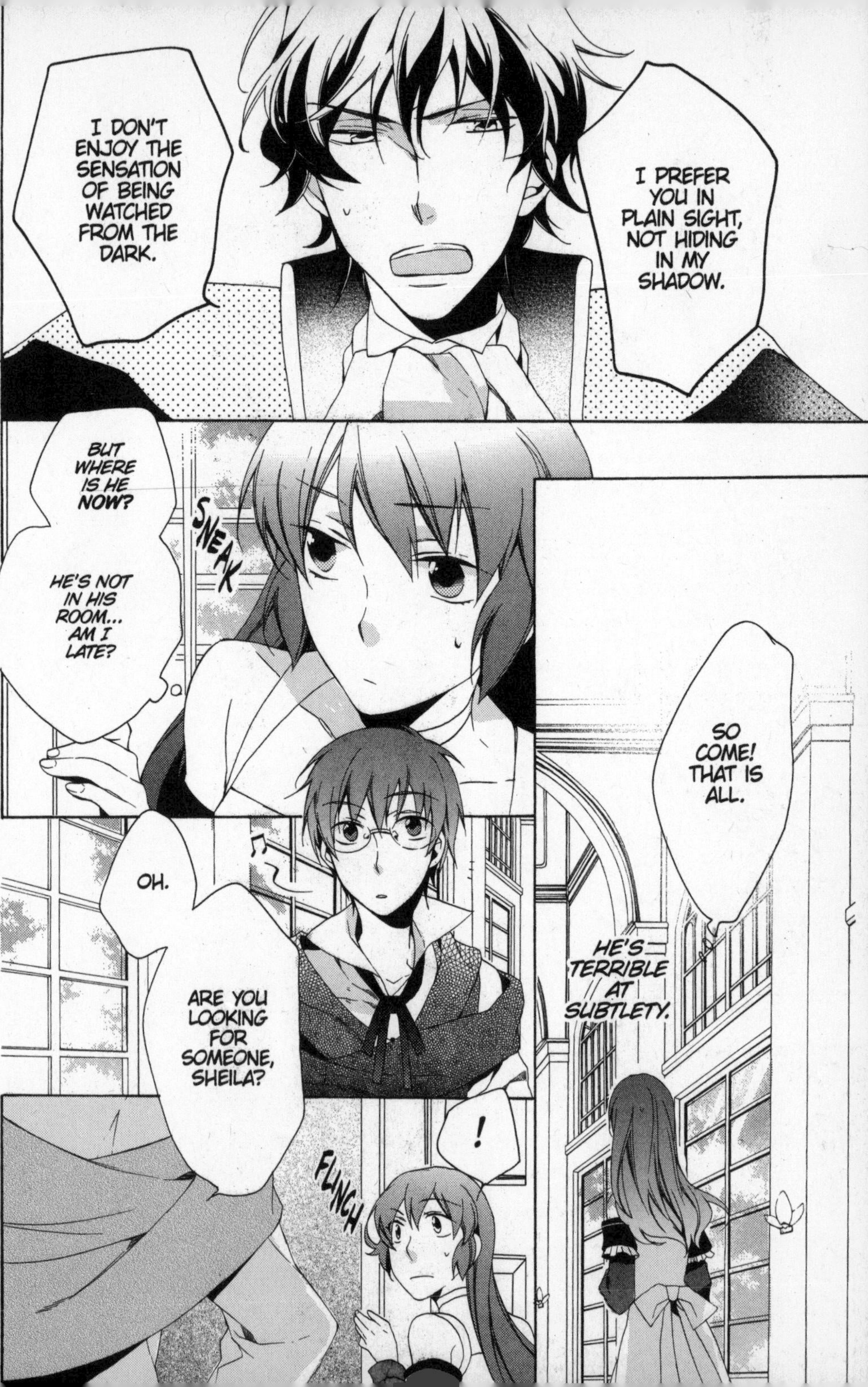
I DON'T ENJOY THE SENSATION OF BEING WATCHED FROM THE DARK.
I PREFER YOU IN PLAIN SIGHT, NOT HIDING IN MY SHADOW.
SO COME! THAT IS ALL.
HE'S TERRIBLE AT SUBTLETY.
BUT WHERE IS HE NOW?
SNEAK
HE'S NOT IN HIS ROOM... AM I LATE?
OH.
ARE YOU LOOKING FOR SOMEONE, SHEILA?
!
FLINCH

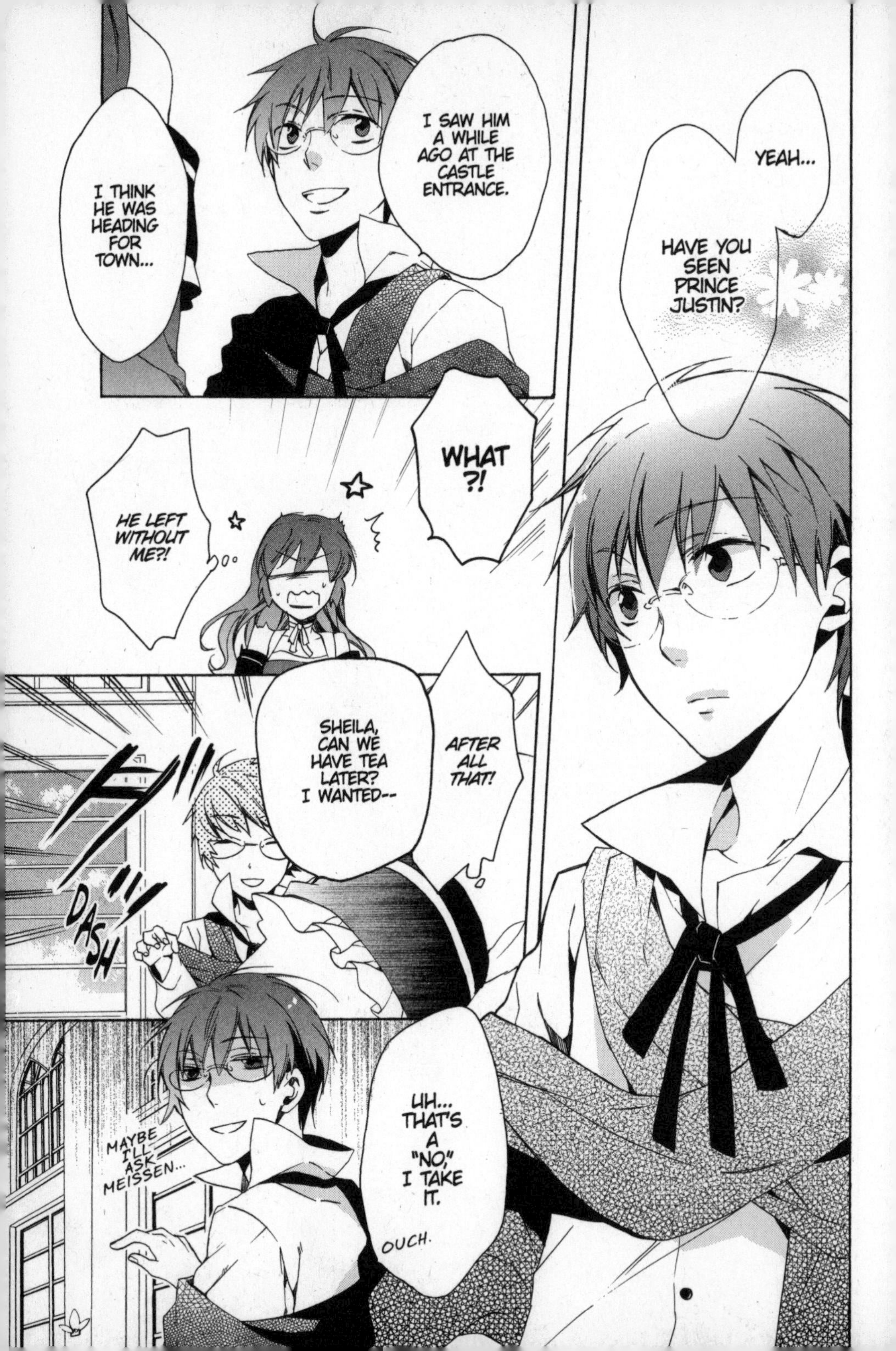
YEAH...
HAVE YOU SEEN PRINCE JUSTIN?
I SAW HIM A WHILE AGO AT THE CASTLE ENTRANCE.
I THINK HE WAS HEADING FOR TOWN...
WHAT?!
HE LEFT WITHOUT ME?!
AFTER ALL THAT!
SHEILA, CAN WE HAVE TEA LATER? I WANTED--
DASH
UH... THAT'S A "NO," I TAKE IT.
OUCH.
MAYBE I'LL ASK MEISSEN...

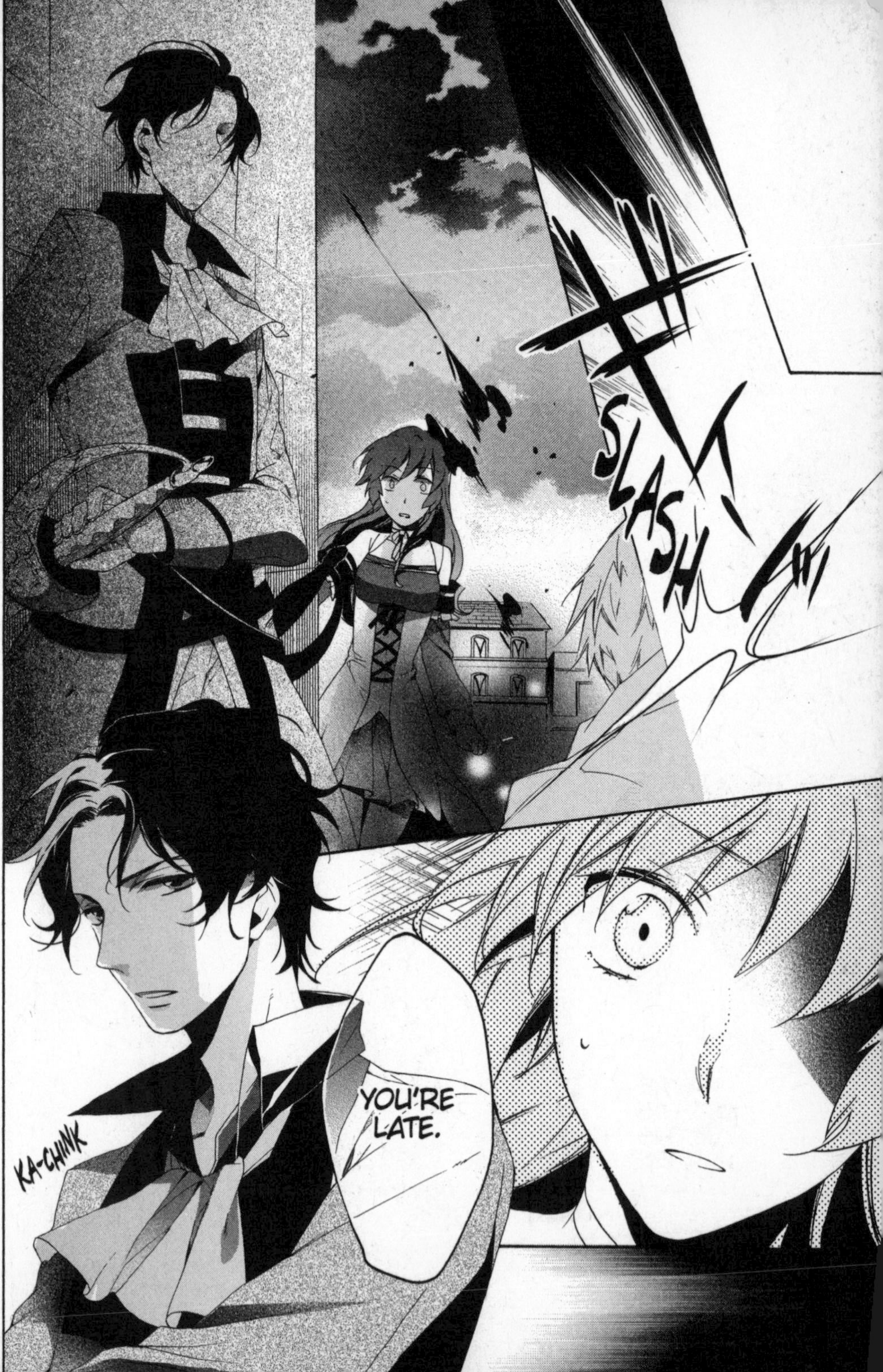
SLASH
YOU'RE LATE.
KA-CHINK

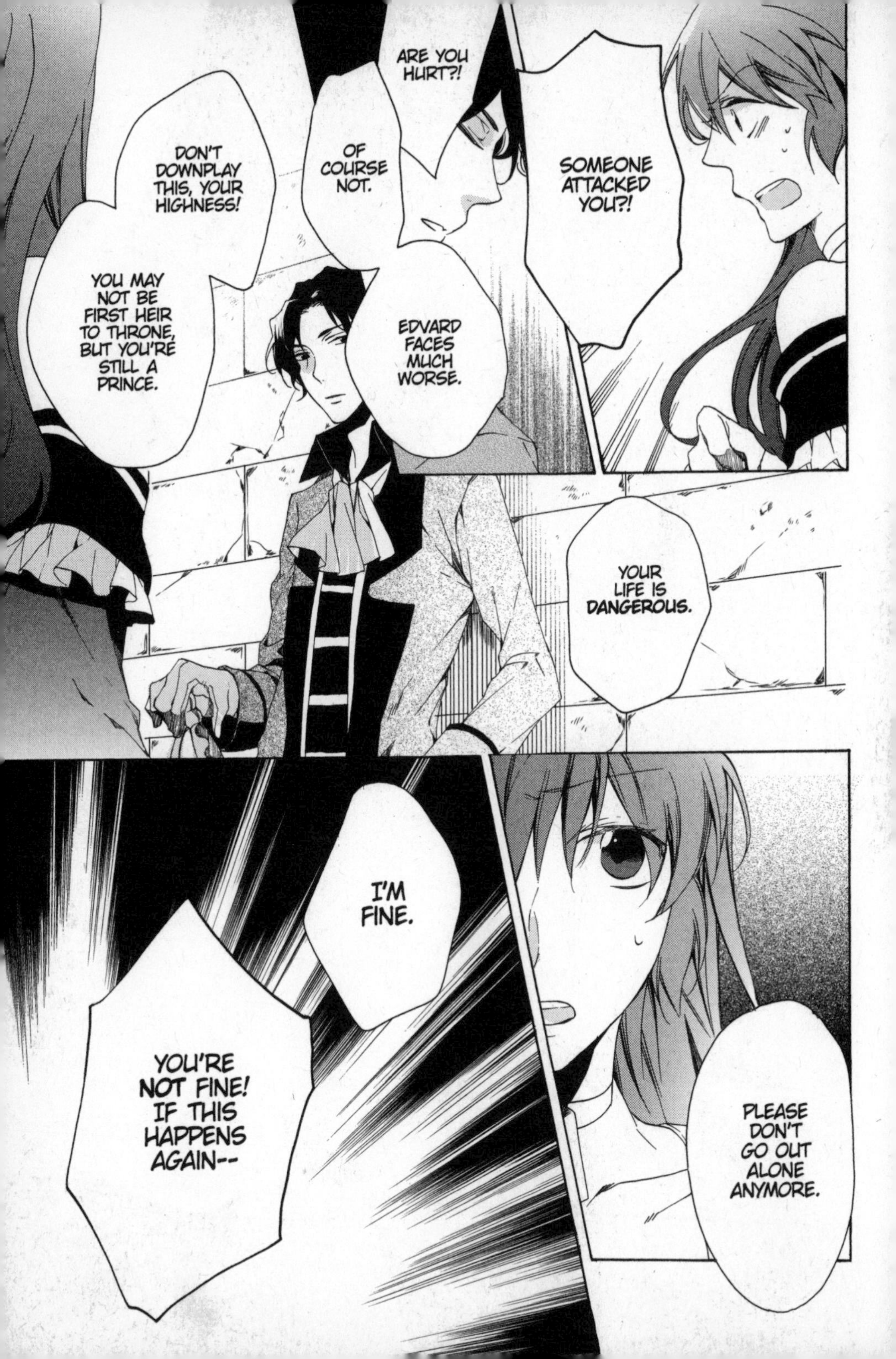
SOMEONE ATTACKED YOU?!
ARE YOU HURT?!
OF COURSE NOT.
EDVARD FACES MUCH WORSE.
DON'T DOWNPLAY THIS, YOUR HIGHNESS!
YOU MAY NOT BE FIRST HEIR TO THRONE, BUT YOU'RE STILL A PRINCE.
YOUR LIFE IS DANGEROUS.
PLEASE DON'T GO OUT ALONE ANYMORE.
I'M FINE.
YOU'RE NOT FINE! IF THIS HAPPENS AGAIN--

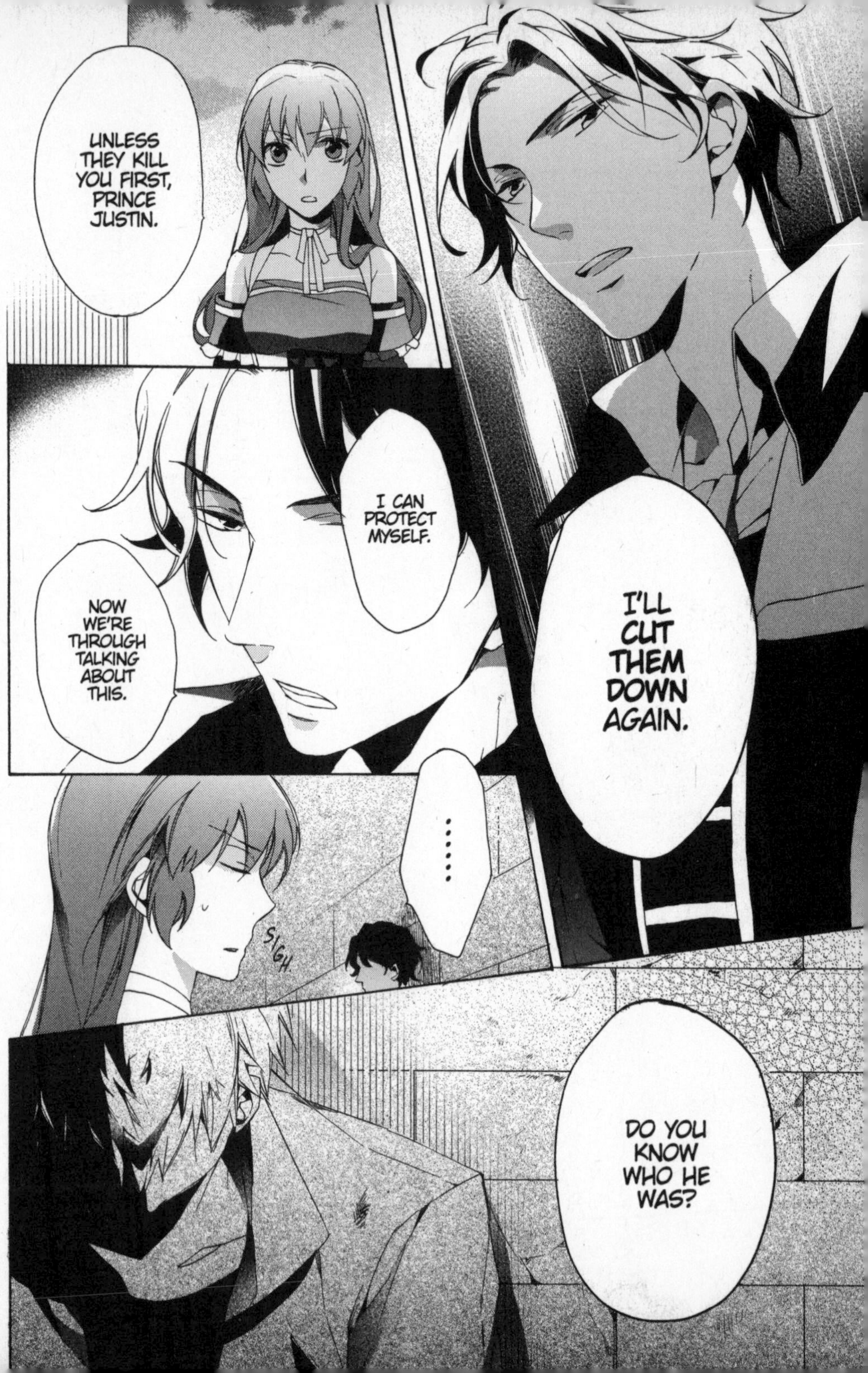
I'LL CUT THEM DOWN AGAIN.
UNLESS THEY KILL YOU FIRST, PRINCE JUSTIN.
I CAN PROTECT MYSELF.
NOW WE'RE THROUGH TALKING ABOUT THIS.
......
SIGH
DO YOU KNOW WHO HE WAS?

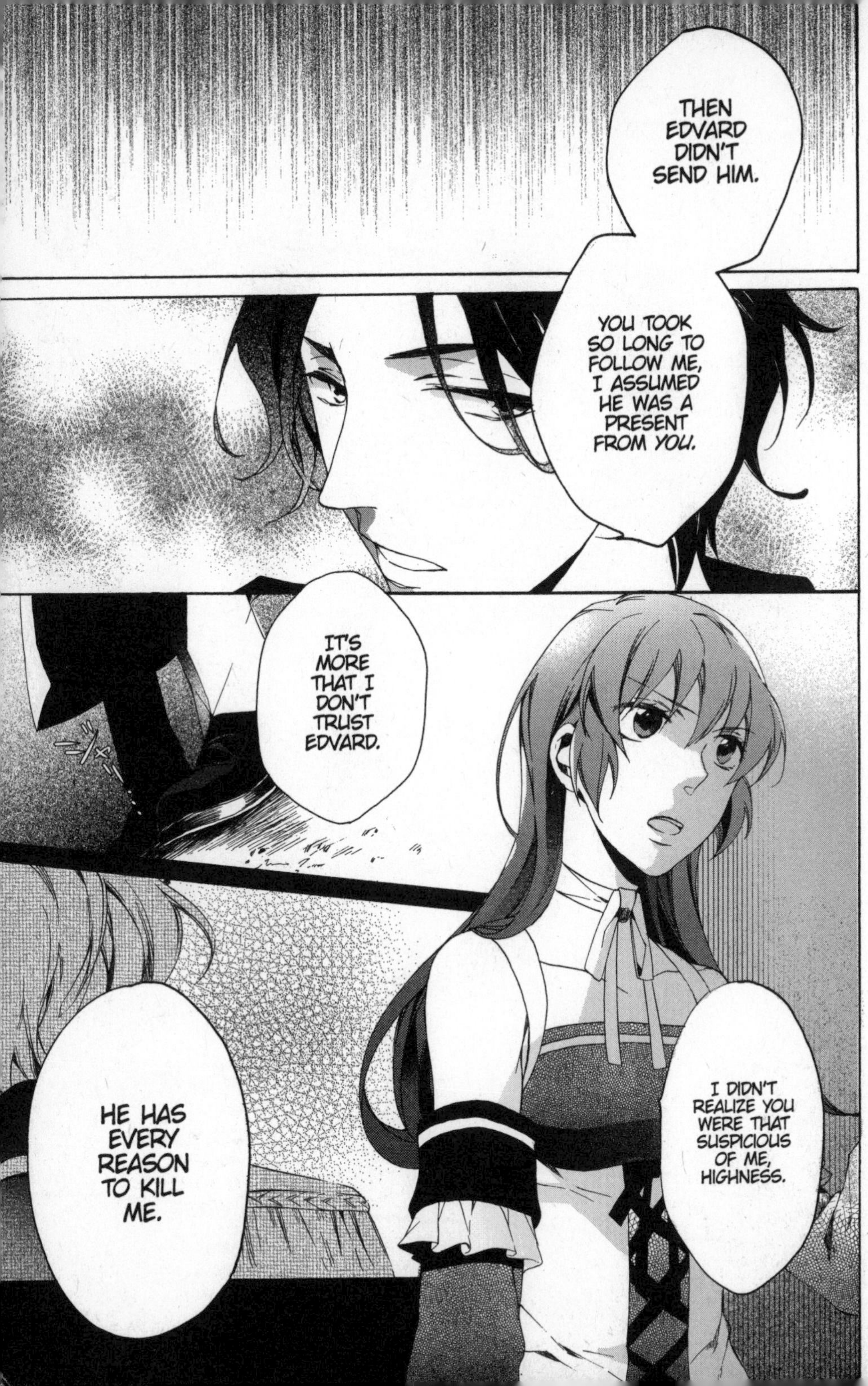
THEN EDVARD DIDN'T SEND HIM.
YOU TOOK SO LONG TO FOLLOW ME, I ASSUMED HE WAS A PRESENT FROM *YOU*.
I DIDN'T REALIZE YOU WERE THAT SUSPICIOUS OF ME, HIGHNESS.
IT'S MORE THAT I DON'T TRUST EDVARD.
HE HAS EVERY REASON TO KILL ME.

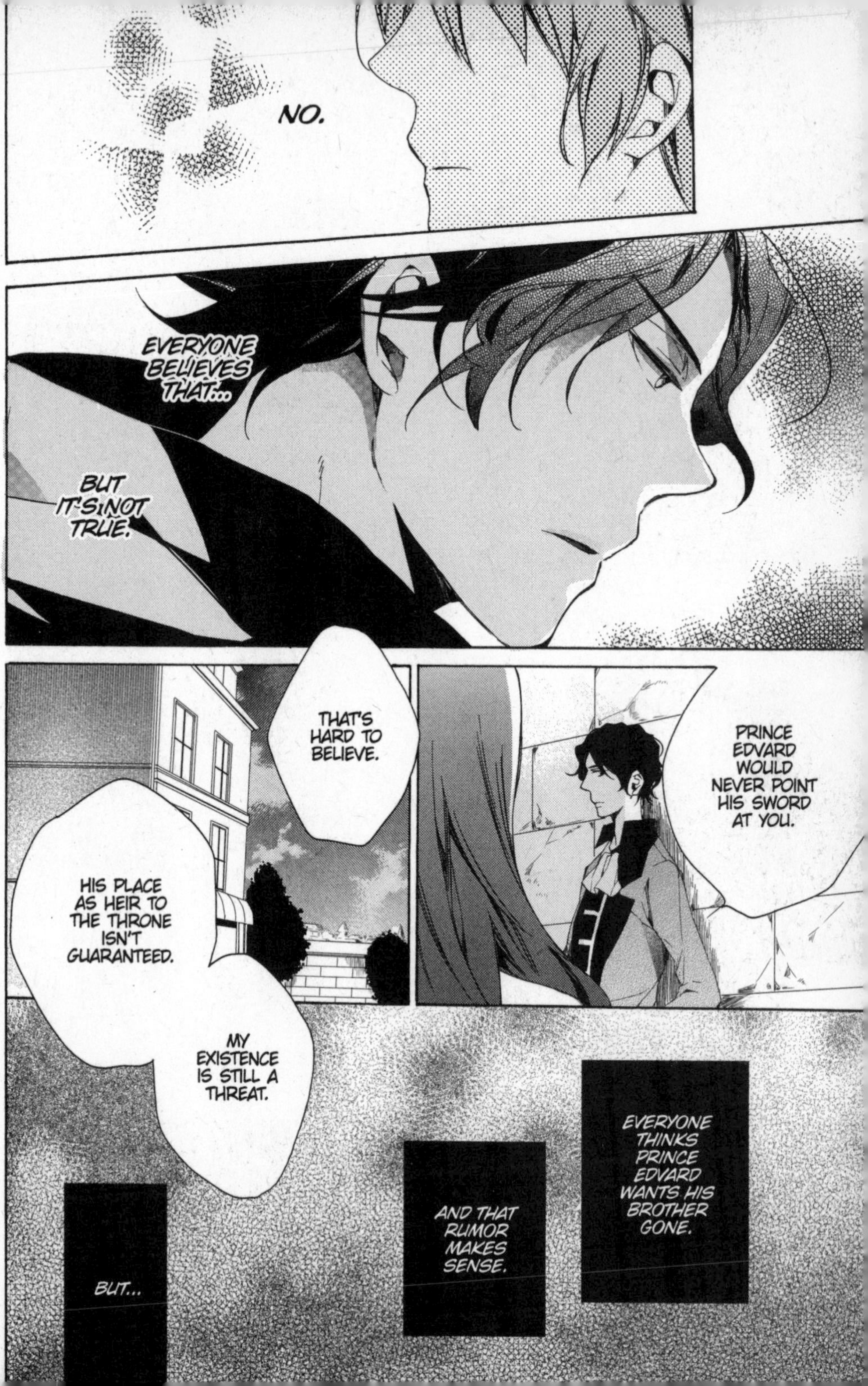
NO.
EVERYONE BELIEVES THAT...
BUT IT'S NOT TRUE.
PRINCE EDVARD WOULD NEVER POINT HIS SWORD AT YOU.
THAT'S HARD TO BELIEVE.
HIS PLACE AS HEIR TO THE THRONE ISN'T GUARANTEED.
MY EXISTENCE IS STILL A THREAT.
EVERYONE THINKS PRINCE EDVARD WANTS HIS BROTHER GONE.
AND THAT RUMOR MAKES SENSE.
BUT...

IT'S NOT REALITY.
IT'S DANGEROUS GOSSIP...
WHISPERED BY HATEFUL, JEALOUS ARISTOCRATS WHO WOULD NEVER CONFESS TO SPREADING RUMORS.
YOU SHOULD KNOW THAT, PRINCE JUSTIN.
I WANT TO TELL YOU THAT.
I WANT TO SCREAM IT AT YOU.

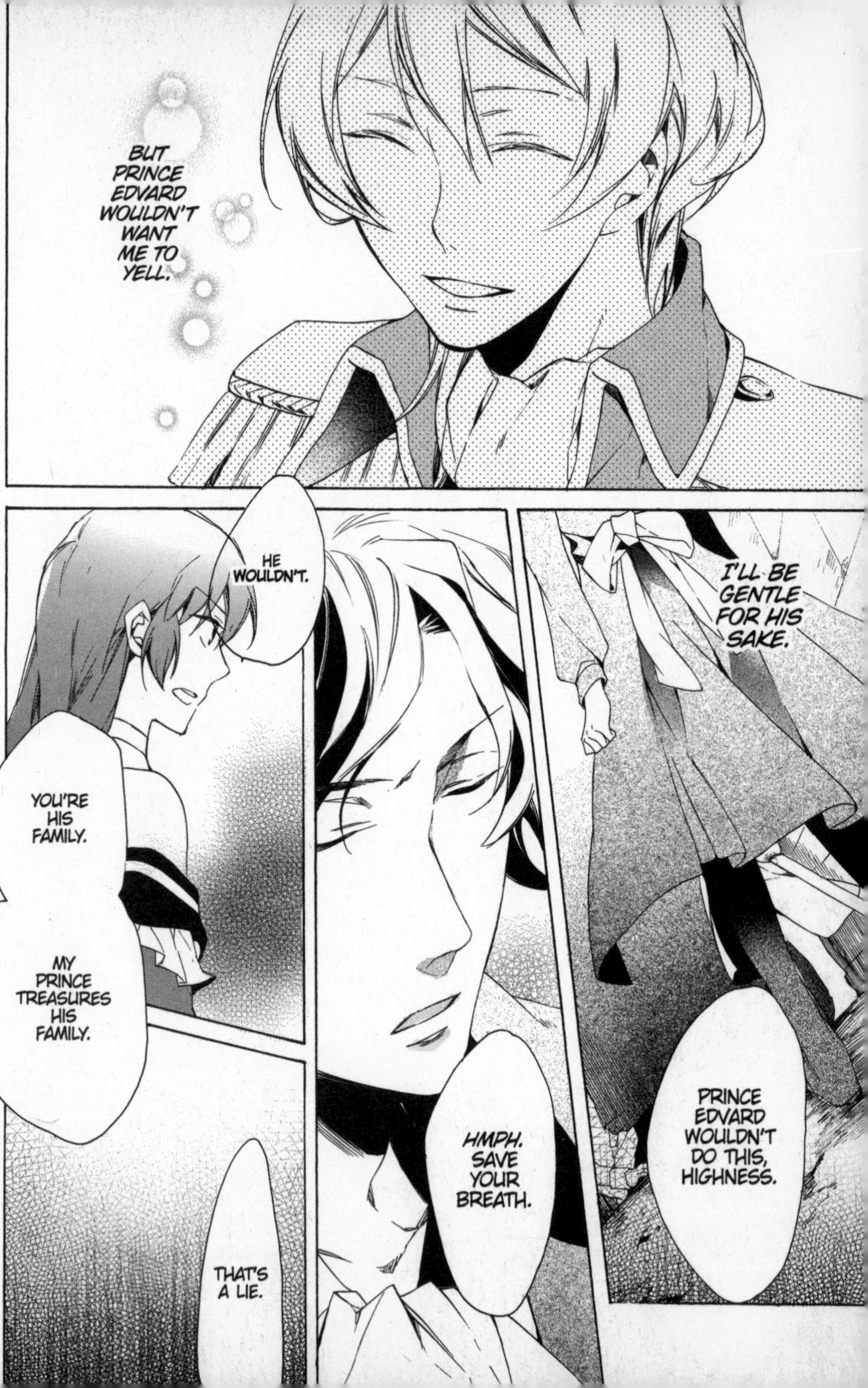
BUT PRINCE EDVARD WOULDN'T WANT ME TO YELL.
I'LL BE GENTLE FOR HIS SAKE.
PRINCE EDVARD WOULDN'T DO THIS, HIGHNESS.
HMPH. SAVE YOUR BREATH.
HE WOULDN'T.
YOU'RE HIS FAMILY.
MY PRINCE TREASURES HIS FAMILY.
THAT'S A LIE.

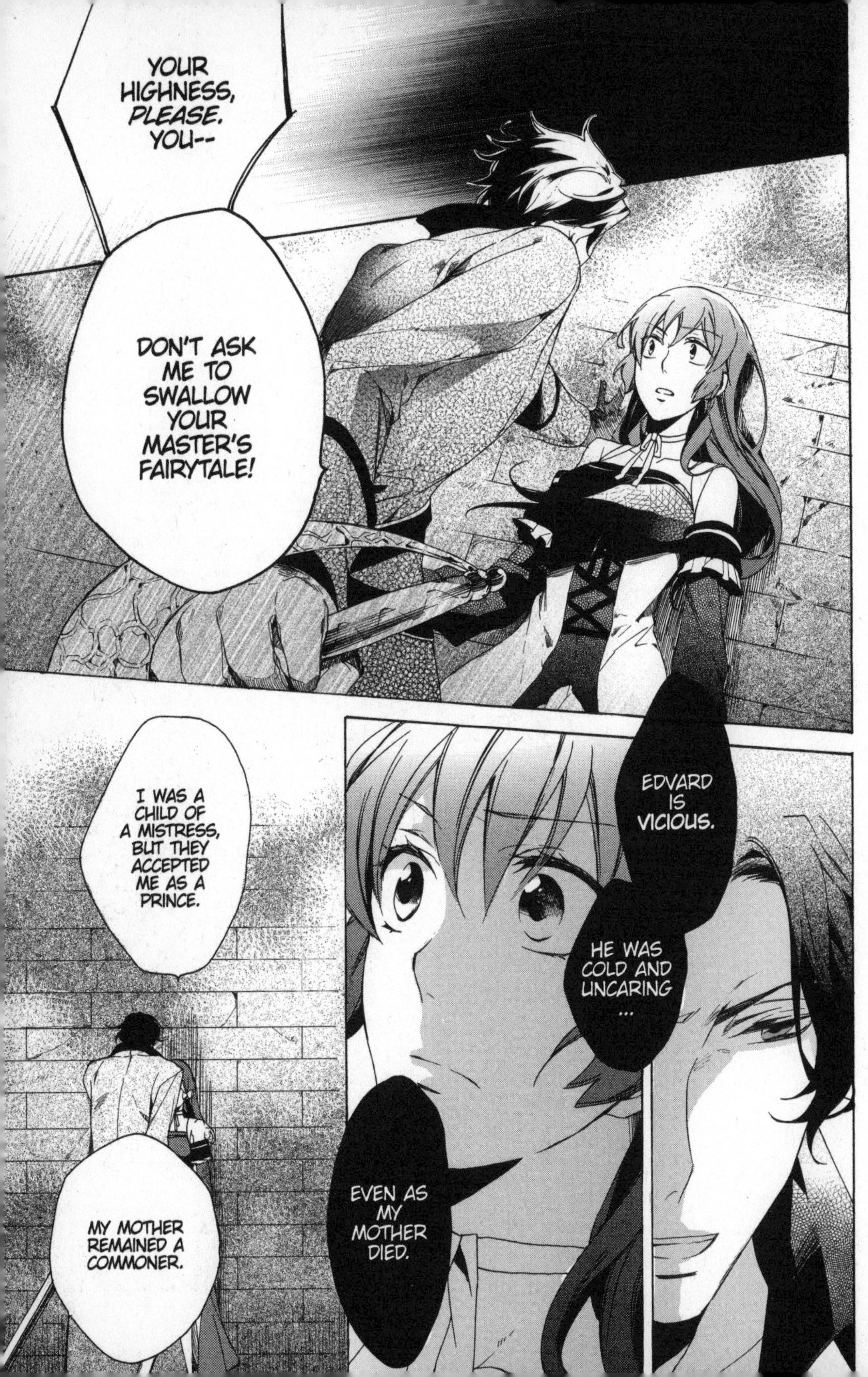
YOUR HIGHNESS, PLEASE. YOU--
DON'T ASK ME TO SWALLOW YOUR MASTER'S FAIRYTALE!
EDVARD IS VICIOUS.
HE WAS COLD AND UNCARING ...
EVEN AS MY MOTHER DIED.
I WAS A CHILD OF A MISTRESS, BUT THEY ACCEPTED ME AS A PRINCE.
MY MOTHER REMAINED A COMMONER.

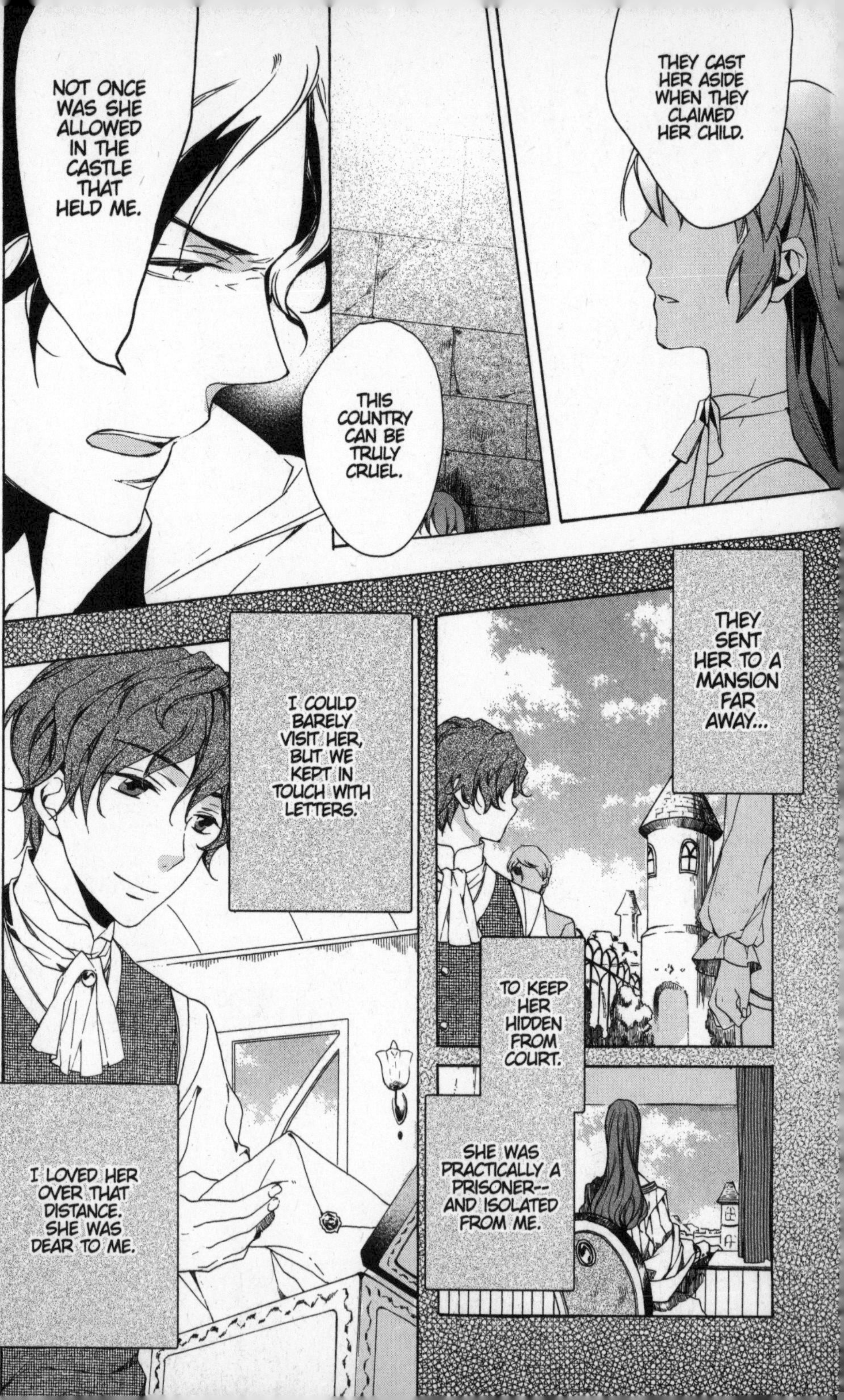
THEY CAST HER ASIDE WHEN THEY CLAIMED HER CHILD.
NOT ONCE WAS SHE ALLOWED IN THE CASTLE THAT HELD ME.
THIS COUNTRY CAN BE TRULY CRUEL.
THEY SENT HER TO A MANSION FAR AWAY...
TO KEEP HER HIDDEN FROM COURT.
SHE WAS PRACTICALLY A PRISONER-- AND ISOLATED FROM ME.
I COULD BARELY VISIT HER, BUT WE KEPT IN TOUCH WITH LETTERS.
I LOVED HER OVER THAT DISTANCE. SHE WAS DEAR TO ME.

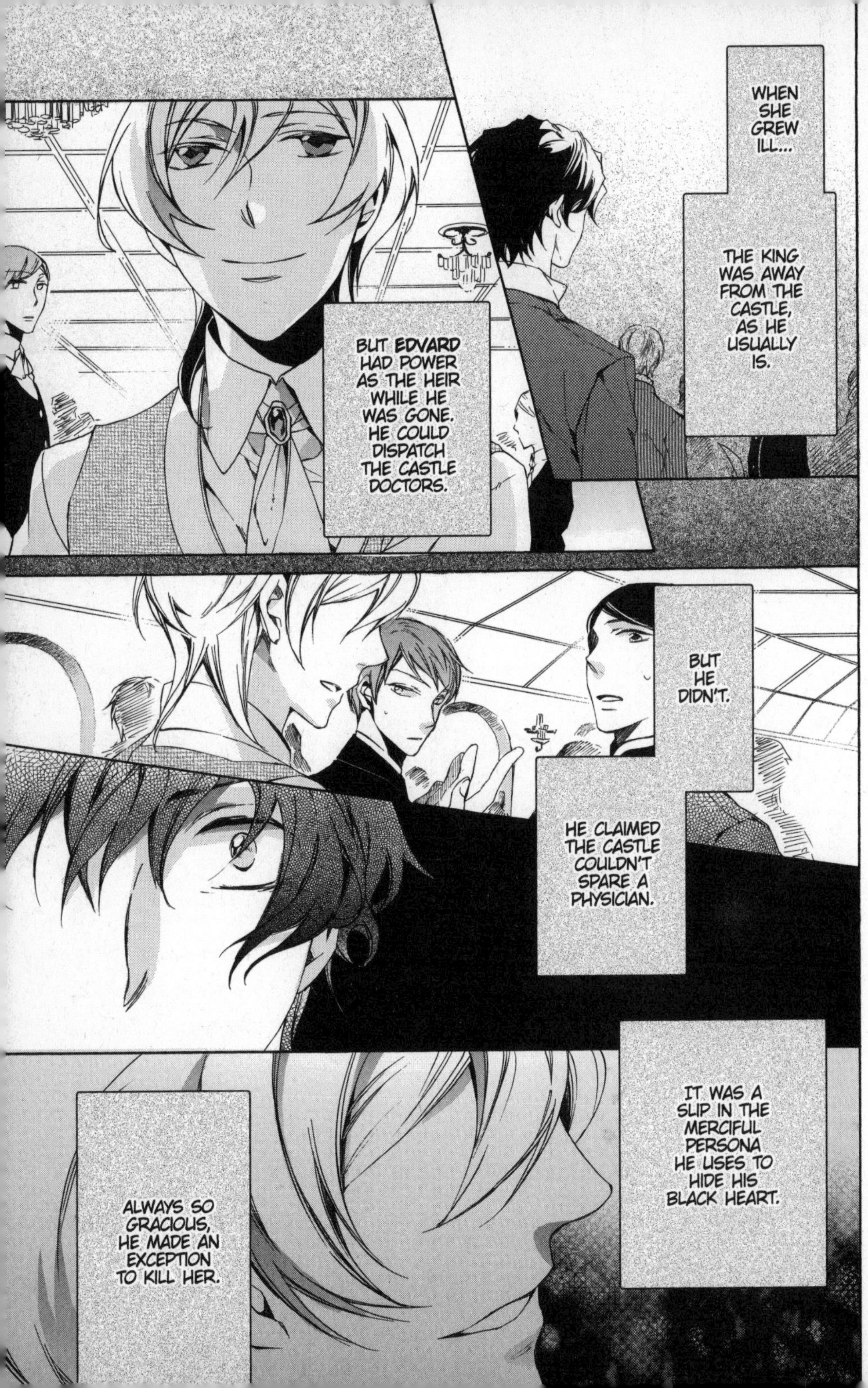
WHEN SHE GREW ILL...
THE KING WAS AWAY FROM THE CASTLE, AS HE USUALLY IS.
BUT EDVARD HAD POWER AS THE HEIR WHILE HE WAS GONE. HE COULD DISPATCH THE CASTLE DOCTORS.
BUT HE DIDN'T.
HE CLAIMED THE CASTLE COULDN'T SPARE A PHYSICIAN.
IT WAS A SLIP IN THE MERCIFUL PERSONA HE USES TO HIDE HIS BLACK HEART.
ALWAYS SO GRACIOUS, HE MADE AN EXCEPTION TO KILL HER.

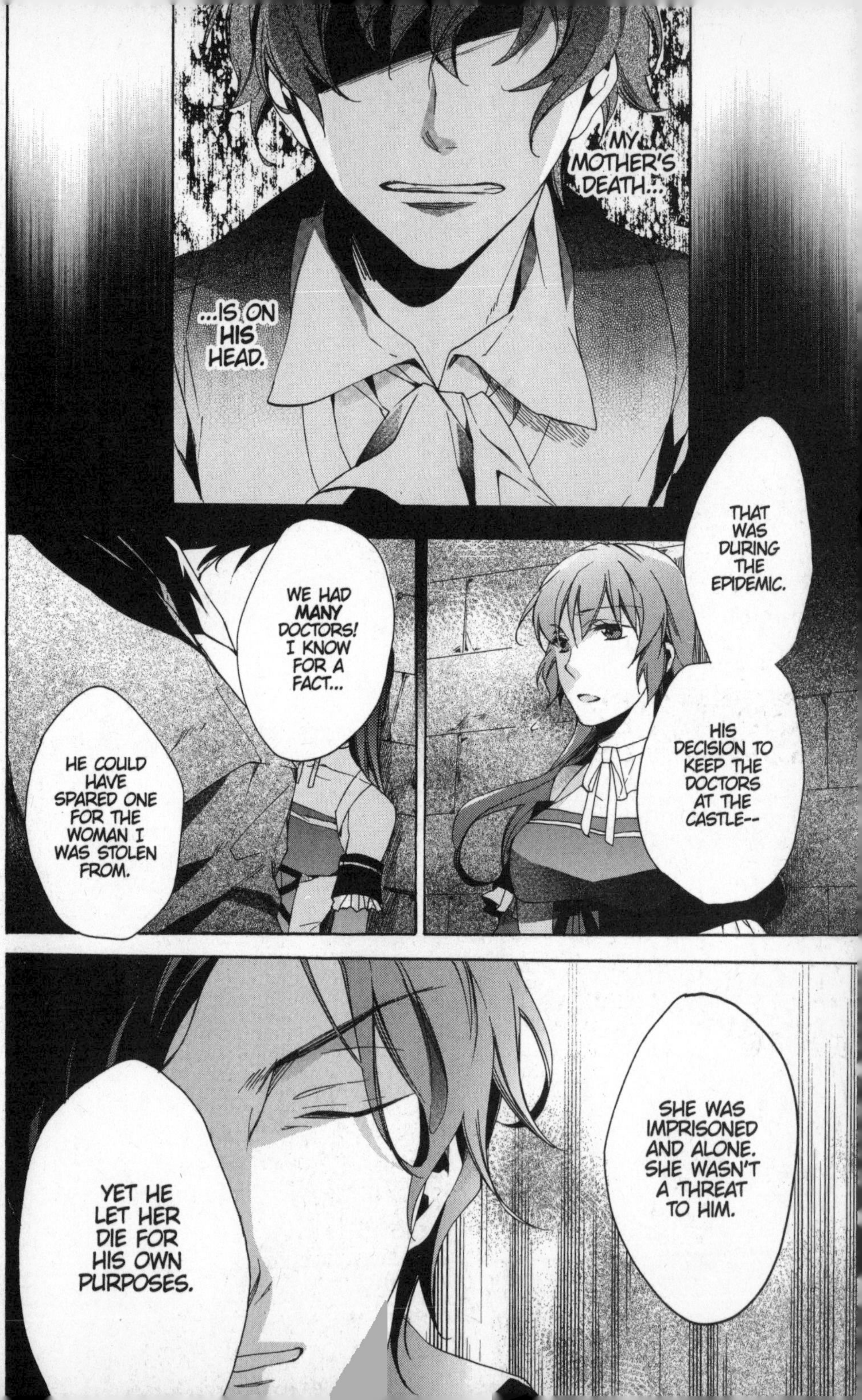
MY MOTHER'S DEATH...
...IS ON HIS HEAD.
THAT WAS DURING THE EPIDEMIC.
HIS DECISION TO KEEP THE DOCTORS AT THE CASTLE--
WE HAD MANY DOCTORS! I KNOW FOR A FACT...
HE COULD HAVE SPARED ONE FOR THE WOMAN I WAS STOLEN FROM.
SHE WAS IMPRISONED AND ALONE. SHE WASN'T A THREAT TO HIM.
YET HE LET HER DIE FOR HIS OWN PURPOSES.

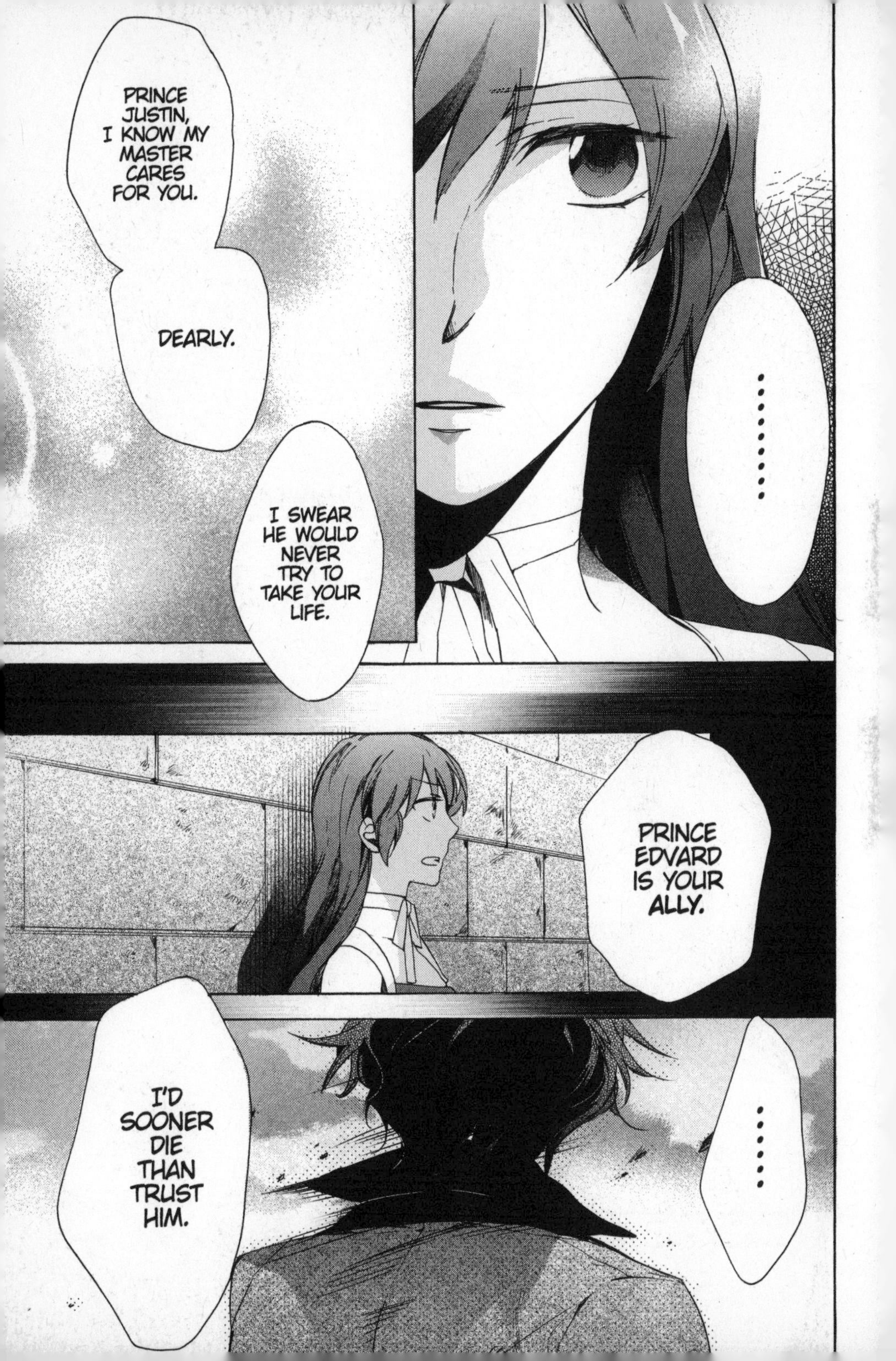
PRINCE JUSTIN, I KNOW MY MASTER CARES FOR YOU.
DEARLY.
I SWEAR HE WOULD NEVER TRY TO TAKE YOUR LIFE.
......
PRINCE EDVARD IS YOUR ALLY.
......
I'D SOONER DIE THAN TRUST HIM.

AND HE WOULD NEVER TRUST ME.
I'M SURE ...
YOU'VE HEARD THE RUMOR.
HIS MOTHER IS ALSO DEAD.
AND I'M THE ONE WHO MURDERED HER.

CRIMSON EMPIRE
Circumstances to serve a noble

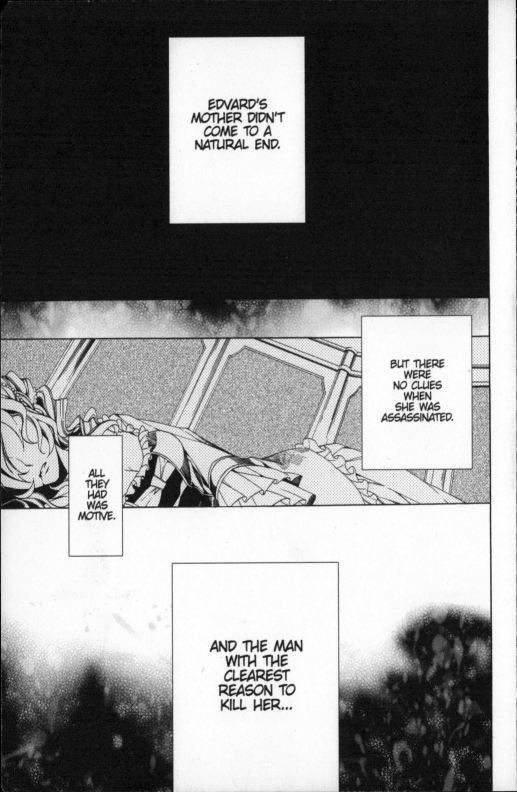

EDVARD'S MOTHER DIDN'T COME TO A NATURAL END.

BUT THERE WERE NO CLUES WHEN SHE WAS ASSASSINATED.

ALL THEY HAD WAS MOTIVE.

AND THE MAN WITH THE CLEAREST REASON TO KILL HER...

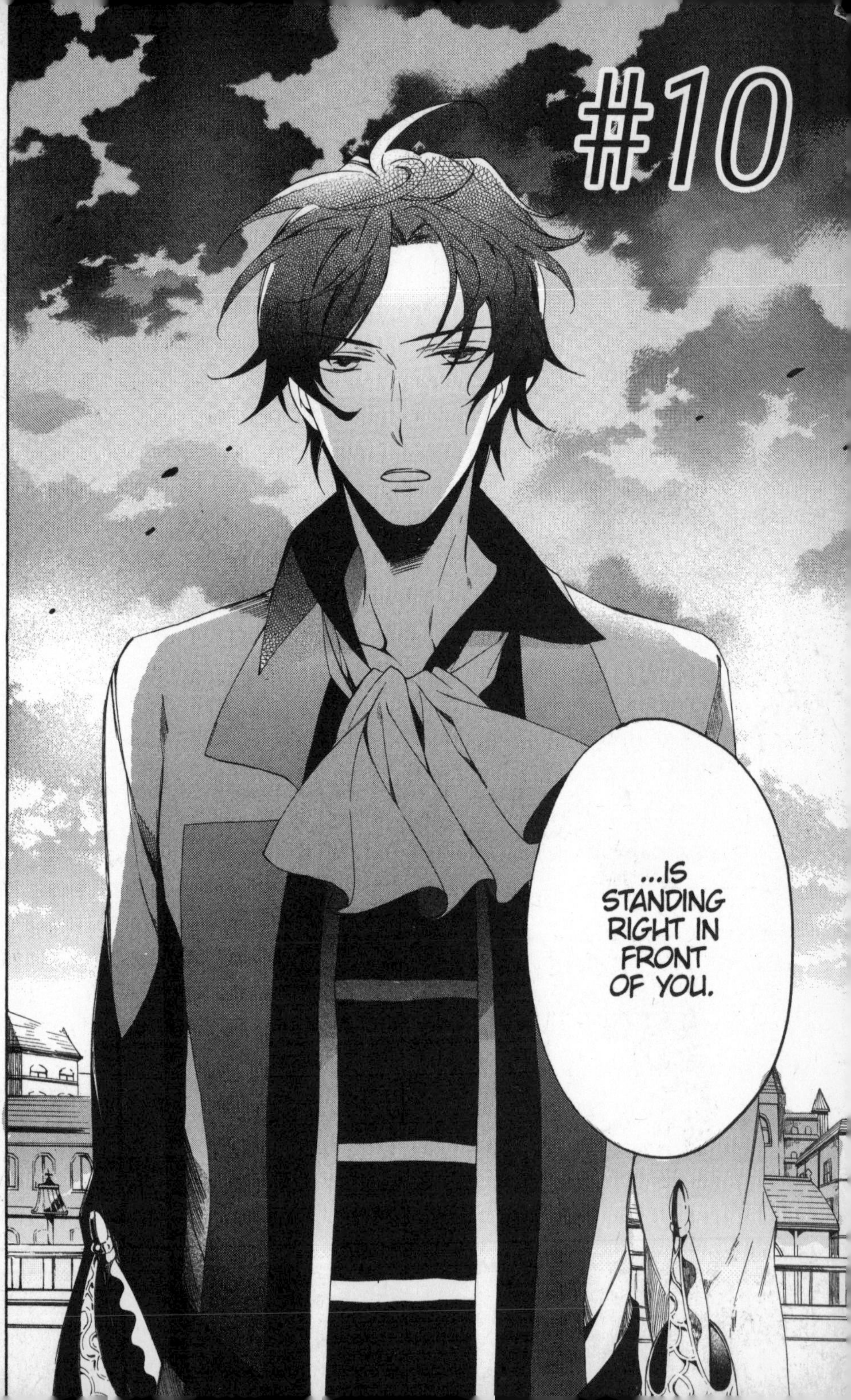
#10
...IS STANDING RIGHT IN FRONT OF YOU.

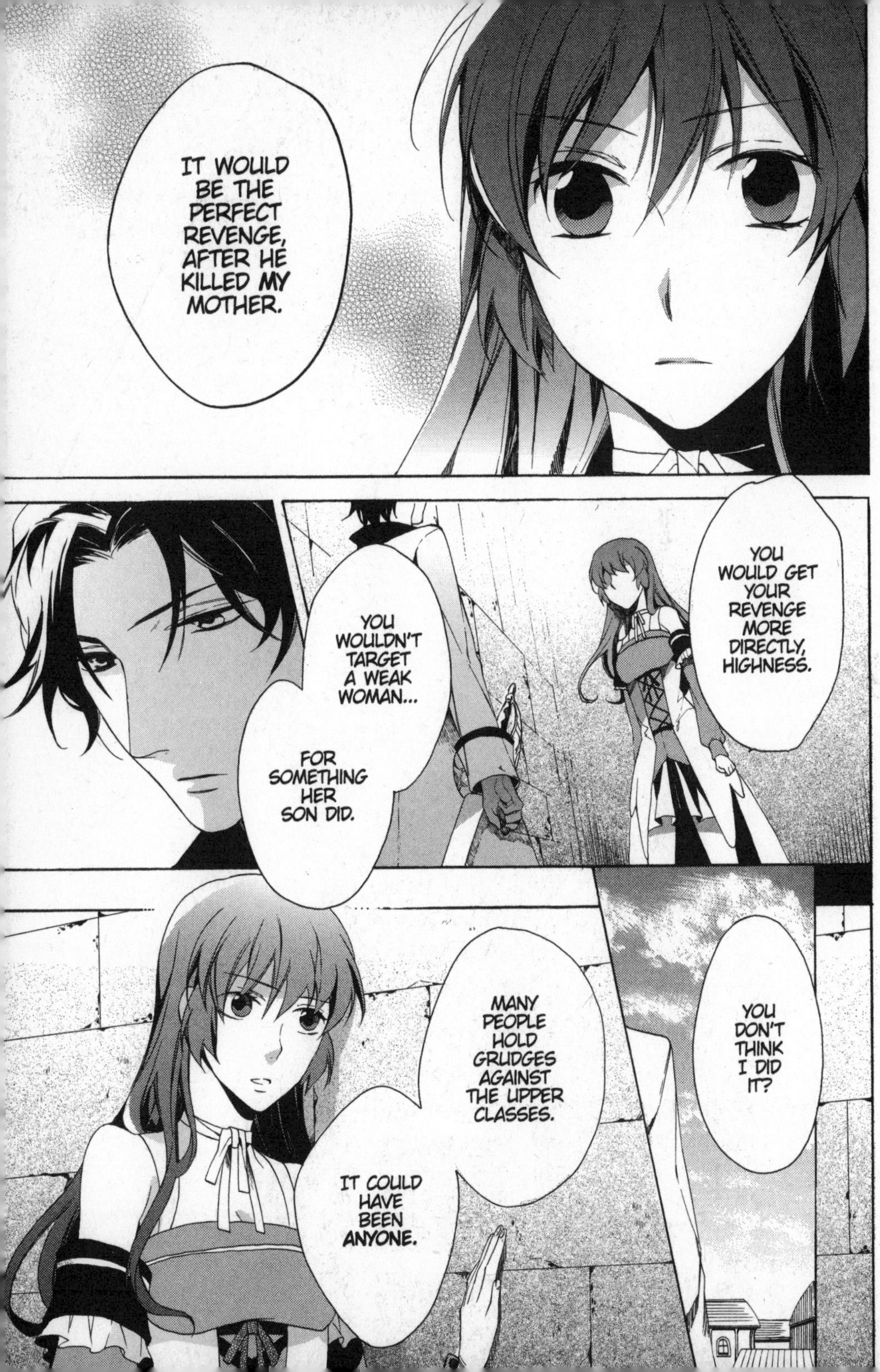
IT WOULD BE THE PERFECT REVENGE, AFTER HE KILLED MY MOTHER.
YOU WOULD GET YOUR REVENGE MORE DIRECTLY, HIGHNESS.
YOU WOULDN'T TARGET A WEAK WOMAN...
FOR SOMETHING HER SON DID.
YOU DON'T THINK I DID IT?
MANY PEOPLE HOLD GRUDGES AGAINST THE UPPER CLASSES.
IT COULD HAVE BEEN ANYONE.

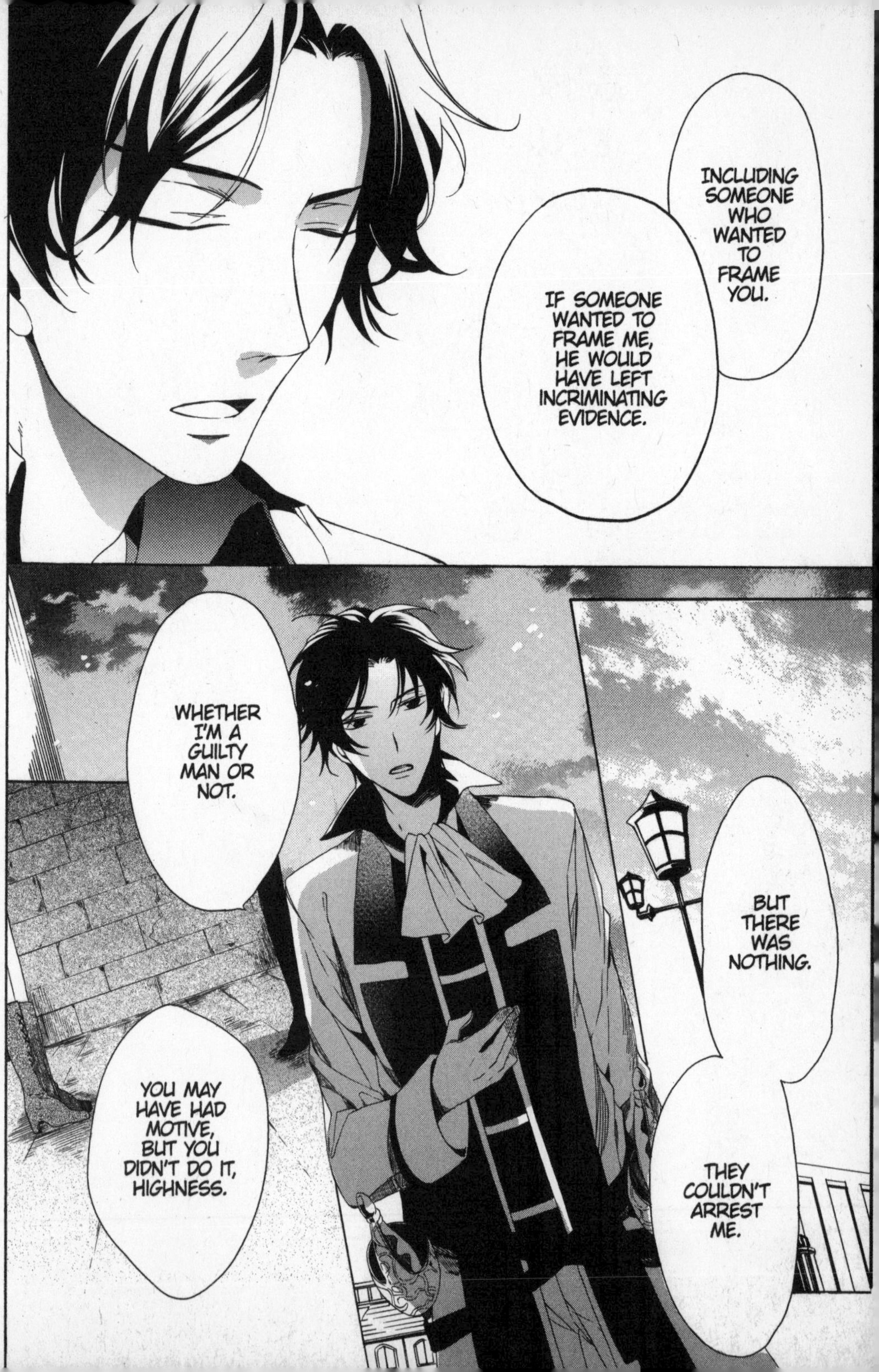
INCLUDING SOMEONE WHO WANTED TO FRAME YOU.
IF SOMEONE WANTED TO FRAME ME, HE WOULD HAVE LEFT INCRIMINATING EVIDENCE.
BUT THERE WAS NOTHING.
THEY COULDN'T ARREST ME.
WHETHER I'M A GUILTY MAN OR NOT.
YOU MAY HAVE HAD MOTIVE, BUT YOU DIDN'T DO IT, HIGHNESS.

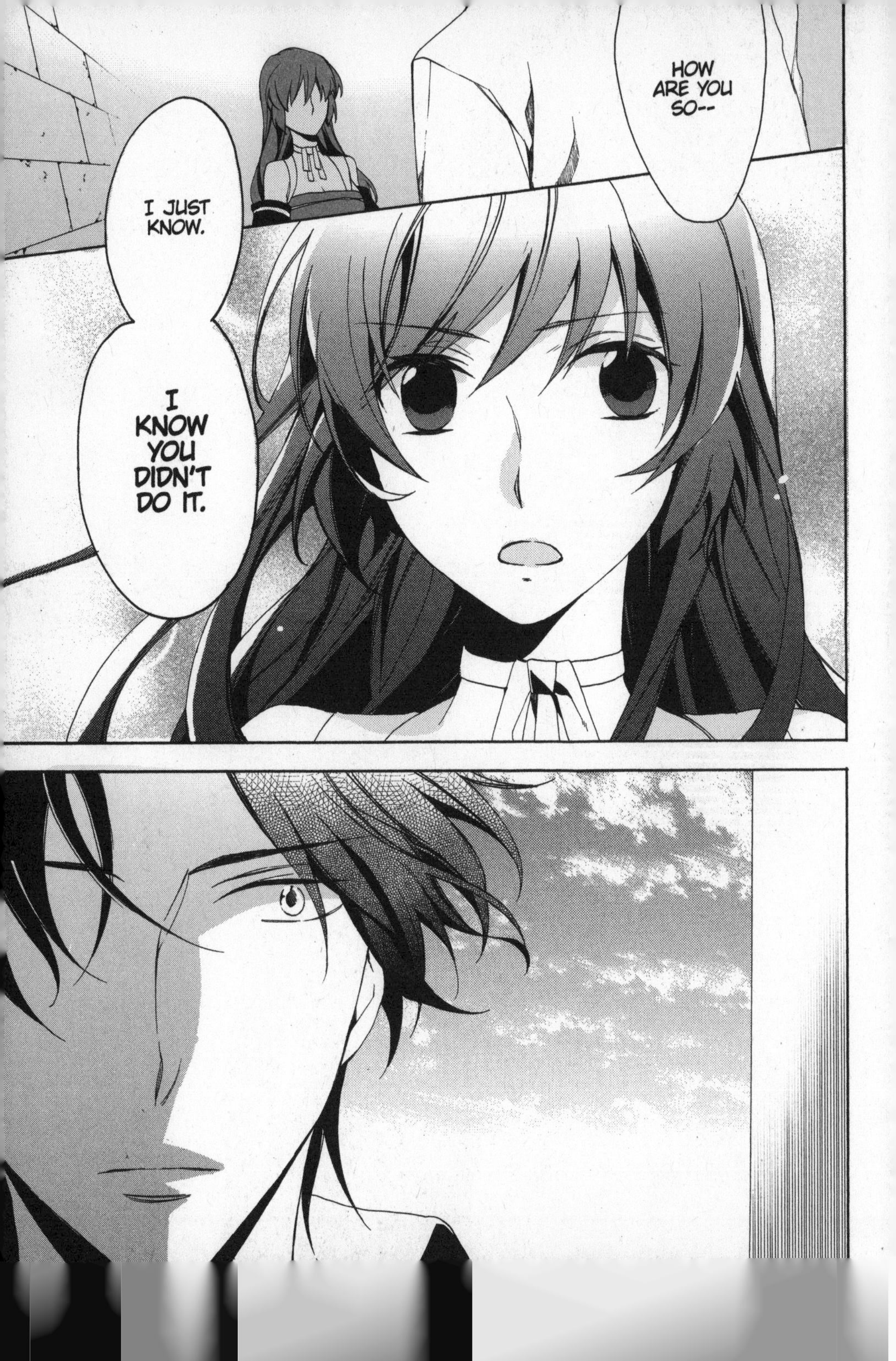
HOW ARE YOU SO--
I JUST KNOW.
I KNOW YOU DIDN'T DO IT.

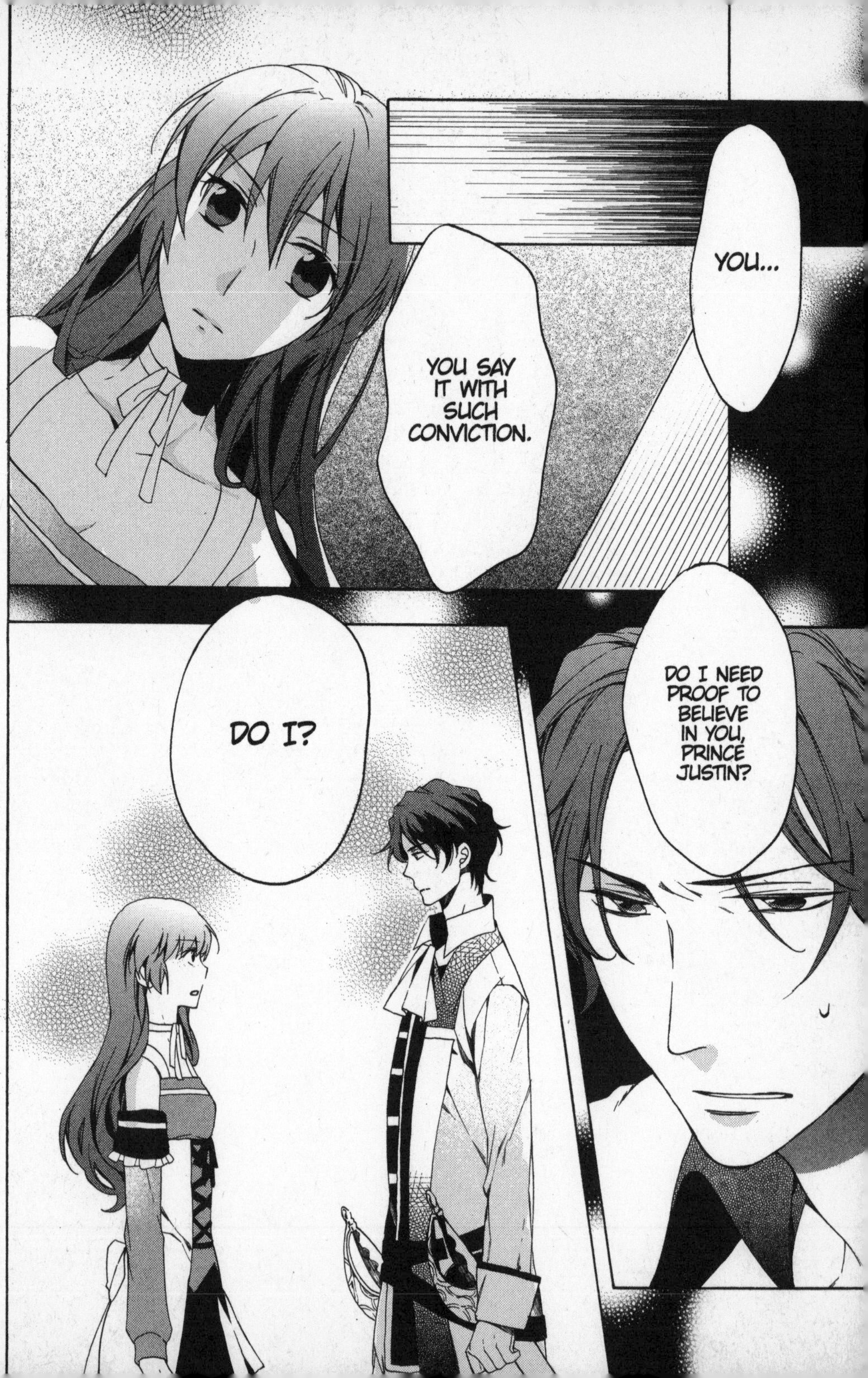
YOU...
YOU SAY IT WITH SUCH CONVICTION.
DO I NEED PROOF TO BELIEVE IN YOU, PRINCE JUSTIN?
DO I?

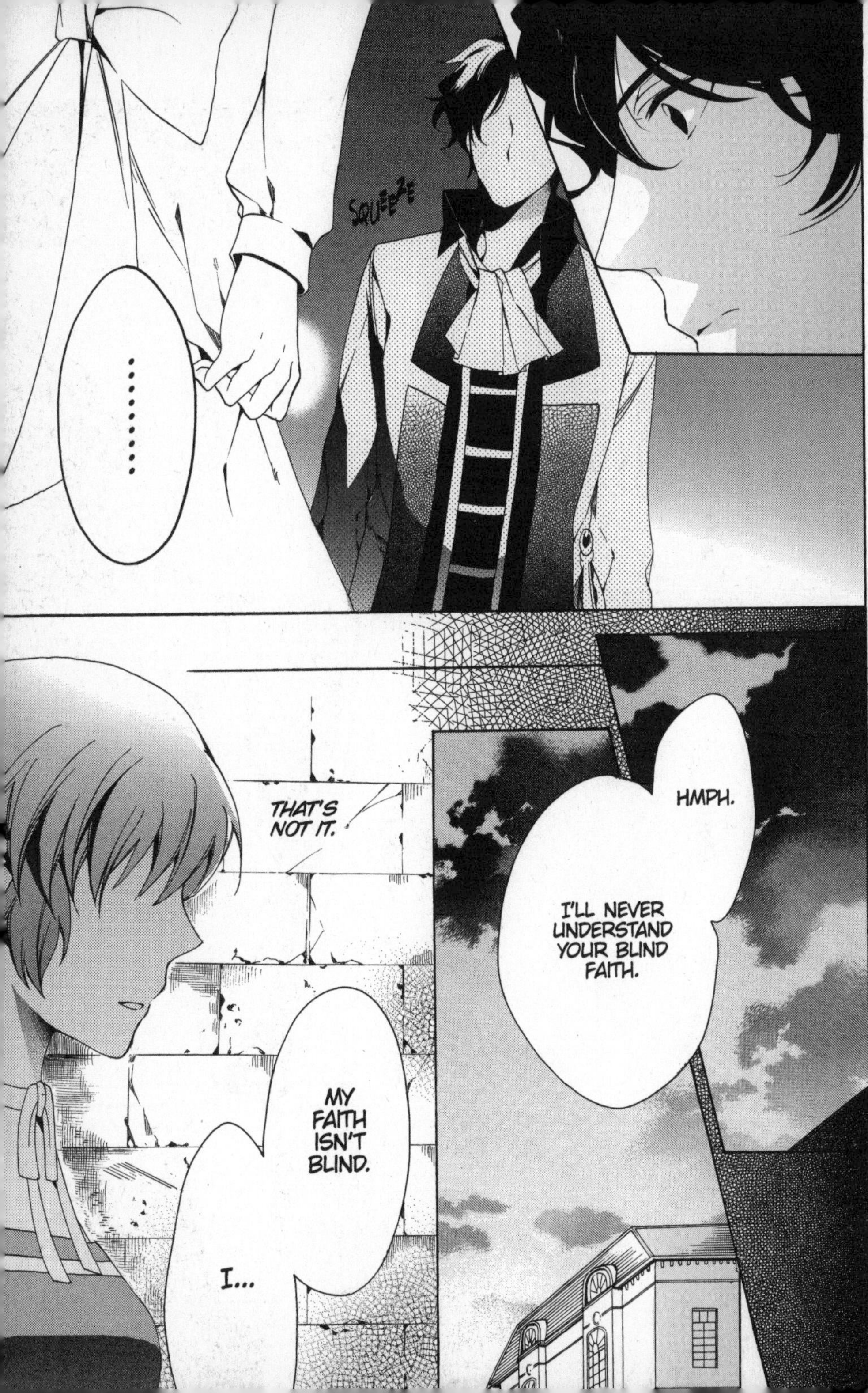
SQUEEZE
......
HMPH.
I'LL NEVER UNDERSTAND YOUR BLIND FAITH.
THAT'S NOT IT.
MY FAITH ISN'T BLIND.
I...

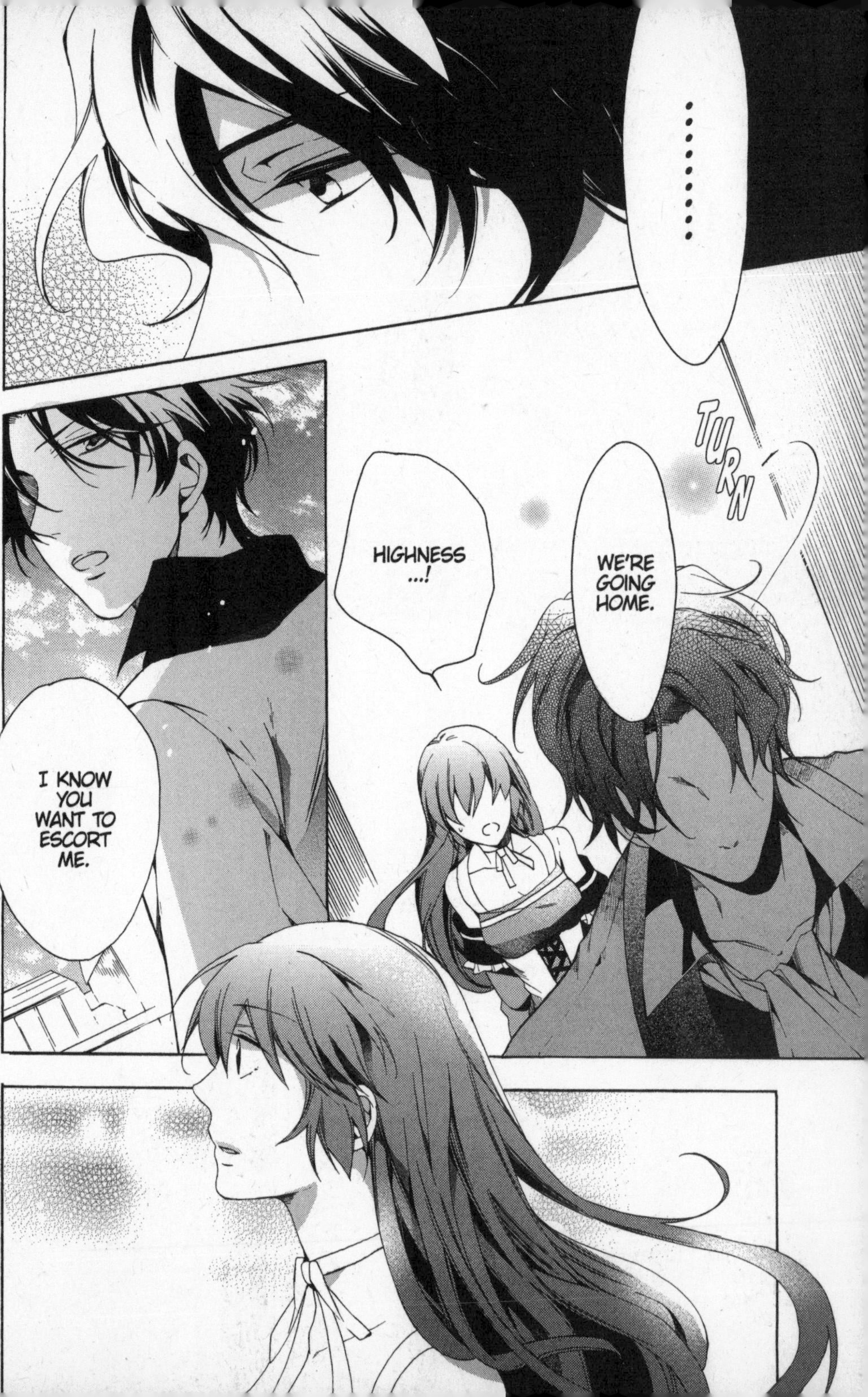
......
TURN
WE'RE GOING HOME.
HIGHNESS ...!
I KNOW YOU WANT TO ESCORT ME.

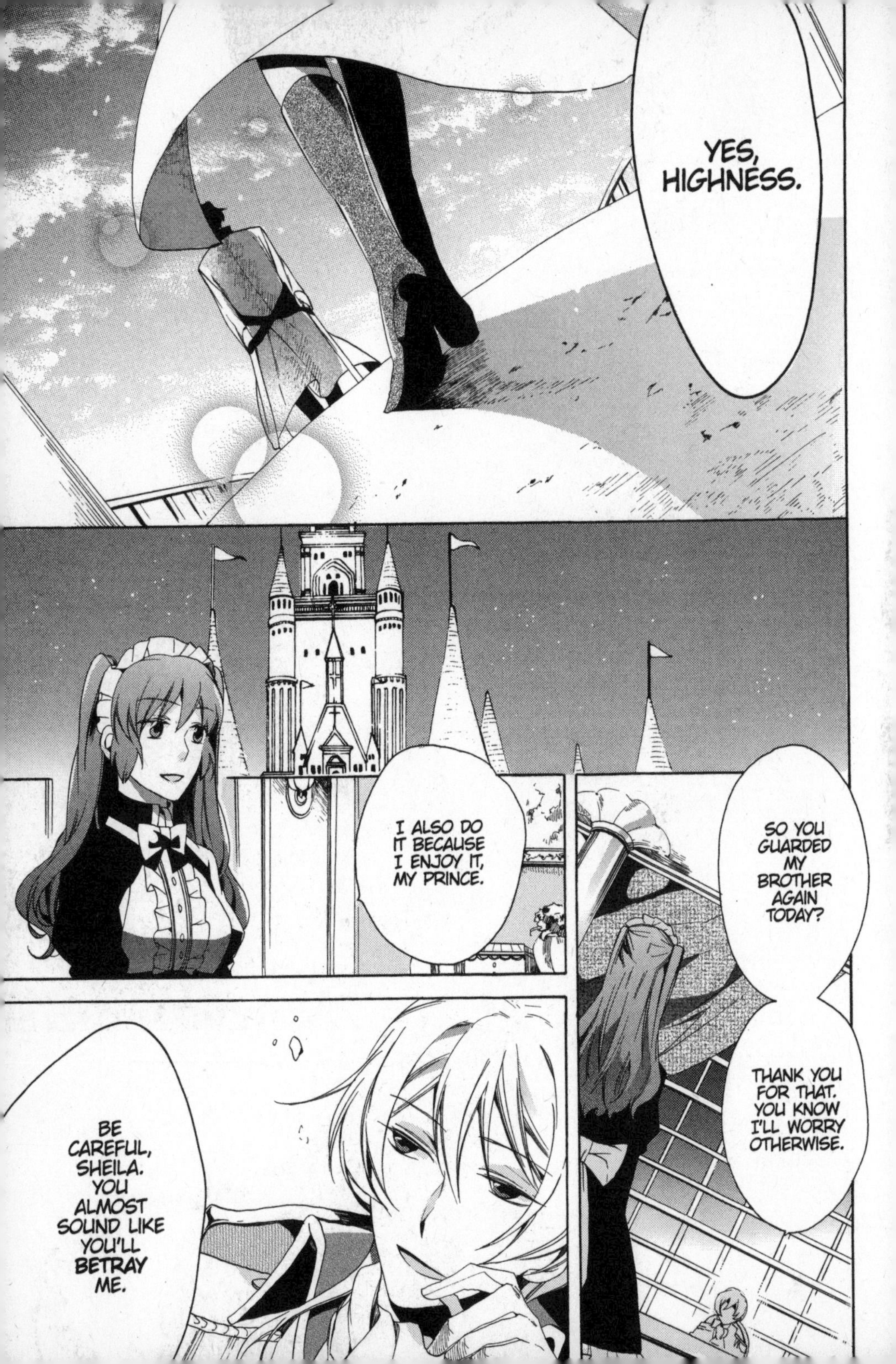
YES, HIGHNESS.
SO YOU GUARDED MY BROTHER AGAIN TODAY?
THANK YOU FOR THAT. YOU KNOW I'LL WORRY OTHERWISE.
I ALSO DO IT BECAUSE I ENJOY IT, MY PRINCE.
BE CAREFUL, SHEILA. YOU ALMOST SOUND LIKE YOU'LL BETRAY ME.

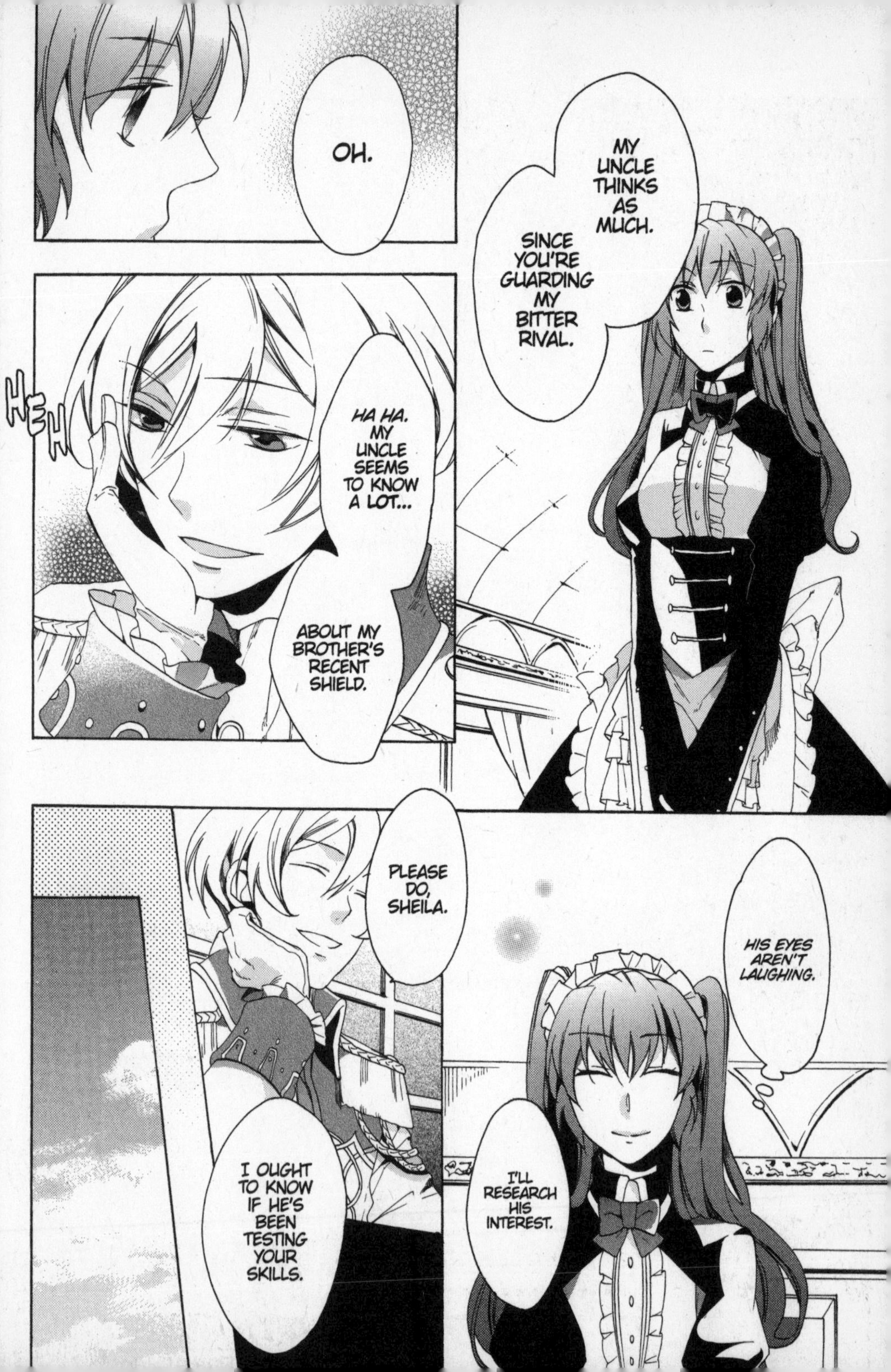
MY UNCLE THINKS AS MUCH.
SINCE YOU'RE GUARDING MY BITTER RIVAL.
OH.
HEH
HA HA. MY UNCLE SEEMS TO KNOW A LOT...
ABOUT MY BROTHER'S RECENT SHIELD.
HIS EYES AREN'T LAUGHING.
I'LL RESEARCH HIS INTEREST.
PLEASE DO, SHEILA.
I OUGHT TO KNOW IF HE'S BEEN TESTING YOUR SKILLS.

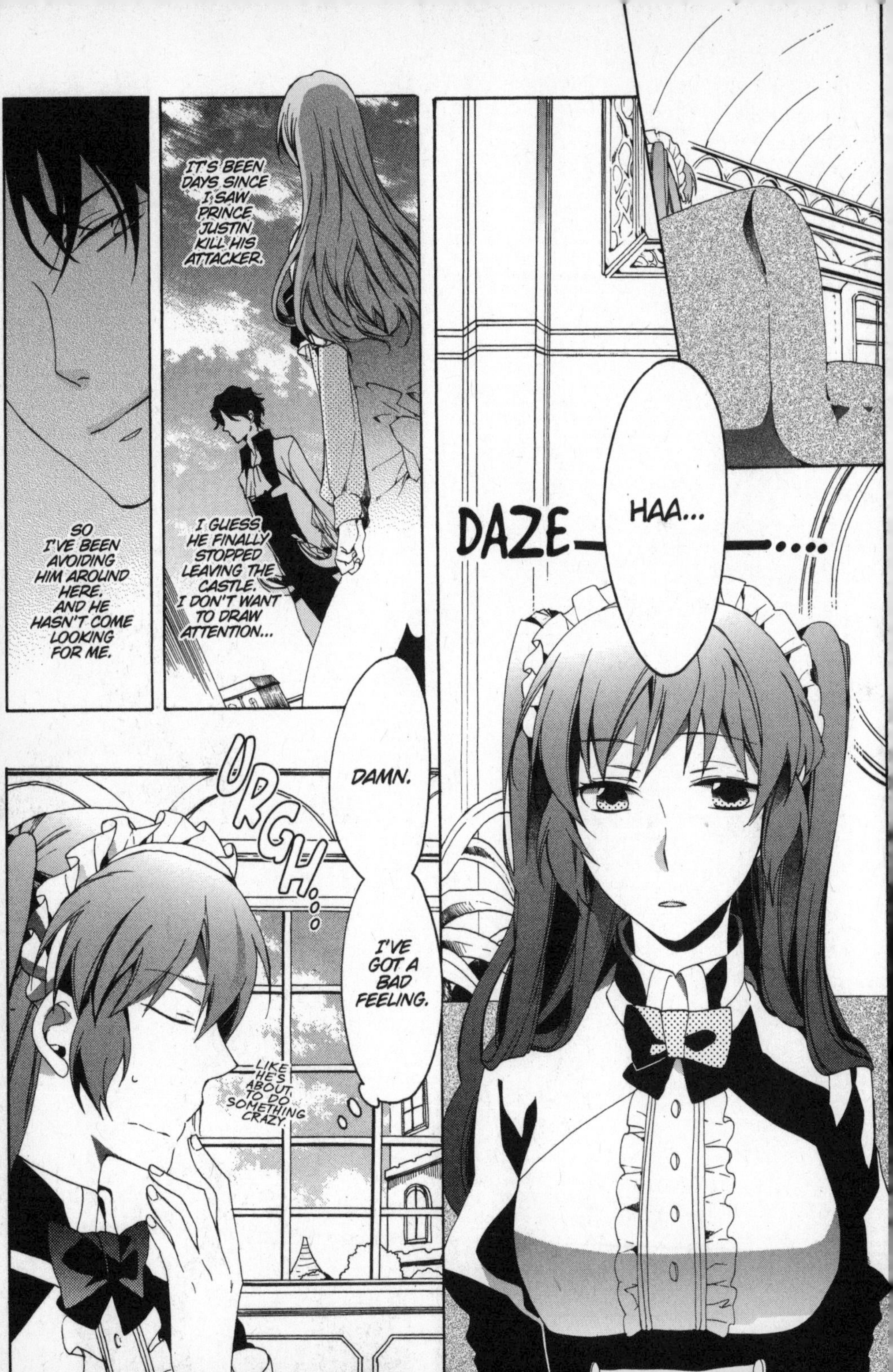
DAZE—
HAA...
—...
IT'S BEEN DAYS SINCE I SAW PRINCE JUSTIN KILL HIS ATTACKER.
I GUESS HE FINALLY STOPPED LEAVING THE CASTLE. I DON'T WANT TO DRAW ATTENTION...
SO I'VE BEEN AVOIDING HIM AROUND HERE. AND HE HASN'T COME LOOKING FOR ME.
DAMN.
I'VE GOT A BAD FEELING.
URGH...
LIKE HE'S ABOUT TO DO SOMETHING CRAZY.

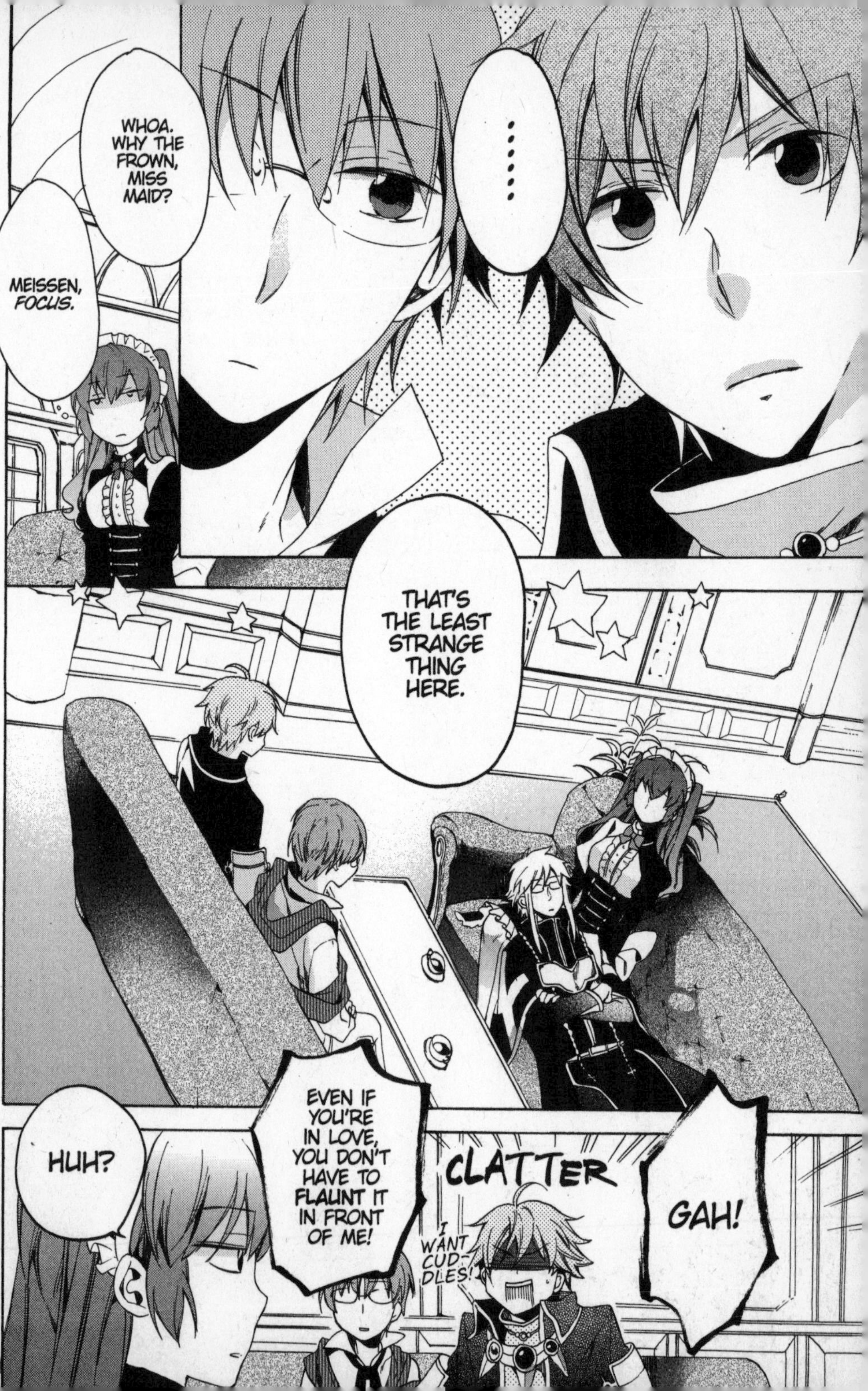
......
WHOA. WHY THE FROWN, MISS MAID?
MEISSEN, FOCUS.
THAT'S THE LEAST STRANGE THING HERE.
GAH!
CLATTER
I WANT CUDDLES!
EVEN IF YOU'RE IN LOVE, YOU DON'T HAVE TO FLAUNT IT IN FRONT OF ME!
HUH?

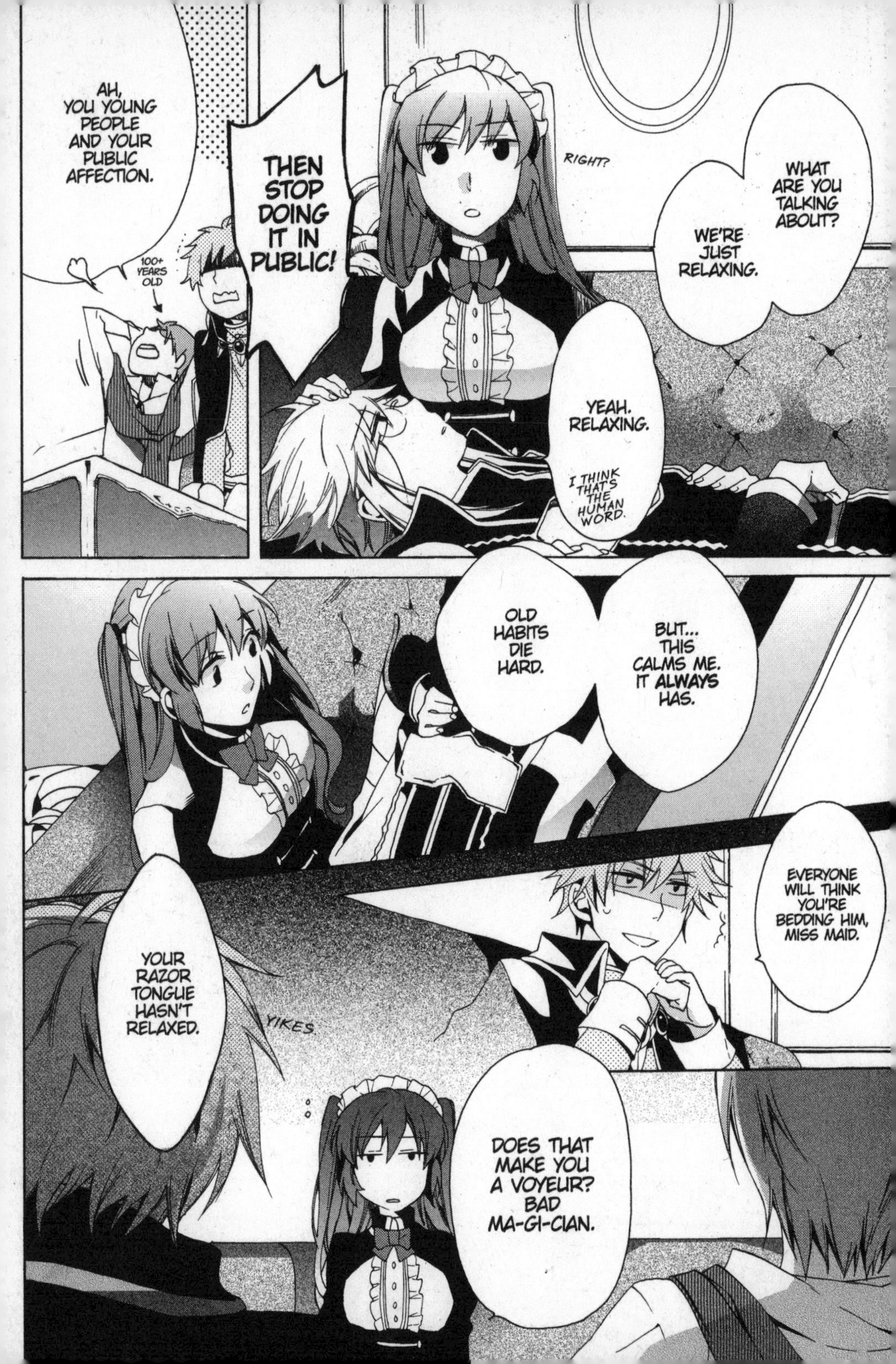
WHAT ARE YOU TALKING ABOUT?
WE'RE JUST RELAXING.
RIGHT?
YEAH. RELAXING.
I THINK THAT'S THE HUMAN WORD.
THEN STOP DOING IT IN PUBLIC!
AH, YOU YOUNG PEOPLE AND YOUR PUBLIC AFFECTION.
100+ YEARS OLD
BUT... THIS CALMS ME. IT ALWAYS HAS.
OLD HABITS DIE HARD.
EVERYONE WILL THINK YOU'RE BEDDING HIM, MISS MAID.
YIKES.
YOUR RAZOR TONGUE HASN'T RELAXED.
DOES THAT MAKE YOU A VOYEUR? BAD MA-GI-CIAN.

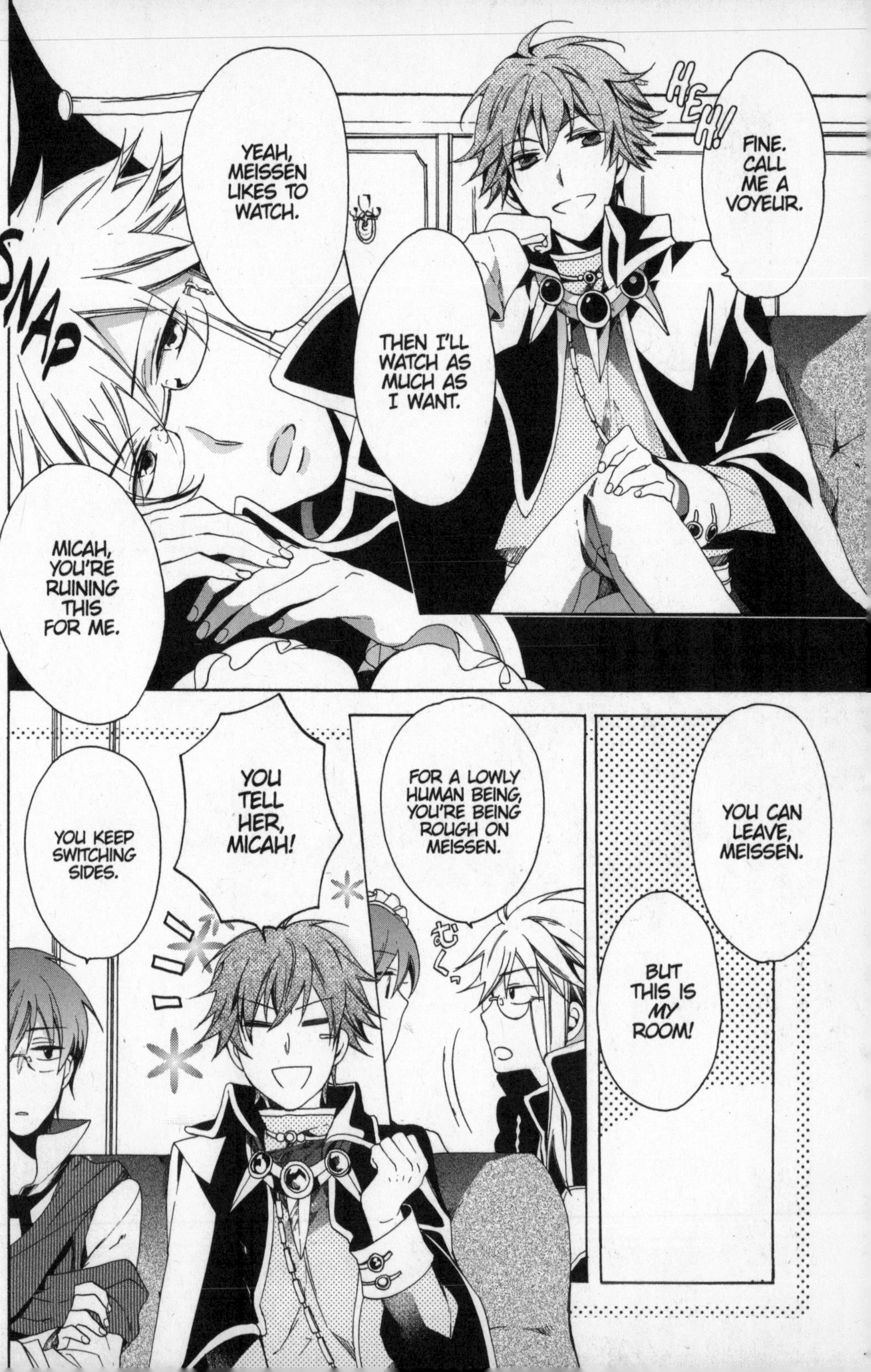

YEAH, MEISSEN LIKES TO WATCH.
HEH!
FINE. CALL ME A VOYEUR.
THEN I'LL WATCH AS MUCH AS I WANT.
SNAP
MICAH, YOU'RE RUINING THIS FOR ME.
YOU CAN LEAVE, MEISSEN.
BUT THIS IS *MY* ROOM!
FOR A LOWLY HUMAN BEING, YOU'RE BEING ROUGH ON MEISSEN.
むくっ
YOU TELL HER, MICAH!
YOU KEEP SWITCHING SIDES.

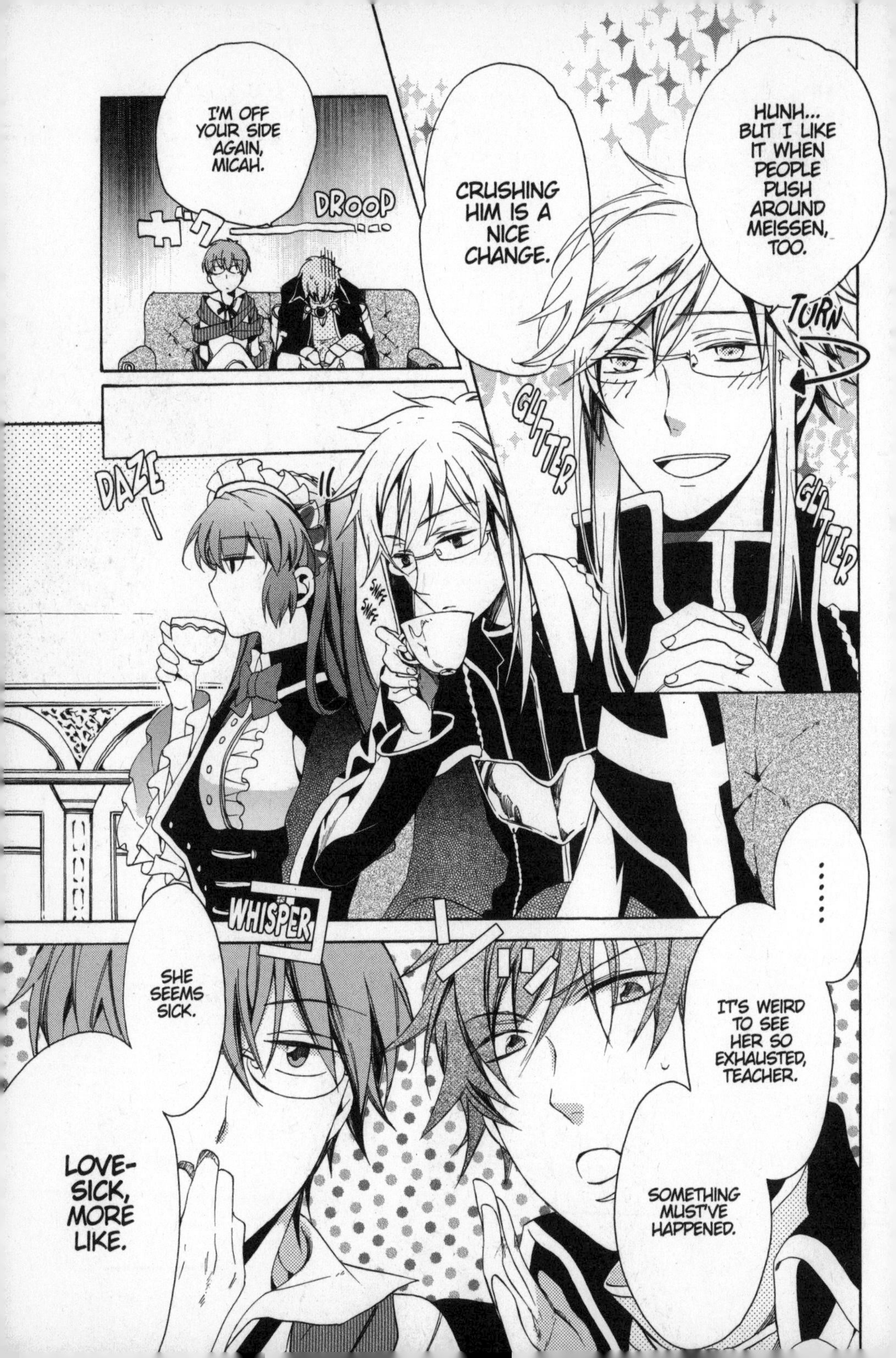
HUNH... BUT I LIKE IT WHEN PEOPLE PUSH AROUND MEISSEN, TOO.
CRUSHING HIM IS A NICE CHANGE.
TURN
I'M OFF YOUR SIDE AGAIN, MICAH.
DROOP
GLITTER
GLITTER
DAZE
SNIFF SNIFF
......
IT'S WEIRD TO SEE HER SO EXHAUSTED, TEACHER.
SOMETHING MUST'VE HAPPENED.
WHISPER
SHE SEEMS SICK.
LOVE-SICK, MORE LIKE.

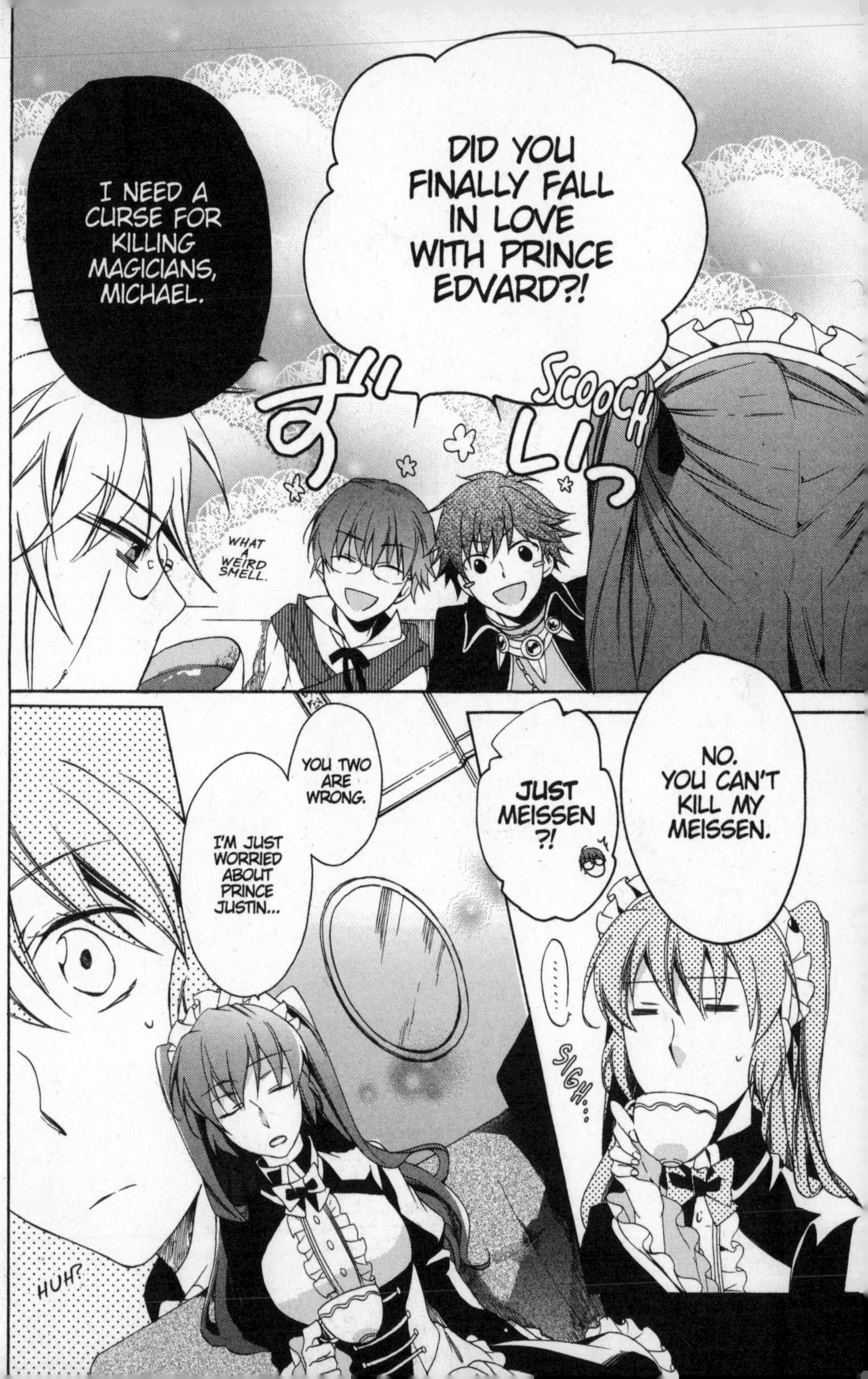
DID YOU FINALLY FALL IN LOVE WITH PRINCE EDVARD?!
I NEED A CURSE FOR KILLING MAGICIANS, MICHAEL.
SCOOCH
WHAT A WEIRD SMELL.
NO. YOU CAN'T KILL MY MEISSEN.
JUST MEISSEN ?!
......
SIGH...
YOU TWO ARE WRONG.
I'M JUST WORRIED ABOUT PRINCE JUSTIN...
HUH?

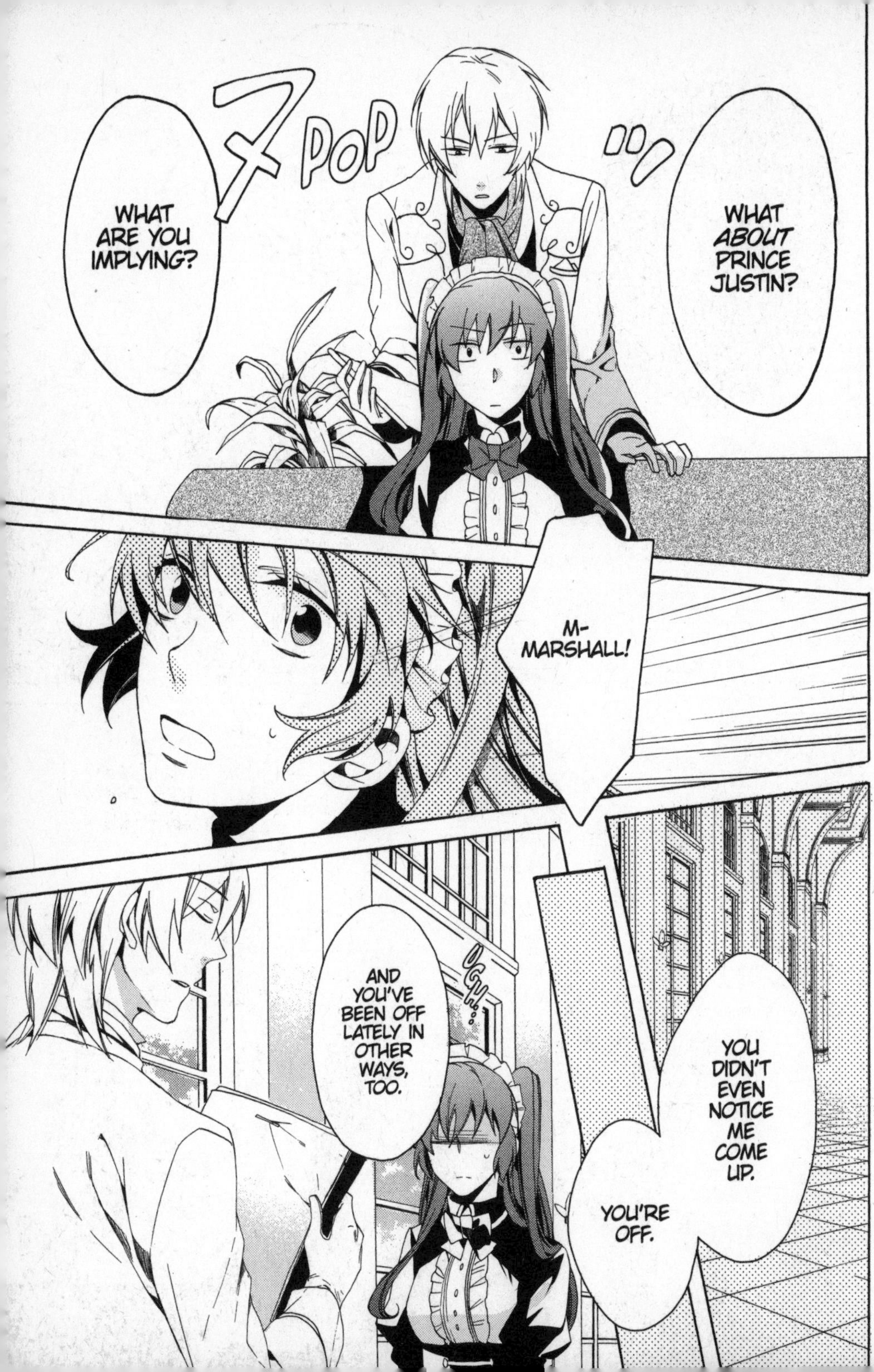
WHAT ABOUT PRINCE JUSTIN?
POP
WHAT ARE YOU IMPLYING?
M-MARSHALL!
YOU DIDN'T EVEN NOTICE ME COME UP.
YOU'RE OFF.
UGH...
AND YOU'VE BEEN OFF LATELY IN OTHER WAYS, TOO.

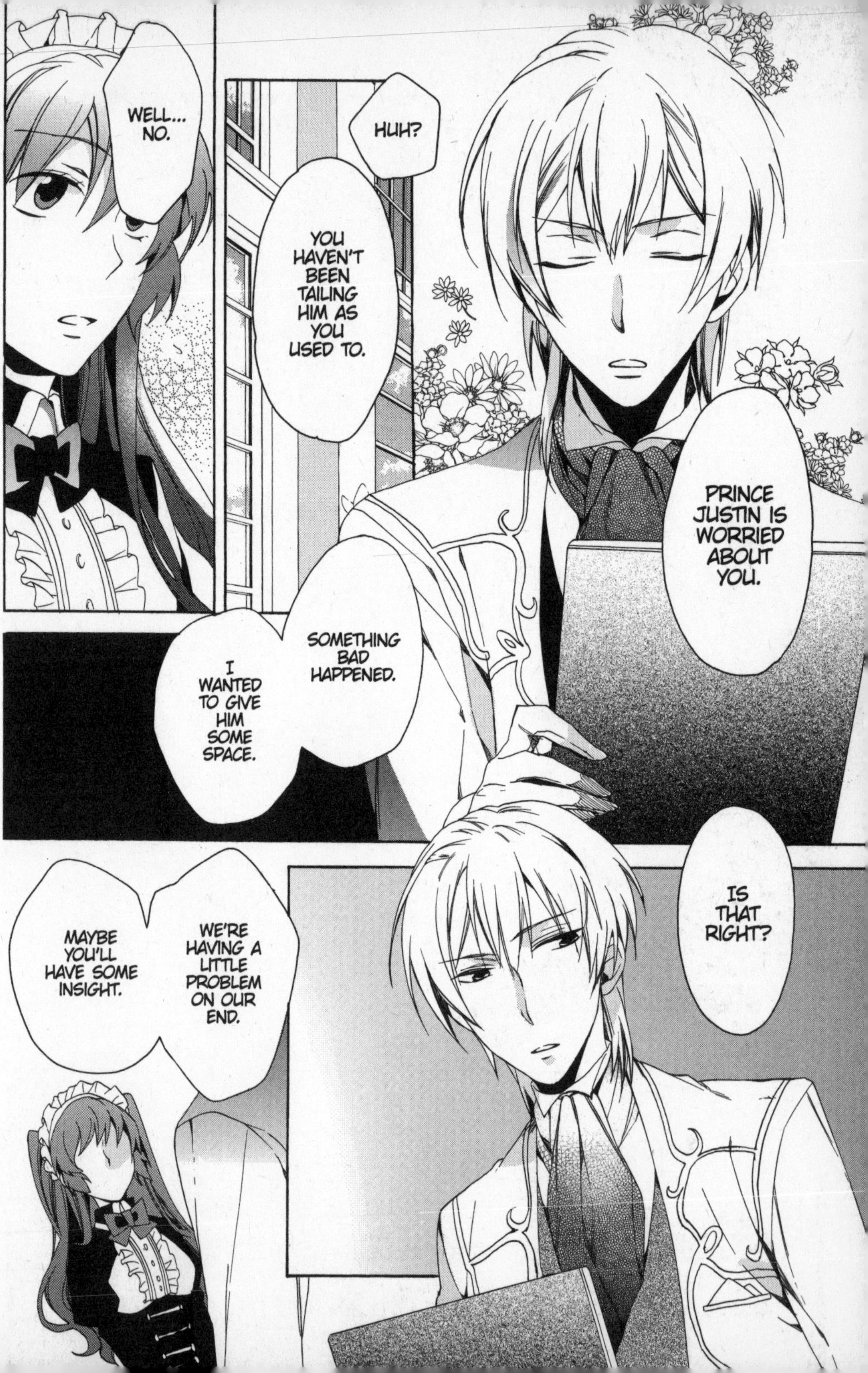
PRINCE JUSTIN IS WORRIED ABOUT YOU.
HUH?
YOU HAVEN'T BEEN TAILING HIM AS YOU USED TO.
WELL... NO.
SOMETHING BAD HAPPENED.
I WANTED TO GIVE HIM SOME SPACE.
IS THAT RIGHT?
WE'RE HAVING A LITTLE PROBLEM ON OUR END.
MAYBE YOU'LL HAVE SOME INSIGHT.

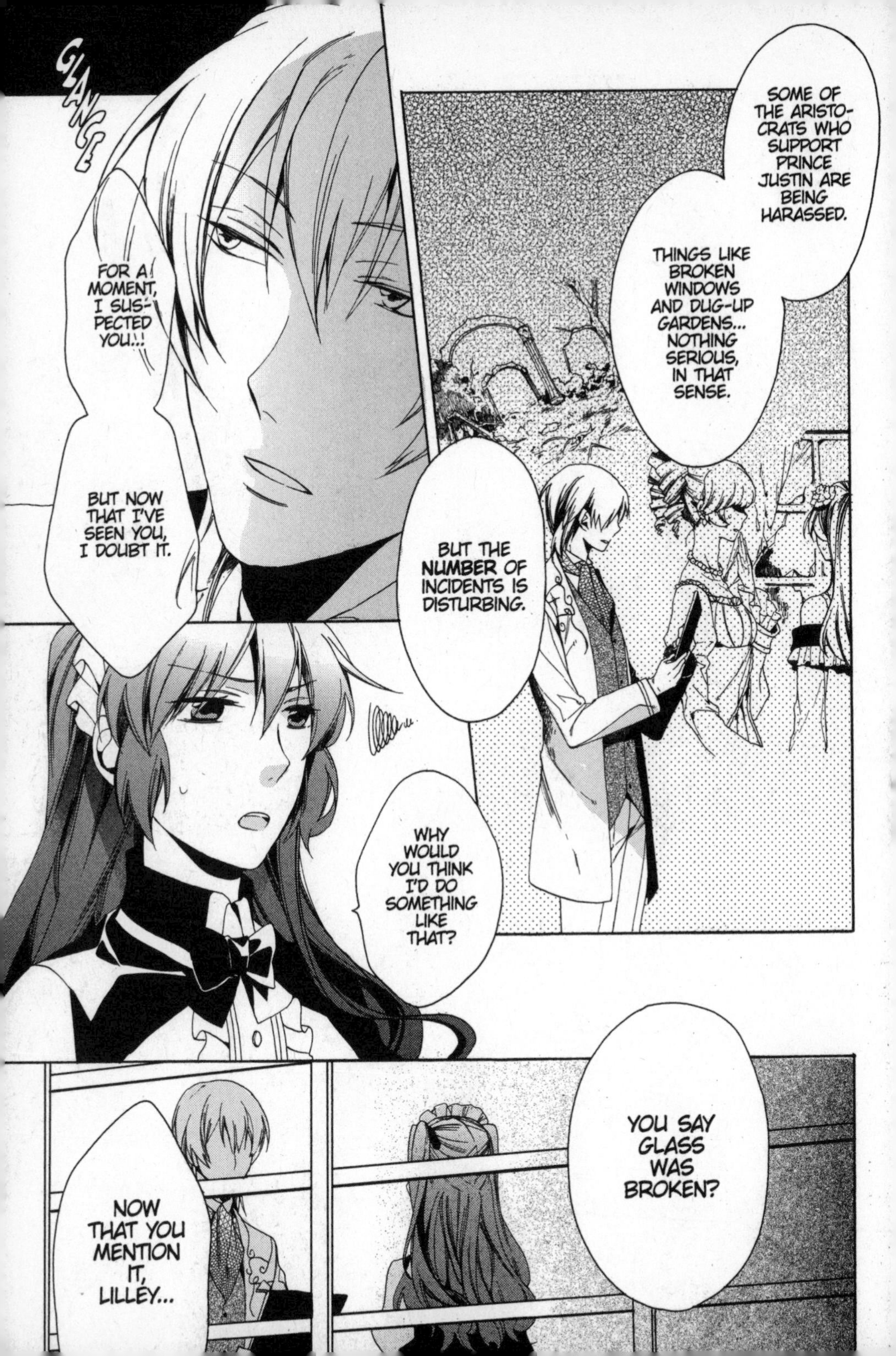
SOME OF THE ARISTOCRATS WHO SUPPORT PRINCE JUSTIN ARE BEING HARASSED.
THINGS LIKE BROKEN WINDOWS AND DUG-UP GARDENS... NOTHING SERIOUS, IN THAT SENSE.
BUT THE NUMBER OF INCIDENTS IS DISTURBING.
GLANCE
FOR A MOMENT, I SUSPECTED YOU...
BUT NOW THAT I'VE SEEN YOU, I DOUBT IT.
WHY WOULD YOU THINK I'D DO SOMETHING LIKE THAT?
YOU SAY GLASS WAS BROKEN?
NOW THAT YOU MENTION IT, LILLEY...

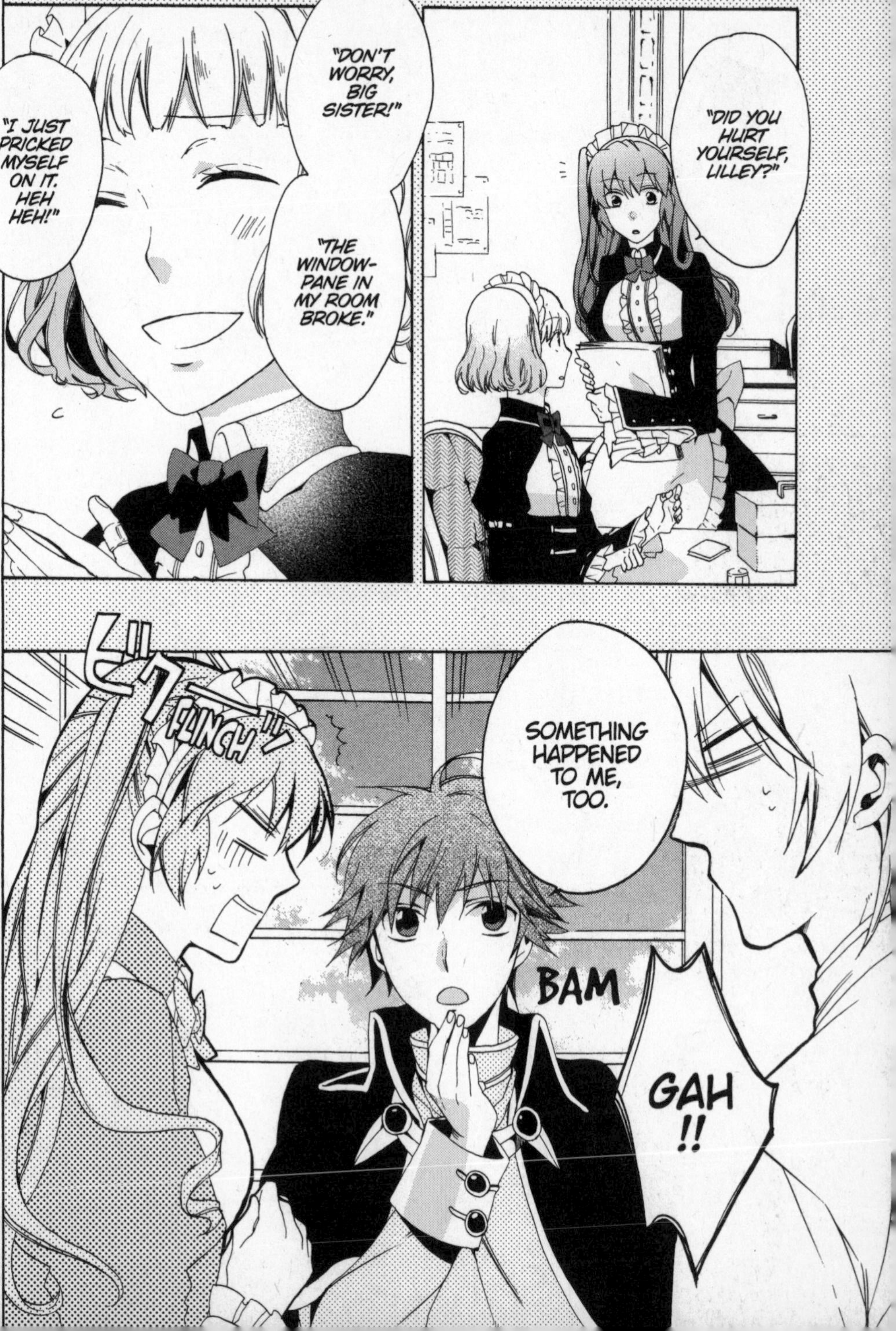
"DID YOU HURT YOURSELF, LILLEY?"
"DON'T WORRY, BIG SISTER!"
"THE WINDOWPANE IN MY ROOM BROKE."
"I JUST PRICKED MYSELF ON IT. HEH HEH!"
SOMETHING HAPPENED TO ME, TOO.
GAH!!
BAM
FLINCH

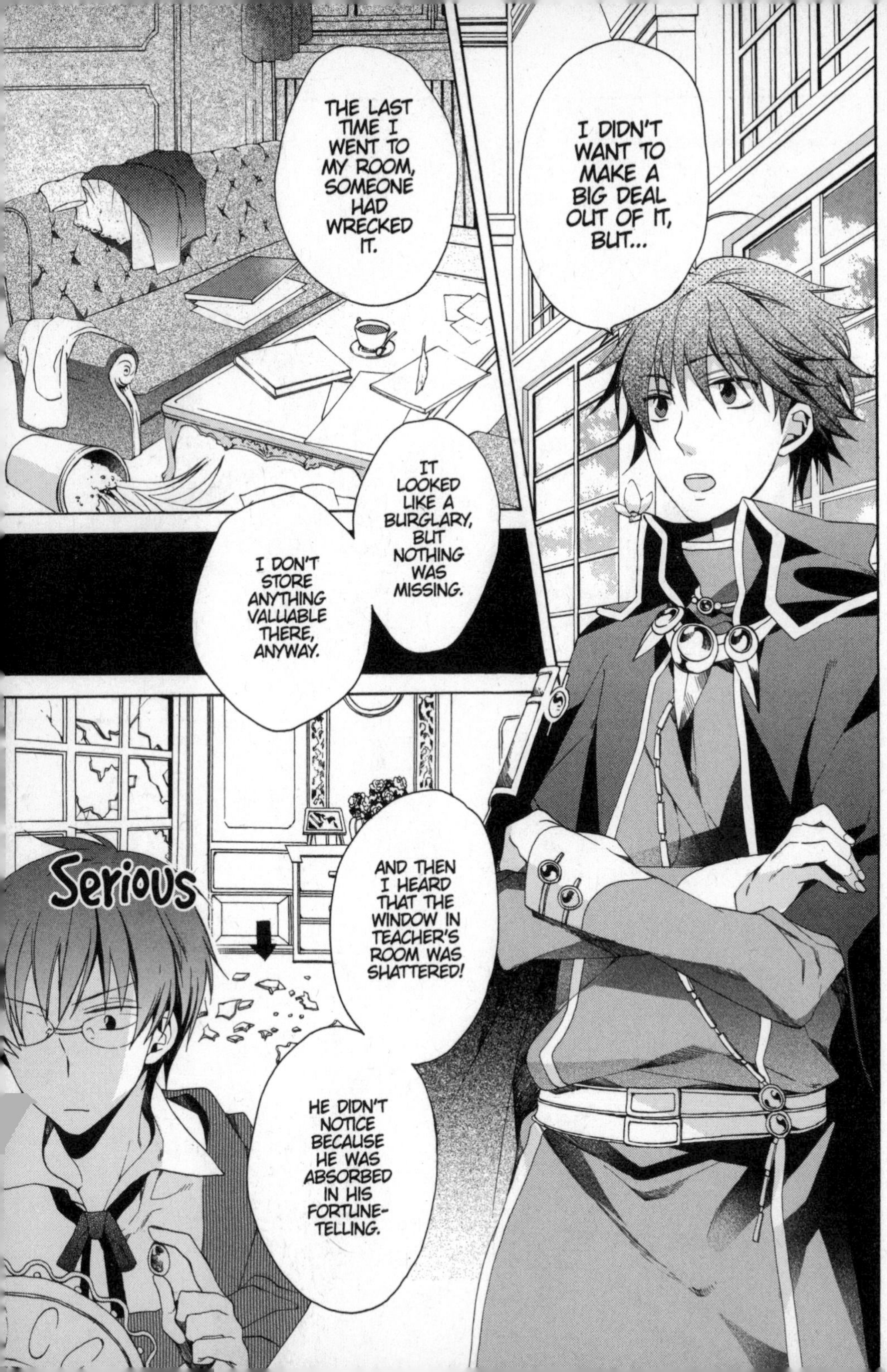
I DIDN'T WANT TO MAKE A BIG DEAL OUT OF IT, BUT...
THE LAST TIME I WENT TO MY ROOM, SOMEONE HAD WRECKED IT.
IT LOOKED LIKE A BURGLARY, BUT NOTHING WAS MISSING.
I DON'T STORE ANYTHING VALUABLE THERE, ANYWAY.
AND THEN I HEARD THAT THE WINDOW IN TEACHER'S ROOM WAS SHATTERED!
Serious
HE DIDN'T NOTICE BECAUSE HE WAS ABSORBED IN HIS FORTUNE-TELLING.

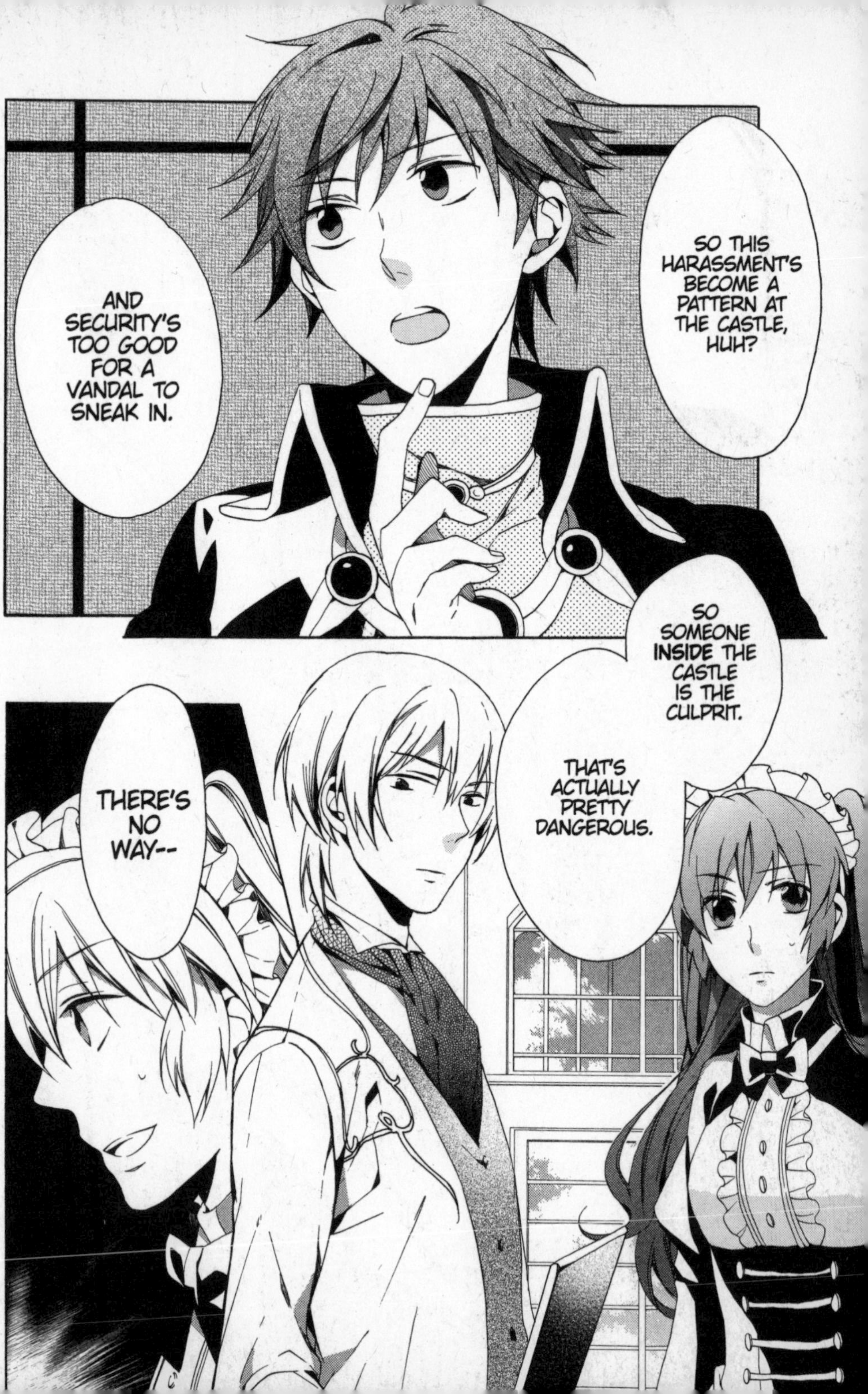
SO THIS HARASSMENT'S BECOME A PATTERN AT THE CASTLE, HUH?
AND SECURITY'S TOO GOOD FOR A VANDAL TO SNEAK IN.
SO SOMEONE INSIDE THE CASTLE IS THE CULPRIT.
THAT'S ACTUALLY PRETTY DANGEROUS.
THERE'S NO WAY--

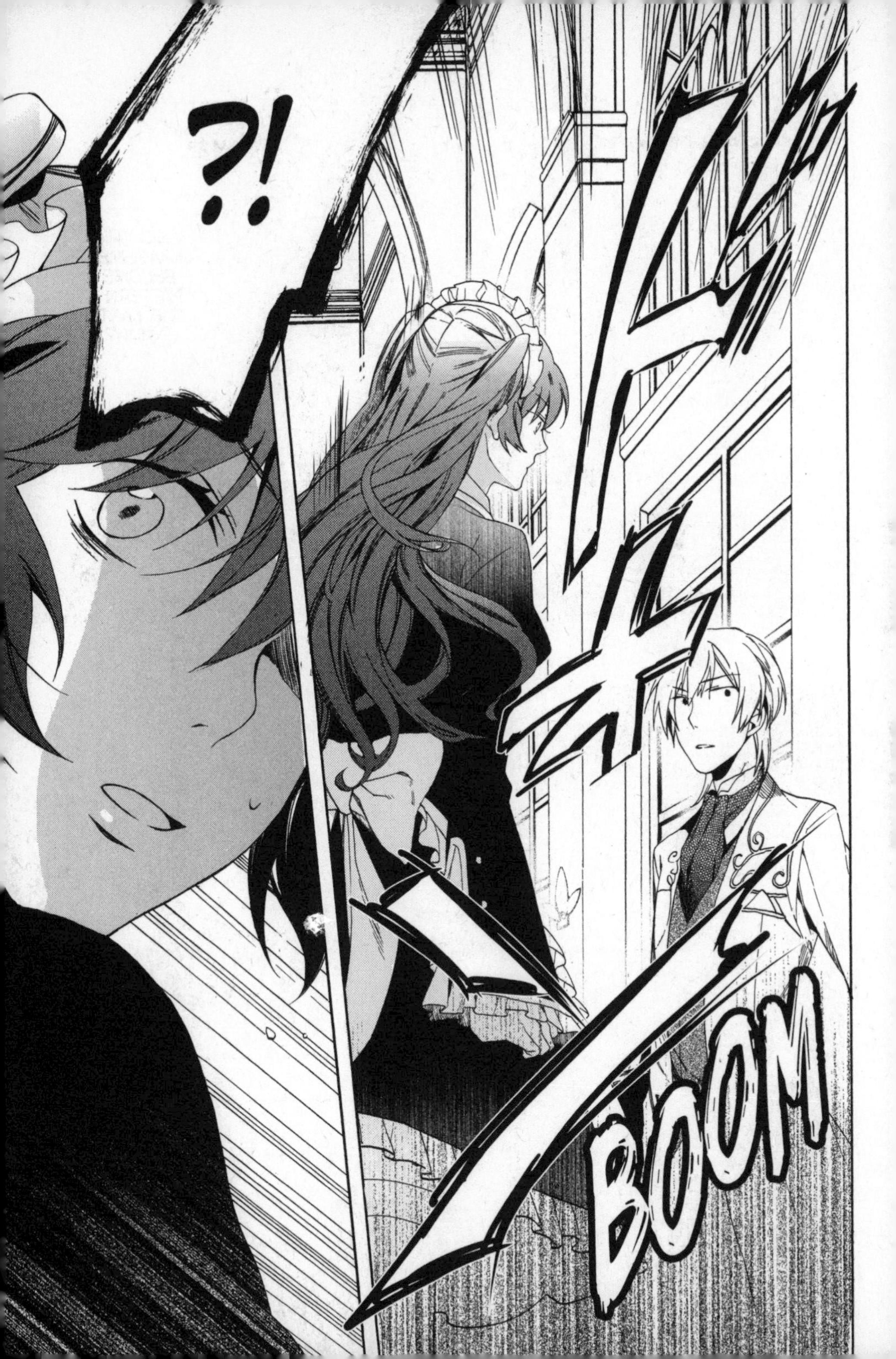
BOOM
?!

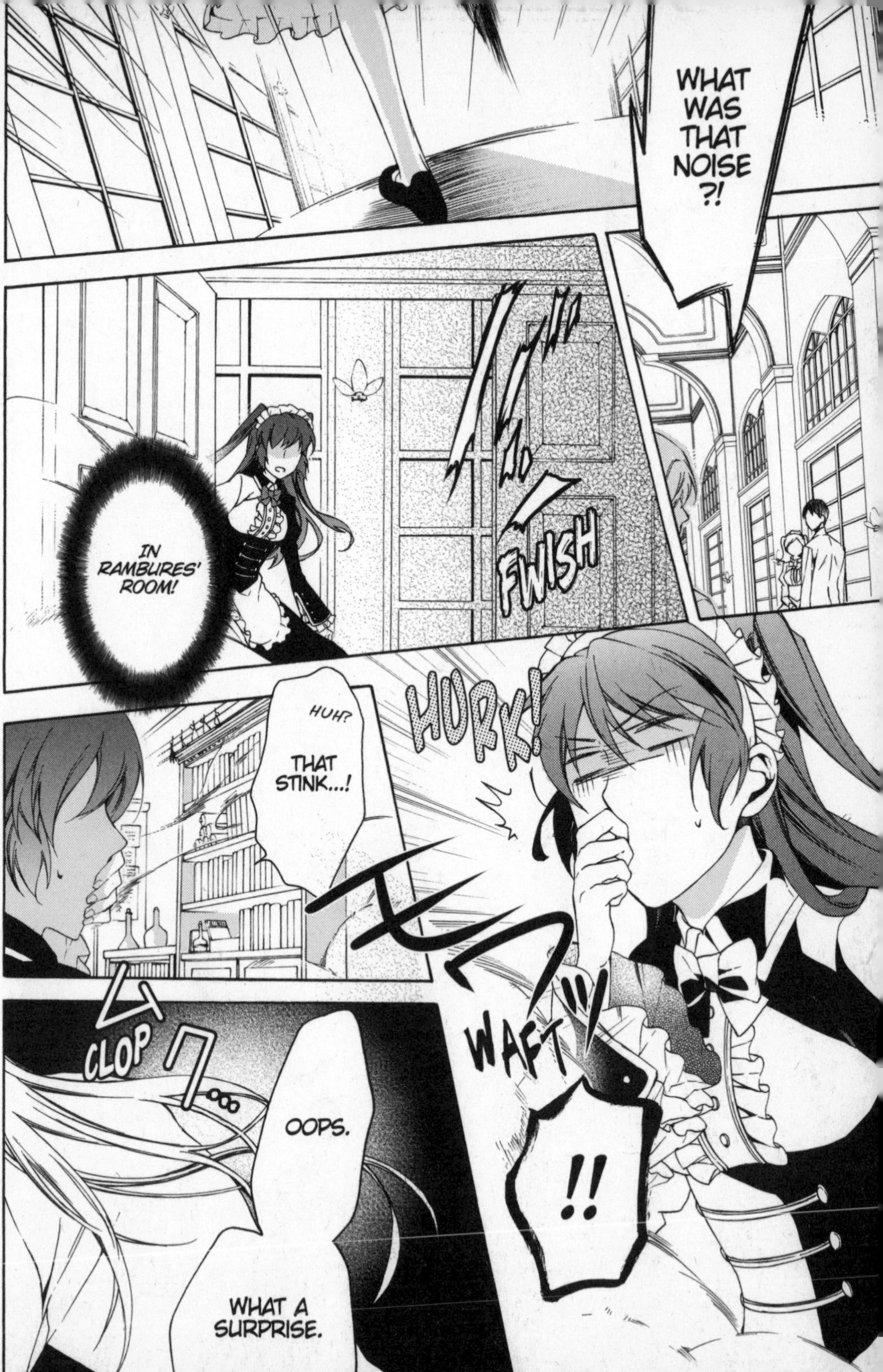
WHAT WAS THAT NOISE ?!
FWISH
IN RAMBURES' ROOM!
HORK!
WAFT!!
HUH?
THAT STINK...!
!!
CLOP
OOPS.
WHAT A SURPRISE.

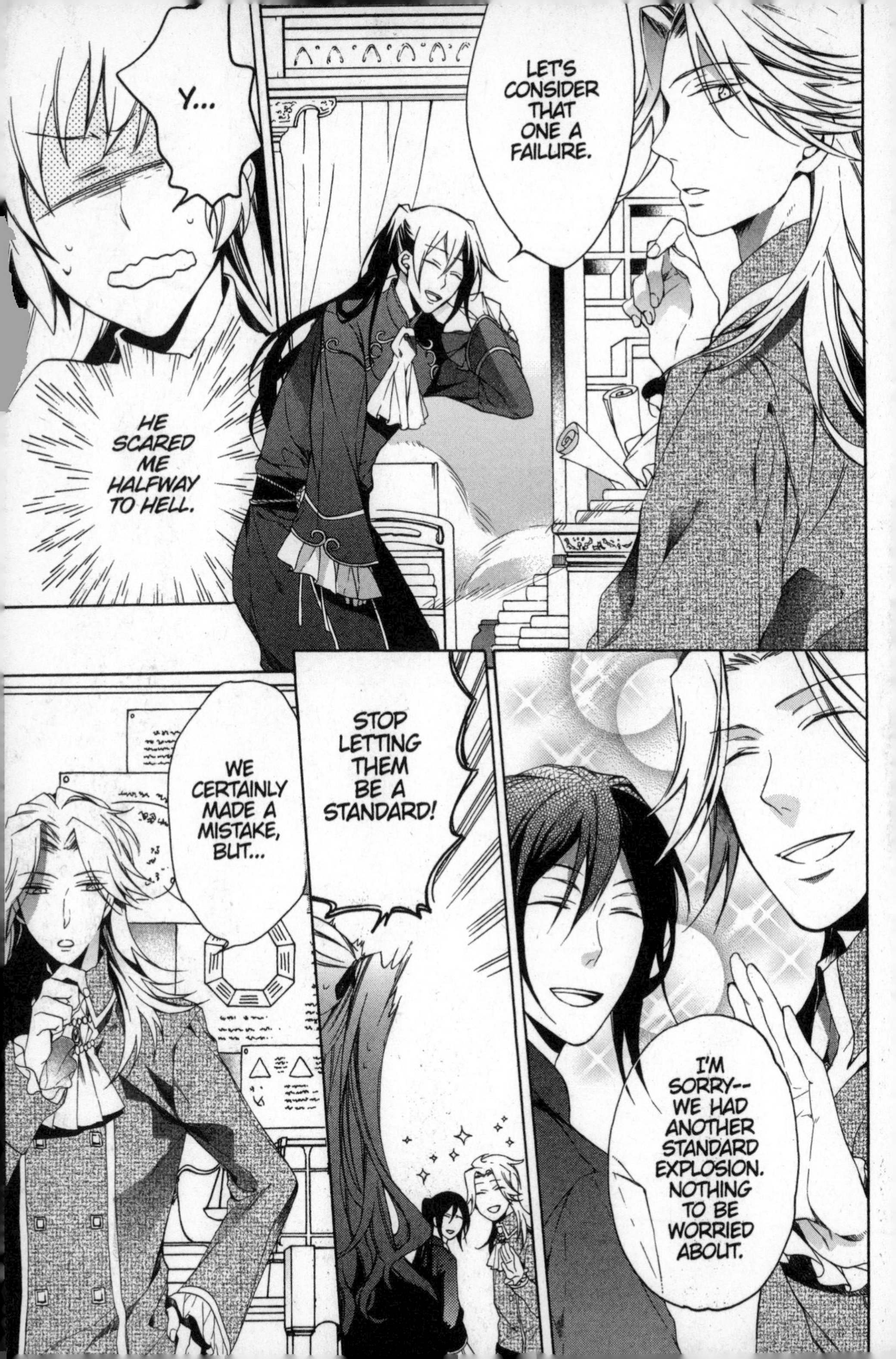
LET'S CONSIDER THAT ONE A FAILURE.
Y...
HE SCARED ME HALFWAY TO HELL.
I'M SORRY-- WE HAD ANOTHER STANDARD EXPLOSION. NOTHING TO BE WORRIED ABOUT.
STOP LETTING THEM BE A STANDARD!
WE CERTAINLY MADE A MISTAKE, BUT...

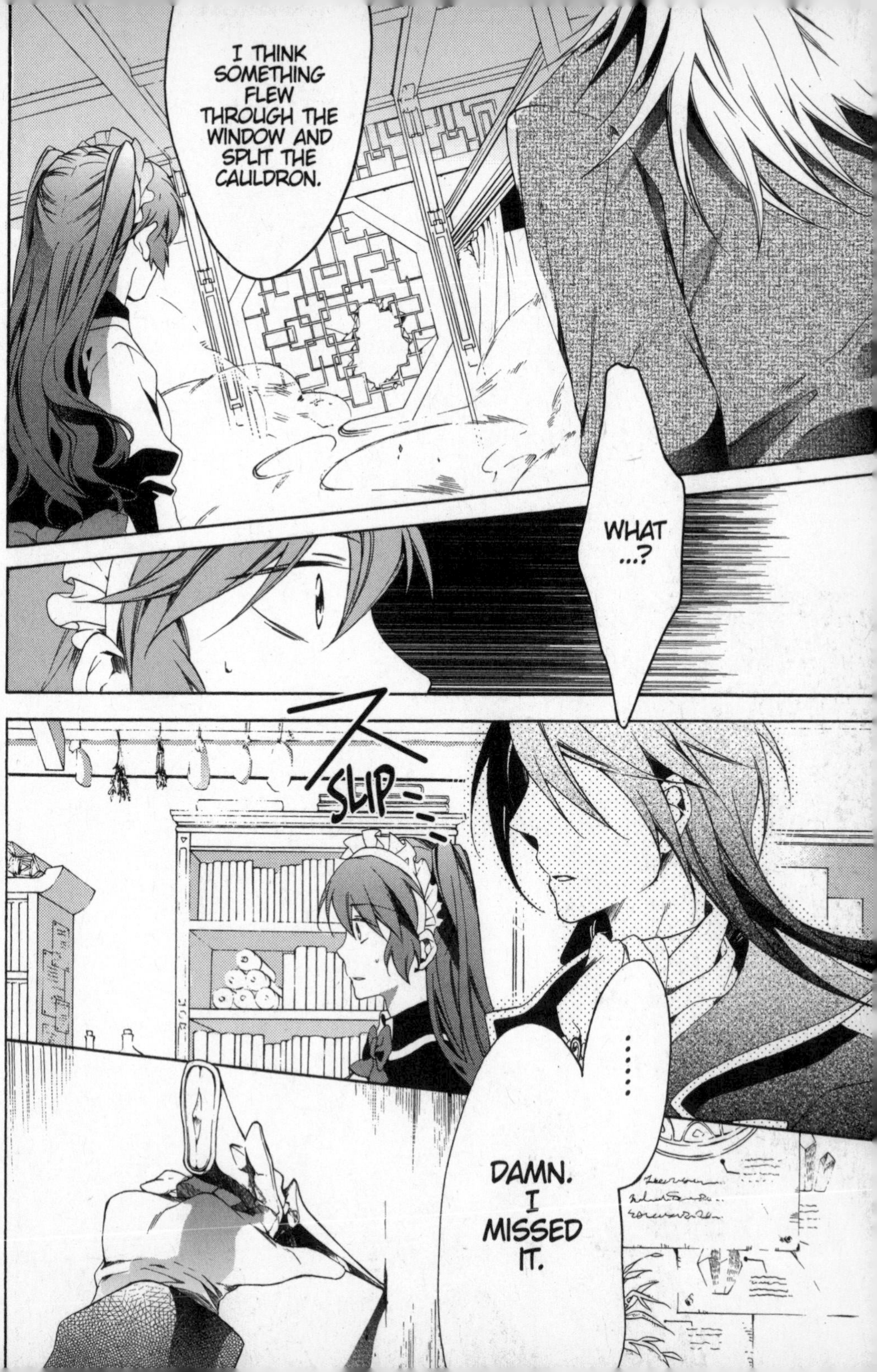
I THINK SOMETHING FLEW THROUGH THE WINDOW AND SPLIT THE CAULDRON.
WHAT ...?
SLIP
......
DAMN. I MISSED IT.

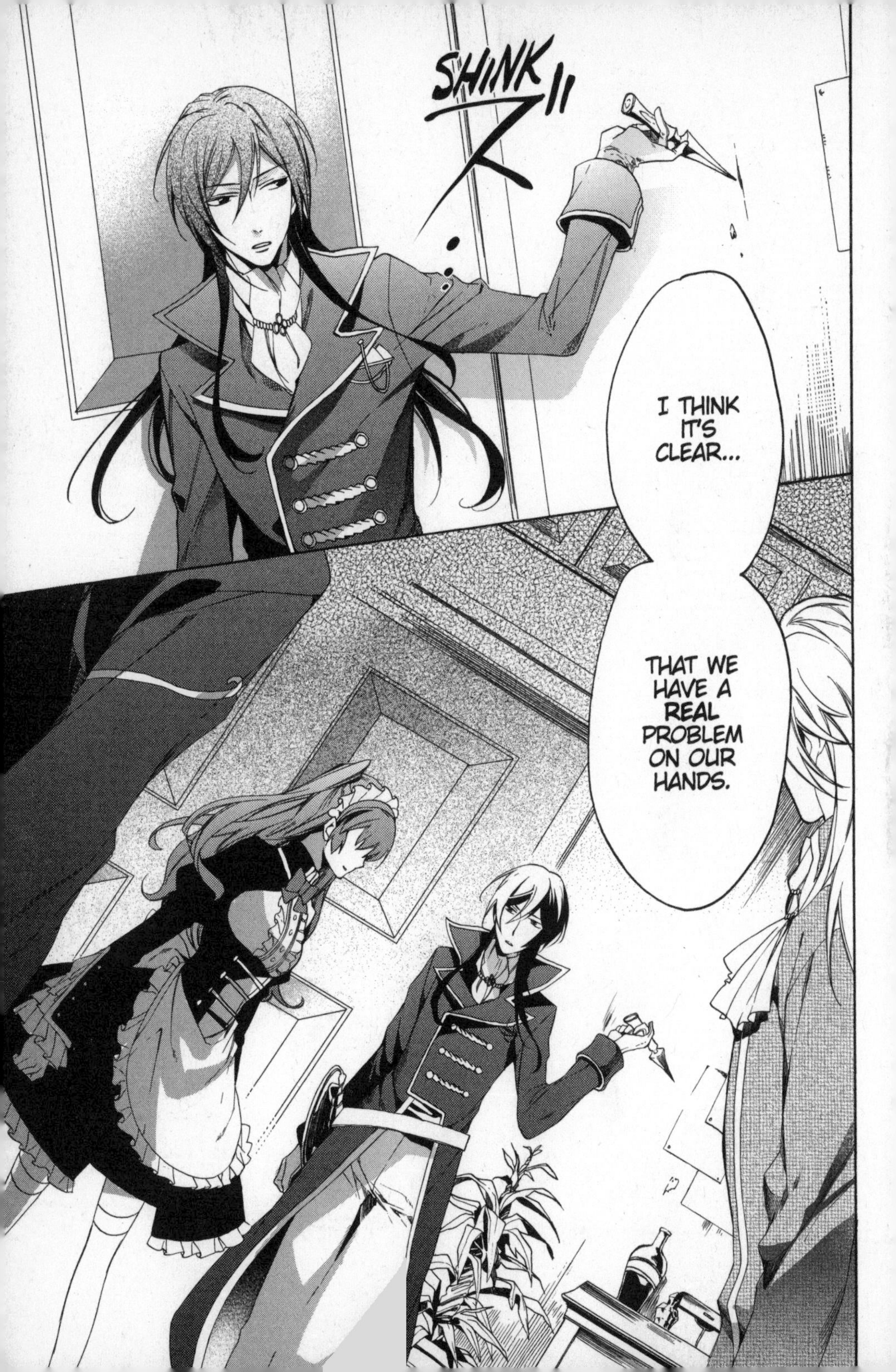
SHIINK
I THINK IT'S CLEAR...
THAT WE HAVE A REAL PROBLEM ON OUR HANDS.

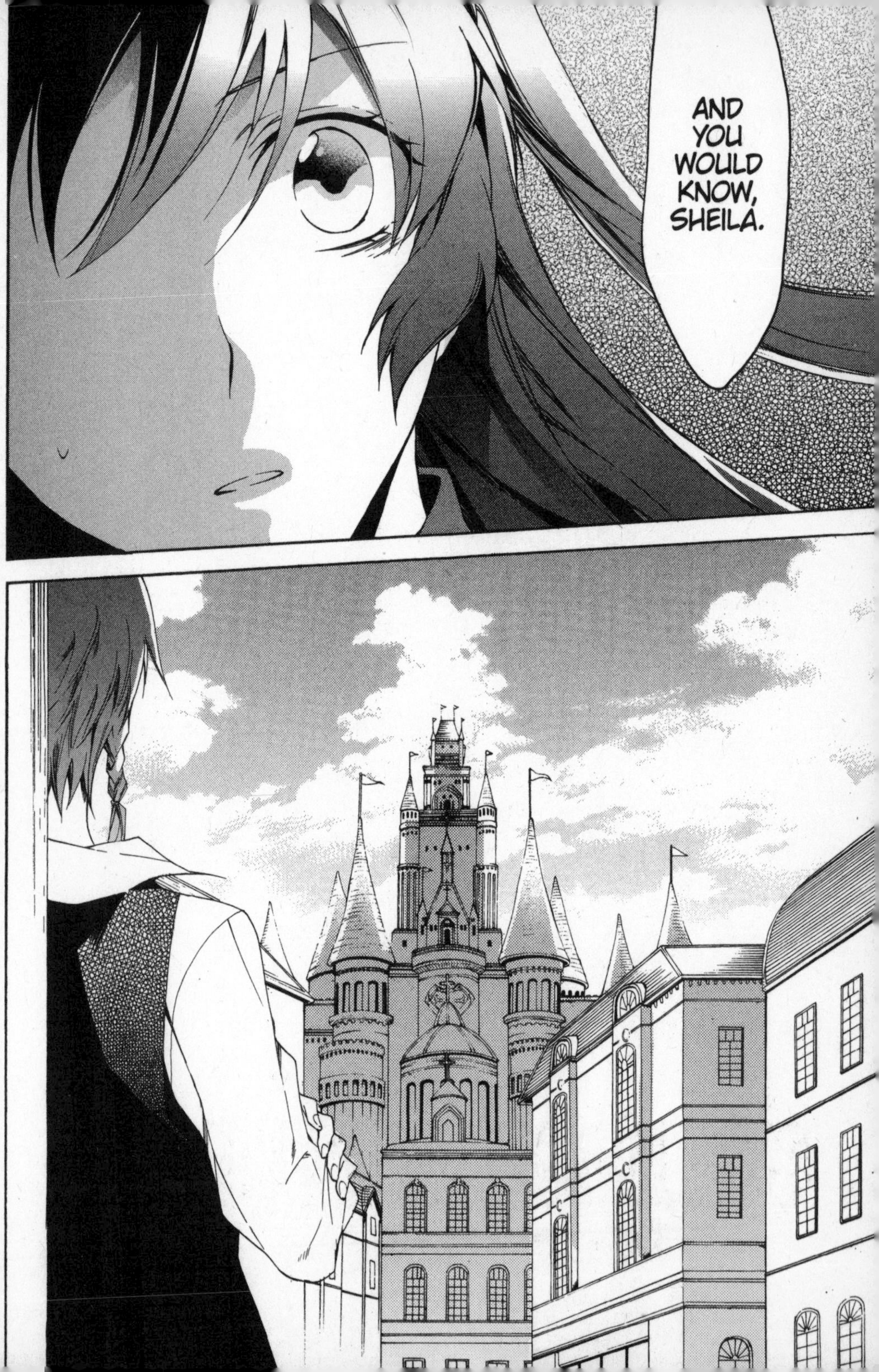
AND YOU WOULD KNOW, SHEILA.

CRIMSON EMPIRE

Circumstances to serve a noble

I DID SOME RECONNAISSANCE IN TOWN.
#11
FLAP
YOU HAVE A VERY DANGEROUS FRIEND, SHEILA.
COULD HE BE CONNECTED TO THE HARASSMENT WE'RE SEEING IN THE CASTLE?
......!

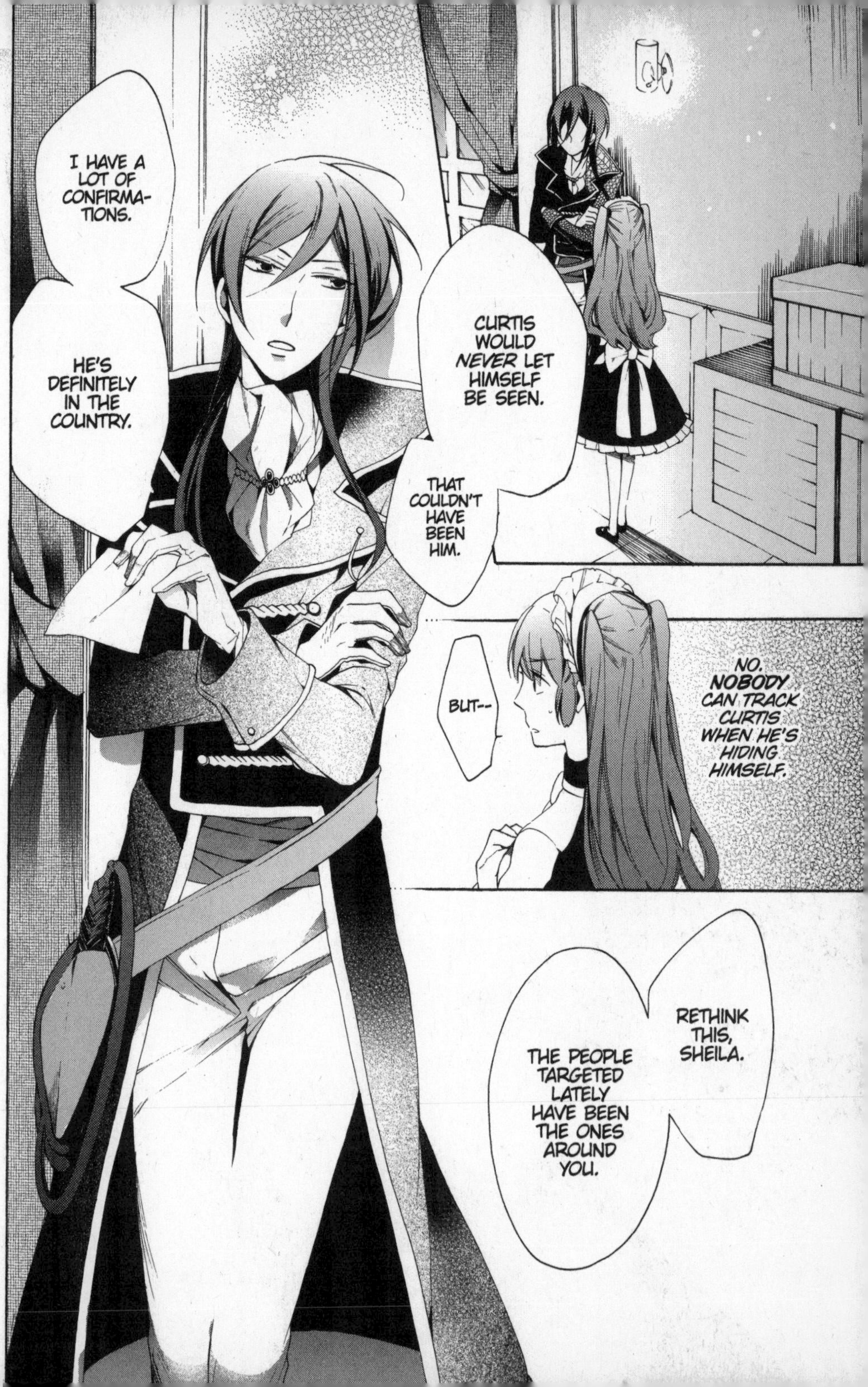
CURTIS WOULD NEVER LET HIMSELF BE SEEN.
THAT COULDN'T HAVE BEEN HIM.
NO. NOBODY CAN TRACK CURTIS WHEN HE'S HIDING HIMSELF.
BUT--
I HAVE A LOT OF CONFIRMATIONS.
HE'S DEFINITELY IN THE COUNTRY.
RETHINK THIS, SHEILA.
THE PEOPLE TARGETED LATELY HAVE BEEN THE ONES AROUND YOU.

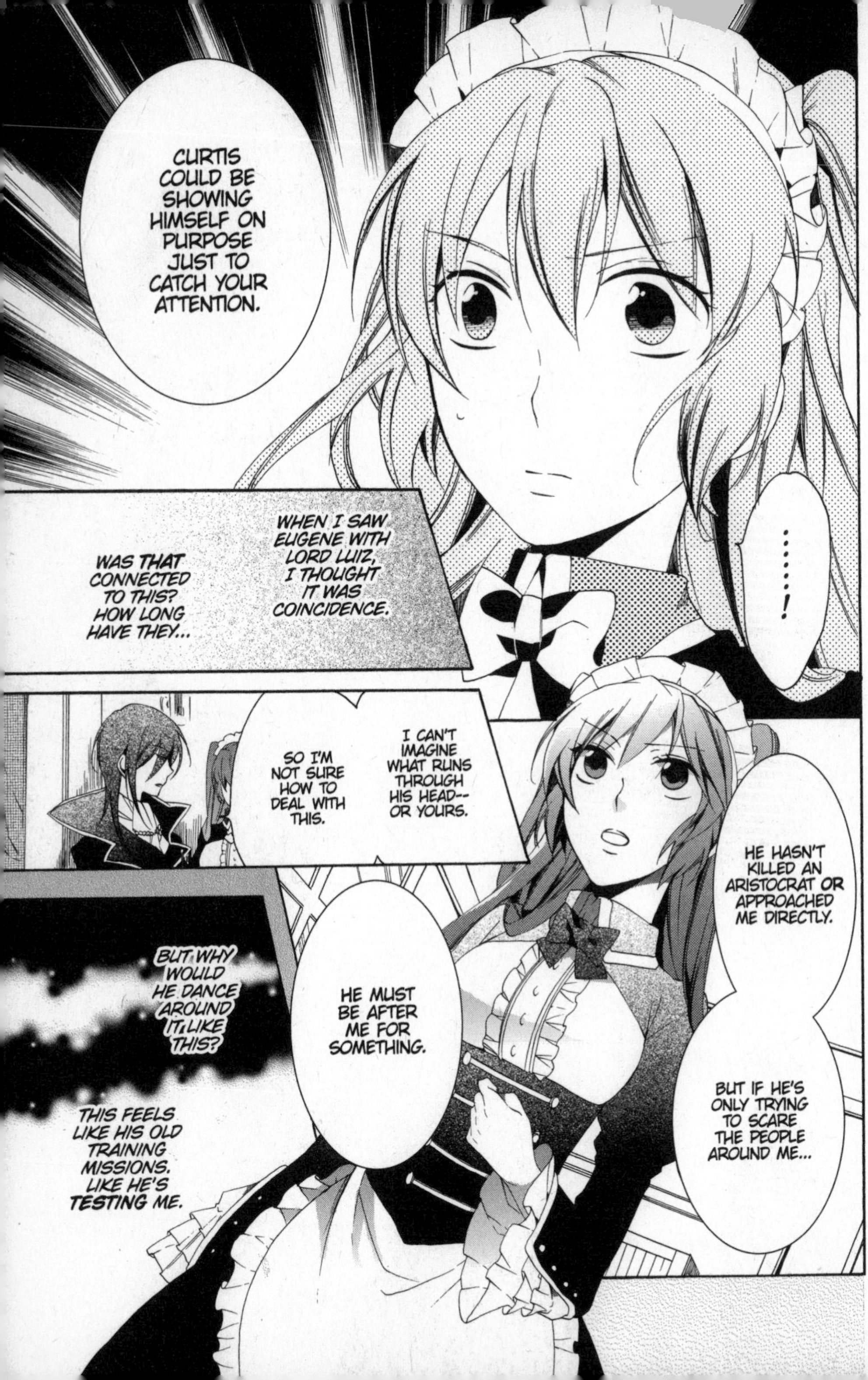
CURTIS COULD BE SHOWING HIMSELF ON PURPOSE JUST TO CATCH YOUR ATTENTION.
......!
WHEN I SAW EUGENE WITH LORD LUIZ, I THOUGHT IT WAS COINCIDENCE.
WAS THAT CONNECTED TO THIS? HOW LONG HAVE THEY...
HE HASN'T KILLED AN ARISTOCRAT OR APPROACHED ME DIRECTLY.
BUT IF HE'S ONLY TRYING TO SCARE THE PEOPLE AROUND ME...
HE MUST BE AFTER ME FOR SOMETHING.
I CAN'T IMAGINE WHAT RUNS THROUGH HIS HEAD--OR YOURS.
SO I'M NOT SURE HOW TO DEAL WITH THIS.
BUT WHY WOULD HE DANCE AROUND IT LIKE THIS?
THIS FEELS LIKE HIS OLD TRAINING MISSIONS. LIKE HE'S TESTING ME.

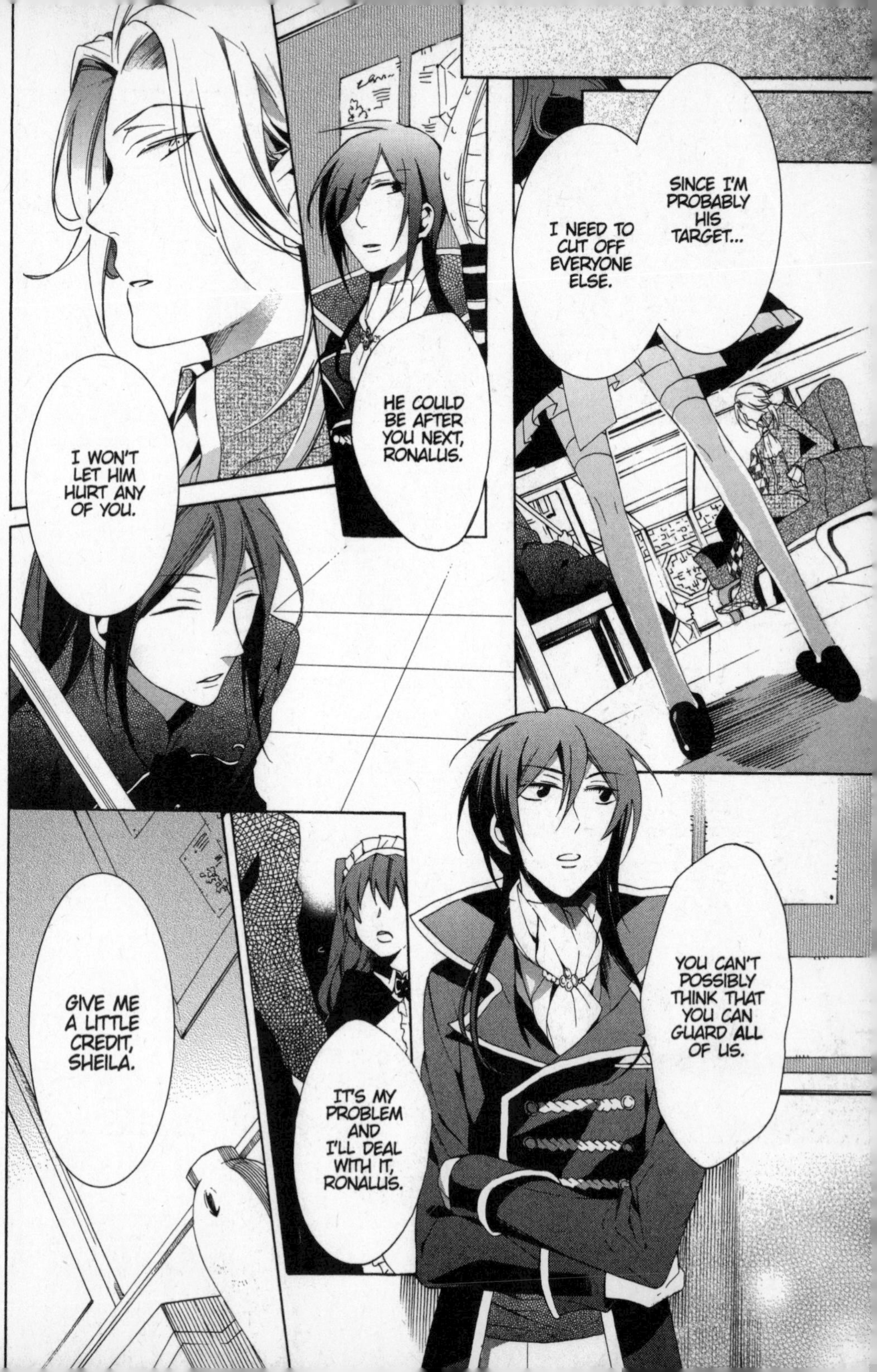

SINCE I'M PROBABLY HIS TARGET...
I NEED TO CUT OFF EVERYONE ELSE.
HE COULD BE AFTER YOU NEXT, RONALUS.
I WON'T LET HIM HURT ANY OF YOU.
YOU CAN'T POSSIBLY THINK THAT YOU CAN GUARD ALL OF US.
IT'S MY PROBLEM AND I'LL DEAL WITH IT, RONALUS.
GIVE ME A LITTLE CREDIT, SHEILA.

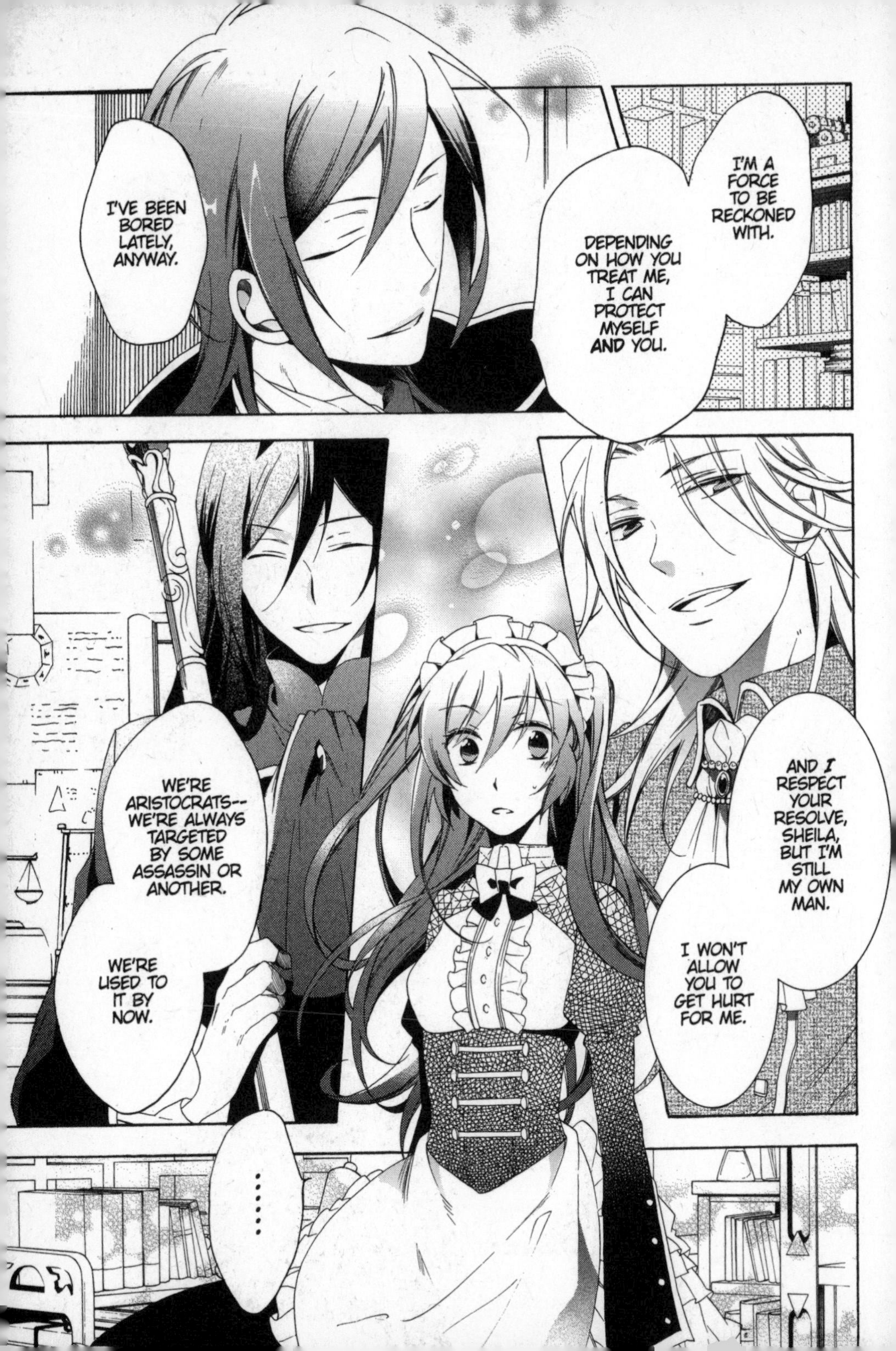
I'M A FORCE TO BE RECKONED WITH.
DEPENDING ON HOW YOU TREAT ME, I CAN PROTECT MYSELF AND YOU.
I'VE BEEN BORED LATELY, ANYWAY.
AND I RESPECT YOUR RESOLVE, SHEILA, BUT I'M STILL MY OWN MAN.
I WON'T ALLOW YOU TO GET HURT FOR ME.
WE'RE ARISTOCRATS--WE'RE ALWAYS TARGETED BY SOME ASSASSIN OR ANOTHER.
WE'RE USED TO IT BY NOW.
......

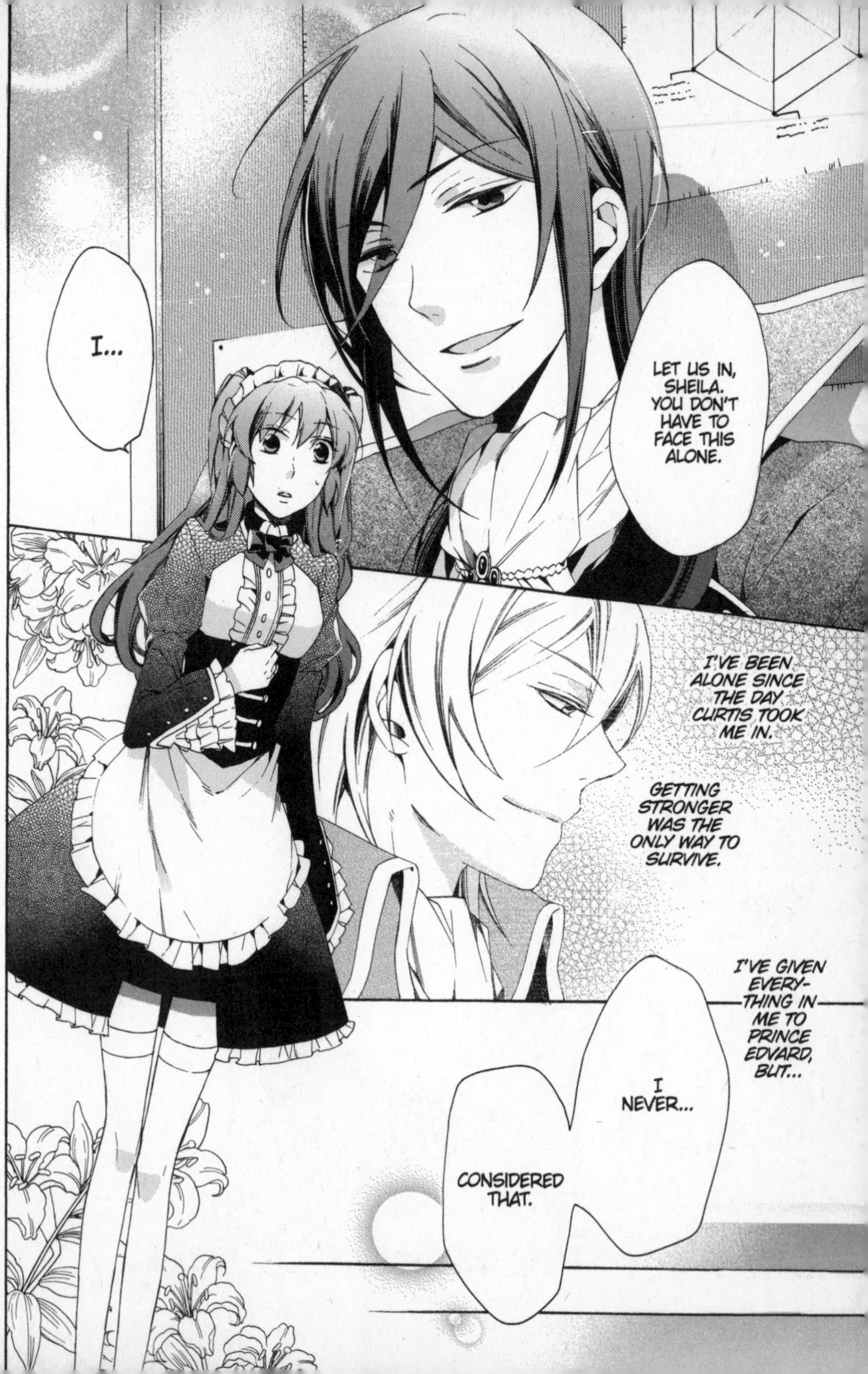
LET US IN, SHEILA. YOU DON'T HAVE TO FACE THIS ALONE.
I...
I'VE BEEN ALONE SINCE THE DAY CURTIS TOOK ME IN.
GETTING STRONGER WAS THE ONLY WAY TO SURVIVE.
I'VE GIVEN EVERY-THING IN ME TO PRINCE EDVARD, BUT...
I NEVER...
CONSIDERED THAT.

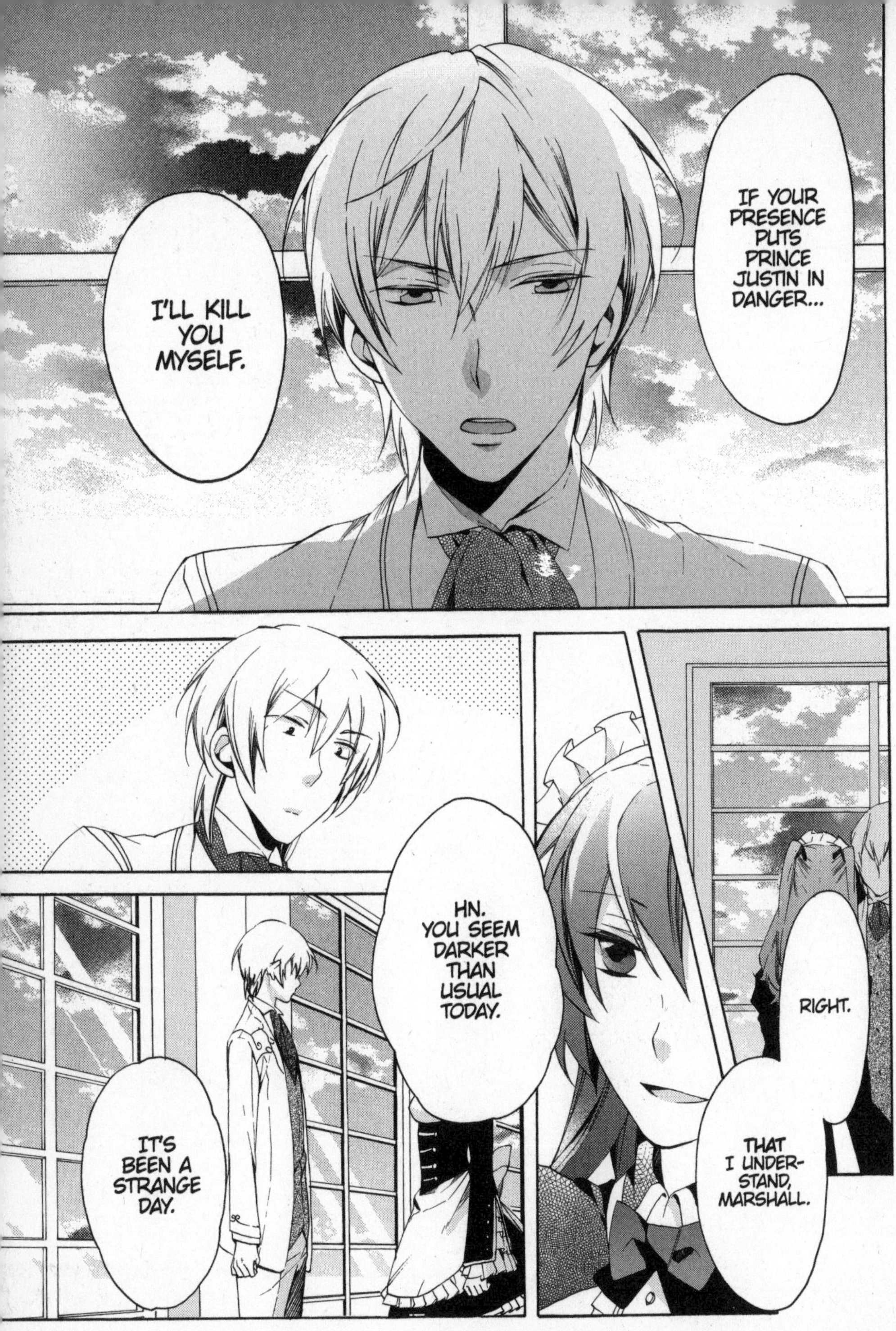
IF YOUR PRESENCE PUTS PRINCE JUSTIN IN DANGER...
I'LL KILL YOU MYSELF.
HN. YOU SEEM DARKER THAN USUAL TODAY.
IT'S BEEN A STRANGE DAY.
RIGHT.
THAT I UNDER-STAND, MARSHALL.

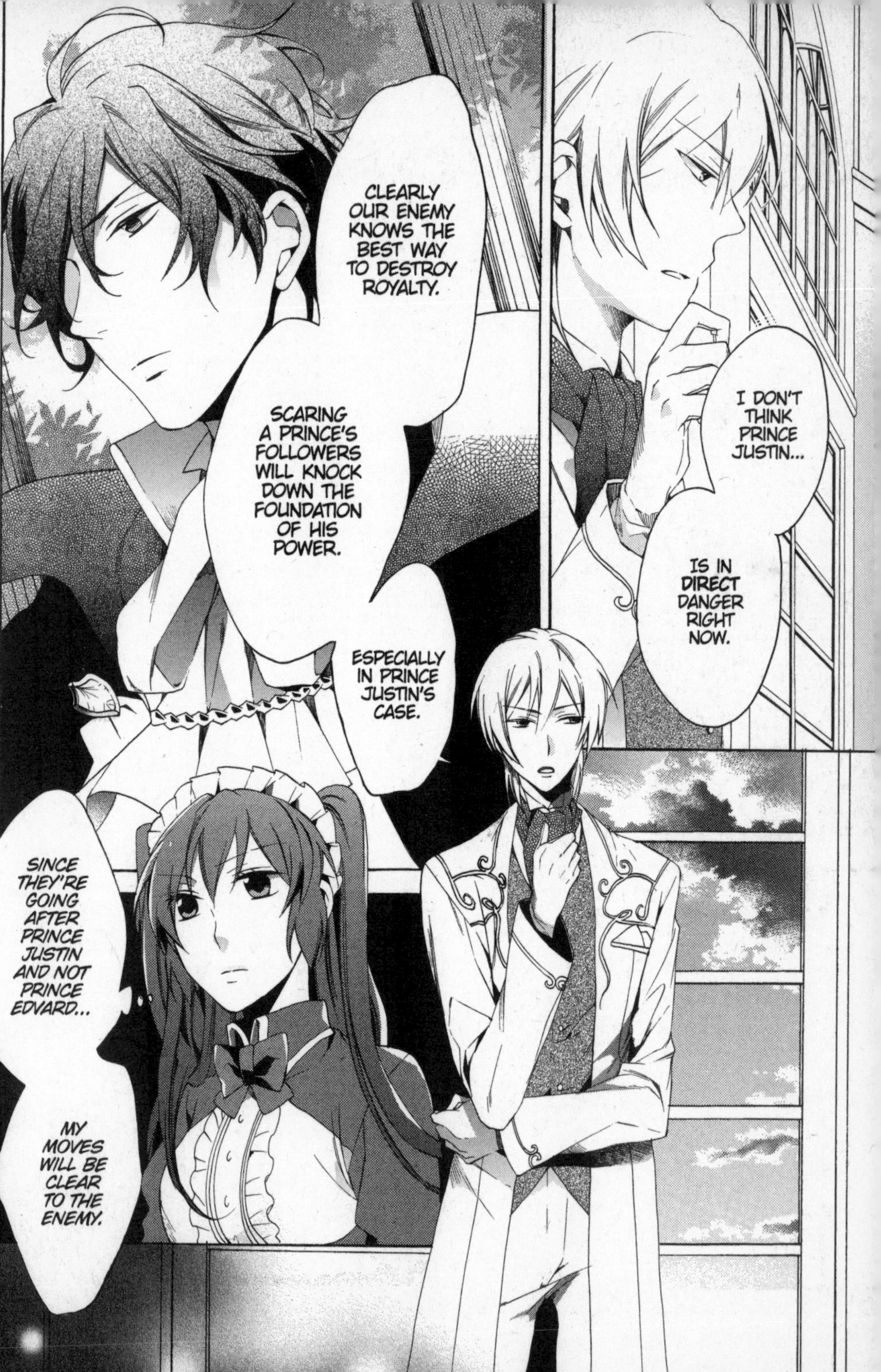
I DON'T THINK PRINCE JUSTIN...
IS IN DIRECT DANGER RIGHT NOW.
CLEARLY OUR ENEMY KNOWS THE BEST WAY TO DESTROY ROYALTY.
SCARING A PRINCE'S FOLLOWERS WILL KNOCK DOWN THE FOUNDATION OF HIS POWER.
ESPECIALLY IN PRINCE JUSTIN'S CASE.
SINCE THEY'RE GOING AFTER PRINCE JUSTIN AND NOT PRINCE EDVARD...
MY MOVES WILL BE CLEAR TO THE ENEMY.

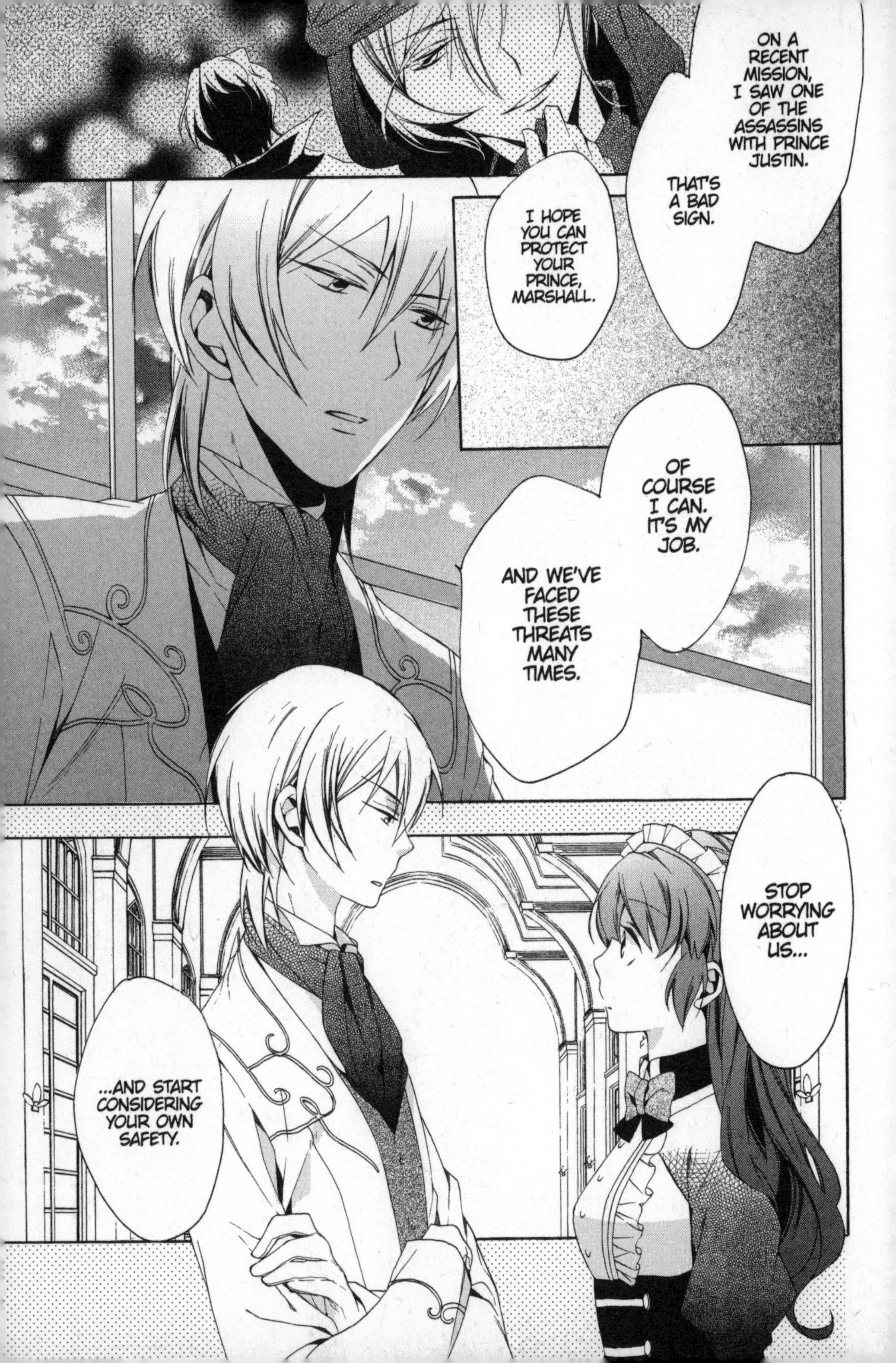
ON A RECENT MISSION, I SAW ONE OF THE ASSASSINS WITH PRINCE JUSTIN.
THAT'S A BAD SIGN.
I HOPE YOU CAN PROTECT YOUR PRINCE, MARSHALL.
OF COURSE I CAN. IT'S MY JOB.
AND WE'VE FACED THESE THREATS MANY TIMES.
STOP WORRYING ABOUT US...
...AND START CONSIDERING YOUR OWN SAFETY.

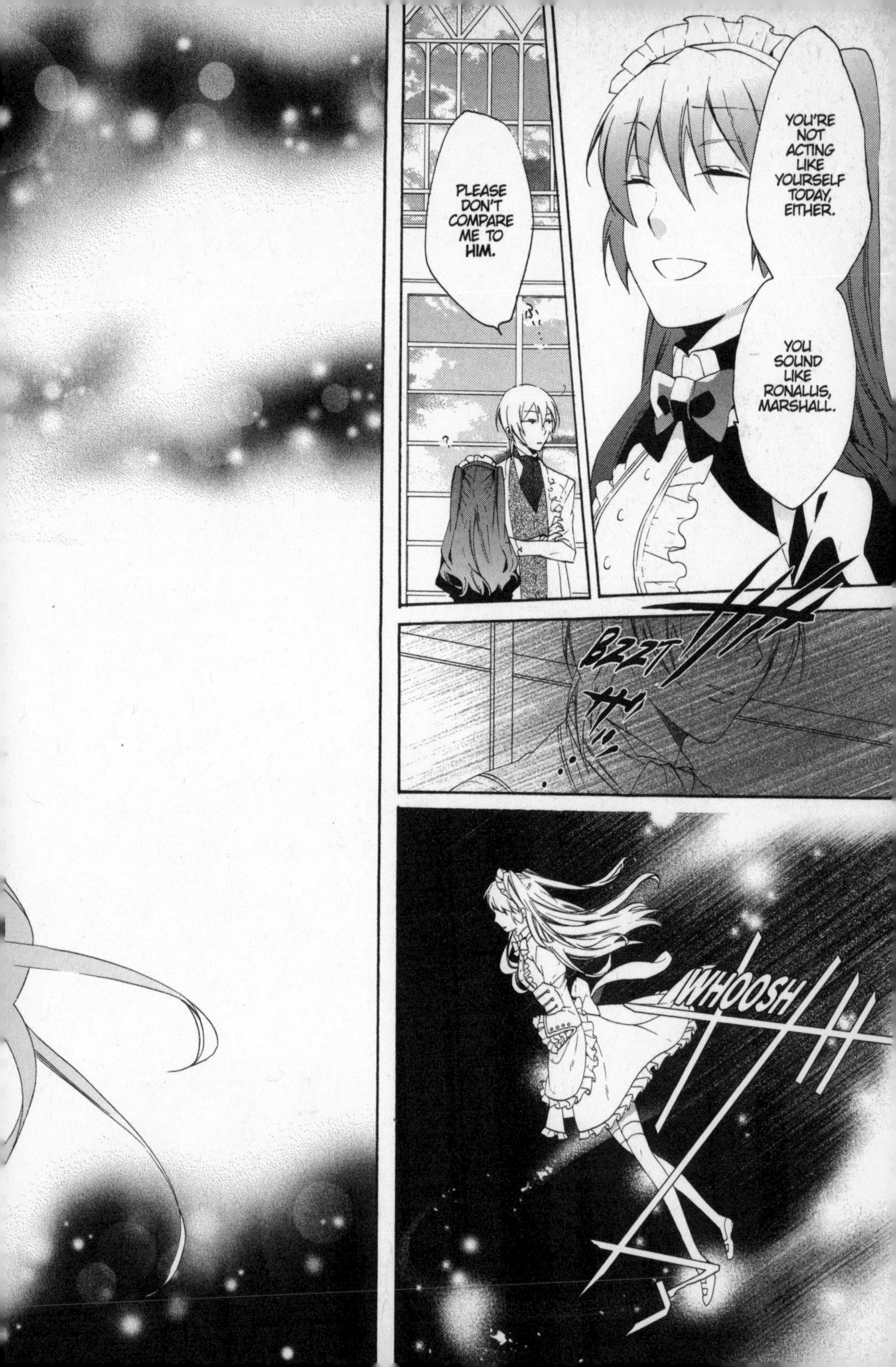
YOU'RE NOT ACTING LIKE YOURSELF TODAY, EITHER.
YOU SOUND LIKE RONALUS, MARSHALL.
PLEASE DON'T COMPARE ME TO HIM.
BZZT
WHOOSH

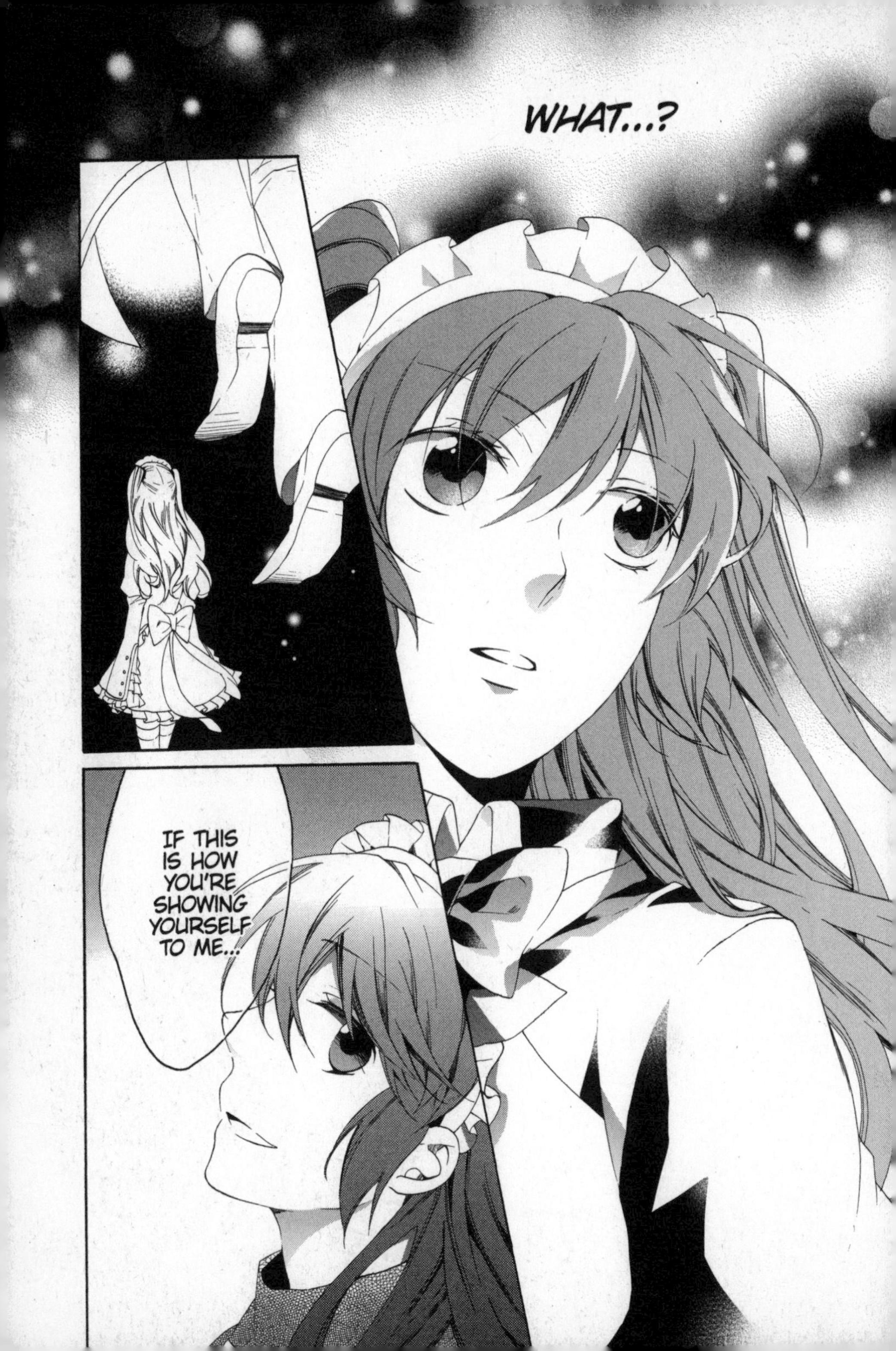
WHAT...?
IF THIS IS HOW YOU'RE SHOWING YOURSELF TO ME...

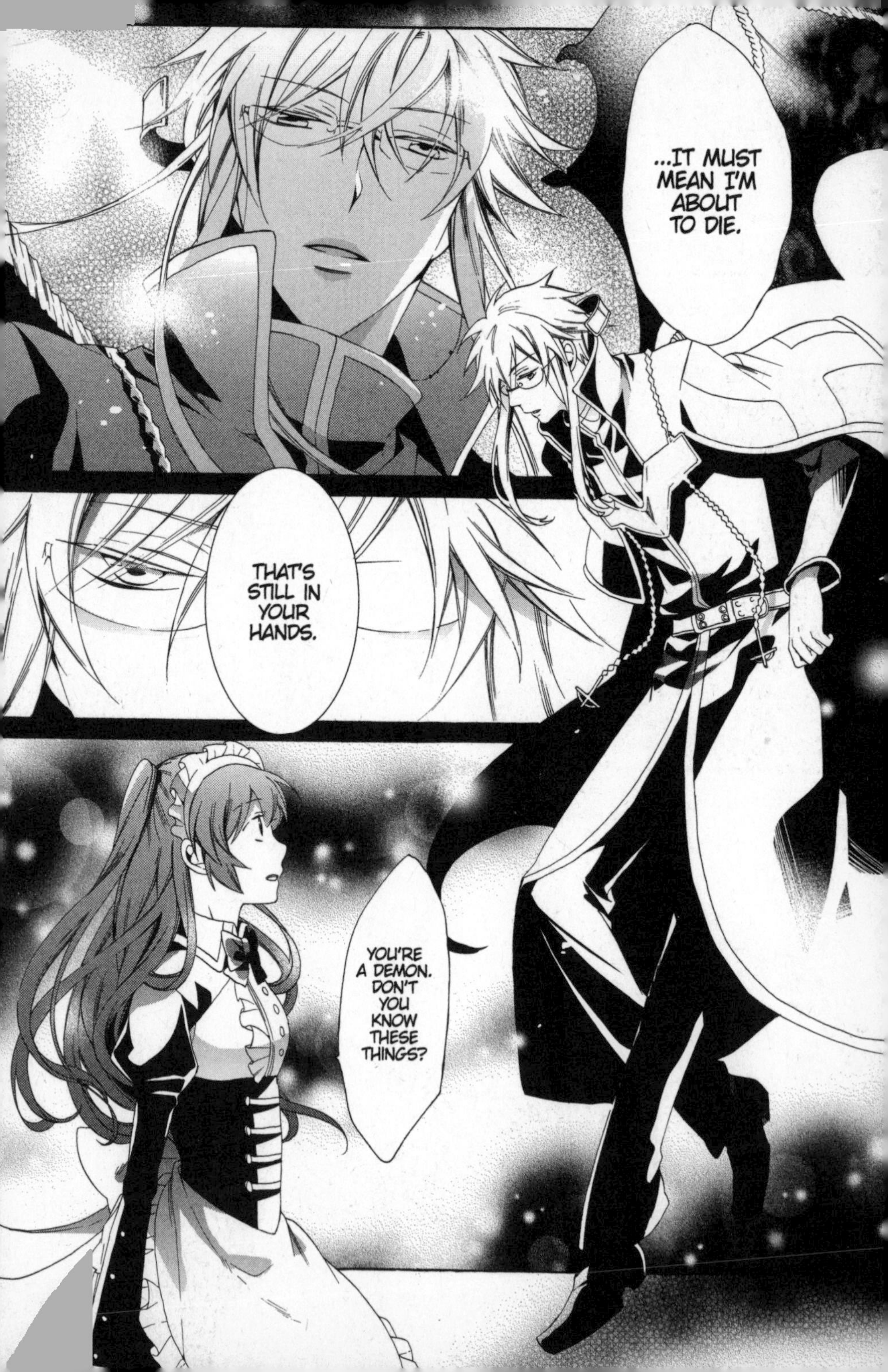
...IT MUST MEAN I'M ABOUT TO DIE.
THAT'S STILL IN YOUR HANDS.
YOU'RE A DEMON. DON'T YOU KNOW THESE THINGS?

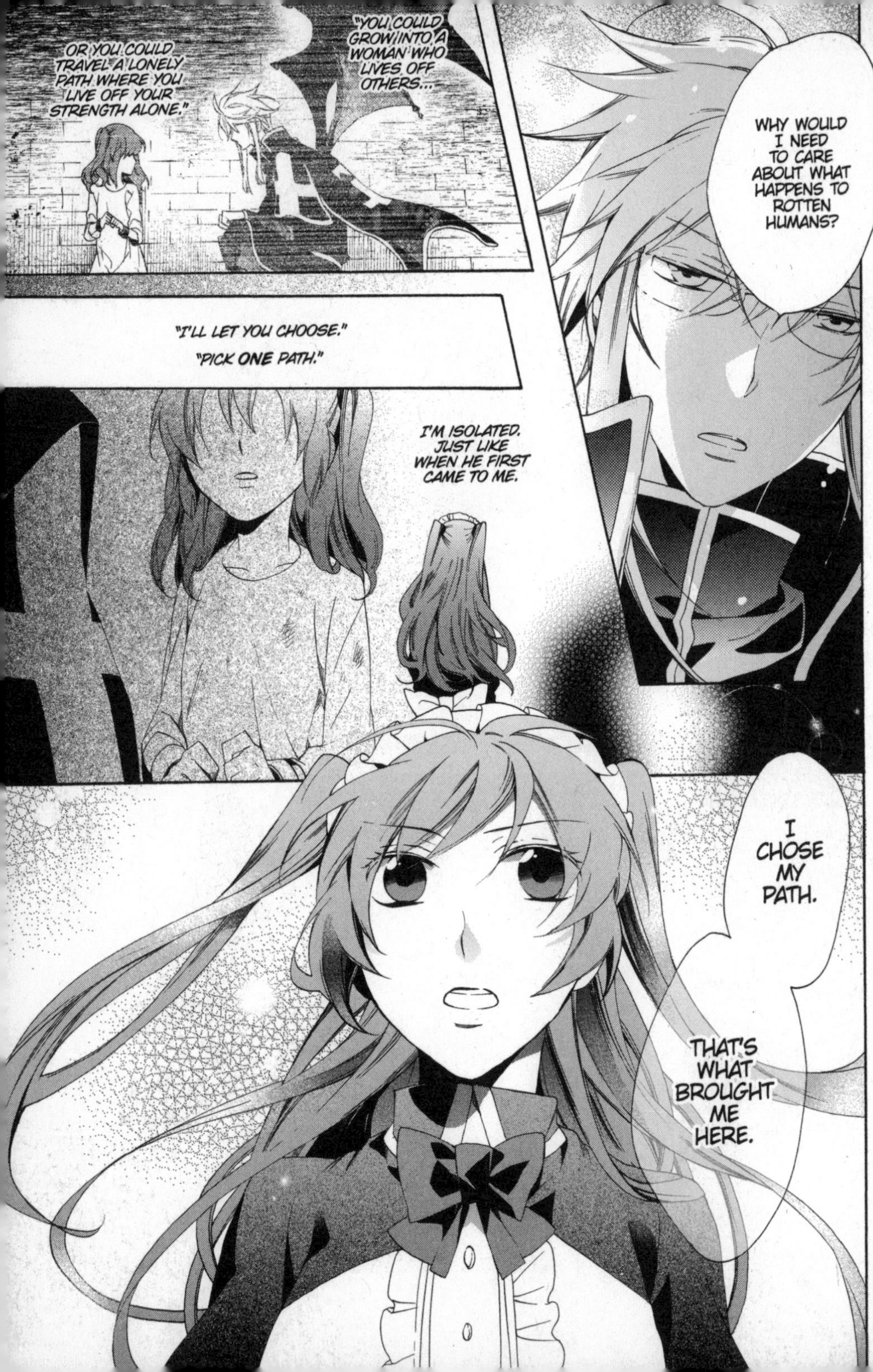
WHY WOULD I NEED TO CARE ABOUT WHAT HAPPENS TO ROTTEN HUMANS?
"YOU COULD GROW INTO A WOMAN WHO LIVES OFF OTHERS...
OR YOU COULD TRAVEL A LONELY PATH WHERE YOU LIVE OFF YOUR STRENGTH ALONE."
"I'LL LET YOU CHOOSE."
"PICK ONE PATH."
I'M ISOLATED. JUST LIKE WHEN HE FIRST CAME TO ME.
I CHOSE MY PATH.
THAT'S WHAT BROUGHT ME HERE.

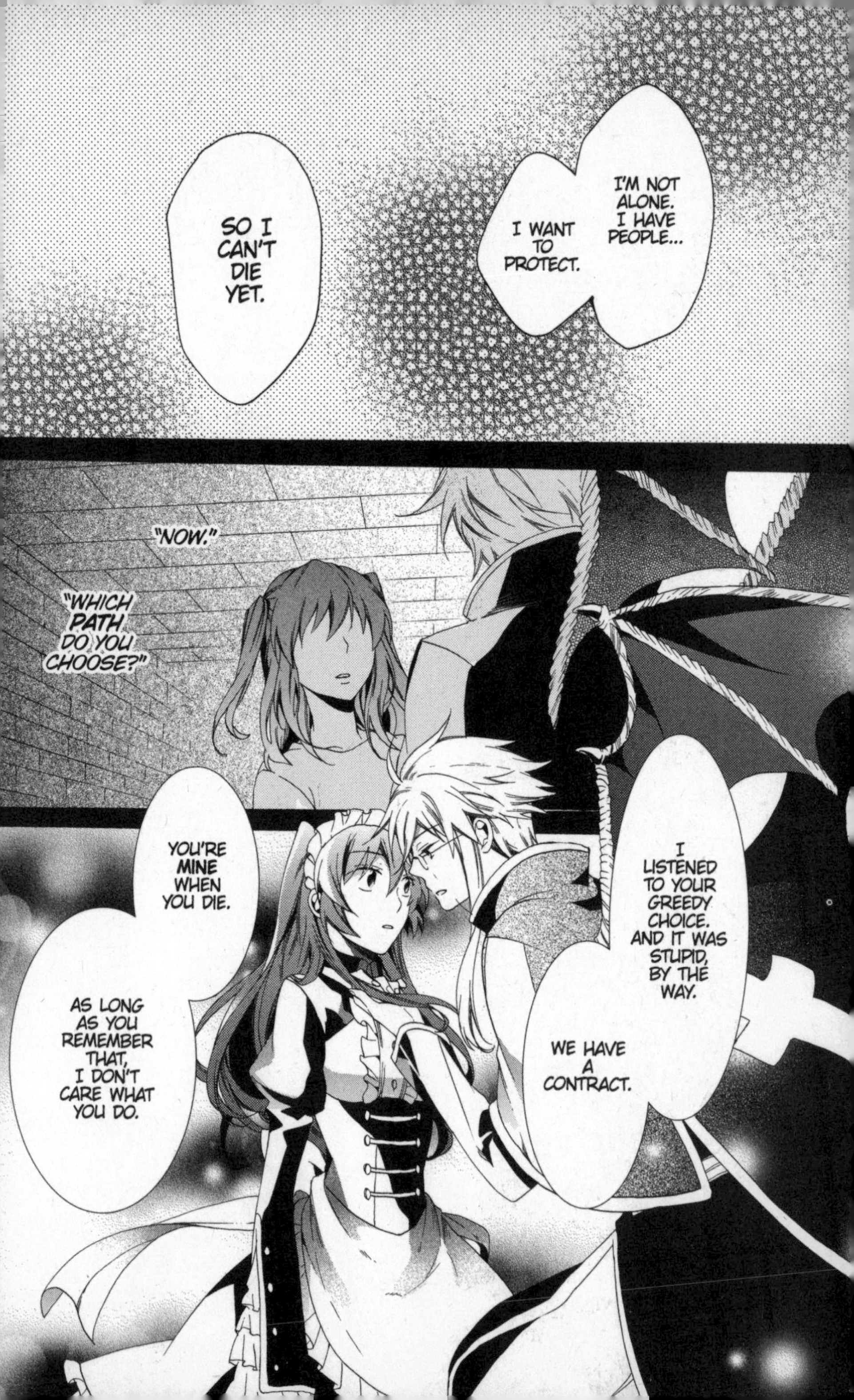
I'M NOT ALONE. I HAVE PEOPLE...
I WANT TO PROTECT.
SO I CAN'T DIE YET.
"NOW."
"WHICH PATH DO YOU CHOOSE?"
I LISTENED TO YOUR GREEDY CHOICE. AND IT WAS STUPID, BY THE WAY.
WE HAVE A CONTRACT.
YOU'RE MINE WHEN YOU DIE.
AS LONG AS YOU REMEMBER THAT, I DON'T CARE WHAT YOU DO.

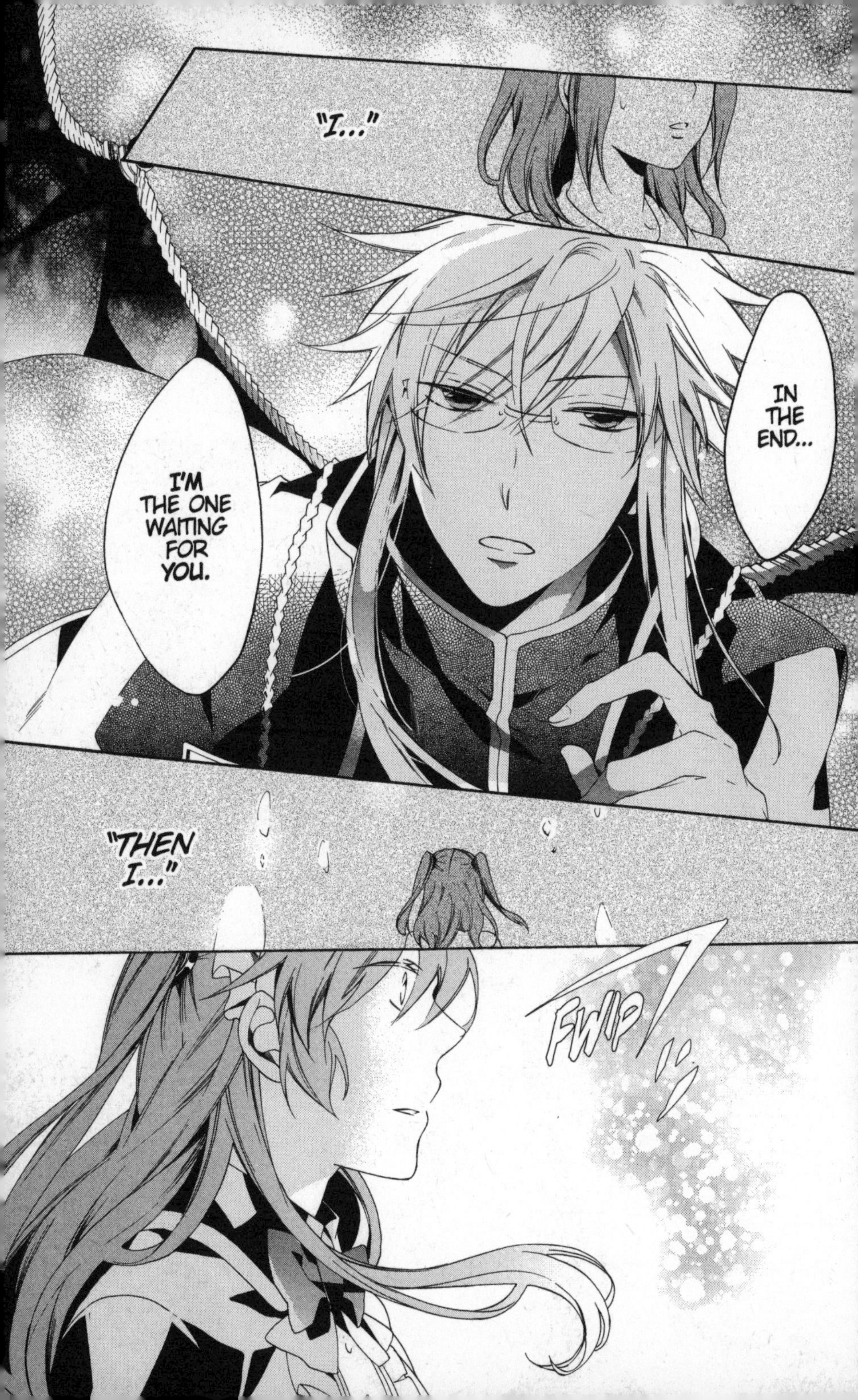
"I..."
IN THE END...
I'M THE ONE WAITING FOR YOU.
"THEN I..."
FWIP

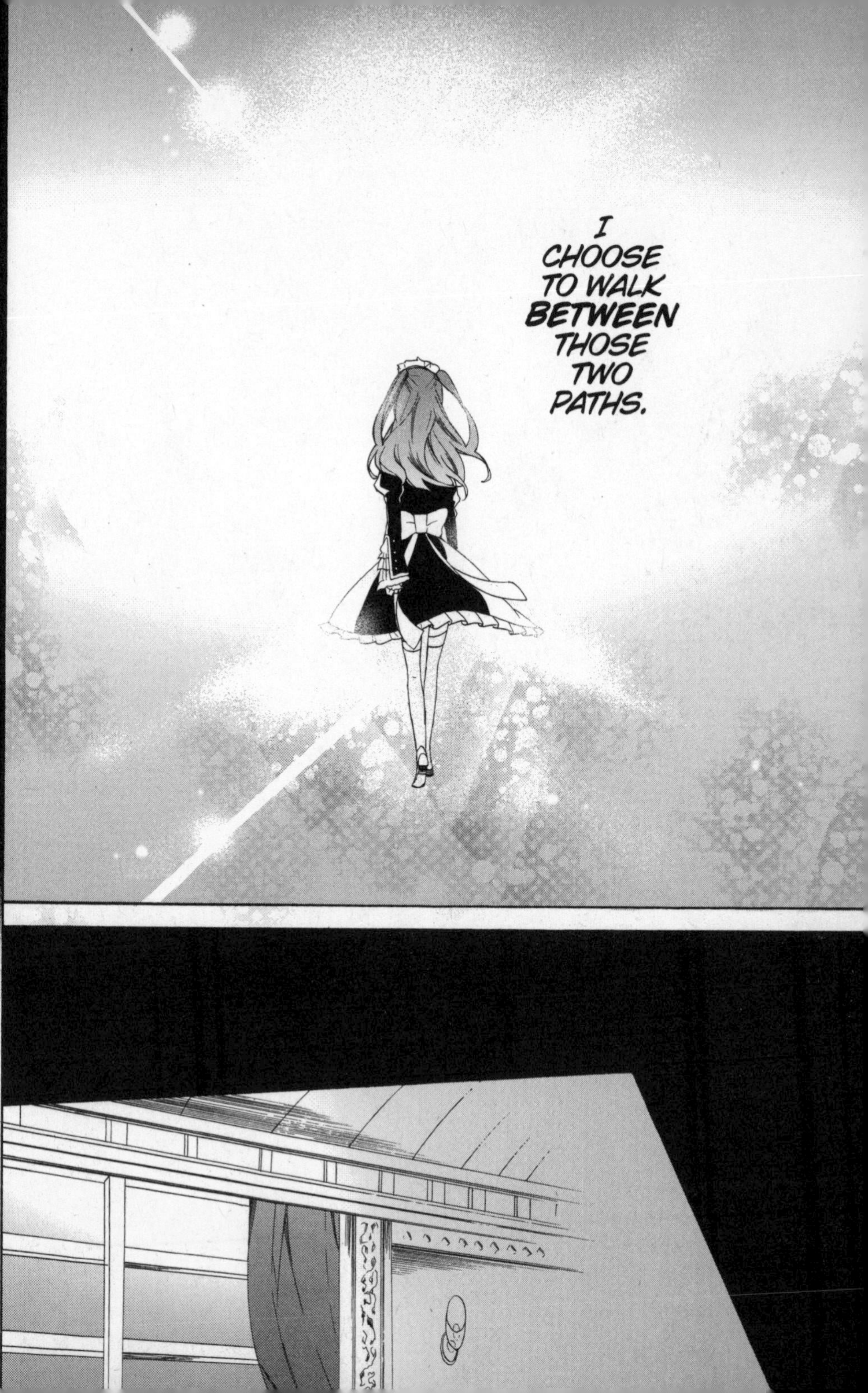
I CHOOSE TO WALK BETWEEN THOSE TWO PATHS.

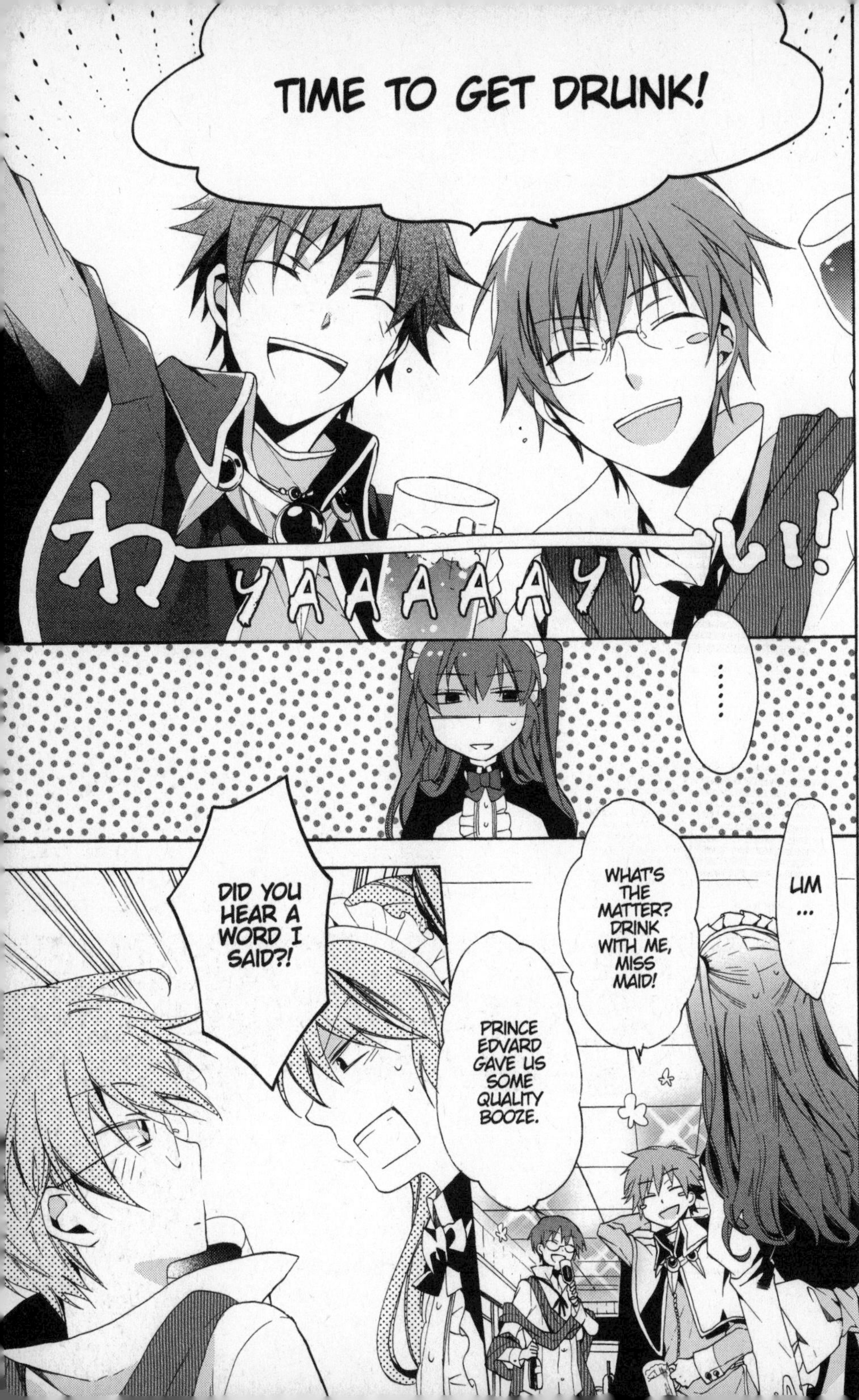
TIME TO GET DRUNK!
わ YAAAAAY! い!!
......
UM ...
WHAT'S THE MATTER? DRINK WITH ME, MISS MAID!
PRINCE EDVARD GAVE US SOME QUALITY BOOZE.
DID YOU HEAR A WORD I SAID?!

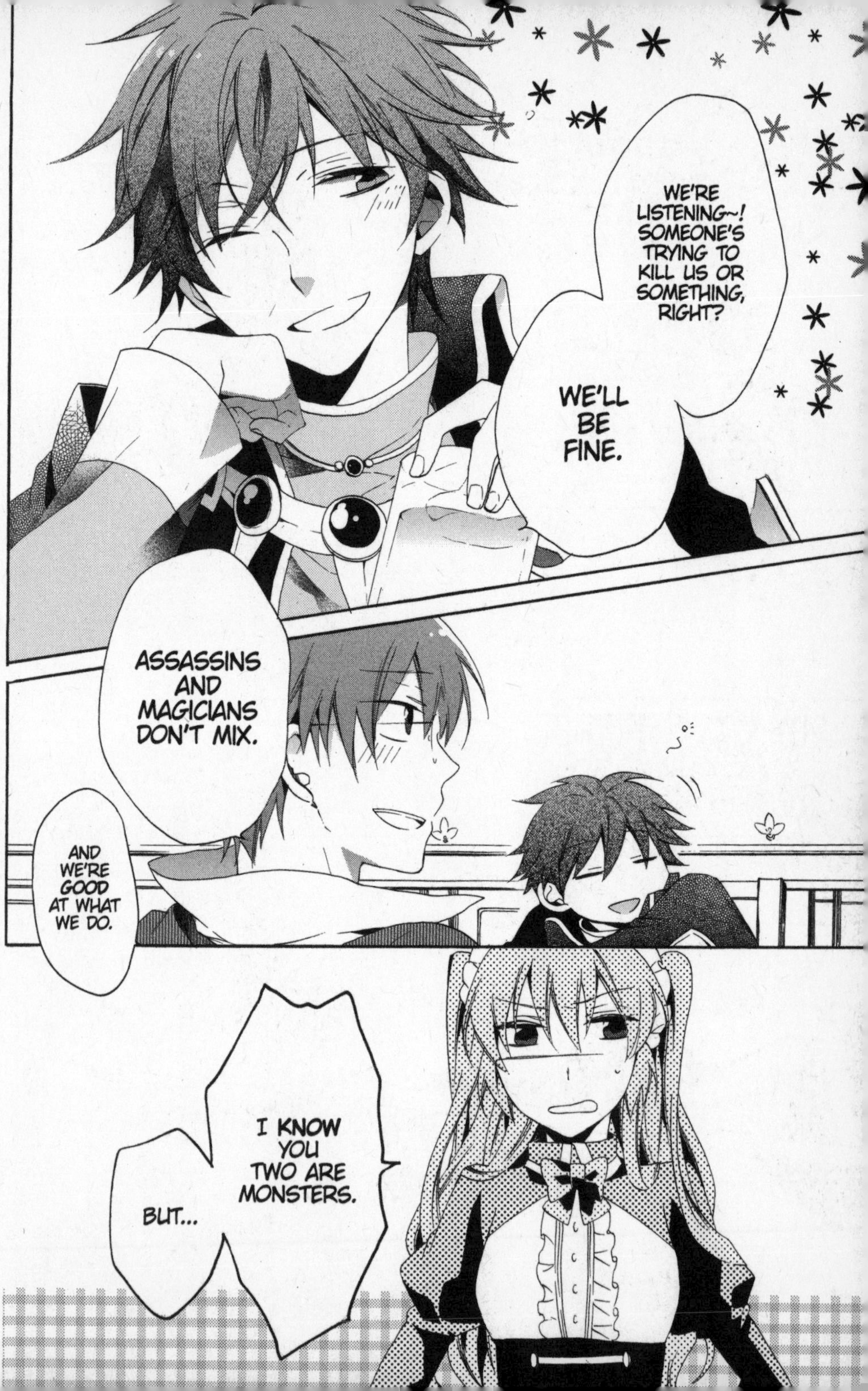
WE'RE LISTENING~! SOMEONE'S TRYING TO KILL US OR SOMETHING, RIGHT?
WE'LL BE FINE.
ASSASSINS AND MAGICIANS DON'T MIX.
AND WE'RE GOOD AT WHAT WE DO.
I KNOW YOU TWO ARE MONSTERS.
BUT...

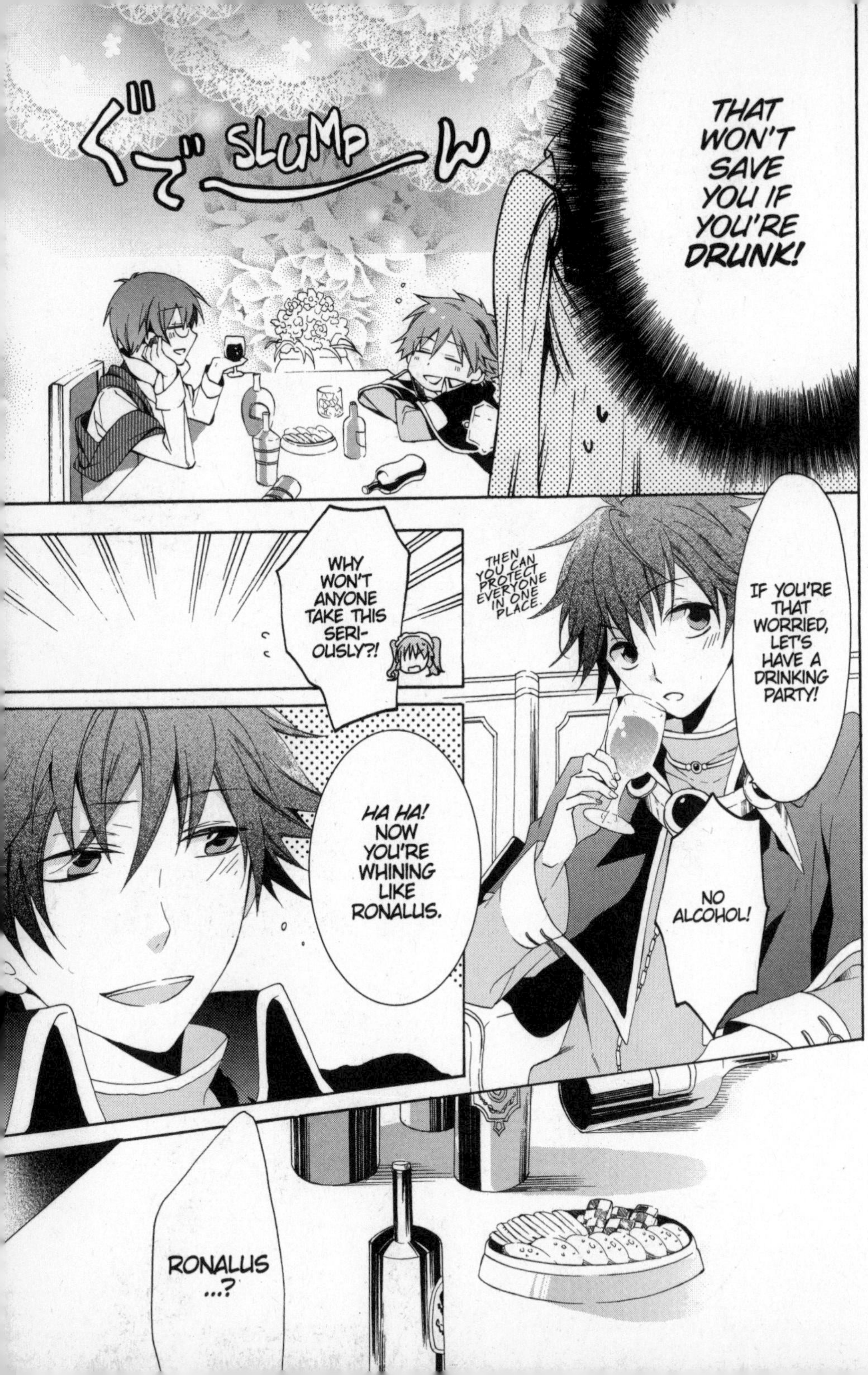
THAT WON'T SAVE YOU IF YOU'RE DRUNK!
ぐでーん
SLUMP
IF YOU'RE THAT WORRIED, LET'S HAVE A DRINKING PARTY!
THEN YOU CAN PROTECT EVERYONE IN ONE PLACE.
NO ALCOHOL!
WHY WON'T ANYONE TAKE THIS SERI-OUSLY?!
HA HA! NOW YOU'RE WHINING LIKE RONALUS.
RONALUS ...?

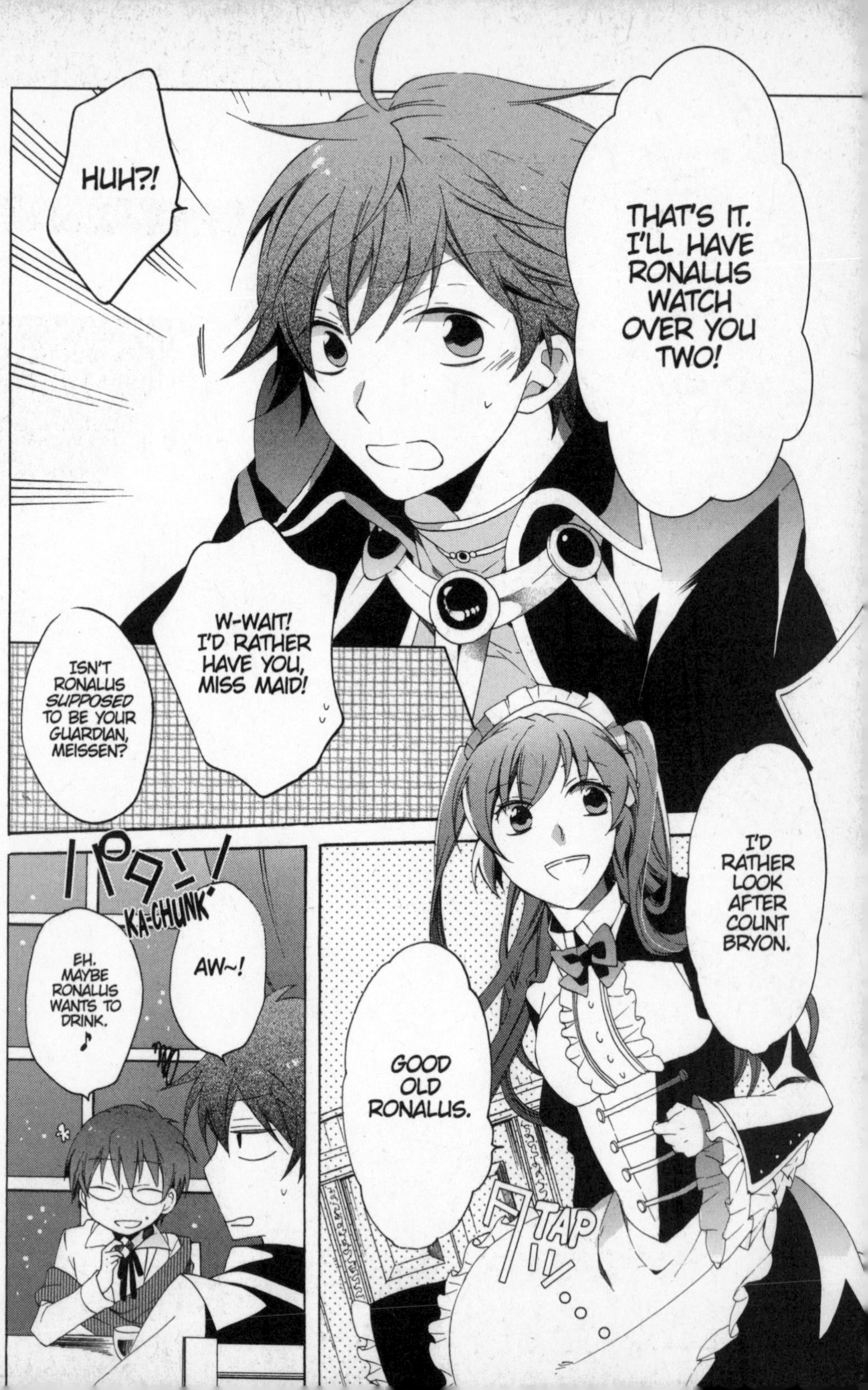
THAT'S IT. I'LL HAVE RONALUS WATCH OVER YOU TWO!
HUH?!
W-WAIT! I'D RATHER HAVE YOU, MISS MAID!
ISN'T RONALUS *SUPPOSED* TO BE YOUR GUARDIAN, MEISSEN?
I'D RATHER LOOK AFTER COUNT BRYON.
GOOD OLD RONALUS.
TAP
パタン!
KA-CHUNK
AW~!
EH. MAYBE RONALUS WANTS TO DRINK. ♪

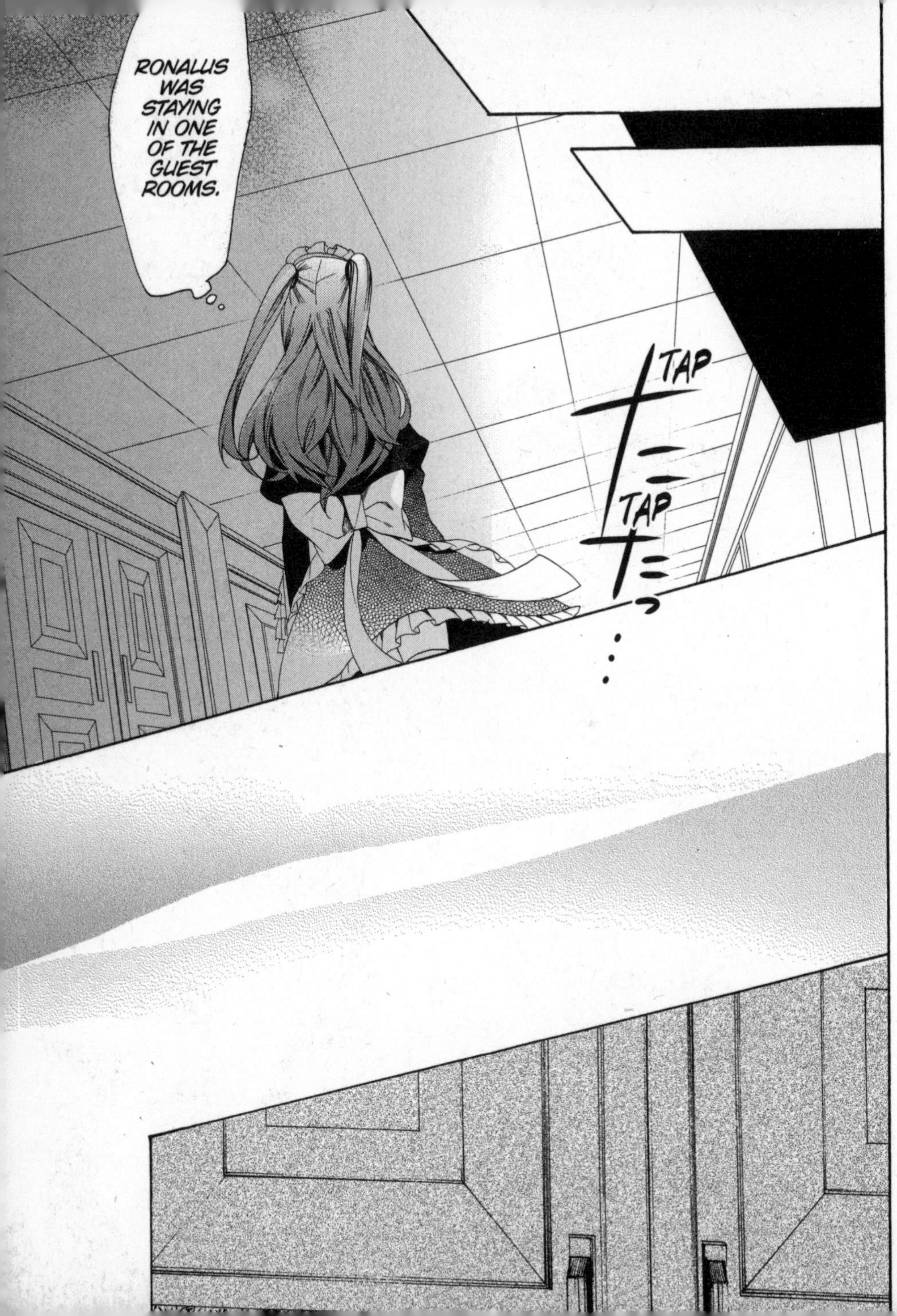
RONALUS WAS STAYING IN ONE OF THE GUEST ROOMS.
TAP
TAP

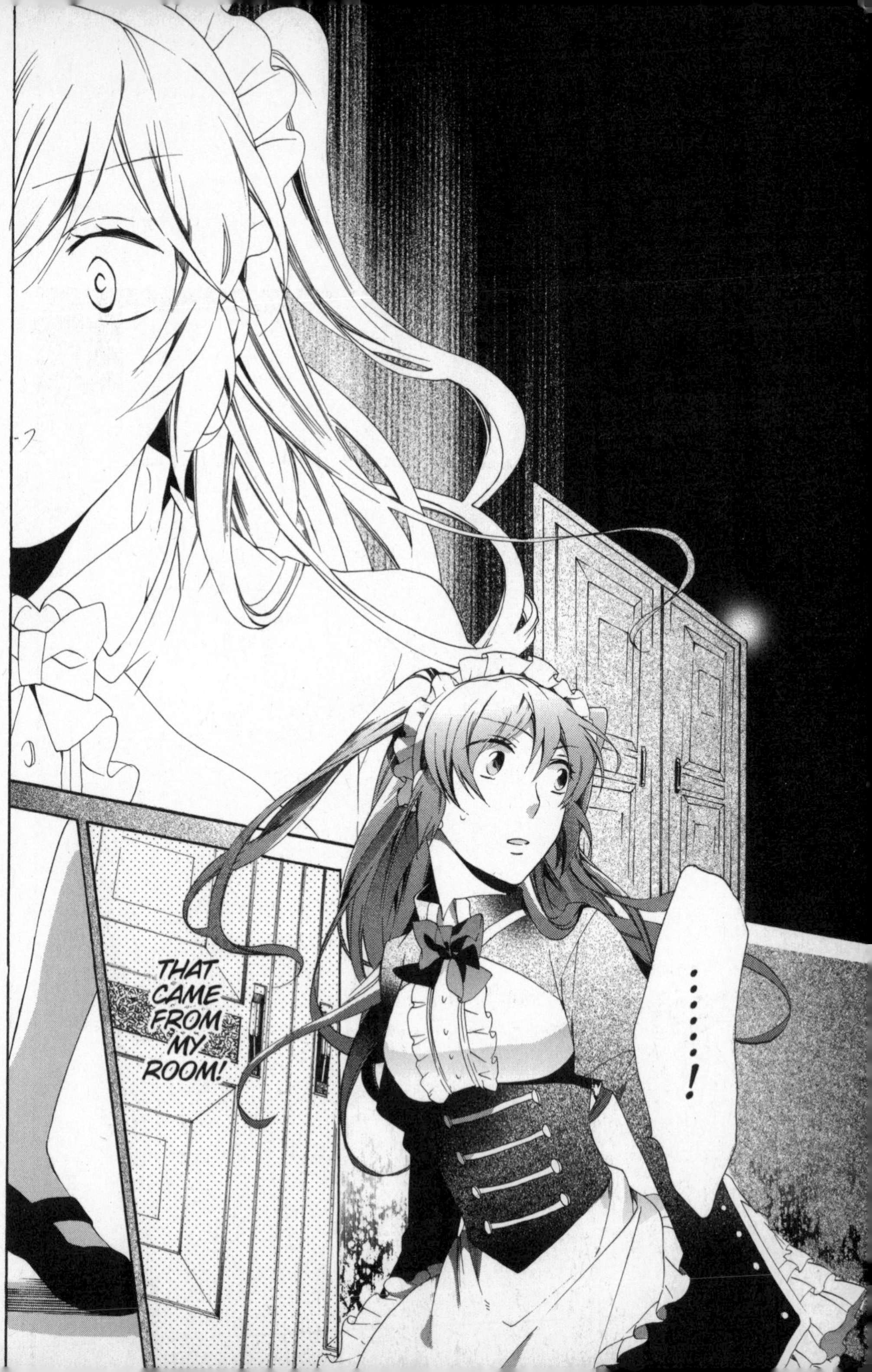
......!
THAT CAME FROM MY ROOM!

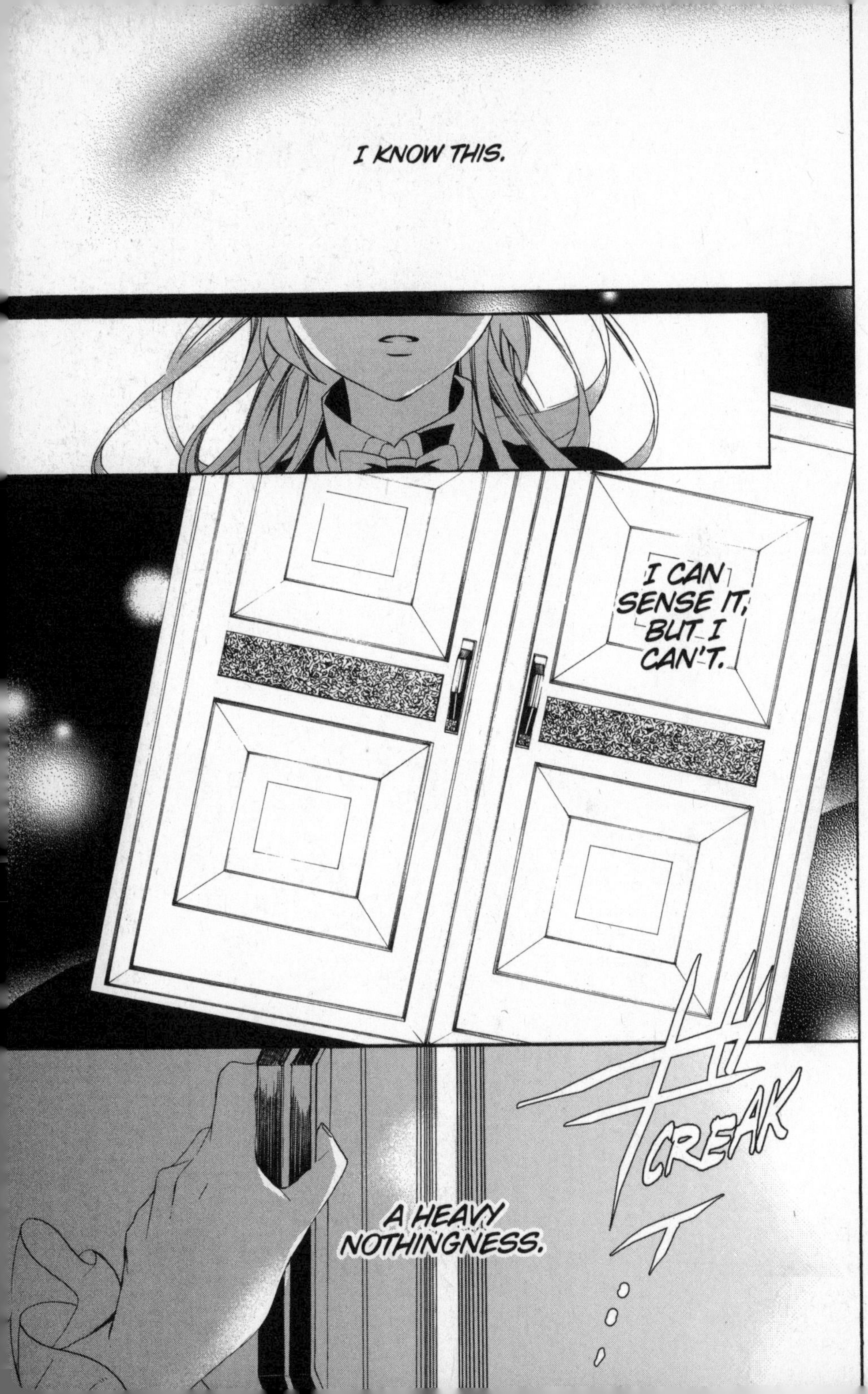
I KNOW THIS.
I CAN SENSE IT, BUT I CAN'T.
CREAK
A HEAVY NOTHINGNESS.

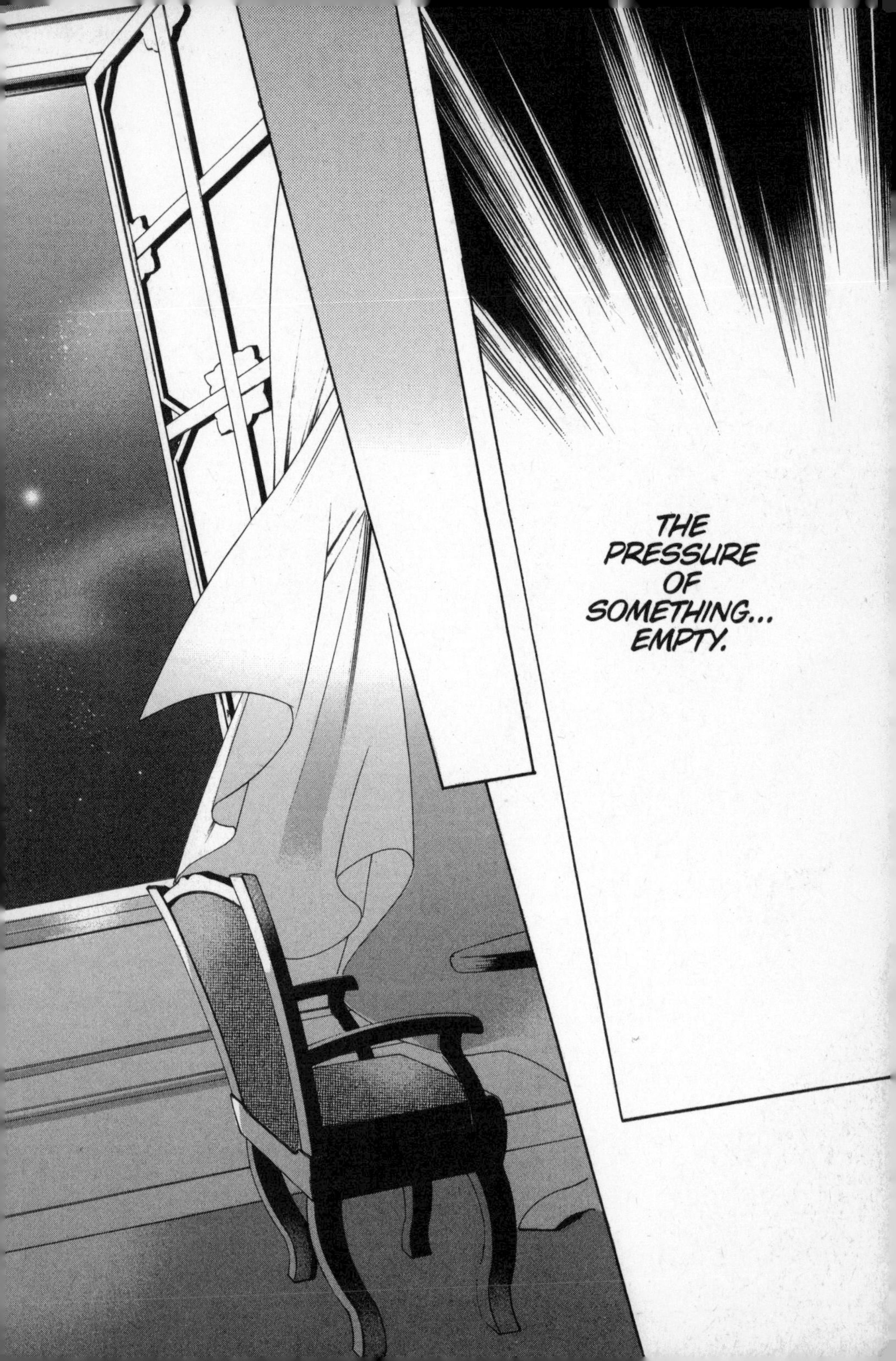
THE PRESSURE OF SOMETHING... EMPTY.

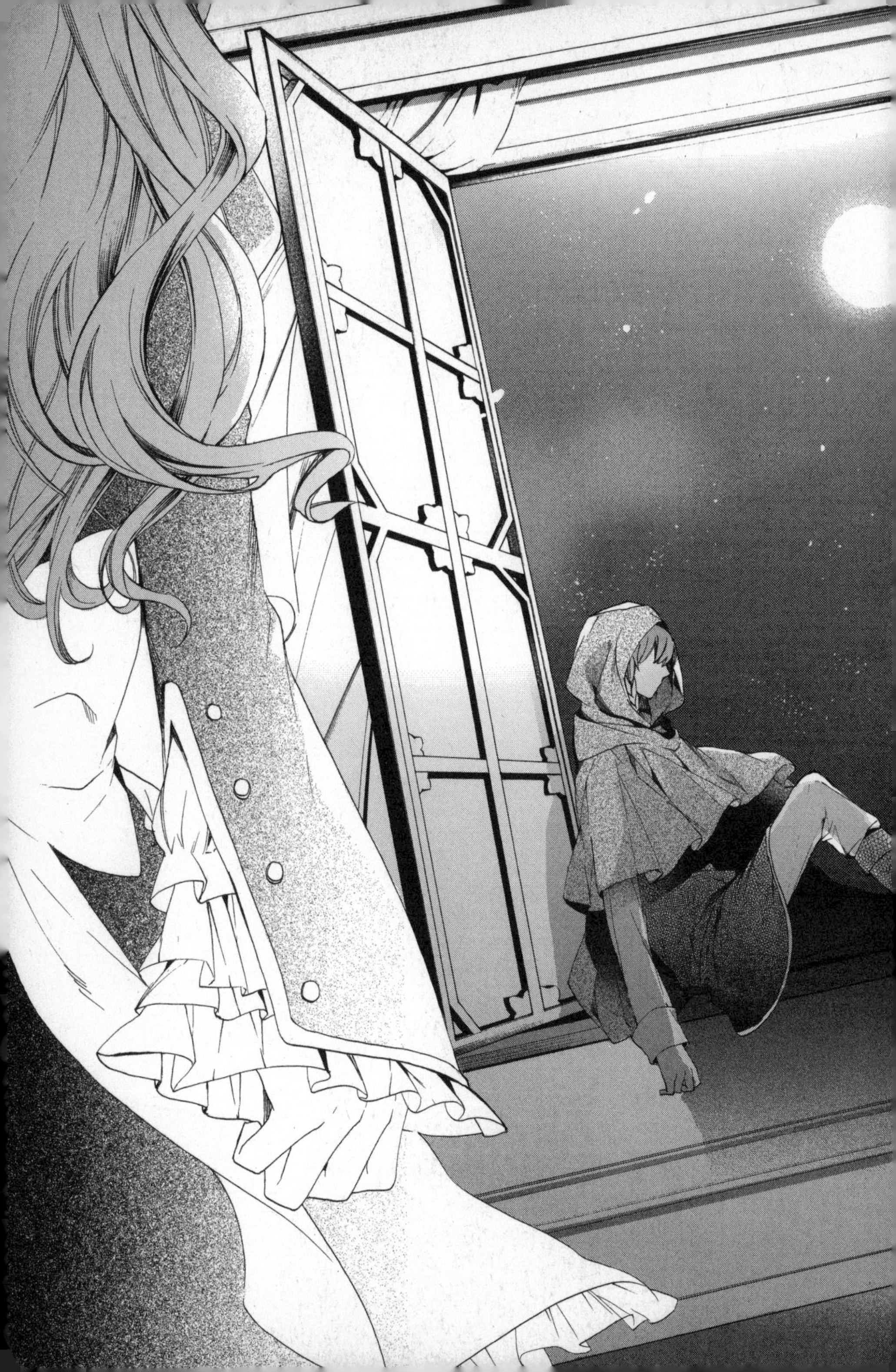

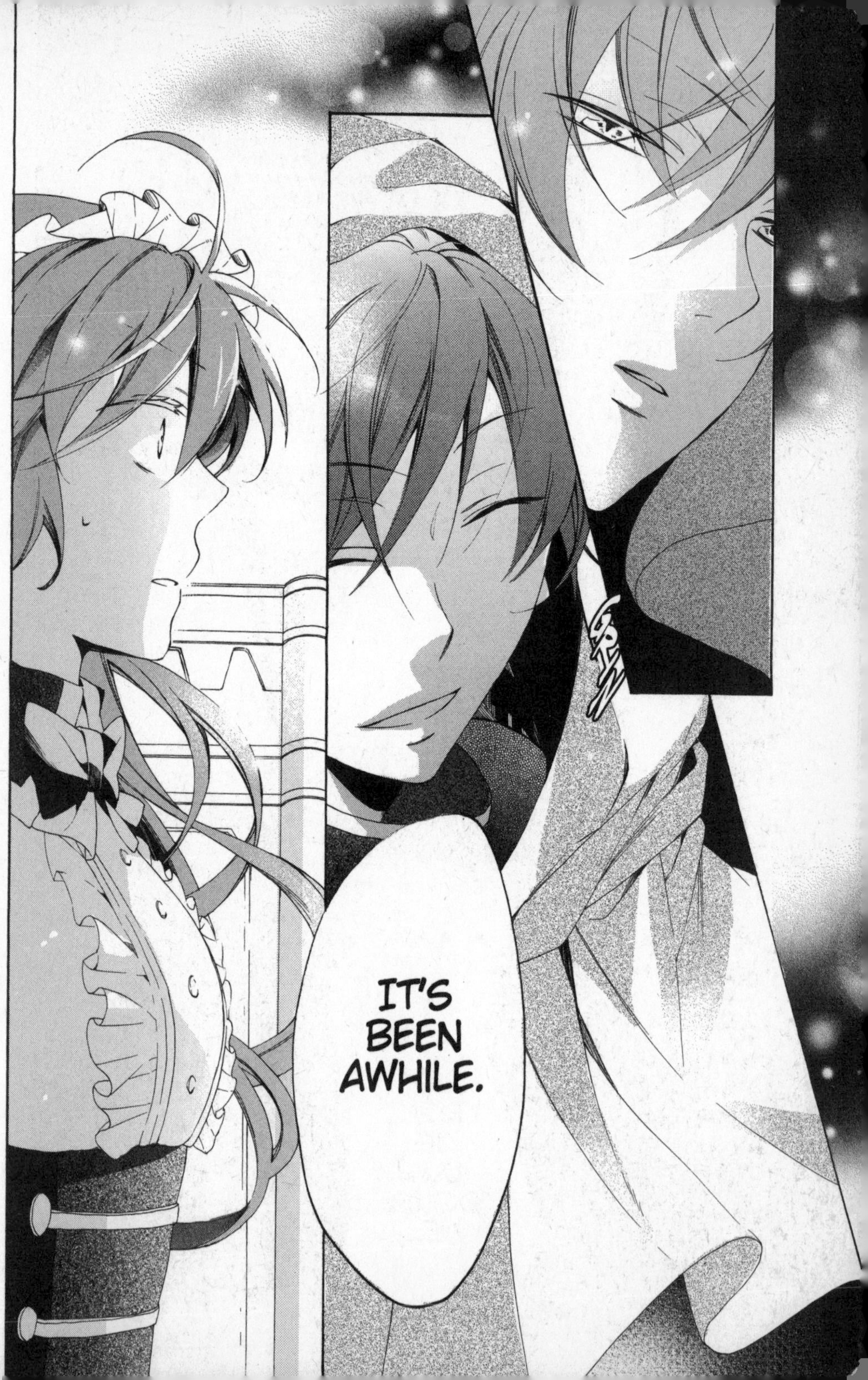
GRIN
IT'S BEEN AWHILE.

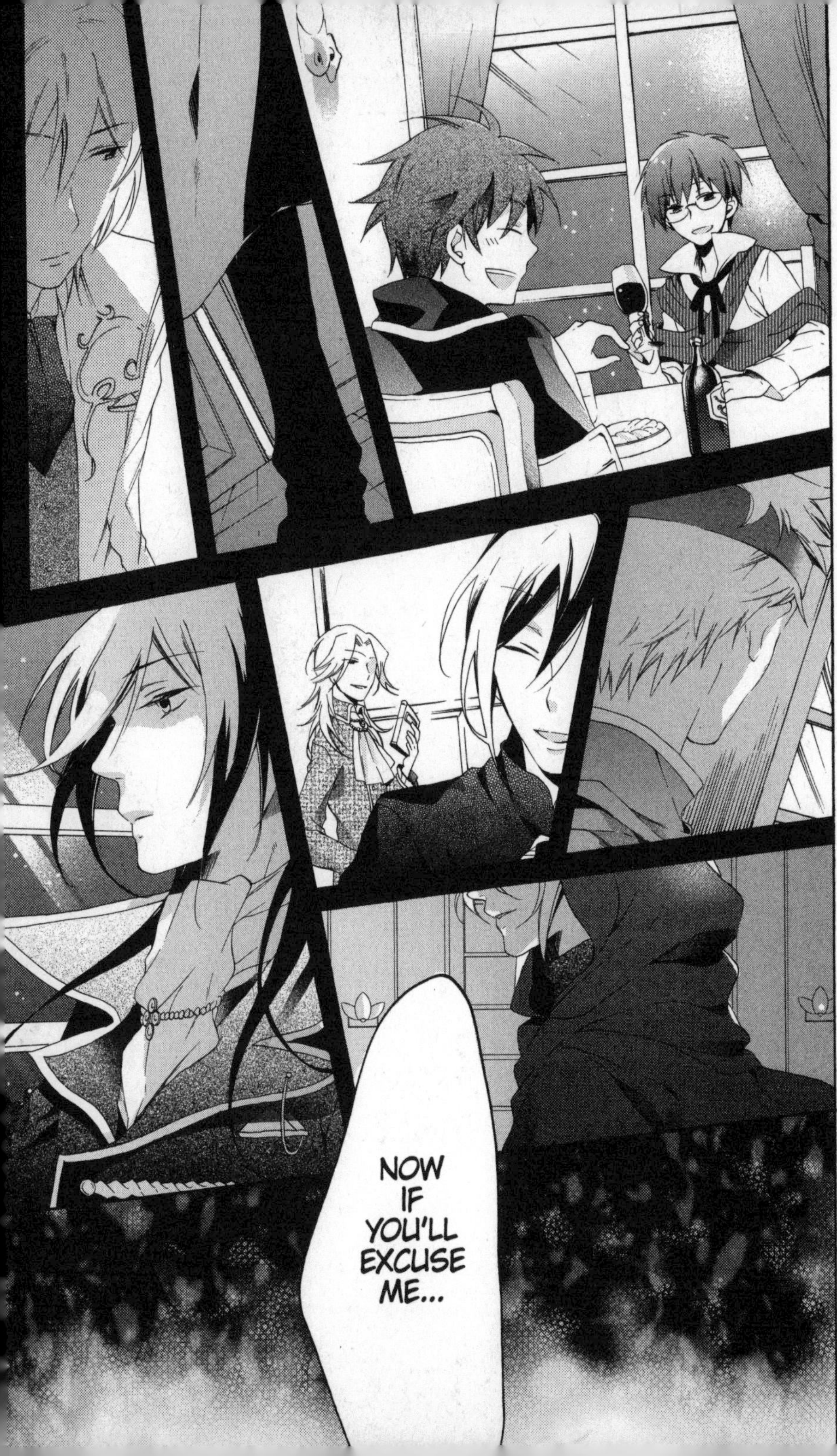
NOW IF YOU'LL EXCUSE ME...

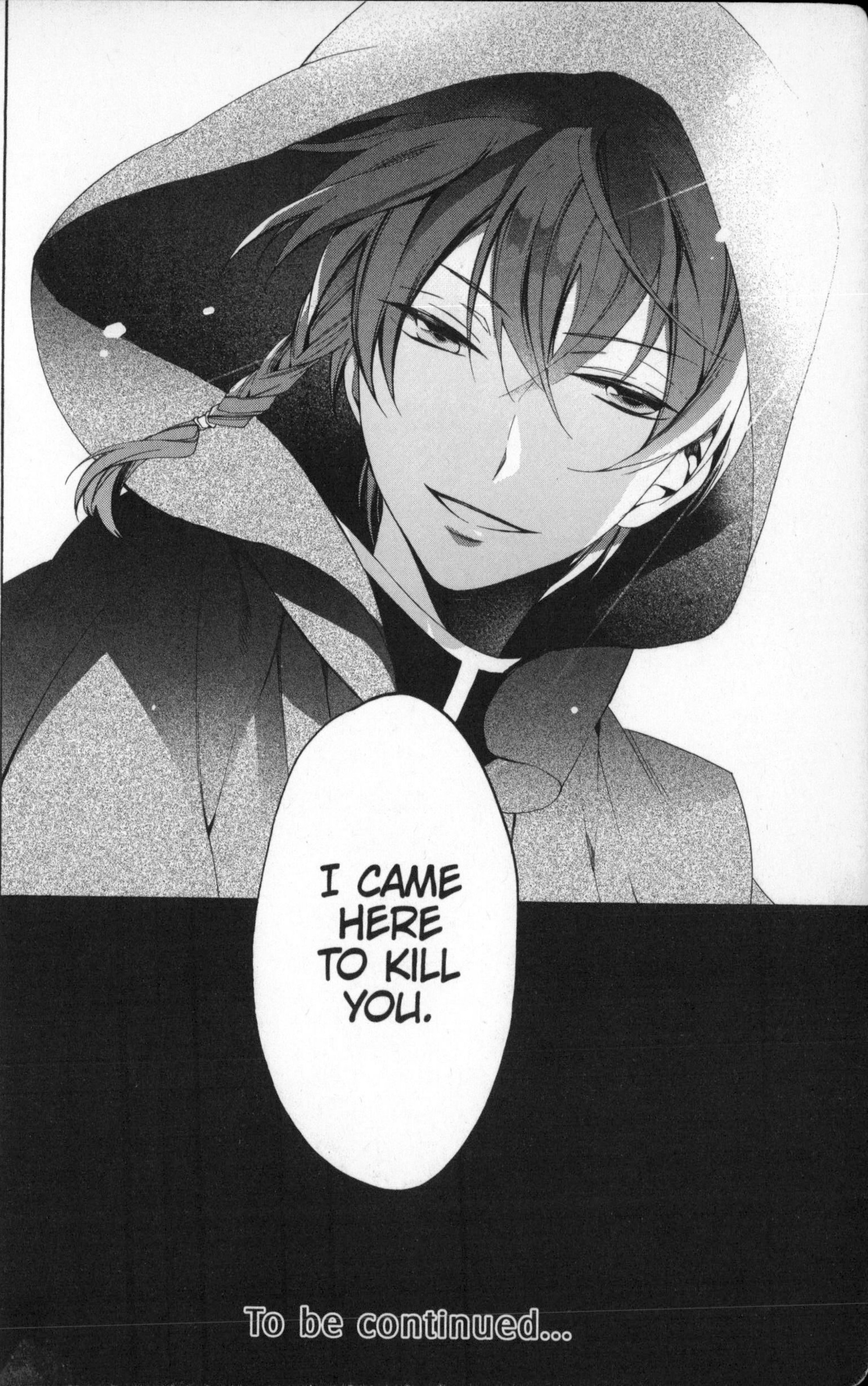
I CAME HERE TO KILL YOU.
To be continued...

CRIMSON EMPIRE
CIRCUMSTANCES TO SERVE A NOBLE

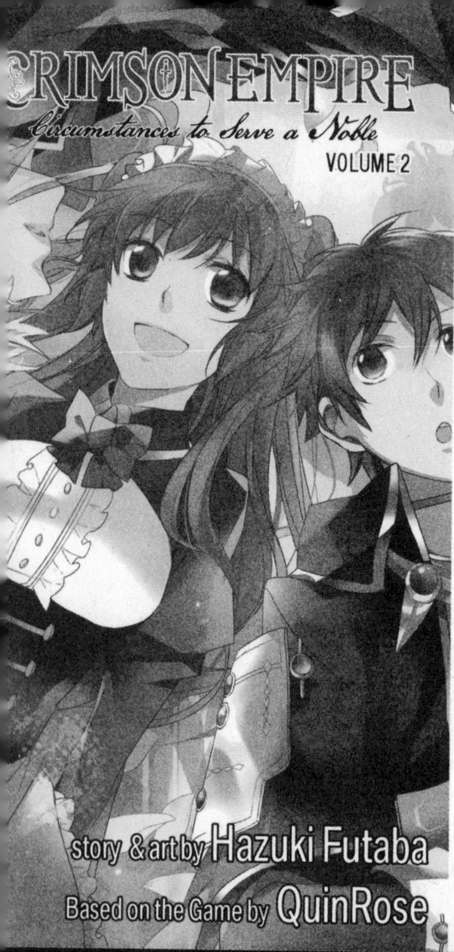
CRIMSON EMPIRE
Circumstances to Serve a Noble
VOLUME 2
story & art by Hazuki Futaba
Based on the Game by QuinRose

STAFF CREDITS

translation Angela Liu
adaptation Lianne Sentar
lettering Roland Amago
layout Bambi Eloriaga-Amago
cover design Nicky Lim
proofreader Danielle King, Conner Crooks
editor Adam Arnold

publisher Jason DeAngelis
Seven Seas Entertainment

CRIMSON EMPIRE: CIRCUMSTANCES TO SERVE A NOBLE VOL. 2

First published in Japan in 2010 by ICHIJINSHA Inc., Tokyo.
English translation rights arranged with ICHIJINSHA Inc., Tokyo, Japan.

ISBN: 978-1-937867-44-7

Printed in Canada

First Printing: August 2013

10 9 8 7 6 5 4 3 2 1

READING DIRECTIONS

This book reads from ***right to left***, Japanese style. If this is your first time reading manga, you start reading from the top right panel on each page and take it from there. If you get lost, just follow the numbered diagram here. It may seem backwards at first, but you'll get the hang of it! Have fun!!

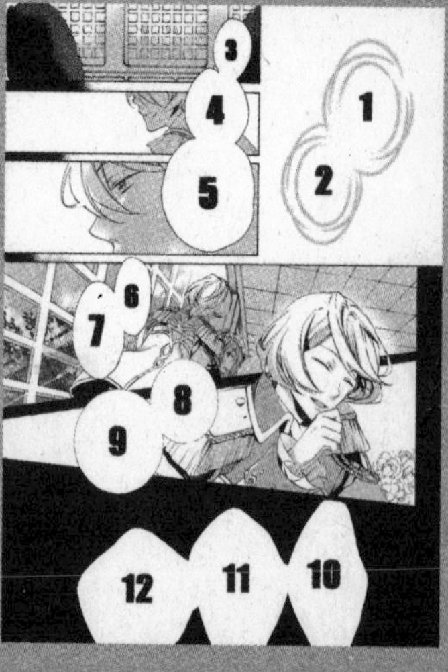
1
2
3
4
5
6
7
8
9
10
11
12